D1291528

Horror Film and Psychoanalysis

In recent years, psychoanalytic theory has been the subject of attacks from philosophers, cultural critics, and scientists who have questioned the cogency of its reasoning as well as the soundness of its premises. Nevertheless, when used to shed light on horror cinema, psychoanalysis in its various forms has proven to be a fruitful and provocative interpretative tool. This volume seeks to find the proper place of psychoanalytic thought in critical discussion of cinema in a series of essays that debate its legitimacy, utility, and validity as applied to the horror genre. It distinguishes itself from previous work in this area through the self-consciousness with which psychoanalytic concepts are employed and the theorization that coexists with interpretations of particular horror films and subgenres.

Steven Jay Schneider is a scholar of cinema and philosophy. He is the author of *Designing Fear: Aesthetics of Cinematic Horror* and editor of *New Hollywood Violence,* among other publications.

Cambridge Studies in Film

General Editors

William Rothman, *University of Miami*

Dudley Andrew, *University of Iowa*

Cambridge Studies in Film is a series of scholarly studies of high intellectual standard on the history and criticism of film. Each book examines a different aspect of film as a social and cultural phenomenon, setting standards and directions for the evaluation and definition of film scholarship. Designed for both film enthusiasts and academic readers, the series is international in scope of subject matter and eclectic in terms of approach and perspective. Cambridge Studies in Film provides a foundation in the theory and philosophy of the emerging visual media that continues to shape our world.

Selected titles from the series

The 'I' of the Camera: Essays in Film Criticism, History, and Aesthetics, by William Rothman

The Cinema of Satyajit Ray, by Darius Cooper

Documentary Film Classics, by William Rothman

John Huston's Filmmaking, by Lesley Brill

Projecting Illusion: Film Spectatorship and the Impression of Reality, by Richard Allen

Interpreting the Moving Image, by Noel Carroll

Horror Film and Psychoanalysis

FREUD'S WORST NIGHTMARE

Edited by

STEVEN JAY SCHNEIDER
New York University and Harvard University

CAMBRIDGE
UNIVERSITY PRESS

PUBLISHED BY THE PRESS SYNDICATE OF THE UNIVERSITY OF CAMBRIDGE
The Pitt Building, Trumpington Street, Cambridge, United Kingdom

CAMBRIDGE UNIVERSITY PRESS
The Edinburgh Building, Cambridge CB2 2RU, UK
40 West 20th Street, New York, NY 10011-4211, USA
477 Williamstown Road, Port Melbourne, VIC 3207, Australia
Ruiz de Alarcón 13, 28014 Madrid, Spain
Dock House, The Waterfront, Cape Town 8001, South Africa

http://www.cambridge.org

First published 2004

Printed in the United States of America

Typeface ITC New Baskerville 10/13 pt.   *System* LATEX 2$_\varepsilon$ [TB]

A catalog record for this book is available from the British Library.

Library of Congress Cataloging in Publication Data
Schneider, Steven Jay, 1974–
Horror film and psychoanalysis : Freud's worst nightmare / Steven Hay Schneider.
    p.   cm. – (Cambridge studies in film)
    Includes bibliographical references.
    ISBN 0-521-82521-0
    1. Horror films – Psychological aspects.   I. Title.   II. Series.
PN1995.9.H6S33   2004
791.43/6164 – dc22   2003060604

ISBN 0 521 82521 0 hardback

For Mom and Dad, with love

Contents

Acknowledgments

For their support, encouragement, and assistance throughout the development of this project, I would like to extend my sincerest thanks to Richard Allen, Wheeler Winston Dixon, Micheline Frank, Andrea Sabbadini, Daniel Shaw, Judith Stevenson, Damien Treffs, Fiona Villella, and Ivan Ward. Thanks go as well to all of the contributors for their hard work and patience. Beatrice Rehl at Cambridge University Press made the editing process incredibly smooth and easy. As always, the support and understanding of my family and friends – Elyse, Stuart, Katheryn, Pam, Owen, Suzy, Max, Erin – was essential. And most of all, a huge thanks goes to William Rothman for believing in this book from the start, and for assisting me with it every step of the way.

Andrew Tudor's chapter (excluding the Afterword) first appeared as sections in his essay, "Why Horror? The Peculiar Pleasures of a Popular Genre," *Cultural Studies* 11:3 (1997), pp. 446–53. It is reprinted here with permission of the publisher, Taylor & Francis Ltd. (http://www.tandf.co.uk/journals).

An earlier version of Cynthia Freeland's chapter, "Explaining the Uncanny in *The Double Life of Véronique*," appeared under the same title in *Film & Philosophy*, Special Edition, 2001, pp. 34–50. Material is reprinted here with kind permission of the editor.

An earlier version of Steven Jay Schneider's chapter, "Manifestations of the Literary Double in Modern Horror Cinema," appeared under the same title in *Film & Philosophy*, Special Edition, 2001, pp. 51–62. Material reprinted here with kind permission of the editor.

An earlier and shorter version of Michael Grant's chapter, "'Ultimate Formlessness': Cinema, Horror, and the Limits of Meaning," appeared under the title "Psychoanalysis and the Horror Film" in *Free Associations* vol. 5, part 4 (no. 36), 1995, pp. 483–91. Material is reprinted here with kind permission of the editor.

Foreword: "What Lies Beneath?"

In 1979, Richard Lippe and I organized and hosted a retrospective of the (primarily) American horror film at the Toronto International Film Festival, then known as the "Festival of Festivals." We invited a number of filmmakers to give seminars, and Brian de Palma, George Romero, Wes Craven, and Stephanie Rothman all made public appearances and answered questions, Richard and I interviewing each on stage before turning the questioning over to the audience. As part of this event, we produced a small booklet, to which Andrew Britton and Tony Williams also contributed essays, entitled (like the retrospective) *The American Nightmare.* My sections were subsequently included in my book *Hollywood from Vietnam to Reagan*, with an extension dealing with the genre's development – "degeneration" would be a more appropriate term – in the 1980s.

Looking back, it seems to me that our primary motivation was what Howard Hawks always claimed for making his movies – "having fun" – though I would add that, like Hawks, we wanted to make as good a professional job of it as possible and we took our work very seriously. Of course, we would never have done it had we not believed that we had something to say, at the root of which was our sense that this most despised and ridiculed of genres deserved serious attention. I don't think it occurred to us that what we were doing would come to assume the historic importance that seems to be the case. We never asserted (or believed) that ours was the only way of looking at horror films or that our theories explained every horror film that had ever been made, although much of what has been written since appears to accuse us of exactly that.

At the core of our ideas was the belief (which I doubt anyone is likely to dispute) that a genre's evolution is strongly influenced by cultural-political evolution at least as much as by the genre's internal evolution (the fact that later films in a given cycle are nourished by and grow out of their predecessors). How else could one account for the astonishingly abrupt shift in the American horror film from the progressive, exploratory, often radical late 1960s–70s to the reactionary and repressive 1980s? Michael Myers, Jason Voorhees, Freddy Krueger – they did not develop out of the characteristic monsters of the 1970s, but represent a refusal of everything embodied earlier.

What was crucially determinant of *The American Nightmare* was our political commitment – leftist, radical, and with at least an interest in Marxist ideology and especially the confluence of Marx and Freud in 1970s thought. That commitment was vastly more important to us than any desire to tell "the whole truth and nothing but the truth" about the horror film. Here I must acknowledge the key importance of Andrew Britton: his contributions to our booklet were relatively brief but his influence pervaded the entire enterprise. For myself, Andrew has been for many years the most important film critic writing in English; his neglect within academic circles seems to me disgraceful.

If one approaches the American horror film from a radical perspective one must inevitably find great positive interest in the achievements of the late 1960s–70s and reject almost everything that has followed. My social-political position has not changed essentially since that time, though in honesty I must admit that two decades of reaction and conservatism have somewhat dulled its edges. In the 1970s one felt supported by, at the least, a general disquiet and dissatisfaction, and at best, a widespread desire for change, which came to a focus in the period's great social movements – radical feminism, the black movement, gay rights, environmentalism. Those movements still exist but have lost much of their momentum, perhaps because of the advances they made: advances that have, to some degree, been recuperated into the establishment at the cost of losing their dangerousness. Perhaps the new administration will goad people into a new sense of outrage and fury, but it may take the equivalent of the Vietnam War.

Criticism of *The American Nightmare*'s approach has in fact concentrated not on politics but on psychoanalysis, which to us was a valuable weapon that could be used politically. Relatively speaking, our radical political commitment has been generally ignored, despite the fact that it embodies the foundation of our arguments. I would agree today that building an analysis of the horror genre on Freudian theory made it readily vulnerable to attack by those uneasy with our politics. The (supposed) demolition and repudiation of Freud is another 1980s phenomenon, again (I would claim) strongly influenced by the social-political climate. Part of the problem lies in that distressingly common tendency either to totally accept or totally reject, as opposed to the principle of *examining critically*. Few today appear to read Freud or Marx with a view to sorting out what is still valid, what can be cast off, and what needs to be rethought.

Freudian theory is vulnerable to attack on many points, but not, in my opinion, on the one that formed *The American Nightmare*'s psychoanalytic basis: the theory of repression and the "return of the repressed." We can all trace the workings of this, surely, in our own personal histories and daily lives; it continues to have great resonance in relation to the horror film, but only insofar as it is melded with a political awareness. Murnau's *Nosferatu* (1921), made in the very shadow of Freud, strikes me as almost textbook Freudianism – the monster as "return of the repressed" (and its ultimate re-repression) in almost diagrammatic (yet extremely powerful) form. The Freudian analogy holds good for Whale's *Frankenstein* (1931), but here, in Karloff's make-up, clothing, gestures, and performance, his threats and pleadings, we can also see the working class, the poor, the homeless, and the dispossessed, suggesting a parallel between psychological *re*pression and social *op*pression. The possibility that the monster (hence, "the repressed") might be seen as sympathetic or pitiable as well as horrifying was perhaps inherent in the genre from the outset (it is clearly there in Whale's two *Frankenstein* movies). But it is in the 1970s, with the development of radicalism and protest, that the figure of the monster develops a widespread tendency to become (though never unambiguously) the emotional center of many horror films.

That the "return of the repressed" formula does not exhaustively explain all horror movies was demonstrated already in the 1970s/1980s by what seems in retrospect the period's greatest achievement, George Romero's *Living Dead* trilogy. It has not, I think, been sufficiently recognized that the meaning and function of the zombies changes radically from film to film. It is consistent, in fact, in only one way – that the zombies constitute a challenge to the humans, not merely to survive but to *change*. But the nature of the challenge differs from film to film.

Of the three, *Night of the Living Dead* (1968) corresponds most closely to the psychoanalytic formula – the first zombie emerges not merely from a graveyard but from the precariously repressed familial tensions between brother and sister, tensions derived directly and explicitly from the structures of the nuclear family. Having established this in the first few minutes, however, Romero relegates the zombies to a subservient and functional position; though powerful because they are so numerous, they quite lack the dynamic, rebellious energy of other, more characteristic, monsters of the period – the baby of *It's Alive* (1974), Danielle (Margot Kidder) of *Sisters* (1973), Regan (Linda Blair) of *The Exorcist* (1973), or, going farther back, the Irena (Simone Simon) of *Cat People* (1942), the Tootie (Margaret O'Brien) of *Meet Me in St Louis* (1944), or the Erlking of Goethe and Schubert – whose function is *to demand recognition*. The zombies destroy all the main characters (the existing nuclear family, the "young couple" who represent the future nuclear family) but one, simply because they are incapable of change and will merely repeat the repressive patterns of the past. The exception, the film's hero and sole black character, hence an outsider, survives the zombies but, in the film's final irony, is shot down by the sheriff's posse.

The theme is carried over into *Dawn of the Dead* (1978), but with an important difference: the zombies of the shopping mall are the products of consumer capitalism, drawn back to the mall that embodies their utmost desires, the pitiful non-satisfactions of material possessions by which their culture has taught them to live. The totally passive (literally traumatized) woman of *Night* is here transformed into an active and increasingly resourceful heroine who eventually learns to free herself from male domination and all the social formations (marriage, traditional family, dependency) that support it, taking over the film's primary symbol of masculine power, the helicopter. Finally, in *Day of the Dead* (1985), the trilogy's lamentably unrecognized crown ("Easily the least of the series," according to the lamentably influential Leonard Maltin) – at once the darkest, most desperate, and ultimately most exhilarating of the three films – the woman becomes the central figure, the heart of sanity in a world of masculinity gone mad.

I suspect that the almost total incomprehension (more precisely, *refusal* of comprehension) with which *Day of the Dead* has been received is simply the result of its late date: by 1985 we had already entered the era of hysterical masculinity that countered the radical feminism of the 1970s, Stallone and Schwarzenegger were already major presences, and the reactionary horror movie had already fully established itself. No one wanted to hear about how science and militarism were male-dominated, masculinist institutions threatening to destroy life on the planet (*Day*'s essential theme, even more timely today than it was then, though no one seems willing to pay attention any more). Though made by a man, it stands (and will probably be recognized as, when it is too late) one of the great feminist movies. It is also, for me, the last great American horror film.

Are significant horror films being made outside America? in the East? in Italy? I am not qualified to answer this question, although it seems necessary to raise it. The Italian horror films of Bava and Argento have their defenders; the few I have seen struck me as obsessively preoccupied with violence against women, dramatized in particularly grotesque images. One European film perhaps qualifies, though it must be seen as marginal to the genre: Michael Haneke's profoundly disturbing and troubling *Funny Games* (1997). Although it barely evokes the supernatural, its relationship to the horror film becomes apparent quite early on.

Two young men enter a bourgeois household on a pretext, then swiftly proceed to make prisoners of the family (father, mother, young son) and subsequently humiliate, torment, and finally kill all three before going off cheerfully to visit the nearest neighbors for the same purpose. No obvious "explanation" of the young men is offered: they are not noticeably impoverished or underprivileged (rather the contrary); we learn nothing of their background and so cannot see them as victims of the conventional nuclear family structure; they appear to humiliate, torment, and kill just for the pleasure of it. One is clearly dominant and he is credited with the film's only hint of supernatural powers – the ability to rewind the film when things go wrong and replay a scene to his own specifications. Are they "the return of the repressed"? The worst the bourgeois couple can be accused of is complacency, which is what Hitchcock said *The Birds* (1963) is about, and the couple's punishment (if that is how it is to be read) is only a step worse than that meted out to Melanie Daniels (Tippie Hedren).

Funny Games can also be read (and this links it thematically to Haneke's other work) as suggesting that our civilization, by dehumanizing its inhabitants, intrinsically produces psychopaths who therefore require no further explanation. This is one of the most disturbing films I have ever seen (no surprise, really, that it is probably the most widely hated film in modern cinema – critics react to it with such an intense resentment of what it does to them that it becomes a tribute to the film's power). Haneke allows his chief "monster" an intimate relationship with the audience, inviting us into the film with his knowing look into camera, and implicating us in the violence (which is for the most part more psychological than physical): do we *want* to punish this affluent and complacent, yet generally pleasant and harmless, couple? But, simultaneously, we are implicated in an opposed violence, the deliberate tormenting of helpless people reaching a point where we would like to leap into the movie and kill the two young men with our own hands. The film's great danger, it seems to me, is that it might (given that the tormentors appear in-explicable and therefore unreformable) be read as advocating capital punishment.

Aside from *Day of the Dead*, is there *any* American horror movie made since 1980 that could be championed as any sort of radical statement about our impossible (so-called) civilization? I ask the question seriously, hoping it may get answered in this anthology (for myself, the only possible candidate is Neil Jordan's fascinating and underrated *In Dreams* [1998]). Or is the genre as "living dead" as Romero's zombies who, while immensely powerful, have nothing to offer but a kind of subhuman nothingness and survive without any real life? The genre's deterioration is easy to chart. Around 1980 it moves crucially from the release of repressed (and therefore terrifying) energies to "teenagers endlessly punished for having sex." And why has this perversion of the genre been so popular with teenagers? Presumably because, while it is exactly what, at their age, they ought to be doing (besides protesting vigorously about almost everything happening in the dominant culture), their parents make them feel guilty.

From there to the spoof is an easy leap (about two inches), stupidity (of the characters, of the films themselves) being already generically inherent. Actually, the "spoof" horror film (unnecessary to give titles, I think) simply carries the "slaughter of sexual teenagers" 1980s subdivision of the genre one step further: all those naughty teenagers can now enjoy themselves without taking their punishment seriously. There is just one small problem: in all the films I can recall (and they have fused themselves into one horrible confused image of sex and slaughter) the teenagers hardly ever achieve orgasm. The popularity of these films with teenagers is vastly more interesting, and even more depressing, than the films themselves ever are. Given that all these films operate on a very low level of artistic or thematic interest, it is (I suppose) still possible to make certain distinctions. The original *Halloween*, which had the dubious distinction of initiating the entire cycle, and is therefore of historic interest, was a well-made and effective film; the entire *Friday the 13th* series fully deserves to go, with Jason, to hell; the *Nightmare on Elm Street* films have a marginally more interesting monster and (especially in the first) a certain flair in invention and design. What more can one say?

STEVEN JAY SCHNEIDER

Introduction: Psychoanalysis in/and/of the Horror Film

THE MYTH OF META-THEORY

Over the past thirty years, a plethora of publications have argued in favor of a specific psychoanalytic approach to some dimension or convention of cinematic horror. Included among these are articles and books by such influential scholars as Robin Wood, Carol Clover, Stephen Neale, Linda Williams, Barbara Creed, even Noël Carroll in an earlier incarnation. These efforts have typically taken the form of either interpretive analysis (of a particular film, subgenre, or the genre as a whole) or depth-psychological explanation (of the symbolic/mythic import of horror film monsters; of the horror affect and how it is generated; of the possibly perverse pleasures viewers obtain from being frightened by visible fictions). And despite the often vitriolic criticisms of psychoanalysis both inside and outside academic film studies, the horror genre has continued to see a steady stream of *new* psychoanalytic approaches, as well as new variations on existing ones.

As originally conceived, the present volume was to be a collection of "meta-theoretical" essays on psychoanalysis and the horror film – not essays that simply (or not so simply, as the case may be) make use of Freudian, Jungian, Kleinian, Jonesian, or Lacanian principles, theses, arguments, or purported discoveries in an effort at shedding light on aspects of the horror film. Instead, it was envisaged that contributors would take a step back to address the relative strengths and weaknesses of such approaches. This was to be a book *about* psychoanalytic theories of the horror film rather than a book that offered still more psychoanalytic theories of the horror film.

But of course there is no such neutral space outside, much less "above," the fray from which to conduct an investigation of this sort. Those who

defend a psychoanalytic approach to horror cinema typically have pet
applications of their own. Similarly, those who see fit to critique psychoanalytic theories of the horror film almost always have alternative,
incompatible (or so it may seem) paradigms in mind.[1]

Especially since the late 1970s, there has been a tremendous diversity of psychoanalytic approaches to the horror film. These approaches
differ, and often conflict, in substantial ways. But the objections levied
in recent years by analytic philosophers, film aestheticians, sociologists
and cultural theorists, cognitive and feminist film theorists, and empirical psychologists, many of whom position themselves well outside the
circle of Freud and his followers, constitute a far more serious threat, or
challenge, to psychoanalytical horror film theory. This is because such
objections would be fatal to psychoanalysis if proven correct.[2]

To refuse to hear such critics out, to assume *a priori* that none of their
objections are powerful enough to warrant serious treatment, and to es-
chew making any effort at responding in turn is more than just irrespon-
sible scholarship. It adds strength to the already potent criticisms that
psychoanalytic thought is hermetic and self-confirming, that its film theoretical applications produce "closed, self-justifying systems" (Jancovich
1995: 147). And it weakens the power of those *prima facie* affinities holding between psychoanalytic concepts and explanations, on the one hand,
and the manifest content of much horror cinema, on the other. The existence of such affinities is often cited as additional evidence in support of
whichever psychoanalytic theory of the horror film brings them to bear in
the first place; consider, for example, Marguerite LaCaze's (2002) look
at how the relationship between mourning and melancholia – a relationship about which Freud had much to say – is thematized in M. Night
Shyamalan's *The Sixth Sense* (1999).

Most psychoanalytic horror film theorists to date have not proven very
open to revising their particular accounts as a result of critical engagement with the work of others operating even from *within* the psychoanalytic paradigm. As Malcolm Turvey details in his contribution to this
volume, for instance, a survey of the various explanations offered by psychoanalytic film theorists concerning the puzzling pleasures of horror
film viewing reveals a host of structurally similar but still more or less conflicting positions. All of these positions depend on the Freudian notion
of repressed mental content – anxieties, fears, even fantasies and wishes
that get relegated to the unconscious during childhood either because
they are too unpleasurable in and of themselves or because they conflict

with more acceptable/appropriate mental content. While the diversity Turvey refers to might be held up as indicative of the fertility of psycho-analysis in this area, "from the point of view of critics of psychoanalytical film theory, there is no genuine disagreement among psychoanalytical theorists of the horror film – simply pluralism." This is because such theorists typically "do not dialectically engage with each others' theories by (a) showing why candidates for repressed mental content proposed by other theorists cannot explain the phenomenon they want to explain; or (b) showing why their candidate does explain the phenomenon better than others" (*n.* 9).

Clearly, the pluralism Turvey has in mind here is not of the "method-ologically robust" type advocated by Noël Carroll. According to Carroll, methodologically robust pluralism only occurs when competing theories are held up against one another for the purpose of weeding out the weak ones. Rather, Turvey seems to be thinking of "a situation in which everyone just rattles around in their own paradigm" (Carroll 1996: 334); only here, the theorists in question are held to be "just rattling around" in the *same* paradigm, broadly construed as psychoanalysis.[3] Although questions have been raised about the presupposed neutrality and external stance of the arbiter in Carroll's own problem–solution model of research,[4] and although it is certainly possible for there to be different ways – *all* fruitful – of looking at a particular phenomenon, Carroll's methodological imperative makes sense when it comes to the consideration of theories that appear to be in competition or conflict with one another.

Arguably, one example of the sort of unproductive pluralism Turvey is referring to centers on the poststructural psychoanalytic claim that at the heart of cinematic horror lies a patriarchal fear of female sexuality. In order to tap into this fear, it is held that the genre defines female sexuality "as monstrous, disturbing, and in need of repression" (Jancovich 1992: 10). Such a claim can be considered "poststructural" in that it ultimately locates meaning not within individual films or the work of particular writers or directors, but in the signifying codes of horror cinema itself – also because it casts itself in political terms, purporting to identify and analyze the ideological effects of a specific visual-narrative structure.[5]

A number of poststructural psychoanalytic horror film theorists, including Barbara Creed and Xavier Mendik (1998), employ Julia Kristeva's (1982) notion of abjection to argue that women in the genre – mothers especially – are frequently presented as monstrous beings who pose a fatal threat to men. According to Creed,

the horror film attempts to bring about a confrontation with the abject (the corpse, bodily wastes, the monstrous-feminine) in order finally to eject the abject and redraw the boundaries between the human and the non-human. As a form of modern defilement rite, the horror film attempts to separate out the symbolic order from all that threatens its stability, particularly the mother and all that her universe signifies. (1993: 14)

Meanwhile, Stephen Neale and others argue that horror film monsters are typically defined as *male*, with *women* as their primary victims: "In this respect, it could well be maintained that it is women's sexuality, that which renders them desirable – but also threatening – to men, which constitutes the real problem that the [*sic*] horror cinema exists to explore" (1980: 61). If these intuitions were applied to different films within the genre, they would be quite compatible. But unless and until the necessary qualifications are proffered, they stand in evident conflict with one another (as the predominant genders of monster and victim are reversed in each).

Unfortunately, the trend has been for psychoanalytic horror film theorists to downplay the tensions between their respective positions rather than attempt to address them. This has meant that those externally motivated criticisms that *cut across* various psychoanalytic theories of the horror film – as many, if not most of them, do – are typically ignored, their implications unacknowledged, precisely because their very scope encourages a passing of the dialectical buck.[6]

The same cannot be said of psychoanalytic film theory in general, which has certainly seen its fair share of internal controversy. One need only consider the objections of neo-Lacanians such as Joan Copjec (1995) and Slavoj Zizek (2001) to earlier claims concerning apparatus theory and the suture effect; Constance Penley's (1989) critique of screen theory;[7] Linda Williams on the problematic (because ambiguous) "terms of perversion used to describe the normal pleasures of film viewing" (1984/1999: 706); and the heated mid-1980s debate in *Cinema Journal* concerning *Stella Dallas* and the Mulvey–Metz model of female spectatorship. In fact, the feminist-inflected psychoanalytic theories of horror proposed by Williams (1984/1996), Clover (1987; 1992), and Creed (1986; 1993) can all be understood as revisions, rather than outright rejections, of the original Mulveyan paradigm. According to this paradigm, the threat of castration (absence and lack) posed by images of the female form in Hollywood cinema is contained through a sexualized objectification of that form, whether fetishistic–scopophilic (woman displayed as erotic spectacle, rendered unthreatening by the controlling male look) or sadistic–voyeuristic (woman investigated, demystified, and eventually controlled through punishment) in nature.

As Richard Allen has observed, both Williams and Creed contest aspects of Mulvey's position by identifying "scenarios of female empowerment in the horror film in which the threat of castration [i]s not contained, but acted out in the narrative" (1999: 140). This acting out takes place either through the figure of the "monstrous-feminine" (Creed), or else through the female character's sympathetic "look" at the monster – "a potentially subversive recognition of the power and potency of a nonphallic sexuality" (Williams 1984/1996: 24). Clover, meanwhile, argues for a primarily masochistic and empathetic, rather than sadistic–voyeuristic, identification on the part of both male and female spectators with the originally suffering but ultimately empowered "Final Girl" of the slasher movie. But due to the fact that each of these accounts constitutes a revision/ refinement of a highly politicized and psychoanalytically motivated feminist film theory whose implications extend far beyond the boundaries of the horror genre – just recall Mulvey's sweeping claims, e.g., that "unchallenged, mainstream film code[s] the erotic into the language of the dominant patriarchal order" (1975: 835) – they do not really qualify as debates taking place within the domain of psychoanalytic *horror* film theorizing. Rather, they are debates taking place within psychoanalytic film theory in general.

Eschewing the bogus idea of "pure" meta-theoretical inquiry conducted by people with no first-order attachment to their arguments and conclusions, this volume responds to the need for critical dialogue among psychoanalytic horror film scholars and those of other theoretical and disciplinary stripes. It also responds to the need for internal debate among otherwise (at least potentially) sympathetic psychoanalytic theorists of the horror genre. What all of the essays exhibit is something a great deal more practical than meta-theorization, and also a great deal more valuable: namely, *self-conscious theorizing*. It is hoped that the concerted efforts made by each of the contributors to question their methods and motives (past and present), anticipate and respond to objections (actual and possible), and situate their work (historically and across disciplinary lines) will help pave the way for future scholarship on the horror film – of whatever theoretical persuasion – committed to dialogue, progress, and conceptual openness.

In the remainder of this introduction, I will attempt to carve out a space
for psychoanalytic theory in horror film studies that is both substantive –
more than just an identification of the genre's many direct and indirect
references to Freudian (and post-Freudian) ideas – and "epistemically
neutral." By this latter term I mean a use of psychoanalytic theory whose
validity and usefulness does not depend on the underlying truth or falsity of such theory according to some independent objective standard,
scientific or otherwise.

PSYCHOANALYTIC (HORROR FILM) THEORY AT A MINIMUM

Just as it important for us to "be clear about *which* psychoanalysis it is that
we are talking about, and so about which claims are and are not being
made for psychoanalysis" (Donald 1991: 2) with respect to the horror
genre, it behooves us to acknowledge the enormous debt this genre owes
to Gothic literature – a debt that has been traced by Judith Halberstam
(1995), David Punter (1996), Philip Simpson (2000), Jack Morgan
(2002), and others – as well as the past susceptibility of the Gothic to psychoanalytic, especially Freudian, theorizing. William Patrick Day hardly
overstates things when he writes that "no discussion of the Gothic can
avoid discussing Freud; one of the most obvious ways of thinking about
the genre is to read it in terms of Freud's system. . . . We cannot pretend
that the striking parallels between Freud's thought and the Gothic fantasy
do not exist" (1985:177).

Day seeks to account for the obvious correspondences between
Freudian psychoanalysis and Gothic literature at the level of theme (e.g.,
the drama of selfhood played out within the family; the struggle to contain and control sexual energy; the conflict between masculine and feminine modes of identity) as well as narrative (e.g., the subversion of linear
plot structures; the substitution of mechanisms such as transformation,
condensation, and projection for clearly defined patterns of cause and
effect; the prioritization of subjective experience and the dynamics of
"inner life"). He first rejects the orthodox and uncritical psychoanalytic
view according to which these correspondences were *inevitable* because
the Gothic simply anticipated truths soon to be discovered by Freud. He
also rejects the pragmatic and hermeneutic view that these correspondences were *fortuitous* because, regardless of whether Freud was right or
wrong, the Gothic simply lent itself to allegorization in psychoanalytic
terms.

Instead, Day argues that the two systems – one imaginative-literary, the other intellectual-scientific – have a "common, or at least related, origin":

The Gothic is not a crude anticipation of Freudianism, nor its unacknowledged father. Rather, the two are cousins, responses to the problems of selfhood and identity, sexuality and pleasure, fear and anxiety as they manifest themselves in the nineteenth and early twentieth centuries. The Gothic arises out of the immediate needs of the reading public to escape from conventional life and articulate and define the turbulence of their psychic existence. We may see Freud as the intellectual counterpart of this process.... The Gothic ... acclimatized the culture to the types of ideas Freud was to present as truth by presenting them as fiction. (179)

Notice how questions concerning the logical or referential status of orthodox Freudian psychoanalysis are bracketed here. Instead, we get an account that takes the narrative and thematic affinities holding between this theoretical paradigm and traditional Gothic literature to be historically and culturally conditioned, even determined. Such affinities are neither immutable nor traceable, at least in the first instance, to the intentions of individual authors – not those of the Gothic novelists, and certainly not Freud's own. This latter is the case despite the Gothic tone of some of Freud's case histories. Rather, the affinities in question are to be understood primarily in formal and generic terms, the two systems developing, changing, and subdividing in what may well be read as a strange but significant sort of tandem.

A parallel can be drawn here, and perhaps an intellectual debt is owed, to the work of Stanley Cavell. In his 1987 collection of essays, *Disowning Knowledge in Six Plays of Shakespeare*, and even earlier, in *The Claim of Reason*, Cavell makes a convincing case for the affinities between Shakespearean tragedy and what philosophy (in Descartes) calls "skepticism":

Shakespeare could not be who he is – the burden of the name of the greatest writer in the language, the creature of the greatest ordering of English – unless his writing is engaging the depth of the philosophical preoccupations of his culture.... My intuition is that the advent of skepticism as manifested in Descartes's *Meditations* is already in full existence in Shakespeare, from the time of the great tragedies in the first years of the seventeenth century, in the generation preceding that of Descartes. (1987: 2, 3)

Elsewhere, Cavell writes "that tragedy is the working out of a response to skepticism – as I now like to put the matter, that tragedy is an interpretation of what skepticism itself is an interpretation of..." (1987: 5–6).[8] If Freud and the Gothic both provided responses (of a sort) to "the

problems of selfhood and identity, sexuality and pleasure, fear and anxiety" as these were manifested in the nineteenth and early twentieth centuries, Shakespearean tragedy and Cartesian skepticism both concern,
e.g., "the sense of the individual human being not only as now doubtful
in his possessions, as though unconvinced that anything really belongs to
him, but doubtful at the same time whether there is a place to which he
really belongs" (10).

Whether Freudianism, or any other species of psychoanalytic thought,
can successfully shed light on filmic horror's textual processes and the
nature and mechanics of its effects on viewers, while presenting itself as
one among a number of rival candidates for the job, remains an open
question. It is one that depends at least in part on the truth value of the
various claims and arguments made in support of psychoanalysis more
generally – if not as medical-therapeutic practice, then as theory of human development. (As noted above, precisely *how* such truth or falsity
is to be determined is yet another open question.) Many of the essays
included herein – e.g., those by Freeland, Schneider, and Prince – make
reference to, and in a sense creatively "apply," findings in the broader
philosophical and scientific literature to support their arguments, pro,
con, and otherwise.

But even if, for the sake of discussion, psychoanalysis at this more general level is somehow proven *false*, its value as a tool for shedding light
on specific horror films, cycles, and subgenres – particularly those with
identifiable Gothic linkages – can hardly be denied. Many such films
and groups of films have been interpreted as thematizing, narrativiz-
ing, and embodying ideas and constructs similar to those found in orthodox psychoanalytic theory and its revisions. One example of this is
Margaret Tarratt's influential examination of the distinctly, though not always overtly or self-consciously, Freudian manner in which many science-
fiction/horror films of the 1950s and 1960s explore "the problem of
reconciling the desires of the individual as both sexual animal and social
being" (1971: 276). Another, very different, example is Julian Hoxter's
look at how, in the Italian *giallo* horror films of Dario Argento, the
"complex, shifting connection between individuals and . . . the world of
objects which they inhabit" (1998: 99) exemplifies certain key principles
of Kleinian object-relations theory.

Carroll (1990: 172–78) seeks to undermine the numerous Freudian-
derived explanations of horror film monsters as projections of repressed
infantile anxieties. These anxieties are in turn held to be either necessary and inescapable (e.g., Gabbard and Gabbard 1999; Schneider 2000)

or socially and culturally specific (e.g., Wood 1979; Moretti 1983). In addition to such negative emotions as fear and disgust, the return to consciousness of these anxieties in the more or less disguised form of the monster is typically held to produce spectatorial pleasure, whether directly (Carroll 1981; cf. Creed 1993) or indirectly (Urbano 1998; cf. Pinedo 1997), depending on the nature of the repressed material they are taken to incarnate – unacceptable wishes in the former case (enjoyed at the cost of feeling simultaneous horror), primal fears or traumas in the latter case (enjoyed because here worked through or "mastered"). With a few *prima facie* counterexamples in hand, Carroll concludes that psychoanalysis "fails to provide a comprehensive account of the figures of horror" (1990: 174).[9]

Looking at the same glass half-full, however, we might say that psychoanalysis nevertheless *succeeds* in providing insight into many of the figures of horror – not so much into what they metaphorically *mean* as into what they literally *say*, or at least suggest, in terms taken from the languages of Gothic fantasy, childhood nightmare, popular culture, and the cinema itself. Although the issue is by no means settled, it is possible that Freud's theory of anxiety, one which he himself found necessary to revise in 1926, is fatally flawed for one or more of the reasons suggested by various philosophers, psychologists, and neurobiologists (for discussion, see the essays by Freeland, Urbano, and Levine in this volume).[10] If so, then neither the terror nor the pleasure generated by horror film monsters can truly be said to stem from their returning certain repressed fears or desires to consciousness. But this wouldn't mean that such beings still do not represent or stand for something very much like a return of the ideologically or instinctually repressed. The monsters of horror cinema, or at least some of them (if we grant Carroll his counterexamples), may still be plausibly analyzed as embodiments of the *idea* or *belief* that, e.g., "in a society built on monogamy and family there will always be an enormous surplus of sexual energy that will have to be repressed; and that...must always strive to return" (Wood 1979: 177), or that "the anxiety of castration and the fantasies woven around the mother's phallus produce horror forms" (Dadoun 1989: 52).

Carroll qualifies his critique of psychoanalytic horror film theory in a manner that would seem to anticipate the epistemically neutral position advocated here: "If psychoanalysis does not afford a comprehensive theory of horror, it remains the case that psychoanalytic imagery often reflexively informs works within the genre which, of course makes

psychoanalysis germane to interpretations of specific instances of the
genre" (1990: 168). In a 1997 essay, part of which has been reprinted
in this volume, Andrew Tudor makes a similar point, albeit even more
cautiously: "Although the genre's self-conscious borrowing from psychoanalysis is not without significance for the theoretical frameworks invoked
in its understanding, such an emphasis does not *entail* any specific theoretical consequences" (446). This last point is most likely true, though
just *how* true will of course depend on what one counts as "specific theoretical consequences." In any case, the role for psychoanalytic theorizing
of the horror film I have in mind here is not restricted to the "reflexive informing" or "self-conscious borrowing" of pop-Freudian (or pop-Jungian)
concepts, images, self-understandings, and explanatory models.[11] The
evident kinship between particular horror films and particular psychoanalytic ideas may be (and often is) the result of a calculated decision on
the part of the film's writer or director, but this is by no means a necessary condition for bringing to bear the psychoanalytic ideas in question.
What really matters is whether these ideas can be shown to be present in
the text – *not* whether they were self-consciously appropriated, or even
whether they were appropriated at all.

   Richard Allen comes closest to articulating the position being argued
for here when he admonishes those psychoanalytic film theorists who
would equate their purported discoveries with the therapeutic explanation of a patient's symptoms:

Symptomatic readings purport to show the meaning behind the text that is
concealed by its manifest content, but it is not clear that this is what psychoanalytic readings of Hollywood cinema achieve.... [A]rguably, far from
providing an objective code to unlock the real (hidden) meaning of the text,
psychoanalytic criticism quite frequently describes what is going on at the
surface of it.... However, if this is the case, the psychoanalytic critic posing
as theorist erroneously claims for himself the insight that rightly belongs to
the text itself. (1999: 142)

Allen cites "the innumerable psychoanalytic interpretations of the work
of Hitchcock" (142) – a director who made self-conscious, often ironic
use of Freudian themes, ideas, and explanations of behavior – as evidence
in support of his charge. Nevertheless, he refrains from overvaluing authorial intention, stressing the fact that, through close examination of
its formal structure, a particular film "itself" can be "understood as a
work of symptomatic criticism" (142). My only suggestion would be to
give the psychoanalytic critic a little bit more credit, particularly in those

cases where the relevant textual material is not especially self-conscious or reflexive.

If Day is right, then one of the key tasks performed by the psychoanalytic literary critic is *neither* revelation of the Gothic novel's "real (hidden) meaning" *nor* mere description of its surface characteristics. Rather, it is the in-between one of *translation*, of writing and rewriting the Gothic novel's "thematized, narrativized, and embodied" ideas and constructs in terms that are more explicitly Freudian, Jungian, Kleinian, Lacanian, etc. Similar tasks might well be called for, and have in fact been performed, by film scholars examining the horror output of such auteur directors as Tod Browning, Tobe Hooper, Alejandro Jodorowsky, and Kathryn Bigelow.[12]

None of this is to rule out the possibility that horror texts may think in their own ways about the things that psychoanalytic theory, in *its* own ways, thinks about, and that such texts cannot provoke us to revise our views on these matters. Horror films and novels can participate in the conversation themselves, thereby "challeng[ing] the concepts of analysis being applied to them" (Cavell 1996: 91).[13] And while the psychoanalytic critic-as-translator should not be credited with the discovery of something that was present at or just below the "surface" of the text to begin with, like any translator hers is still a task which can be performed well or poorly, which has the potential to elucidate those previously unfamiliar with (or unsympathetic to) the new language, and which requires expertise, interpretation, and insight.

PSYCHOANALYTIC SUPPLEMENTATION

Just as "one should not assume, *prima facie*, that either Freudian psychology or one singular version of psychoanalytic theory is the key to understanding a text" (Allen 1999: 142), one should not assume that any version of psychoanalysis, not even any *combination* of versions, is the key to understanding *every* horror text. Most critics object to what they perceive as psychoanalytic horror film theory's unsupportable claims of explanatory sufficiency. This objection appears in a number of forms and cuts across the distinction I have been drawing between a minimal, epistemically neutral use of psychoanalytic theory and a use of such theory which depends on the truth of at least some of the particular version's substantive theses.

Jonathan Lake Crane, for example, charges those theorists who offer depth-psychological explanations of canonical horror film monsters and narratives (e.g., Evans 1984; Twitchell 1985) with ahistoricity: "In irrevocably linking horror to the unconscious we dismiss, all too hastily, the possibility that horror films have something to say about popular epistemology, about the status of contemporary community, or about the fearsome power of modern technology" (1994: 29). Jancovich emphasizes the reductiveness of a post-structural psychoanalysis that defines horror "as [a] necessarily repetitive form which reproduce[s] the dominant ideology" (1992: 11–12). We have already made mention of Carroll's (1990) argument-by-counterexample against the comprehensiveness of standard "return of the repressed" analyses of horror film monsters. And Tudor finds fault with those "universalizing" explanations of the pleasure viewers get from watching horror films on the grounds that "it is only possible to speak of the appeal of a genre in a particular sociotemporal context. . . . [P]sychoanalytic models, arguably already reductive, will be particularly misleading, conceptually inclined to neglect the variability of audience responses in the name of a spurious generality" (1997: 456).

In fact, I would second any objection to the effect that the majority of psychoanalytic film scholars – of horror and other areas – have displayed an unfortunate tendency to write "Grand Theoretical" checks that they have no intention of cashing.[14] The clarification and delimiting of one's position should certainly be among the tasks of the psychoanalytic horror film scholar. (Wood, leading the way here as usual, writes in the Preface to this volume: "We never asserted [or believed] that ours was the only way of looking at horror films or that our theories explained every horror film that had ever been made.") What I would like to close with is a brief look at how the kind of "culturally embedded, interpretive use of psychoanalysis" (Allen 1999: 142) advocated here allows for constructive replies to those who criticize psychoanalytic horror film theory for what they see as its ahistorical and universalizing tendencies.

Note first that different psychoanalytic paradigms can stand as more or less accurate "translations" of different horror films, cycles, subgenres, and national traditions. Just as particular strains of psychoanalytic thought have proven dominant, at least *en vogue*, in different periods and cultural zeitgeists, particular horror themes, narratives, conventions, and stylistic signatures may well have special affinities with the dominant psychoanalytic strain(s) of the time/place in question. Because it provides room for a sensitivity to generic development and variation, psychoanalytic horror film theorizing need not be homogenizing or reductive. It also allows for the possibility that some horror films, cycles, subgenres, and national traditions (especially non-Western ones?) may not be open to reasonable or convincing translation in psychoanalytic terms *at all*.[15] Finally, because it is neutral with respect to the underlying truth or falsity of the theses and explanatory models it invokes, the mode of psychoanalytic horror film theorizing advocated here is in principle capable of being buttressed by non-, possibly even *anti-*, psychoanalytic film theoretical explanations of certain "deep" features of cinematic horror, e.g., the co-mingled affective responses of pleasure, fear, and disgust generated in many viewers by horror film narratives and images. (The question raised by a number of the contributors to this volume, e.g., Crane and Turvey, concerning just what constitutes a *legitimate supplementation* of theoretical and interpretive models, like the question of just what constitutes a *productive pluralism*, is of central importance for future theorizing of the horror film.)

In his fascinating discussion of David Cronenberg's *Dead Ringers* (1988), Michael Grant – often highly critical of the use of psychoanalysis in horror film scholarship (see Grant 1995; 2003) – suggests an interpretation that combines a Freudian/Rankian analysis of the film's doppelgänger motif with a textual close-reading in terms of Shakespearean/Elizabethan tragedy. At one point, he asserts that

If we are to understand the deaths of the twins . . . we have to integrate them into the narrative in a way that can account for how they acquire their imaginative force, an account that will need to be both critical and evaluative. A psychoanalytic reading can assist in this only insofar as it helps clarify the artistic function of the deaths in the film, a clarification that is in turn inseparable from recognising what kind of film *Dead Ringers* is. (1997: 20–21)

Remove the word "only" from the sentence above, and I would say we are off to a great start.[16]

NOTES

1. In the case of the critic, the presence of an alternative theory need not be readily apparent, and finding fault with a particular take on the horror film (psychoanalytic or otherwise) does not *require* having a substitute ready at hand. In fact, however, close attention to a critic's own methodological commitments, invocation of authorities, and what Matt Hills in his contribution to this volume identifies as *performative theorization* – "the cultural work that theory performs as a persuasive, legitimating, affective, and valorizing form" – typically indicates the presence, however emergent, of a possible replacement for the psychoanalytic theory of horror being attacked.
2. A big if!

3. Elsewhere, Carroll labels this "peaceful coexistence pluralism," which he characterizes/caricatures as follows: "Everyone has his own theory; if you want to conjoin theories, well, that's a matter of personal taste. You can accept some cognitivist hypotheses, but if you also like some aspects of psychoanalysis (at this point, it is usually said, 'I find it useful'), you can have that too" (1996: 63).

4. Slavoj Zizek writes that "while the problem-solution model . . . can undoubtedly lead to a lot of precise and enlightening insights, one should nonetheless insist that the procedures of posing problems and finding solutions to them always and by definition occur within a certain ideological context that determines which problems are crucial and which solutions acceptable" (2001: 17).

5. See Jancovich (1992: 9).

6. For an exception to this claim, see the useful exchange between Creed (1990b: 242) and Tudor (1997: 449).

7. "Screen theory" refers to the loose collection of articles published in the British film journal *Screen* in the 1970s, all of which advocated (in various ways, and to various degrees) a blend of Althusserian Marxism and Lacanian psychoanalysis. For an introduction and critical discussion, see Jancovich (1995).

8. Cf. *The Claim of Reason*: "the form of tragedy is the public form of the life of skepticism with respect to other minds . . ." (1979: 478).

9. For critical discussion of Carroll's counterexamples, see Schneider (2000: 177–79).

10. It is also possible that the arguments presented by the critics in question are fatally flawed themselves.

11. See Iaccino (1994) for an extended look at the "striking correlation" between a number of Jungian archetypes and "the manifest content expressed consistently throughout a number of horror films" (4).

12. See, respectively, Herzogenrath (2002); Brottman (1996); Larouche (1985); and Schneider (2003a).

13. Elsewhere, Cavell writes that "Sympathy with my project depends . . . on unsettling the matter of priority (as between philosophy and literature, say) implied in the concepts of illustration and application. The [Shakespeare] plays I take up form respective interpretations of skepticism as they yield to interpretations by skepticism" (1987: 1). For an excellent example of what Cavell is talking about with respect to horror films and psychoanalytic theory, see LaCaze 2002.

14. According to its critics, "Grand Theory" sees itself as "an indispensable frame of reference for understanding all filmic phenomena" (Bordwell and Carroll 1996: xiii).

15. The presence of counterexamples is not deadly here, but instead provokes a call for alternative translation (perhaps by a different translator) in other, *non*-psychoanalytic language.

16. Thanks to Harvey Roy Greenberg, Matt Hills, Fiona Villella, and especially William Rothman for their constructive comments on earlier versions of this essay.

PART ONE

THE QUESTION OF HORROR-PLEASURE

"What's the Matter with Melanie?": Reflections on the Merits of Psychoanalytic Approaches to Modern Horror Cinema

The past decade has been hard on psychoanalysis. When *Time* magazine commissions a leading contemporary psychoanalytic scholar, historian Paul Gray, to write a cover story on "The Assault on Freud" (November 29, 1993), it is clear that the bashing has become so predominant and widespread to have entered, in fact, the mainstream. The attacks have come from many fronts, indeed from all angles – new critics joining forces with older, more famous opponents. The few staunch (or shall we say obtuse?) defenders circle the wagons and hope, at most, to be able to sustain the assault a little longer.... Perhaps, though, the gravest danger doesn't come from these critics, who are, after all, still mere thinkers. How can practitioners and scholars of psychoanalysis worry about theoretical challenges when the dire twins of psychopharmacology and HMOs appear so steadfastly intent on starving Freud's creature to death? Forget the academic debates! Today what is truly doing psychoanalysis in is capitalism's good old-fashioned market logic.

In these unusually difficult times for psychoanalysis, it is not surprising that its influence within film theory has been fading as well. The first (and perhaps the last) nail in the coffin was the 1996 publication of David Bordwell and Noël Carroll's massive anthology, *Post-Theory: Reconstructing Film Studies*. The title is admirable for the economy with which it expresses both major claims made by the book's editors, namely that (a) psychoanalytic film theory had acquired so much status as to become Film Theory *tout court* (note their ironic use in the book of capital letters F and T); and (b) the damages caused to the field by psychoanalysis' alleged predominance have been such that the first task of the "post-" phase of film studies is one of "reconstruction."

Seven years later comes the present book, whose aim is "to host a series of debates concerning the legitimacy, utility, and claims to validity

of psychoanalytic theories of horror cinema." Are we to convince ourselves that horror is psychoanalysis' last bulwark? That horror cinema,
due to some intrinsic qualities, particularly "lends" itself to psychoanalytic approaches? That, as Andrew Tudor suggests, "the genre itself invokes psychoanalytic considerations, at times borrowing its imagery from
the symbolic apparatus of dream interpretation as well as allowing fictional characters to advance pseudo-Freudian accounts of their own and
others' motivations" (1997: 446)? Provided that psychoanalysis does not
make further claims, even Carroll is willing to concede that "nevertheless, [it] may still have much to say about particular works, subgenres,
and cycles within horror" (1990: 168).

Nevertheless?

How are we to defend a theoretical approach, how are we to argue for
its validity and usefulness, if we accept that this validity and usefulness
are all along *de facto* limited either to a genre (Tudor), or even to "particular works, subgenres, and cycles within" the genre (Carroll)? More
importantly, why would we *want* to do this? What kind of "defense" would
this be?

   Psychoanalysis cannot be defended through some limited, albeit successful, applications of it to texts chosen *by its opponents*. These opponents,
after all, have attacked psychoanalysis as a methodology, as a "unified"
theory. They have not been satisfied to criticize specific applications of
it (many of which, I admit, have been notoriously ponderous and un-
convincing), but have attempted to limit its scope by dismissing some of
the very claims upon which its reasoning is founded. In order to *truly* defend psychoanalysis, we must defend it *qua* discipline, *qua* interpretative
methodology, and avoid the trap of arguing for the validity of only *some* of
its particular interpretations, or, even more useless, of humbly offering
up new such "particularistic" ones.

   Thus, although common sense would suggest (given our limited space
and the magnitude of the issues) that all we could hope for in this forum is
to use psychoanalysis to "explain" horror, I shall instead try to use horror
to defend what the opponents of psychoanalysis most unrelentingly call
into question: that is to say *precisely* its epistemological claims.

VICIOUS CIRCLES

Arguably the two most recurring and forceful criticisms of psychoanalysis
qua interpretative methodology are (i) its "distinctive circularity," that

is to say, the "real danger" that the discipline and its applications are enmeshed in a "self-fulfilling vicious circle" whereby "[i]t is impossible for the non-adherent to be convinced of . . . an interpretative account without being first convinced by the whole apparatus of structural psychoanalysis" (Tudor 1997: 451); and (ii) its "universalizing" fallacy – that is, its alleged attempt to offer explanations that are universal (hence the accusations that psychoanalysis is ahistorical, sexist, etc.).

I shall begin by addressing the charge of "circularity." Tudor argues that "[t]he pitfalls of methodological circularity [can be] avoided . . . by invoking psychoanalytic concepts to explain phenomena only after they are first described in ways which do not depend on an initial psychoanalytic reading" (453). The idea that it is possible to "objectively" describe phenomena from a hypothetical place *outside* the framework of one (*any* one) interpretative methodology has, however, already and convincingly been disproved. Summarizing Oswald Ducrot's theory of argumentation, Slavoj Zizek writes:

[the] basic notion is that one cannot draw a clear line of separation between descriptive and argumentative levels of language: *there is no neutral descriptive content*, every description (designation) is already a moment of some argumentative scheme; descriptive predicates themselves are ultimately reified-naturalized argumentative gestures. This argumentative thus relies on *topoi*, on the "commonplaces" that operate only as naturalized, only in so far as we apply them in an automatic, "unconscious" way – a successful argumentation presupposes the invisibility of the mechanisms that regulate its efficiency. (1994: 11; emphasis added)

As a discipline psychoanalysis cannot be exempt from this fate, although we might speculate that a key reason for much of the opposition to psychoanalysis throughout its history has more than a little to do with its inability – or rather, I would suggest, its unwillingness – to conceal the underlying assumptions behind its naturalized "commonplaces." Freud admitted as much in 1921: "Nor, on the other hand has psychoanalysis any interest in going out of its way to defend [exact] authority, for it itself stands in opposition to everything that is conventionally restricted, well-established and generally accepted" (178).

The same cannot be said for cognitive film theory. This is how Bordwell illustrates his methodology:

Most important, the middle-level research programs [that the cognitivists propose] have shown that *you do not need a Big Theory of Everything to do enlightening work in a field of study.* Contrary to what many believe, a study of United

Artists' business practices or the standardization of continuity editing or the
activities of women in early film audiences need carry *no* determining philosophical assumptions about subjectivity or culture, *no* univocal metaphysical
or epistemological or political presumptions – in short, no commitment to a
Grand Theory. (1996: 29; emphasis added)

Here one is left wondering. When Bordwell refers to "business practices,"
does he really believe that it is possible to look at them, let alone study
them, from a standpoint that is not all along political? Isn't the very *definition* of a "business practice" bound to be determined by some "philosophical assumption about culture," if not by "political presumptions"?
Yet Bordwell's claim seems to be that middle-level research programs
are able to look, objectively, at business practices as if these were plain
and simple "facts." As Zizek writes when explaining the work of Michel
Pêcheuz, "one of the fundamental stratagems of ideology is the reference to some self-evidence – 'Look, you can see for yourself how things
are!'. 'Let the facts speak for themselves' is perhaps the arch-statement of
ideology – the point being, precisely, that facts *never* 'speak for themselves' but are always *made to speak* by a network of discursive devices"
(1994: 11). To be sure, these are precisely the "sort" of arguments
Bordwell and Carroll are rebelling against. But if one agrees with the
idea that *any* "research program" is bound to be based upon a number
of "metaphysical or epistemological or political presumptions," then one
would expect to find a number of such presumptions, more or less successfully hidden, in the cognitivists' arguments as well.

I would suggest that the first, and perhaps most basic, of these presumptions is that there is an ontological difference between rational and
irrational mental processes, a belief which, it could be argued, Freud's
entire work tried to dispute. So much rides on this belief (which the cognitivists want us to accept as a "fact") that we can see why psychoanalytic
and cognitive film theory do indeed appear mutually exclusive. Given
the radical differences in their presumptions, in fact, not only are the
conclusions they reach bound to be irreconcilable – the very *objects* they
study are almost never the same.

Let us take a "classic" instance of this split. Whereas the cognitivist sets
out to examine how perception and cognitive processes are inscribed
in film viewing and how they determine filmic texts, the psychoanalytic
theorist, having been convinced that "nothing but a wish can set our
mental apparatus at work" (Freud 1965: 606), will necessarily ("naturally,"
one is tempted to say) turn his attention to where and how desire and

pleasure – the twin anathemas of the cognitivist! – appear in and shape these same texts. The question at this point is this: how can someone still uncommitted to either theory decide which one is more "convincing"? Or, to put it differently, is it possible to adjudicate the merits and flaws of one theory compared to the other? I believe the answer is yes, though not in the way indicated by Tudor, according to which a good theory is first able to describe the phenomena "objectively" and then offer an explanation for them.

Instead, my answer is suggested in the following statement by Jonathan Culler: "If readers do not accept the facts one sets out to explain as bearing any relation to their knowledge and experience of [cinema], then one's theory will be of little interest; and therefore the analyst must convince his readers that meanings or effects which he is attempting to account for are indeed appropriate ones" (111). Culler's point here is that the ultimate test we can put a theory through is the following: does the theory choose to focus on, and attempt to illuminate, the phenomena that I deem to be central and crucial for an understanding of the text? That is, do I agree with this theory's choice of object(s) of study? Only if such agreement exists can the reader, at a second stage, evaluate whether the theory has produced valuable insights concerning the object(s) in question and eventually compare it with other theories, but – and this is crucial – *only if and when this second theory is concerned with the same object(s).*

Note the telling slippage with which Culler moves from "the facts one sets out to explain" to the much more accurate and sophisticated idea that what the analyst is attempting to account for are "meanings and effects." If the first requirement of a good theory is that it be able to zero in on something essential to the "knowledge and experience" of the text, it is also clear that Culler does not see this "something" as a tangible, self-evident *fact*, but rather as a *result* of the process of the text's fruition – a "meaning" or an "effect." A good theory will therefore be one that sets out to investigate, first and foremost, not the text or its parts but the specific ways in which the text engages its readers or viewers. In the case of horror cinema this will arguably be a theory that focuses not on the monster's qualities (à la Carroll) but on the *effects* these have on viewers, a point to which I will return.

Conflicting theories, then, can and should be evaluated not simply on the basis of the coherence and comprehensiveness of the *answers* they provide, but above all on the basis of the pertinence and appropriateness of the *questions* they pose. Let us take an actual example. According to Carroll,

if we are studying horror films, it strikes me as incontrovertible that filmmakers often play upon what psychologists call the "startle response," an innate human tendency to "jump" at loud noises and to recoil at fast movements. This tendency is, as they say, impenetrable to belief; that is, our beliefs won't change the response. It is hardwired and involuntary. Awareness of this response enables theorists like me to explain the presence of certain audiovisual patterns and effects in horror films, without reference to politics and ideology. Indeed, insofar as the startle response is impenetrable to belief, it could be said to be, in certain respects, beyond politics and ideology. Moreover, such examples indicate that there is a stratum of theoretical investigation at the level of cognitive architecture that can proceed while bracketing questions of ideology. (1996: 50)

Now it strikes *me* as incontrovertible that what Carroll has explained here, by his own admission, is the "presence" of certain audiovisual patterns and effects in these films. Given his awareness of the "innate, hardwired, and involuntary" startle response, he can argue that we do not need ideology, or anything else for that matter (except, of course, cognitive theory), to understand that filmmakers "play upon" such response through their deployment of audiovisual patterns.

It also strikes me as incontrovertible that such an argument in fact "explains" very little, if anything at all. Carroll claims that he is explaining the presence of certain audiovisual patterns, but all he is really doing is *pointing out* a characteristic of modern horror films, namely their tendency to play upon the startle response. This in itself does not explain the presence of the audiovisual patterns in question; it only suggests that viewers jump in their seats because of the startle response. But is this suggestion significant, useful, or interesting? Now that we know the cause of the viewer's jump (the innate, hardwired, involuntary startle response), are we satisfied that we have a convincing explanation? And, more importantly, an explanation of *what?*

I will make my point bluntly. It seems to me that, while Carroll is satisfied with pointing out the cause of the viewer's jump, he is not in the least interested in asking *why* the viewer knowingly (voluntarily) goes into the theater in the first place. Instead of claiming that the *cause* of the viewer's jump is the involuntary startle response, a psychoanalytic theorist would look for the *reason* the viewer voluntarily places him or herself in a situation in which s/he will be startled. This is because the psychoanalytic theorist is convinced that explaining the presence of specific audiovisual patterns in a cultural product without taking into consideration their function is ultimately impossible. Hence, such a theorist would conclude that although horror filmmakers' "playing upon" the startle response might describe *how* certain audiovisual patterns frighten viewers, it certainly does not explain *why* these viewers want to be frightened.

Here one is reminded of the (in)famous question often heard in discussions about horror films. The question is usually posed with a certain urgency by a viewer whose very tone implies serious dissatisfaction with a particular moment in the film being discussed – say, for example, Hitchcock's *The Birds* (1963): "Why the hell does Melanie go up the stairs at the end of the film?" Naturally, the rhetorical point being made here is that Melanie (Tippi Hedren) should be more than able to assume that the noises she hears are made by birds that have managed to invade the rooms upstairs. What does she think her searchlight is going to throw light on up there? Is she stupid or what?

The posing of this question might be understood, I submit, as a sort of evidence that the questioner is insufficiently familiar with horror cinema, or else, while familiar, is still unable to relate to it – i.e., is not a fan or admirer of the genre. Indeed, no true horror fan would ever ask such a question. This is because any true horror fan would somehow feel, would in fact *know*, that it is a moot point. S/he would understand that wondering why Melanie climbs the stairs even while knowing what she is going to find up there, is the same as wondering why people pay to go see a horror film even while knowing that the film will frighten or otherwise disturb them. The true horror fan, in other words, does not ask the question because s/he already knows there could only be one answer: Melanie goes upstairs because *she wants to.* And this suggests that unless one is willing to accept that Melanie's reason for going upstairs is *irrational*, one will never be able to fully enjoy *The Birds.* Nor will one be able to fully understand the reasons for either the film's or the genre's success. In order to grasp these reasons one must first realize that the main question to ask is not "Why does Melanie/the viewer choose to walk into a traumatic experience?" but rather "Why does Melanie/the viewer walk into it *willingly*?"; not "Why does she go?" but (since we know that she goes because she wants to) "Why does she *want* to go?"

If we now return to Carroll, it will perhaps be clearer why I claim that his critical acumen is largely misdirected. One of his most well-known assertions is that "horror attracts because anomalies command attention and elicit curiosity" (1996: 195). This is arguably one way of *describing* what happens in our scene: both Melanie and the viewer are presumably struck by the "anomaly" of flocks of birds attacking human dwellings. But even if we agree that this results in an "attraction" (given that our attention and curiosity are automatically elicited by a confrontation with anomalous monsters), can we not still wonder *why* this happens? Or should we be satisfied by the mere claim that it *does* happen? A claim that, moreover, does not appear so self-evident: isn't it more likely that the attention commanded by "anomalies" has more to do with "fear and disgust" (Carroll's terms) than with curiosity? Why, then, isn't the "reasonable" reaction to the sight of anomalies one of repulsion (i.e., escape) rather than attraction?

Even more significant than these doubts, however, is the feeling that, in dealing with horror in these terms, Carroll is way off target. As the Melanie scene suggests, the so-called paradox of horror has much more to do with the question of an apparently inexplicable attraction toward a situation of expected *danger* than with the fear and disgust presumably provoked by the sight of an "impure" *monster* (Carroll calls them "metaphysical misfits" [54], because they are "categorically interstitial, categorically contradictory, incomplete, or formless" [32]). Our focus, then, ought not be on monsters *qua* objects (e.g., the birds) who produce fear and disgust because they are "anomalous," thereby (but *why?*) attracting our "attention" and "curiosity," but on the mental conflict at work in both Melanie and the viewer – on that underlying ambivalence that mysteriously drives the subject caught in the grip of (at least fictional or "art-") horror *toward* rather than *away from* its precipitating causes. But now, assuming the reader agrees with these points, is it not reasonable to suggest that we have already moved into psychoanalytic territory, the key words here of course being "conflict" and "ambivalence"?

There is no denying the importance of monsters in horror cinema. And yet, if monsters are so important, it is in large part because of what they *do* (or threaten to do) rather than simply because of what they are. Consider Hitchcock's *Psycho* (1960). As is well known, despite the film's enormous and undeniable influence on the genre, Carroll does not consider it a work of art-horror because Norman Bates (Anthony Perkins) is not, "technically speaking," a monster (1990: 39). Carroll also argues that his own theory of art-horror is not rendered questionable by such an exclusion. On the contrary, because Norman, "in virtue of his psychosis, *resembles* the impure beings at the core of the concept of art-horror," Carroll's theory can "explain why it is that viewers are so *tempted* to think of *Psycho* as a horror film" (1990: 39; emphasis added).

The problem here is that Carroll, with his benevolent, fatherly conceit (is it among the critic's prerogatives to decide that viewers are "tempted" or "led" to think something, when in fact they *are* thinking it?) is so determined to maintain his theory that he willingly blinds himself. Indeed, he is quick to acknowledge that there are many reasons why viewers and scholars consider *Psycho* a veritable paradigm of the genre, including its isolated setting, the chance arrival of a sexually appealing young woman, a number of typical narrative structures and shock tactics (including Bernard Herrmann's music), the imagery, the lighting, etc. The monster, however – especially in Carroll's terms – is *not* one of them: first, because Norman is not a "metaphysical misfit," and second (I would add), because he is not the killer *until the very end of the film.* (As far as the audience is concerned, the killer is Norman's deranged old mother.) But despite the monster's relative absence in *Psycho,* many have been tempted to think that this is *the* horror film of the past forty years. What is Carroll's solution? It is to forget all the possible reasons for this "temptation" that he himself has just listed, and to suggest instead that it is simply because Norman "resembles" (when? in the film's very last scene?) his own definition of monstrosity that we are led into error.

The "truth" seems to me to be quite different. What *Psycho* proves is that, *pace* Carroll, what is essential to the modern horror film is *not* the mere presence of a monster but a set of peculiar and specific *feelings* that the films elicit in their viewers. Elsewhere (Urbano 1998), I have argued that these feelings are manifestations of the many forms of anxiety identified by Freud in his second, revised theory of anxiety, and I have also suggested that modern cinematic horror deploys four basic formal strategies (the representation of the monster being, incidentally, one of them) to elicit them. At the core of my argument, therefore, lies the idea that what is characteristic of, and necessary to, the modern horror film is neither its monsters nor its typical narrative patterns, but rather a specific spectatorial affect, namely anxiety.

UNIVERSALIZING TENDENCIES

I suspect that mine is what Tudor would criticize as an "inappropriately reductive" theory, for it attempts to pose a "general" explanation "of the appeal of the modern horror film" (1997: 443). Here we encounter the second main criticism aimed at psychoanalysis: its alleged tendency to offer "universalizing" explanations of the phenomena it studies.[1] According to Tudor, it is problematic to assume that there is a "uniquely distinctive

trait of horror. Indeed, perhaps there can be no uniquely distinctive trait
of a constantly evolving genre" (1997: 456). While I appreciate Tudor's
open-mindedness in leaving that "perhaps" in his statement, I am well
aware that he would nonetheless view my claims with great skepticism.
For I *am*, after all, arguing that viewers, on the basis of a number of
sources (advertising strategies, word of mouth, and above all past personal experiences), form the expectation that horror films will attempt
to elicit in them a state of anxiety. And I *am* suggesting that this is a
"uniquely distinctive trait" of modern horror cinema.

But note: I am *not* arguing that this is the only reason why viewers,
in every single case, go to see horror films. Advocates of particularistic
approaches to the genre are right in claiming that we cannot assume
everyone has the same agenda. Some horror fans might very well be
attracted primarily by the visual displays of gore. Others might, to use
Robin Wood's words, "enjoy and surreptitiously condone the working
out of [civilization's] destruction" which horror movies frequently depict
(1979: 19–20). Still others might count themselves as horror fans simply
because their friends or dates are. Regardless, all of these viewers will
share, or so I argue, the *expectation* that (at least non-parodic) horror
films will try to make them anxious.

Defending particularistic approaches, Tudor vehemently argues
against the "presumed homogeneity of horror" (456). My claim, on the
contrary, is that so long as we are invoking the category of genre we are
de facto talking about groups of texts that can be distinguished from *other*
groups precisely on the basis of some presumed homogeneity (which
may nonetheless be a product of many distinct factors). A recognizable
uniformity among certain films, in other words, is precisely why we speak
of Hollywood genres in the first place. And, as suggested earlier, I believe
that in the case of the modern horror film such homogeneity can be
found in the specific attempt(s) the films make to elicit anxiety (not fear,
not disgust, not self-conscious laughter) in their viewers.[2]

If at any given time in the history of a Hollywood genre we can argue that there is (by definition, I am tempted to say) some quality of its
texts perceived to be constant, this still does not mean that this quality,
much less the genre itself, is "universal" or "immutable": individual texts
always introduce changes. It *does* mean that, if and when such changes
are sufficiently radical, the texts that introduce them enter into a different relationship with the genre (they criticize it, deconstruct it, satirize
it, etc.). In this sense, perhaps the genre never does truly change in a
profound way. It either lives on, adapting to different times with what

we might call "non-radical" changes (e.g., the self-referentiality of *Scream* [1996] and its ilk), or it is effectively superseded. This latter can occur in two ways: the genre either disappears (in the sense that the musical and the western are non-existent *as genres* at the time of this writing), or it becomes the *subject matter* of films which, by virtue of their thoroughly "disrespectful" attitude, can be said to lie outside the genre proper (e.g., Mel Brooks' *Blazing Saddles* [1974] and *High Anxiety* [1977]).[3]

The most obvious examples of non-radical changes are horror's various monsters. Clearly, what makes us anxious can and does change. Bela Lugosi's Dracula does not horrify us today, but – if we are to believe the film's contemporary reviews – viewers *at the time* were very much horrified by Lugosi's performance. Interestingly, this argument is also made in one of the more recent attempts at formulating a monster taxonomy. Working within a psychoanalytic framework quite different from my own, Steven Jay Schneider (2000) nonetheless reaches the same conclusion: both monsters and the manner in which they are depicted change *precisely so* that their effects can remain the same.

Certainly, changes within a Hollywood genre are always interesting. But we should not rule out the possibility that what is constant within a genre can *also* be interesting. The preceding reference to Lugosi's Dracula, for example, might suggest that the elicitation of anxiety might not be limited to the genre's most recent period, but was already crucial in horror films of the 1930s. Such a claim would no doubt be deemed dangerously "universalizing" by many, but in fact in making it I would still be referring to a historically well-defined object (Hollywood) and its audiences (viewers from capitalist, and by and large Western, countries).[4] That is, I would not be arguing that the centrality of anxiety applies necessarily to the horror cinemas of *all* countries, nor would I presume to be able to fathom the kind of emotional relationship members of cultures deeply different from ours might have with its products when exposed to them. I would not, in short, presume the validity of my claim to be universal.

Let us turn to an example of the particularist approach. Tudor apparently endorses the argument according to which,

the characteristic ambiguity and fluidity of bodily boundaries in modern horror is seen to be substantially different to the typical boundary-breaching of earlier periods, because it gives expression to postmodern "experience[s] of social fragmentation and to the constantly threatening confrontation between embattled 'selves' and the risky and unreliable world that they inhabit." (1997: 459)

First of all, let me point out this argument's own "spurious generality" (Tudor 1997: 456). Who is the subject of the "postmodern experience of social fragmentation"? Are we to understand that *every* modern horror film viewer is assumed by the particularists to be such a subject? Every North American one? (Do contemporary Italians experience social fragmentation to the same degree?) Every *urban* North American one? Perhaps, despite Tudor's claims, to make a certain kind of argument inevitably entails making a certain kind of generalization.

But where is the difference, then, between my generalization about the presence and importance of anxiety and Tudor's generalization about the postmodern experience? It is in the length of the period examined (mine is longer). However, insofar as both are general suggestions stemming from the analysis of texts that are perceived to share fundamental traits (think of Tudor's "characteristic ambiguity and fluidity of bodily boundaries in modern horror"), and insofar as both can presumably be verified – Is spectatorial anxiety crucial to the American horror film? Is the ambiguity and fluidity of bodily boundaries typical of postmodern horror? – then the two approaches just do not seem to be so radically different.

The true difference between them – for of course there *is* one – lies in the fact that my approach presumes the necessity of referring to a psychoanalytic theory of psychical functioning (although not to such a theory *alone*) in order to understand the relationship between viewers and mainstream horror films. The particularist rejects this presumption and invites us instead to choose, case by case, from a plurality of "discourses," among which we are supposed to be able to find the one most appropriate for illuminating the films under examination. Psychoanalysis may or may not be included among these discourses.[5]

ANXIOUS VIEWERS

What follows is a series of suggestions. Although Tudor never mentions anxiety, the concept of anxiety (understood in psychoanalytic terms) is used precisely to account for, among other things, the feelings evoked by Tudor's words – uncertainty of bodily boundaries, fragmentation, being under a constant threat, etc. Perhaps, in the context of the American horror film, it could be argued that different sources of anxiety have been represented (or rather hidden behind the film's manifest content) throughout the genre's history. The Bomb and Communism marked the 1950s. Wood's so-called return of the repressed (feminism, the sexual revolution, Black Power) stamped the 1970s. And, as Tudor notes, the risk of bodily and social fragmentation is easily recognizable as our very own contemporary form of anxiety.

This, of course, is where psychoanalysis meets cultural history, and here I am in total agreement with Tudor that the two *must* meet. The suggestion implicitly raised by my argument is that a specific affect, anxiety, quite rapidly assumes (for reasons that would be well worth examining) a much greater importance in Western societies in the twentieth century than in the past. Following this line of thought, we might consider rephrasing the question about the paradoxical nature of horror spectatorship. We might pause to wonder why film – the twentieth century's most powerful and successful form of popular culture – far from simply "giving expression" to anxiety, has produced with the horror genre a body of works able to *generate* anxiety through highly sophisticated formal strategies; that is, through a combination of specific narrative structures and audiovisual (re)presentations.

Let us look at a couple of specific examples. In the essay cited earlier (Urbano 1998), I argue that, like the Melanie scene from *The Birds*, two scenes from the *Alien* series can also be read as (almost self-reflexive) embodiments of two different accounts of the nature of horror film spectatorship. The first scene occurs near the end of *Alien*'s (1979) final sequence. It begins with Ripley's (Sigourney Weaver) discovery that the alien is with her in the escape shuttle. Terrified, she hides in the space-suit compartment. From this moment on, I take her actions as paralleling what one school of thought believes are the actions and motives of horror viewers.

What does Ripley do? She gets into a spacesuit and re-enters the capsule's main area, walking slowly to the control panel and *tying herself down* into the pilot's chair. She then starts releasing powerful air jets over the alien's hiding place in an attempt at forcing it out. When the alien does come out and can be seen standing on the capsule's floor, Ripley, *not being able to look at it*, swivels around in her chair and turns her back to the monster. Now the alien starts to move slowly toward the chair, effectively forcing Ripley *to peek at it from the side of her helmet*.[6] This is the most suspenseful moment of the sequence and arguably of the entire film. Clearly Ripley cannot bear to look at the alien, and yet she also knows that she *must* look at it.

It is only when the alien is about to attack her that the reason for Ripley's actions becomes evident. She slams her fist on the button that controls the opening of the craft's main door and the alien is sucked out into deep space. Now we understand why she willingly submitted to the terrible experience of tying herself down into the chair, luring the monster out from its hiding place, and forcing herself to look at it: to wipe the alien out. Read as a self-reflexive commentary on the genre, this scene would seem to suggest that Ripley's thinking is somehow at work in the horror film viewer as well. One submits to the horror experience in order to get rid of the monster(s). The pain and discomfort experienced during the watching of the films is considered something necessary and inevitable in order to achieve the (presumably pleasurable) final victory.

Even when embraced by psychoanalytic film scholars (who usually suggest that the monster signifies the return of the repressed), I tend to find this account of horror spectatorship very unsatisfying, mainly because it seems totally inadequate to explain the fascination, and often the great commercial success, of horror films in which there is no ostensible monster (e.g., *The Haunting* [1964]), or in which a final victory is *not* achieved (e.g., *Night of the Living Dead* [1968], *The Texas Chainsaw Massacre* [1974], *The Omen* [1986]). Moreover, this account seems inappropriate if one considers the genre *itself*. Think of this particular case, the *Alien* series. In a move extremely typical for the genre, Ripley not only comes back to fight the first alien's numerous siblings seven years later (in *Aliens*), and then again six years after that (in *Alien³*), but, in a nice twist on the "return" theme, in *Alien Resurrection* (1997) she turns up as a clone. In each film, poor Ripley (truly the Sisyphus of horror) is condemned to repeat essentially the same task, and it is precisely this all-too-evident repetition-compulsion of the genre that should lay what we might call the "catharsis explanation" of the paradoxical nature of horror spectatorship definitively to rest.

Our second self-reflexive scene comes from the first of Ripley's returns, James Cameron's *Aliens* (1986), and offers us, I believe, a much better model for horror film spectatorship. Again this is actually a brief scene within a longer sequence. As the marines are exploring the cavernous structure in which the colonists have been turned into cocoons by the aliens, Ripley is watching the action from the control room of the marines' spaceship. Various monitors display the images taken by mini-cameras attached to the marines' helmets. When one of the soldiers walks by a cocoon, the woman trapped inside suddenly opens her eyes wide and, with fear and pain ringing in her voice, begs him to kill her. At this point the woman's midsection begins to bulge, and we immediately recognize the upcoming moment as the series' trademark shock: one of the aliens is about to burst out of the woman's stomach. What is fascinating about this scene is the fact that *Ripley* is watching it on a screen as well. That is, she is depicted in what is clearly a passive (and very painful) *spectatorial* role. Far from the action like ourselves, she can only watch and clutch her stomach in empathy with the victim.

The scene thus stands as a perfect literalization of both major claims made by Carol Clover in the final chapter of her 1992 book, *Men, Women, and Chain Saws: Gender in the Horror Film.* Here Clover argues that horror spectatorship is (1) predicated upon the viewer's alignment with the victim, and (2) a feminine or feminizing experience. Her work is part of a long-overdue effort to stress the importance of masochistic fantasies for an understanding of popular cinema's appeal, in contrast and response to the overemphasis paid previously to theories of sadistic voyeurism. Instead of assuming a desire for mastery on the part of the viewer (typically held to be, first of all, a male viewer), the suggestion is now often made that the central desire may in fact be for precisely the opposite of this: a (controlled) *loss* of mastery.

Clearly this scene literalizes Clover's argument so well because it is also a literalization of the Moloch fantasy which Clover, following Kaja Silverman's work on male masochism, draws on and analyzes from Theodore Reik's *Masochism in Modern Man.* As Silverman points out, this fantasy, needed by a thirty-seven-year-old married man to achieve orgasm during intercourse, is remarkable for the fact that its author "is not its overt 'star'" (1992: 206). The fantasy concerns a complex ritual in which a number of young men are to be sacrificed to an ancient barbaric idol. The patient does not imagine *himself* being mutilated and killed by the high priest; rather, he operates through a third-person surrogate. As Silverman notes:

the fantast is "bound to the scenario through a complex imaginary network. His immediate point of insertion occurs via the young man who will be the next to fall victim ... but that figure himself identifies closely with the victim presently suffering that mutilation." The fantasy's imaginary protagonist, in other words, stands in the same relation to the person ahead of him in line that the fantast stands to his imaginary protagonist. (quoted in Clover 1992: 220)

This last sentence uncannily describes the mechanisms at work in our brief scene from *Aliens.* Like the fantast, the viewer's entry point into the narrative is not through the victim, but through someone else (clearly figured as a potential future victim) who identifies with the victim's plight and pain. Ripley's reactions to the gruesome death of the woman colonist, seen by her on a screen, clearly mirror our own reactions to the gruesome deaths we see on *our* (filmic) screens. But the high degree of self-reflexivity present in this scene is above all a function of the fact that it dramatizes/visualizes the importance of *intermediary identification* with the hero figure as someone who knows that they are next in line, and who must *see* upon another's body all of that pain which the narrative suggests is coming to (for) them.

Many, including Tudor, have found this line of psychoanalytic inquiry fascinating. This is mainly, I submit, because we have the sense that Clover is asking the right questions. And while her answers are perhaps not always completely convincing (I am not so sure, for example, that masochism necessarily results in a radical denaturalization of gender roles), nevertheless her account of spectatorial activity seems right on target. Presumably, this is because it corresponds to the experience of viewing these films as we remember it, and because it is more cogent and coherent than the alternative hypothesis discussed earlier (the catharsis explanation). Note, however, that *both* explanations – Clover's and the catharsis one – are psychoanalytic in nature. The reason Clover's is better is that it is subtler and more complex. Tudor is *wrong* to argue that it is better because it avoids "the pitfalls of methodological circularity." In fact, Clover's psychoanalytic approach *does* predetermine the focus of her analysis:

[The Final Girl] is feminine enough to act out in a gratifying way, a way unapproved for adult males, *the terrors and masochistic pleasures of the underlying fantasy*, but not so feminine as to disturb the structures of male competence and sexuality. (quoted in Tudor 1997: 452; emphasis added)

Far from objectively describing some phenomenon, Clover is here presuming the existence of an "underlying fantasy" and the ability to identify not only with someone of the other gender, but with a fictional character as well. She is, in other words, knee-deep in psychoanalytic "doctrine" (cf. the cognitivists' extended critique of the concept of "identification"), a fact Tudor himself admits: "[Clover's explanation] rests on more general theoretical presuppositions, including a number of precepts drawn from structural psychoanalysis" (1997: 453). Clearly, Tudor is caught in a dilemma here – how to justify the cogency and validity of a specific psychoanalytic interpretation *without* simultaneously praising the discipline that produced it.

I have suggested that one reason why Clover's argument is so interesting is that it focuses not on the *objects* of horror (the films), but on the *subjects* (the viewers). Well versed in psychoanalysis as she is, she believes that texts are significant neither in themselves nor because they give expression to our experience – the ancient theory of Art as a mirror of Life – but because they help us to understand *how* we experience. She does not "use" psychoanalysis to "explain" horror films, but instead seeks to bring into focus a set of historically specific fantasies *through* the study of horror cinema. And insofar as one of the main goals of psychoanalysis has traditionally been the unraveling of unconscious fantasies (those of the patient in clinical situations; those of society at large in the application of psychoanalytic theory to cultural products), Clover's work strikes me as one of the very few examples to date of what Christian Metz wished for more than twenty-five years ago, namely that "the theory of the cinema may some day contribute something to psychoanalysis" (57).

Perhaps, were there more psychoanalytic studies along the lines of Clover's, scholars like Carroll and Bordwell would not feel so alienated by the past predominance of psychoanalysis in the field. On the other hand, perhaps they would feel even *more* alienated, for, after all, it is easier to push aside weak, repetitive, and dogmatic works than strong, well-rounded, and intriguing ones. Indeed, it is evident that the current "fall from grace" of psychoanalysis, in both film studies and the world at large, must be blamed, at least in part, on the discipline itself.

It remains to be seen whether, at this point in its history, psychoanalysis is able – and willing – to try to regain the ground that has been lost.

NOTES

1. A criticism that, of course, is aimed not only at psychoanalysis. Carroll's theory of art-horror, for example, also offers a universalizing account of the genre and is therefore similarly opposed by Tudor.

2. There is another, perhaps even greater, problem with particularist approaches. Although Hollywood genres certainly do "sustain differently constructed audiences," shall we overlook or undervalue the observation that arguably they have been used in precisely the opposite way? That is, haven't generic conventions been one of the most effective means by which Hollywood has pursued the ideological effect of making widely different audiences *feel as one* (we all cry when DiCaprio dies in *Titanic* [1998]; we are all startled when Mother draws back the shower curtain; etc.)? Here the following quote from a contemporary review of *The Exorcist* (1973) is particularly illuminating: "[I]f the message doesn't pull people together, the experience of it does. I, for one, spoke to more Puerto Ricans during my two hour wait in front of a New York theatre than I did the entire two years I lived in New York. And the vomit-splattered bathroom after the show (you couldn't even get near the sink) may well be the closest the Melting Pot ever comes to blending literally" (Ringel).

3. Texts like Brooks' films can perhaps be said to be "based on" the genre, just like certain texts are "based on" pre-existing material (a novel, a play, etc.).

4. Cf. Freud's own acknowledgment of the *relative* nature of psychoanalytic discoveries: "In general, *so far as we can tell* from our observations of *town children belonging to the white races and living according to fairly high cultural standards,* the neuroses of childhood are in the nature of regular episodes in a child's development" (1959: 80; emphasis added).

5. Moreover, but clearly related to this point, its opponents blame psychoanalysis not so much for its "spurious generality" – they generalize just as much – but for focusing on "deep" elements *shared by* viewers, rather than on the numerous (potentially endless) differences among them.

6. The helmet's wide visor clearly resembles a screen here, reflecting the alien while simultaneously allowing us to see Ripley's terrified eyes.

A Fun Night Out: Horror and Other Pleasures
of the Cinema

Psychoanalytic theories of film, and of the horror film in particular, have been subject to attack from various quarters. This essay responds to these attacks, defending a psychoanalytic approach to horror cinema from objections raised by theorists such as Stephen Prince, Andrew Tudor, Jonathan Crane, Noël Carroll, and Berys Gaut. Some of these objections do little more than wheel out the familiar charge – a common one even in Freud's time – that psychoanalysis is "unscientific." But even if it is true that psychoanalysis is unscientific (by some often objectionable standard), this does not *ipso facto* show that it is false. Adolf Grünbaum's critique of Freud's so-called Tally Argument (see below) is an example of one such "objectionable standard." This critique is basically a gussied-up version of the claim that psychoanalysis is not falsifiable. However, the falsifiability (in principle) of a scientific theory has to be interpreted in a way suitable to the theory in question. It is clear that psychoanalysis is not going to be falsifiable (in principle) in the way that the physical or biological sciences are – that is, by producing an experiment that can conclusively falsify it. Nevertheless, as I will argue, *aspects* of psychoanalysis certainly are falsifiable, and indeed have been falsified.[1]

It is also not difficult to produce examples of disciplines and theories that are (by certain standards) unscientific but true, or likely to be true. Many philosophical theories – whether broadly or narrowly construed – are unscientific and true, though it may be difficult to say which are the true ones. Similarly, some very general theories in social science may be true but unscientific according to the standards of the physical and biological sciences. Thus, Clifford Geertz's enormously influential theory of "religion as a cultural system" (1973: 90) is in my view true but not experimentally falsifiable.

Other objections are based on a misunderstanding of fundamental aspects of psychoanalysis.[2] Though most of the criticisms directed at psychoanalytic film theory are founded on well-worn criticisms of psychoanalytic theory generally, there *are* more specific objections to the application of psychoanalysis to film, especially film spectatorship, and to particular film genres such as horror. In what follows, I shall discuss the general objections before considering a sample of more specific ones. I argue that the general objections to psychoanalysis are unfounded, whereas the specific ones are often based on a misunderstanding of fundamentals of psychoanalysis. This is the case even allowing for the wide variety of disparate views among psychoanalytic theorists themselves.

One final preliminary note: Psychoanalytic approaches to film are often contrasted with cognitive approaches, those who support the latter typically eschewing the former. Freud, however, would have rejected this dichotomy. A psychoanalytic approach to film would be regarded by Freud and most psychoanalytic theorists as a cognitive approach. Those who favor cognitive approaches to film err in not recognizing this that is how it sees itself and in pointing to cognition as a firm basis for distinguishing their own approach from that of psychoanalysis.[3] Whether psychoanalysis is a fundamentally flawed cognitive approach is of course another matter.

GENERAL OBJECTIONS TO PSYCHOANALYSIS

Until recently most, but by no means all, philosophical work in connection with Freud has been concerned with the question of whether Freud's work was scientific – whether it was testable, verifiable, or falsifiable in accordance with accepted scientific procedure. Grünbaum (1984; 1993), Erwin (1993; 1996), Macmillan (1997), Cioffi (1985; 1988), and others (see Robinson 1993) have been far less concerned with the significance and wide-ranging philosophical implications of psychoanalytic theory, or even with the truth of such theory, than with the nature and methods of science.[4] But arguably the scientific status of psychoanalysis has always been a problem for the philosophy of science in general, rather than having any intrinsic connection to psychoanalysis. What constitutes a scientific theory?[5] What are appropriate scientific inductivist canons?[6] Furthermore, even if psychoanalysis is not a "science" given some agreed-upon inductivist canons, it may nevertheless be more or less true. Because a theory can be true without being scientific it is a mistake to see psychoanalysis as *false* if not scientific. Its support may come from various sources and considerations – both theoretical and empirical.

Grünbaum's account of Freud's Tally Argument shows that Freud *himself* was responsible for focusing so much attention on the scientific status of his theories. Freud says that, "After all, his [the patient's] conflicts will only be successfully solved and his resistances overcome if the anticipatory ideas [i.e., psychoanalytic interpretations] he is given tally with what is real in him. Whatever in the doctor's conjectures is inaccurate drops out in the course of analysis. . . . It has to be withdrawn and replaced by something more correct" (1917a: 452). Grünbaum interprets this "as a conjunction of the following two causally necessary conditions: (1) Only the psychoanalytic method of interpretation and treatment can yield or mediate for the patient the correct insight into the unconscious causes of his neuroses; and (2) The patient's correct insight into the conflictual cause of his condition and into the unconscious dynamics of his character is in turn causally necessary for the durable cure of his neuroses" (1988: 14). He refers to the conjunction of these claims as the Necessary Condition Thesis. Such claims appear subject to inductive assessment in accordance with scientific (inductivist) canons, and Freud's apparent adherence to the Necessary Condition Thesis suggests that he agrees.[7]

No doubt Freud believed his theories to be scientific and testable to a degree. However, it should not be overlooked that, whether or not he had sound and/or ulterior motives in claiming scientific status for psychoanalysis, it was probably a good thing for psychoanalysis that he did. It is unlikely that psychoanalysis would have received the attention it did had it not associated itself early on with the mystique of science in a scientistic age. At any rate, even a cursory reading of Freud suggests that his theories were not based solely on clinical data and "evidence," but also, and perhaps even more so, on his observations of everyday life. He understood only too well the presence of mitigating factors and the difficulty of achieving a psychoanalytic cure. Textual evidence notwithstanding, he never strictly adhered to the Necessary Condition Thesis. Freud carried his couch around with him. In psychoanalysis, like anything else, too selective or too close a reading can at times be as misleading as the alternatives.

What then is the evidence for the validity of psychoanalytic theory? According to Jim Hopkins, psychoanalytic explanation is an extension of commonsense or folk psychology. The relevance of thematic affinity (e.g., dreaming of drinking water when one is thirsty) – how it supports Freud's theory – is crucial to his defense of psychoanalysis. Hopkins says

that Grünbaum objects to the idea that "claims as to a causal connection between mental items can be cogently supported by a connection
in content – a 'thematic affinity' – between them" (1988: 59), quoting
Grünbaum's remark that "thematic affinity alone does not vouch for
etiologic linkage in the absence of further evidence." He continues:

Grünbaum has made no case against the view . . . that much of Freud's reasoning can be regarded as cogently extending commonsense psychology. If
Grünbaum has missed something about the connection between content and
wish-fulfillment [i.e., the significance of thematic affinity], and if what he has
missed constitutes reason to accept Freudian claims, then his conclusions
systematically understates the support for Freudian theory. (59)[8]

In addition, and related to instances of thematic affinity found in dreams
and neurotic symptoms, ordinary experience of the kinds Freud relied
upon should not be discounted in support of psychoanalysis. Thus, the
view that our strongest denials are often affirmations; that slips of the
tongue are (often) meaningful; that individuals regularly deploy a variety of ego defence mechanisms at their disposal – all are Freudian insights
that have now become commonplace. They can jointly be taken as part
of the evidence for the truth of psychoanalytic theory. Together, they
allegedly support the inference that psychoanalytic explanations of these
phenomena are often the most plausible ones.[9] When judged against
alternative explanations, psychoanalytic explanations of phenomena like
racism and sexism can also allegedly support fundamental psychoanalytic
truths.[10] Whether or not Woody Allen's psychoanalysis reaches a successful conclusion is – except for Woody – relatively unimportant.

Prince states that "the primary and to my mind insurmountable problem with basing general theories of spectatorship on psychoanalysis is
that such theories must remain unsupported because psychoanalysis is
a discipline without reliable data" (1996: 72–73). However, just as hard
science's notion of falsifiablity is too narrow as applied to psychoanalysis,
so too is Prince's notion of "reliable data." They are too narrow given the
kind of "science" psychoanalysis is. Prince endorses Colby and Stroller,
who claim that "psychoanalytic evidence is hearsay, first when the patient
reports his or her version of an experience and second when the analyst
reports it to an audience. . . . Reports on clinical findings are mixtures of
facts, fabulations, and fictives so intermingled that one cannot tell where
one begins and the other leaves off" (1988: 3, 29). This charge of unreliable data is just another way of systematically rejecting the kinds of
support for psychoanalysis that are in fact available. The criticism falsely

assumes that what constitutes reliable and accurate psychoanalytic data and interpretation is up for grabs – that there are *no* criteria for judging what is and is not correct in psychoanalysis. Of course there is going to be disagreement among theorists as to what those criteria are, both generally and in specific cases. And of course those criteria are going to be very different from the criteria for theoretical adequacy in, say, the physical sciences. But the idea that psychoanalytic practice and theory necessarily employ "unreliable data" is a roundabout way of failing to recognize what *does* constitute psychoanalytical data and why.

Far from regarding his work as final, Freud frequently reiterated that psychoanalysis has a bright future regarding "further discoveries" about the individual, civilization, and the connections between them. Freud constantly revised his theories in view of theoretical concerns and new data. Perhaps the most (recently) notorious example is his revision of the seduction theory. Freud first claimed that actual childhood seductions were the cause of various neuroses. He later claimed that imagined seductions could suffice in terms of the aetiology of neuroses, given all the other conditions of susceptibility, instinctual endowment, etc. Wishful fantasies of various sorts came to be considered important, including fantasies of seductions (e.g., fantasies of parental intercourse). Both the original and altered positions were heavily and vehemently criticized, although for different reasons.

Another example is Freud's (1920) introduction of the death instinct to supplement the sexual/libidinous instinct. The conflict between libido and ego-instincts becomes a conflict between eros and the death instinct. There is also his revision of the account of anxiety in 1926: first he thought that anxiety was transformed libido; then he realized that (signal) anxiety was a reaction to threat from the external world, the superego, and instinctual forces. And then there is Freud's change in topography from Uc.-Pcs.-Cs. to id, ego, and superego in 1923. Such revision – and the extent to which he revised truly is striking – goes hand-in-hand with the falsification of earlier theory and interpretation. So aspects of Freud's theory were (and are) not only falsifiable, but were indeed *falsified* and recognized by Freud as such. Subsequent developments in psychoanalysis build on aspects of Freud's views without regarding those earlier views as sacrosanct. The work of Melanie Klein, for example, and of David Winnicott accept as well as revise aspects of Freud. The ongoing development of psychoanalysis is indicative of the fact that it continues to be revised, refined, and in many cases corrected. By its own light, aspects of psychoanalysis – even key aspects – are falsifiable.

The standards or criteria for falsification are different for psychoanalytic theory than they are, e.g., for physics. But even those in psychoanalysis who claim that it is science have never claimed the standards to be the same – or if they did, they were confused and mistaken. If the demand for criteria of falsification is a demand for criteria of the falsification of psychoanalysis in its entirety, then this is a different kind of demand and standard. It is more akin to asking for criteria of falsification not just for a theory or aspect of physics, but for physics *per se*. And it would seem that there is no more readily acceptable standard of falsification for physics *per se* than there is for psychoanalysis as such.

OBJECTIONS TO PSYCHOANALYTIC ACCOUNTS OF (HORROR) FILM SPECTATORSHIP

Psychoanalytic explanations of spectatorship in relation to horror films – for example, why some people like them and what this says about spectators – are for the most part an aspect of psychoanalytic accounts of film spectatorship more generally. Categories like perversion, voyeurism, fetishism, masochism, and sadism that are used to psychoanalytically explain film spectatorship are the same as those used to explain the (seemingly inexplicable) attractions of horror. Nevertheless, there remain some psychoanalytic concepts and theories – like repression, the "uncanny," and "doubling" – that seem relevant primarily to horror films.

Prince

Prince couples his rejection of psychoanalytic approaches to horror with an endorsement of what he sees as a more empirically oriented research program. He writes that

The empirical research on factors affecting levels of attention and comprehension can give us a more nuanced portrait of spectatorship than does psychoanalysis, and this, in turn, can help us to construct theories that are sensitive to the differences, as well as the similarities, among viewers. Rather than continuing to base theories on a concept of the scopically driven, fixated (or "positioned") viewer, I suggest that we begin to derive our theories and research from the constructs of "attention" and "attentiveness." This will enable us to make a key advance in the way we model viewing behavior. It will enable us to conceptualize, and study, viewing processes in terms of levels of information processing and emotional response. (1996: 78)

His claim about a "key advance" notwithstanding, it is hard to see what the merits of Prince's proposed research program may be in regards to a theory of film spectatorship. His is a program that is concerned with "viewing behavior" in a limited sense, for some vague purpose. It appears to focus on the nature of reception rather than interpretation. Or perhaps he is asking for an explanation of the processes by which film is able to do what it does. (Even if psychoanalysis explains content, it does not explain the remarkable fact that flickering images on the screen can evoke this content.)[11] But what Prince calls for abandons film theory's traditional concerns with the elucidation of an account of film spectatorship – e.g., how and why certain kinds of films engage spectators in certain ways, and what these ways are.

Here is an example of the empirical research to which Prince refers:

A great deal of research has studied the ways young children watch television. Preschool children in a room furnished with toys and containing other adults or children do not stare with steady fixation at the screen. Instead, the child will repeatedly glance away from the screen, averaging about 150 looks toward and away from the screen per hour. Furthermore, glances at the screen are quite brief, and most last no longer than 15 seconds. Observations of adult television behavior reveal a similar pattern: looks at the screen are extremely brief and are punctuated by regular glances away from the screen, with non-looking pauses averaging as high as 22 seconds. (77)

He contrasts this with psychoanalytic film theory:

Aside from psychoanalytic film theory's failure to model a sophisticated perceptual process, the claims it does make ill fit the available evidence on how viewers watch film and television. The problem with the "scopic drive" is that it models viewing as a driven and reactive process during which the viewer's passion for looking is cathected by particular formal cues (for example, "fetishizing" close-ups). The scopic drive implies a unifocal fixation within the viewer maintained by a match of formal features and inner fantasy. (77)

But the empirical research Prince cites does not conflict in any obvious (or otherwise) way with a psychoanalytic account of spectatorship partly in terms of a scopic drive.[12] The fact, if it is one, that "glances at the screen are quiet brief" does not conflict with it. It has nothing at all to do with such claims! (A brief glance can be as scopically driven as a long look.) The concerns of the research, the aspects of spectatorship being investigated, are different. Prince's perception that psychoanalytic film theory about spectatorship "ill fit[s] the available evidence on how viewers watch film and television" is not supported by the evidence he cites. Where is the connection? Why *should* psychoanalytic film theory seek to "model a sophisticated perceptual process?" Such theory has rightly been concerned with interpretation and understanding – not with perceptual models.

Prince goes on to say that "[p]sychoanalytic theory fails to grasp [that] . . . when watching media presentations, the viewer simultaneous executes multiple levels of information processing and engages in a se- ries of interpretive moves. Psychoanalytic theory tends to collapse the viewer's responses into a single dimension fed by primary process en- ergy and the unresolved childhood traumas associated with it" (79). But Prince has not shown that psychoanalytic film theory is reductive in the way he claims, and there is nothing in psychoanalysis that prevents it from grasping what Prince claims it fails to understand. What grounds are there for claiming that psychoanalysis would deny that "the viewer simultane- ous executes multiple levels of information processing and engages in a series of interpretive moves?" Psychoanalysis would be foremost among the original champions of such a view, for it seeks to explain various in- terpretive moves in terms of its theoretical resources. If one is suffering from castration anxiety, for example, psychoanalysis seeks to explain that anxiety in terms of various interpretive moves without denying that the person sees whatever it is that they see. Repression, it could be argued, *necessarily* involves multiple levels of information processing.

Continuing his critique, Prince says that

> By employing the constructs of "attention" and "attentiveness," film scholars can formulate investigable problems. Indeed, we ought to stipulate as a cri- teria of future theory building that postulated theories be able to generate researchable questions. Current psychoanalytic theories of spectatorship do not do this, in part because psychoanalytic critics often aim only to produce interpretations of particular movies, and because many film scholars employ- ing psychoanalytic theory seem interested in abstract and ideal, as opposed to actual, viewers. (80)

But it is unclear why film scholars, as opposed, say, to cognitive scientists, should be interested in the constructs of "attention" and "attentiveness." After all, film theorists' concerns – and not just psychoanalytic film theo- rists – with spectatorship and horror have been aimed at understanding (e.g.) their appeal; how and why they affect us as they do; and what such films say about us, and what they represent.[13] Additionally, the idea that psychoanalytic theories of spectatorship do not generate researchable questions should be rejected. Prince means, of course, that they are not researchable in the way certain questions in cognitive science/psychology are. But psychoanalytic theorists are not alone in rejecting the standards applicable to those research programs as inappropriate and inapplicable to their own fields. Social scientists, economists, and some psychologists do so too; for that matter, so do individuals working in the humanities. The success and worth of their research is not to be judged by standards appropriate to, e.g., the physical sciences.

Furthermore, it is simply not the case that psychoanalytic theory is "interested in abstract and ideal, as opposed to actual, viewers." Psychoanalysis and the approach lauded by Prince agree that understanding actual viewers requires theory. The concepts psychoanalysis sees as essential to understanding spectatorship generally (e.g., voyeurism, fetishism, sadism, masochism) are also seen as necessary to understanding why and how specific individuals view films as they do. Prince's claim that film theory generally, and psychoanalytic theory in particular, has ignored real spectators is, from a psychoanalytic perspective, false. Such theory does not agree with what Prince thinks is important about spectatorship, but that is another matter. In short, Prince basically ignores the question of why film theory *should* be concerned with the constructs he thinks are key – e.g., those of "attention" and "attentiveness."

Crane

Crane too claims that psychoanalytic approaches to spectatorship tend to be reductionistic. This, he argues, is partly because they are ahistorical and, echoing Prince, because they tend to reduce group dynamics to the operations of the individual psyche. Discussing horror, Crane writes:

Whatever the new terrors mean, they can only be understood in conjunction with a much larger world than that of the solitary misfit coming to grips with his or her own discomfiting sexuality. By consistently reading the audience as an individual psyche, horror films have been turned into tokens of universal, unchanging, and, ultimately, undifferentiable archetypes or psychic black holes with no historical relation to the times of the people who made and understood them. (1994: 39)

The claim that psychoanalysis is ahistorical is only partly true, and Crane's own exposition covers a variety of psychoanalytic approaches that are not, or need not be, reductionistic. Psychoanalytic theory does not deny that human beings are historically conditioned in certain ways – for example,

it allows that the forms particular neuroses take are historically conditioned. Thus, the neuroses that Freud treated in Vienna at the turn of
the century were indeed partly a product of that era and locale. In particular, they were a product of the treatment of women and their role in
society at the time. It is basic mental processes and some contents that
are relatively unconditioned by time. The often heard, but insupport-
able objection that psychoanalysis is only applicable, if applicable at all,
to middle-aged and middle-class Viennese at the turn of the nineteenth
century is perhaps what Crane has in mind. He seems to think it is a
telling criticism of psychoanalytic film theory that versions of one-time
frightening monsters such as Frankenstein and Dracula are now used to
sell breakfast cereals. But psychoanalytic film theory offers explanations
of how and why what frightens us is in some respects historically conditioned and may indeed change over time (see, e.g., Schneider 1997;
2000 for an explanation based on Freud's 1919 essay, "The 'Uncanny'").
Psychoanalysis sees an audience not as an individual psyche, though there
may be group dynamics in an audience. It sees an audience as a group of
individual psyches – which is precisely what it is.[14]

Crane continues by quoting an earlier (1988) article by Prince:

In reading a culture and its attendant texts, Freud and his varied followers
move rather too quickly from the individual to the social, attempting explanations of such collective phenomena as group dynamics, art or religion in
relation to the operations of the psyche, writ large. By collapsing the social
into the psychic life of the individual, Freud risked losing the social, and a
similar problem exists with regard to our theoretical understanding of horror
films. (39)

It is true that for Freud aspects of the social are explainable in terms of
the psychic life of the individual, but he never reduced the former to the
latter. Freud was well aware of, and discussed, various ways in which group
dynamics affect the individual psyche, and vice versa; and he recognized
that groups were often best seen as more or other than the sum of individual psyches. At any rate, neither Prince nor Crane give any substantive examples where the problem they allege interferes with a particular
psychoanalytic explanation of horror.

Tudor

Tudor criticizes Grixti's (1989) "beast within" approach as a way of explaining the attraction of horror. According to Tudor, Grixti traces the

expression of this approach "in the views of such popular horror writers as James Herbert and Stephen King as well as in those academic perspectives which invoke catharsis as a key mechanism or claim that horror appeals to deep-seated, psychoanalytically intelligible repressed desires":

Underlying such arguments, [Grixti] says, is the belief "that human beings are rotten at the core," whether by nature or nurture, and that horror resonates with this feature of the human condition. The genre serves as a channel releasing the bestiality concealed within its users. If the model is that of catharsis, then the process is deemed to be beneficial: a safety valve. If the model is one of articulation and legitimation, then the genre is conceived to encourage consumers in their own horrific behaviour. Either way, the attraction of horror derives from its appeal to the "beast" concealed within the superficially civilized human. (1997: 445)

First of all, there is no psychoanalytic explanation that explains the attraction of horror in terms of a "beast within." Furthermore, a "beast within" approach need not and does not equate to a belief that human beings are rotten to the core. That aside, psychoanalysis does not assume that human beings are rotten to the core, nor does it need such a view to claim that "horror appeals to deep-seated, psychoanalytically intelligible repressed desires" and that the genre serves as a channel for certain kinds of emotional release. If repression was incompatible with decency then we would all be indecent. But psychoanalysis strives to show how repression and its resulting neurotic activities are quite compatible with both "normalcy" and moral decency.

Tudor claims that if all people are supposed to have a "beast within," then explanations of why people like horror in terms a "beast within" fail to explain why only *some* people like horror and not others (445). He rightly points out that other factors must then be employed to explain this differentiation. But those who explain the appeal of horror in psychoanalytic terms such as the return of repressed, the reconfirmation of previously surmounted beliefs, or sadistic tendencies do not deny this. (I have already noted that psychoanalysis does not explain horror's attractions in terms of a beast within or the rottenness of humanity.) Why particular individuals like horror but not others will depend on the individual's particular psychosexual development – a development that depends on nurture as well as nature. Support for this is scattered throughout Freud's writings on the stages of psychosexual development and character types.[15]

Tudor claims that "even if 'beast within' arguments are *prima facie* plausible, they do not really answer 'what is it about people who like horror?' That requires a different kind of explanation" (445). But this is not right. Psychoanalytically conceived, the explanation requires elaboration in terms of both general and particular psychological features of individuals. This is common sense and does not entail that a "different kind" of explanation is required. It is worth noting in the context of Tudor's discussion that, although psychoanalysis offers explanations for the attraction of horror, it also has explanations for the attractiveness of other genres in film and fiction, such as "action" and "romance." It does not single out horror for explanation in the way that Tudor suggests. The only reason it may seem this way is because of the interest the particular question about the appeal of horror arouses. (Even noted horror film theorist Robin Wood has speculated that his "return of the repressed" theory of the horror film may be fruitfully extended to other genres, e.g., the western.[16])

Tudor claims that "an account of horror in terms of the 'return of the repressed' . . . does not directly address the question of the attraction of horror" (449).[17] Though he does not mention them by name, he elaborates this claim by blending together two so-called paradoxes: the paradox of horror and the paradox of fiction. First, if fictional horror produces unpleasurable emotions such as fear, then why do people enjoy it? Second, if emotion requires belief that the objects of said emotion exist or are real, then how is it that fiction can induce emotion? Tudor says, "one might argue that bringing such fearful things to the surface is likely to be far from pleasurable. Freud himself recognizes that the uncanny as experienced in reality (as opposed to in fictions) is a matter for fear, and to understand it as a source of pleasure when induced through fiction requires further elaboration" (449).

Whatever one may think of the interest of these so-called paradoxes, they are not genuine. An explanation of the attraction of horror in terms of the return of the repressed need only deny what in the end most resolutions of the paradox of horror deny. Emotions such as fear, horror, disgust, etc. are not intrinsically unpleasant. In certain circumstances – not just when watching films, but in everyday life – they obviously *can* be enjoyed. Fear and even horror may be enjoyed in certain sporting activities, for example. And disgust may at times be a source of amusement. (In the case of the paradox of fiction, what is usually denied is that belief in the existence of the objects of emotion is required for an emotional response.) If these paradoxes can in the end be resolved – if they are not genuine – then it seems that an explanation of the attraction of horror in terms of "the return of the repressed" is far more direct than Tudor would have it. This doesn't mean that further elaboration of such an explanation might not refer to more general features of emotion, or indeed to additional psychoanalytic mechanisms. But such elaborations do not undermine the "directness" of the psychoanalytic explanation of the attraction of horror in terms of the return of the repressed. There is nothing in the alleged paradoxes that confounds or short-circuits such explanation.

Tudor claims that whatever psychoanalytic explanations are given for the pleasures associated with horror, more is needed than just an account in terms of the "return of the repressed." He says that "it is necessary to pose supplementary mechanisms to bridge the gap between a general account of repression and the specific explanation of pleasure, and these supplementary mechanisms lead away from the pure form of the repression model" (449). But such supplements are not only available, they are also part of any more complete explanation of the attraction of horror in terms of "the return of the repressed." Of course, there are various and often-conflicting accounts of what additional elements are needed to explain the attraction of horror. Thus, Kristeva's notion of "abjection," taken up by Barbara Creed in her (1993) theorization of the "monstrous-feminine" in terms of a Lacanian account of the Real and the construction of the feminine as Other, seeks to give a more complete explanation of the attraction of horror.[18] Whether or not, and to what degree, these notions (and Lacanian psychoanalysis generally) are compatible with what Freud says about horror, and Freudian theory in general, is controversial. But the existence of such psychoanalytically informed theoretical elaborations on the "return of the repressed" do not subvert but instead support this model.

Tudor appears to regard the need for recourse to additional explanation in terms of psychoanalytic theory as a kind of *ad hoc* maneuver, but it is not. In psychoanalysis as elsewhere, a more complete explanation requires additional theoretical detail. The "return of the repressed" may be pleasurable for a variety of different reasons depending on the nature of the repressed element being returned and also on the particular spectator involved. The pleasures of horror, dependent as they are on the effects of the repressed, may involve temporary substitutive satisfactions – much like neurotic activity. Neurotic activity provides a replacement satisfaction for something else that did not occur.[19]

Given that psychoanalytic themes are to varying degrees consciously adopted in some films, including and especially horror films, psychoanalysis may be indispensable in interpreting them. But this is not primarily what those who claim that psychoanalysis is essential to understanding the attraction of horror films have in mind. Their claim is that psychoanalytic theory is relevant because of what it tells us about spectatorship in general and in relation to horror films specifically. If horror films are attractive because they depict and embody the "return of the repressed" in various ways, then they cannot properly be interpreted, nor can their attraction be understood, apart from such theory.

Carroll

The psychoanalytic claim is that horror films *qua* horror films must be psychoanalytically interpreted. Bad horror films – ones that fail to scare or attract, or ones that are really not part of the genre – may of course require no psychoanalytic theory *about horror* to enable interpretation. However, Carroll claims that although psychoanalysis is necessary for interpretation in cases where psychoanalytic themes are consciously built in, it is not essential to understanding and interpreting horror films generally (1990: 168–69). (Note that Carroll is here assuming that authorial intention is relevant to interpretation.) He acknowledges that psychoanalysis may explain the attraction of particular horror films, but says "the psychoanalytic account is not comprehensive for the genre" (174). However, even those who claim that psychoanalysis is essential for understanding the attraction of horror and interpreting horror films need not claim that such theory is "comprehensive for the genre."

No doubt there are some horror films – ones not central to the genre – that may be attractive to spectators and interpretable, for reasons other than those usually given by psychoanalytic explanations of horrors. Indeed, some of these other explanations may themselves turn out to be psychoanalytic. But exceptions can be acknowledged without undermining the claim that psychoanalysis is necessary for understanding horror. To clarify: in claiming that psychoanalysis is *essential* for understanding the attraction of horror, I mean that horror as a genre, and most cases of being attracted by horror, cannot be understood without it. This does *not* mean that psychoanalysis might not need to be supplemented by other theories and explanations in some cases – or even that psychoanalysis might not be immediately necessary in *all* cases.

The distinction between (i) acknowledging that many, if not most, films (or at least horror films) require psychoanalytic interpretation (i.e., that they are *in fact* perverse in some way) and that, (ii) nevertheless, psychoanalytic categories are *not essential* to (horror) films (i.e., that perversion, etc., is not essential to film and spectatorship), so that films need not necessarily be psychoanalytically interpreted, is an important one. This view leaves open the possibility that, contrary to what may now in fact be the case, films *can* be non-perverse and that spectatorship and the pleasures of the cinema need not necessarily involve some combination of voyeurism, fetishism, sadism, etc., to be psychoanalytically understood.[20]

Gaut

Discussing the work of Carol Clover (1992), Gaut writes that she "develops a model of horror film spectatorship which she generalizes to all film spectatorship":

Full of screaming female victims being hacked up by male monsters and serial killers, urged on by an audience of teenage boys, the field of modern horror looks like a happy hunting ground for a Mulveyan in search of unalloyed male voyeuristic sadism. Clover disagrees. For her, "the first and central aim of horror cinema is to play to masochistic fears and desires in its audiences . . ." Sadism has its place, but masochism dominates. In the "slasher" movie, the locus of our identification is the Final Girl, sole survivor of the murderous carnage, who confronts the serial killer and either kills him or escapes. We must identify with her, for in some cases . . . there is at the end of the film no other character left to choose. In adopting her perspective we experience the full force of her terrors, their polymorphous nastiness whipping us up to masochistic delight. (1994: 14)

But Clover's emphasis on masochism hardly undermines the charge of voyeurism. Masochists can also be voyeurists, exhibitionists, fetishists, and any number of other things – including at times sadists; none of these are mutually exclusive. More important, such an emphasis remains incompatible with any view that sees sadism, masochism, fetishism, or voyeurism as *peripheral* to such films. It is incompatible with any account of the genre that dismisses the need for the centrality of a psychoanalytic interpretation. Gaut, however, dismisses such interpretations without ever giving an alternative account.

Gaut also claims that "even if horror viewing centrally involved masochism, Clover gives us no reason to believe that spectatorship in general is based on the perversion" (17). This is not right or, at any rate, is too quick. The question is whether features of horror viewing, like masochism, sadism, voyeurism in various forms, etc., carry over in various ways and in varying degrees to other forms of cinematic spectatorship.

Gaut's supposition that they do not is based on his more fundamental objection to psychoanalysis. Indeed, he seems to have no film-specific objections or grounds for rejecting such views.

Still in relation to Clover's account, Gaut asks whether "the audience's enjoyment of fear and revulsion is to be explained in terms of masochism":

So widespread is horror that its popularity would argue for an extraordinary prevalence of a perversion that many had thought only a marginal phenomenon. Nor should one hold that the audience is only making-believe that it is afraid: it really is scared, for one can experience fear or disgust towards situations one knows to be imaginary, as when one imagines being viciously assaulted, or contemplates stamping on a hamster. (15)

Psychoanalytically speaking, there is no reason to suppose that perversion in general, and masochism in particular, is "only a marginal phenomenon." Masochism is a component of grief, for example, as well as of melancholy and "love-sickness."[21] Gaut seems to think that there is a more or less clear divide between the normal and neurotic, and between the perverse and non-perverse. But one of the cornerstones of psychoanalytic theory is a denial of these divides. Everyone is appreciably neurotic in varying degrees throughout significant parts of their lives. So important is this thesis, and so contrary to many people's way of thinking about themselves, that Freud (1917a) cited it as a reason why many people would reject psychoanalysis outright. Of course, one must be careful to distinguish sadism, masochism, etc. as nosological categories in psychoanalysis and as dispositions that may become mobilized transiently in people, while they watch movies, who would not be classified as sadists by psychoanalysts or psychiatrists.[22]

Gaut claims that "despite the attractiveness of the thought that horror spectators are masochists, masochism is predominantly a sexual perversion, and this severely curtails its applicability to horror. Specific films may incorporate masochistic fantasies, but the appeal of the genre as a whole cannot be explained in terms of the perversion" (16). If Clover's view is that the appeal of horror generally is to be explained in terms of masochistic fantasies, then she may be misstating or overstating her case. For it is not possible, *a priori*, to find out which psychoanalytic categories come into play in which film in relation to which particular viewers. Some films may lend themselves more to one kind of explanation than another for the pleasures they evoke, but how particular people react to particular films is also a function of individuals' personal histories and

psychological makeup. A scene may evoke masochist pleasure for one person and sadistic, fetishistic, or voyeuristic pleasure (or some combination
thereof) for the person with the popcorn in the next seat. Nevertheless,
if masochism is taken as one important element in explaining what psychoanalysis regards as the sexual appeal of the genre – that is, the appeal
is to be explained basically in sexual terms – then whether or not Clover's
account is fundamentally correct depends on whether psychoanalysis is
right in this instance. The acceptability of such accounts of the appeal of
horror will have to be measured in part against the plausibility of other
quite different accounts.

Drawing on his previous (1993) work, Gaut says,

The enjoyment of horror is undoubtedly a puzzle, for it seems to consist in
the enjoyment of painful emotions, whether of fear or disgust. However, the
unraveling of the conundrum starts by noting that many people, whether
they be rock-climbers, bungee-jumpers, or racing-car drivers, enjoy the thrill
of fear. Fear is not intrinsically unpleasant, it merely incorporates an evaluatively negative thought, as to the danger of its object. Typically, fear will
be unpleasant, but there is no conceptual requirement that it always be so.
This leaves plenty of scope for certain individuals to take pleasure in it, and
the possibility of enjoying fear is all the greater when one knows that one
is merely imagining the dangers involved, and that one is safe in the movie
auditorium. Horror seeks to ratchet up fear by picturing every awful situation
it can imagine. (16)

Gaut's account does not explain the enjoyment of horror. It merely notes,
correctly, that people do enjoy certain negative emotions. Observing that
many people enjoy fear does not even begin to unravel the conundrum.
It merely highlights it. Psychoanalysis on the other hand *does* explain why
this is so – in terms of character type and more generally in terms of an
individual's psychosexual development, which is the source of perversion.

Gaut's solution to the paradox of negative emotion is problematic insofar as it requires a conceptual splitting off of the evaluative or cognitive
component of an emotion from its affective component. But what makes
an emotion an emotion, and the emotion that it is rather than some other,
is the dynamic interactions the cognitive and non-cognitive components
of an emotion have with each other.[23] All that Gaut has done is to note
what he thinks are "negative" about negative emotions ("an evaluatively
negative thought"), and then go on to state the obvious – that negative
emotions can be pleasurable. He has not explained *how* or *why* it is possible that negative emotions are pleasurable. Indeed, Gaut (1993) says

that explaining why negative emotions are pleasurable is no part of his thesis or task – a view that he fails to reiterate in this later essay – as if this question was not central or that there was nothing to explain.

Gaut's 1994 discussion confuses or conflates two issues that he previously distinguished. The first is the so-called paradox of horror: how is it possible to like intrinsically negative emotions? His answer is that there is nothing paradoxical about it – we just do – and what makes the emotion negative is the evaluation component. The second and separate issue is *why* we like negative emotions like fear. Formerly he said he offers no explanation of this. But here he seems to suggest that no explanation is needed – perhaps none is even possible – and that the question as to why we like them is basically irrelevant to understanding the horror film's attraction or Mulvey's thesis about voyeurism. From a psychoanalytic perspective, this is not true. Furthermore, Gaut ignores the difficult and interesting issue of why people like such things.

Gaut asserts that "[i]t is possible to enjoy fear without being a pervert, for no psychological malady or distortion need be assumed in these cases; on the contrary, they exhibit if anything a robust attitude to risk-taking" (17). However, the issue is not whether it is possible to enjoy fear without being a pervert, but whether understanding the attraction of horror requires reference to psychoanalytic categories such as perversion. In his blanket statement, Gaut appears to equivocate on the psychoanalytic notion of perversion and substitute a moral or at least non-psychoanalytically understood meaning for the relevant psychoanalytic one. That equivocation takes place is clear in those contexts in which he begins by discussing a psychoanalytic view (e.g., Mulvey's) only to reject it because it seems to run contrary to "perversion" understood in some other (nondescript) way. Given a psychoanalytic approach to horror, the main reason that the attraction of horror films has to be explained in terms of categories such as perversion is because horror itself – what it is about and what it means – cannot be understood apart from psychoanalytic theory. Gaut appears to miss this point altogether in his discussion. Freud, for example, arguably explains horror in terms of the "uncanny" or, more specifically, in terms of the return of repressed ideas and the reaffirmation of surmounted beliefs.

CONCLUSION

One of the general difficulties with the kind of careless rejection of psychoanalytic theory that has become prevalent – the kind, for example, that sees its running contrary to common sense as a reason to dismiss it – is that such rejections are often secondhand. They rely on the critiques and accounts of others, and often show a mistaken and superficial understanding of even the fundamental tenets of psychoanalytic theory.

Psychoanalytic approaches to cinema and an understanding of cinematic spectatorship may well be open to criticism both from its own quarters and others. One need not be an expert in psychoanalysis to criticize its method or theory. But it should go without saying that such criticism must be based on a grasp of the fundamentals of psychoanalysis. An untutored commonsense "let's see what we have here" approach is manifestly insufficient.[24]

NOTES

1. Grünbaum actually claims that psychoanalysis *is* falsifiable, and that by failing the standards set out in Freud's Tally Argument it has been falsified. But this is really just a needless complication, because the Tally Argument's standards of falsifiability are inapplicable. Psychoanalysis can never be falsified by means of the Tally Argument.
2. "Psychoanalysis" refers both to psychoanalytic theory and practice. In this essay it refers mostly to the former.
3. See Glymour (1991).
4. It goes largely unnoticed that much of the recent criticism is a reiteration, in substance and tone, of criticisms Freud faced throughout his career. For essays discussing the implications and significance of psychoanalysis, see Levine (2000b).
5. Cf. Lear (1990: 216ff).
6. See Hopkins (1988: 50).
7. See Hopkins (1988) for a detailed discussion of Grünbaum on the Tally Argument.
8. See Clark and Wright (1988: ix) for a helpful explanation of Hopkins' critique of Grünbaum.
9. See Freud (1901b).
10. See Chodorow (1987) on how psychoanalytic theory illuminates sexism and why feminist thought needs psychoanalytic theory. See Young-Breuhl (1996) for a discussion of psychoanalytic explanations of racism.
11. This is Tamas Pataki's interpretation of Prince.
12. Tudor asks, "So what *is* [horror cinema's] appeal? Although scholars of different disciplinary persuasions have recently researched the genre at some length,...none of them...provides an entirely satisfactory answer to that question. In part the problem is empirical. These studies are unable to marshal any more than anecdotal evidence as to the composition and preferences of horror audiences and so are forced to build their arguments on what may he ill-founded speculations" (1997: 444). However, the problem

is *not* basically empirical, even "in part," but interpretive. How can further evidence of "the composition and preferences of horror audiences" help answer questions about horror's appeal, except by bolstering particular interpretive schema? Are more data needed? Would these data help bolster a psychoanalytic interpretation in terms of "the return of the repressed" or some rival cognitive approach? Try to imagine or invent data that would.

13. Tudor sees these as separate questions: "'What is it about people who like horror?' and 'what is it about horror that people like?'" (444). Psychoanalytically speaking, however, these are two sides of the same coin.

14. See Freud (1920–22), *S.E.* vol. 18.

15. See, e.g., Freud (1915–17).

16. See Wood (1979).

17. See Schneider (1997; 2000) for just such an account. Schneider also explains why certain kinds of monsters and horror films can lose their appeal and fail to frighten by failing to evoke the "uncanny."

18. Tudor (1997: 450) cites various examples of films in which the monstrous-feminine "does play an important role." It is unclear how he can claim this given his apparent rejection of feminist film theory that employs "structural psychoanalysis."

19. See Hopkins' (1982: xxi) discussion of the table-cloth lady.

20. Consideration of this possibility leads to the Paradox of the Depraved Spectator. See Levine (2001).

21. See Freud (1917b).

22. One should also distinguish between "the return of the repressed" as this occurs in neuroses and as it occurs in watching films or other aesthetic experience. Cf. Freud's (1919b) distinction between repressing and surmounting content. Thanks to Tamas Pataki for these points.

23. See Oakley (1993: ch. 1).

24. My thanks to Damian Cox, Tamas Pataki, and Steven Schneider.

Excerpt from "Why Horror? The Peculiar Pleasures of a Popular Genre" with a New Afterword by the Author

THE RETURN OF THE REPRESSED

By far the most common accounts of horror's appeal are grounded in concepts drawn from Freudian theory, and I shall approach them by focusing first on simple repression models and then on the more elaborate analyses offered by "structural psychoanalysis." This psychoanalytic emphasis is not recent – though the Lacanian turn in cultural theory has lent it additional force – and it is tempting to speculate as to why, more than with any other popular genre, those puzzled by horror should so often have turned to psychoanalysis in search of enlightenment. In some part, of course, the genre itself invokes psychoanalytic considerations, at times borrowing its imagery from the symbolic apparatus of dream interpretation as well as allowing fictional characters to advance pseudo-Freudian accounts of their own and other's motivations. Thus, where its typical monsters have been compulsive murderers, as so often in the past thirty years, the genre's common presumption has been of a psychopathology rooted in the psychosexual dynamics of childhood. In this respect, at least, Norman Bates long ago escaped the confines of *Psycho* to leave his distinctive imprint on modern horror.

However, although the genre's self-conscious borrowing from psychoanalysis is not without significance for the theoretical frameworks invoked in its understanding, such an emphasis does not *entail* any specific theoretical consequences and so hardly explains psychoanalytic theory's predominance. More plausible, perhaps, is the suggestion that psychoanalytic theories of horror gain credibility from the widespread belief that horror fans are a peculiar bunch sharing a perverse predilection. A taste for horror is a taste for something seemingly abnormal and is therefore deemed to require special explanation in terms of personality features not usually accessible to the casual observer. How could anyone want to be horrified, disgusted even, unless there was some deeply hidden reason of which they were not aware? Freud himself, in singling out the "Uncanny" for one of his rare expeditions into the domain of literature (1919b), gives some warrant for the notion that this is a distinctive problem meriting specifically psychoanalytic attention, though he is more modest than some of his followers in also leaving room for what he calls "aesthetic enquiry." So let me begin by briefly recalling some of the main features of Freud's approach to the uncanny – less for its own sake than because his terms have informed so much of what has followed.

The heart of Freud's account is captured in a quotation he takes from Schelling concerning the meaning of the German word *unheimlich* (literally "unhomely," but in Freud's essay more appropriately translated as "uncanny"): "'Unheimlich' is the name for everything that ought to have remained . . . secret and hidden but has come to light" (1919b: 345). The uncanny, he suggests, is that class of frightening things that occasion anxiety because they relate to repressed affect: "something which is familiar and old-established in the mind and which has become alienated from it only through the process of repression" (363–64). The experience is simultaneously both *heimlich* and *unheimlich*, uncanny precisely because it was once familiar but has then been repressed. Of course, not all recalling of long-repressed desires gives rise to the uncanny, and Freud singles out two specific classes of the phenomenon. In the one, uncanniness stems from the return of repressed infantile complexes; in the other, from the recurrence of primitive beliefs which have been surmounted. While recognizing that the boundary separating these classes may be blurred, he argues that the form of the uncanny founded on repressed complexes is "more resistant and remains as powerful in fiction as in real experience" (374). In "The 'Uncanny'," he invokes the castration complex, primary narcissism, and the "compulsion to repeat," but, of course, other potential foci for repression and the uncanny are present throughout Freudian theory.

These root ideas have found their way into numerous investigations of horror, especially those centering on what might be called the "repression model." Perhaps the best known of these in recent years is the "return of the repressed" argument advanced by Robin Wood and his colleagues. They make use of the concept of "surplus repression" which, following Marcuse, they distinguish from Freud's original "basic" repression. Surplus repression, Wood argues, is the product of particular cultures, in ours relating mainly to sexual energy, bisexuality, female sexuality, and children's sexuality. Linked to this is the idea of "the Other" and the key ideological operation of "projection on to the Other of what is repressed within the Self, in order that it can be discredited, disowned and if possible annihilated" (1979: 9). In the case of horror movie monsters, then, the repressed is dramatized in the form of the monstrous Other. Furthermore, "in a society built on monogamy and family there will be an enormous surplus of sexual energy that will have to be repressed; and what is repressed must always strive to return" (15). Clearly, then, the general thrust of this analysis is toward an ideological function for horror in sustaining surplus repression and the bourgeois social order upon which it depends, though Wood does argue that in specified instances horror may play a subversive role.

A somewhat different example is James Twitchell's use of a Freudian "return of the repressed" argument, deployed without the additional concept of surplus repression and thus without the distinctive analysis of bourgeois, patriarchal society informing Wood's account. In Twitchell's version, social contextualization is approached via "myth." "Myths inform an identifiable audience about a particular problem at a specific time . . . [Myths] suggest specific behavior that maintains both the social order and bolsters the individual's sense of worth" (1985: 85). Thus, although he recognizes horror's role as counterphobic (overcoming fearful objects) and as a context for the projection of objects of sublimated desire, these functions are caught up in servicing a key rite of passage. The horror movie audience, Twitchell argues, is mainly adolescent, in the process of making the transition "from onanism to reproductive sexuality" (65). To manage this successfully, and to guarantee social order, adolescents need to be informed about the limits of acceptable sexuality. More particularly – here Twitchell invokes Freud's fable of the primal horde in *Totem and Taboo* – they need to learn the horror of incest: "It has to be taught, and shivers are a most efficient teacher" (96). Horror myths, therefore, are primarily concerned with this process of sexual initiation, both expressing the sexual confusions of their youthful audience and, by performing a function similar to initiation ceremonies in other cultures, presenting in disguised form the norms of appropriate sexual behavior.

These two otherwise diverse cases illustrate the major features of this particular tradition in psychoanalytically influenced analyses of horror. They share a number of key assumptions. First and foremost, they see repression as a constitutive feature of human development, the mechanism through which we are constrained to overcome the (anti-social) desires of infancy. The primary focus for this repression is sexuality, and horror, in a variety of ways, acts as a channel for expression of the repressed affect. In so doing it sustains order, whether by cathartic release of otherwise threatening urges or by reinforcing acceptance of repressive taboos presumed to be essential to social survival. So, once given a model of human development that presupposes the necessity of repression, horror can be conceived to act both as a "safety valve" where repressed affect threatens to surface and as a figurative reminder of the fearful consequences if the "rules" of sexual behavior are broken. In a real sense, then, such perspectives see human agents as unaware victims of their cultures, and necessarily so, because on this account our very psychic functioning would be impaired without the mechanism of repression.

Of course, most theories add to and modify this core repression model. Wood, for instance, opens up space to argue for an emancipatory role for at least some horror by virtue of his concern with surplus rather than basic repression. In as much as surplus repression is socially specific, not fundamental to the very process of human development, it can be overcome. However, the line between surplus and basic repression is not clear, and there are those who would want historically and culturally to relativize many of the "basic" repressions as they are formulated within the Freudian tradition. But to pursue that would take us into a critical discussion of the foundations of psychoanalytic theory itself, an enterprise well beyond this essay's scope. Here I shall limit myself to some observations on the repression model and our understanding of horror's attractions.

While an account of horror in terms of the "return of the repressed" may appear to relate certain features of horror texts illuminatingly to our presumed psychosexual constitution, it does not directly address the question of horror's attraction. Indeed, one might argue that bringing such fearful things to the surface is likely to be far from pleasurable. Freud himself recognizes that the uncanny as experienced in reality (as opposed to in fictions) is a matter for fear, and to understand it as a source of pleasure when induced through fiction requires further elaboration. One commonly voiced possibility is that pleasure is gained simply by dealing with fearful matters in what are known to be safe circumstances. Here the specific character of the repression is immaterial; it is securely dealing with fear, which attracts us. Another possibility is that catharsis is a necessary consequence of fictionally evoking repressed affect, and the subsequent relief, if temporary, is pleasurable much as masturbation relieves sexual tension. Or a yet more complex pleasure might be that derived from the unconscious ambiguity of our responses to taboo subjects: pleasure in indulging sublimated infantile desires; pain because the context of this indulgence is one of monstrosity and disgust. As Noël Carroll (1990: 170) suggests in adapting Ernest Jones's approach to nightmares, the fiction allows us the one only at the price of the other – they are inextricably intertwined because this is precisely how repression works. But in all these arguments, note that it is necessary to pose supplementary mechanisms to bridge the gap between a general account of repression and the specific explanation of pleasure, and these supplementary mechanisms lead away from the pure form of the repression model.

THE UNCONSCIOUS OF IDEOLOGY

A move of this kind can be seen more clearly in a second main group of psychoanalytically influenced approaches to horror. This work, partly derived from feminist film theory, invokes "structural psychoanalysis," which it distinguishes from more mechanistic repression accounts. As Barbara Creed (1990b: 242) puts it, in rightly criticizing my own inclination to construe all psychoanalytic perspectives in terms of the repression model, structural psychoanalysis "helps us to see the unconscious as a structuring element at work in all cinematic representation . . . [It] makes possible a comprehensive reading of the construction of fear in horror texts in relation to filmic codes and *mise-en-scène.*" While one might query her claim, indeed any claim, to a "comprehensive reading," what is evident is that in such views psychoanalytic concepts are used in a more hermeneutic mode, revealing complex meanings by close analysis of texts and thereby seeking to uncover the "workings of the unconscious of ideology." In exemplifying this strand of thinking I shall again consider two somewhat contrasting approaches, those of Creed (1986; 1993) and Clover (1987; 1992).

Creed is concerned with exploring the significance of the monstrous-feminine in horror films using Julia Kristeva's Lacan-influenced account of abjection. She follows Kristeva in emphasizing the breaching of boundaries in the creation of abjection and in focusing on the mother–child relationship wherein the mother is made abject in the child's struggle to enter the symbolic. The passage from maternal authority to the law of the father is the basis upon which the monstrous-feminine is constructed. Of course, abjection in the horror film is not *solely* related to the monstrous-feminine, but the latter is of crucial significance:

The horror film brings about a confrontation with the abject (the corpse, bodily wastes, the monstrous-feminine) in order, finally, to eject the abject and re-draw the boundaries between human and non-human.... [T]he horror film works to separate out the symbolic order from all that threatens its stability, particularly the mother and all that her universe signifies. (1986: 53)

This construction of the feminine as Other protects social order by sustaining the symbolic in the service of which "the horror film stages and re-stages a constant repudiation of the maternal figure" (70), a signifying practice that is constructed within patriarchal ideology. Our pleasure in horror, then, is a "perverse" desire to confront such images of the abject and "also a desire, having taken pleasure in perversity, to throw up, throw out, eject the abject (from the safety of the spectator's seat)" (48).

Of course, the plausibility of all this depends on first accepting the larger project of structural psychoanalysis, and therefore my brief summary does limited service to Creed's argument. It is clear, however, that a concept of the monstrous-feminine does play an important role in some horror movies, not least in *Alien* (1979), *Carrie* (1976), *The Exorcist* (1973), *The Brood* (1979), and *The Hunger* (1983), which she discusses at length (1993: 16–83), and, furthermore, that horror's insistence on breaching various kinds of boundaries is of considerable significance in understanding its appeal. Yet neither of these features *requires* psychoanalytic theory for their elucidation, though the theory might be judged to give useful leverage on them, and to understand the mechanism of our "perverse" pleasure in horror calls for supplementary arguments as much as did the unmodified repression model.

But perhaps more interesting than these issues is the dependence of this hermeneutically inflected use of psychoanalytic theory on prior acceptance of a descriptive framework also drawn from psychoanalysis. Consider the following descriptive constructions from Creed's 1986 essay (emphasis added throughout). "The horror film's obsession with blood, particularly the bleeding body of woman, where her body is transformed into the 'gaping wound,' *suggests that* castration anxiety is a central concern of the horror film" (52); "the seven astronauts emerge slowly from their sleep pods *in what amounts to* a re-birthing scene," and "this scene *could be interpreted as* a primal fantasy in which the human subject is born fully developed" (55); "*we see her* [the archaic mother] *as* the gaping cannibalistic bird's mouth ... the mysterious black hole *which signifies* female genitalia" (63). To someone not already committed to the psychoanalytic perspective, these interpretive claims are cause for skepticism. Suggests castration anxiety to whom? Amounts to re-birthing for what reasons? Why should the scene be interpreted as a primal fantasy? Who is the "we" who see the archaic mother in this way? Under what specific circumstances do black holes come to signify female genitalia?

I raise such questions not in a spirit of nihilistic mischief or crude empiricism, but to underline the distinctive circularity of this form of analysis. The analyst provides descriptions of the imagery which presuppose a framework in which representations of the monstrous-feminine are central. Then these descriptions are presented as evidence of the very significance of the monstrous-feminine. Of course, this is not necessarily a self-fulfilling vicious circle, though in some circumstances that is a real danger, but it does force us to recognize that in such approaches the moment of interpretation is also the moment of justification. It is therefore impossible for the non-adherent to be convinced of such an interpretive account without being first convinced by the whole apparatus of structural psychoanalysis. And because these constructions operate, if they operate at all, at an unconscious level, it is difficult to imagine evidential grounds (as opposed to an act of theoretical faith) on which alternative explanations might be preferred or dismissed.

This is not to suggest that psychoanalytic concepts are of no utility in seeking to comprehend horror's appeal. However, because of their totalizing and self-confirming potential when used in direct interpretation, application does require considerable care. One possible moderating strategy is to embed the psychoanalytic element in a more prosaic and socially aware analysis of the texts involved, beginning by establishing those codes of the genre's operation that would readily be understood by consumers of horror themselves, and only then moving on to a range of more esoteric "depth analyses." This has the virtue of establishing a common framework of interpretation in relation to which candidate explanations may be compared. After all, other than by prior agreement that a particular theory has privileged access to the ultimate ontological grounds of human activity – a faith that some psychoanalytic work does seem to exhibit – there is no reason to suppose the necessary primacy of any one perspective. To do so, indeed, would be a pernicious form of reductionism.

In this context Carol Clover's 1992 study of gender in modern horror cinema is particularly instructive in that she deploys psychoanalytic concepts as part of a larger analytic framework. Although her full analysis is too rich and subtle for brief summary, I shall try to explore at least the main outline of her argument. Clover's point of departure is the observation that male spectators are both willing and able to identify with female characters and, more specifically in the horror film, with "females in fear and pain" (5). How is this to be understood? Prevailing views, Clover argues, tend to assume that such cross-gender identification is unlikely or even impossible, and, although she may overstate the extent to which such claims do prevail, it is certainly true that the tradition based in Laura Mulvey's influential work on visual pleasure has emphasized the sadistic/voyeuristic rather than the empathic quality of the male cinematic gaze directed at the screen female. While Clover concedes that horror films may indeed offer such pleasures to male viewers, she does not "believe that sadistic voyeurism is the first cause of horror" and she therefore seeks a critical and political interrogation of "the standard critique of horror as straightforward sadistic misogyny" (19). In pursuing that, she explores some distinctive strands of the modern genre (the slasher film, rape-revenge films, possession films) in terms of the gender-specific pleasures they might afford to male spectators.

The heart of her argument lies in the claim that the availability of the "girl-hero" for purposes of identification allows male viewers to "simultaneously experience forbidden desires and disavow them on grounds that the visible actor is, after all, a girl" (18). Thus, in the slasher film the distinctive figure of the "Final Girl" – the only one to survive the increasingly frenzied attacks of the (male) killer – is a clear focus for such identification: "She is feminine enough to act out in a gratifying way, a way unapproved for adult males, the terrors and masochistic pleasures of the underlying fantasy, but not so feminine as to disturb the structures of male competence and sexuality" (51). Though the Final Girl is strong and resourceful, she is "an agreed-upon fiction" available to male viewers as a focus for their sadomasochistic fantasies. But, Clover argues, this is not the whole story. Gender is much more compromised in the slasher film than even this suggests. The Final Girl is given both masculine and feminine traits; she undergoes the trials and tribulations of pursuit in conventional female-victim fashion but also saves herself as a typical male hero might. Similarly, although the killer wields the phallic weapon, his masculinity is represented as "severely qualified." Accordingly, and on the basis of much more detailed analysis than this, Clover suggests that "the text at every level presents us with hermaphroditic constructions" (55) and, therefore, that the "gender-identity game" is central to modern horror.

So it is the very ambiguity of gender representation in modern horror cinema that is vital to the male spectator's involvement. But where does structural psychoanalysis enter the argument? Essentially, it provides

Clover with terms for explaining this combination of gender slippage and vicarious playing-out by reference to the horror film's scopic regime. Such films, she claims, invite both an "assaultive" and a "reactive" gaze. The former is the familiar (Metzian) sadistic/voyeuristic look associated with our identification with the camera, further developed in its gendered aspect by Mulvey. In modern horror, it is the look of the camera and of the predatory killer with whom the audience is at least temporarily positioned. The latter is the gaze in which we, the audience, are assaulted rather than assaulting, our involvement constructed through our empathic identification with characters and not through our controlling voyeurism. This gaze is gendered feminine and, contrary to the primacy conventionally accorded the sadistic, mastering look, "it is the reactive gaze that has pride of place in the scopic regime of horror" (205). From here it is but a short step to associate reactive involvement in horror with masochism or, more precisely, Freud's "feminine masochism." Indeed, Clover argues that the specific masochistic fears that Freud considers (being copulated with, impregnated, beaten, penetrated, castrated, etc.) are those apparent in the modern horror subgenres she discusses. So, she concludes, "the first and central aim of horror cinema is to play to masochistic fears and desires in its audience" (229).

Note that the pitfalls of methodological circularity are avoided here by invoking psychoanalytic concepts to explain phenomena only *after* they are first described in ways that do not depend on an initial psychoanalytic reading. Thus, Clover's investigation can be reconstructed as beginning with two interrelated empirical observations, one concerning the audience (male audience members can identify empathically with female horror victims), and the other textual (modern horror texts exhibit distinctive ambiguities in their representation of gender). Her account of horror cinema's scopic regime and her analysis of the role of masochism then provide grounds for a linked explanation of the two phenomena. Naturally that rests on more general theoretical presuppositions, including a number of precepts drawn from structural psychoanalysis as well as, beyond that, a version of the repression model. But what is important is that it is possible to make a judgment about the explanation's efficacy without first committing oneself to a psychoanalytic framework of interpretation and, essential to that judgment, it is therefore possible to propose other explanations of the same phenomenon. It is this conceptual openness that distinguishes Clover's approach from Creed's, for the latter's description of horror texts is constructed primarily using psychoanalytic descriptors, thus making non-psychoanalytic explanations difficult to mount without first redescribing the texts. In Clover's work, then, it is possible to see some of the points at which psychoanalytic theories of horror might be enhanced by coordination with other explanations. But what are these alternatives to psychoanalytic theory in constructing general explanations of horror's appeal?

AFTERWORD (MAY 2001)

Several contributors to this volume have been kind enough to refer to my "Why Horror?" essay. Two of them – Cosimo Urbano and Michael Levine – mount extended critiques of various aspects of my argument in the course of their (different) defenses of psychoanalytic approaches to horror. While I am in agreement with some of the points that they make, there remain three basic issues on which we differ. These three issues are (1) the epistemological status of the relation between theory and evidence, both generally and in applications of psychoanalytic film theory; (2) the category of *genre* and the question of generality and particularity of explanations of the appeal of horror; and (3) the status and character of "return of the repressed" arguments. The first two are raised primarily by Urbano; the third by Levine. I shall consider them in turn.

Urbano takes me to task for my claim that there is a potential circularity in the application of psychoanalytic theories, whereby descriptions of the film text are made in distinctively psychoanalytic terms and then these descriptions are invoked as evidence for the plausibility of the psychoanalytic theories from which the descriptive terms are derived in the first place. In "Why Horror?" I suggest that some of these difficulties might be avoided by beginning with more prosaic accounts of the texts to be understood. Only in relation to such evidence would we be able to judge the competing claims of different theories. Urbano's counterclaim is that "the idea that it is possible to 'objectively' describe phenomena from a hypothetical place *outside* the framework of one (*any* one) interpretative methodology has . . . already and convincingly been disproved." In other words, I am mistaken in assuming that an "objective" description is available against which theories might be judged.

If this was what I was assuming then, of course, Urbano would be correct. But it is not. He attributes this assumption to me, although I nowhere make any such claim to "objective" description. Indeed, the term itself – and the quotation marks in which it is enclosed – are Urbano's, not mine. My position on the relation between "evidence" and "theory" remains broadly that advanced over twenty years ago in my book *Beyond*

Empiricism: that evidence, data, facts, descriptions, etc. are all inevitably constituted within theoretical frameworks. However, precisely to avoid problems of circularity, it is essential that the theories used to generate evidence are *not the same theories* as those being assessed against that evidence. As Lakatos famously put it, "the clash is not 'between theories and facts' but between two high-level theories: between an *interpretative theory* to provide the facts and an *explanatory theory* to explain them" (1970: 129). If the interpretative and explanatory theories are the same, then the claim to have made an assessment against evidence is illusory. Accordingly, I remain committed to the view that the dangers of this kind of circularity have to be avoided if we are to have any basis for assessing competing accounts, and I stand by the claim that these problems are often, though not uniquely, found in applications of psychoanalytic film theory.

Urbano, following Culler, goes on to suggest that theories should be evaluated "on the basis of the pertinence and appropriateness of the *questions* they pose." He appears to consider this to be an alternative view to my own, but it is not. Theories are quite properly to be judged against a variety of criteria, including relevance of the questions that they pose, and his suggestion should not be construed as an alternative to my own but as a specification of a *further* complementary criterion. No doubt both of us could come up with yet more equally important criteria – for example, logical coherence, scope, ontological depth, etc.

The second issue that Urbano raises relates to my support for "particularistic" explanations of the appeal of horror. I suspect that our differences on this may be more apparent than real (we agree, as Urbano observes, on the importance of linking psychoanalytic analysis with cultural history), but there are some interesting issues here nonetheless. My "particularism" takes the form of claiming that if we wish to understand the appeal of horror we should not seek to establish some general feature of the genre that is constitutive of its appeal in all circumstances, but that we should ask "why do *these* people like *this* horror in *this* place at *this* particular time." As Urbano recognizes, such a view does not preclude the use of psychoanalytic theories unless, of course, they depend fundamentally on transcultural and transhistorical assumptions that exclude local variation (as not a few critics have argued that they do).

What Urbano takes exception to is my desire to question "the presumed homogeneity of horror," to which he responds, "*so long as we are invoking the category of genre*, we are *de facto* talking about groups of texts which can be distinguished from *other* groups precisely on the basis of some presumed homogeneity." Once more I am obliged here to draw upon a long-standing position which is put more fully in the discussion of genre in my *Theories of Film* (1974) and in the various reprints of that discussion. Essentially I hold the view that genres are what we (their audiences) collectively believe them to be. There is a complex interaction between the context of production, the film texts themselves, and the audiences for those texts. Thus, whereas the term "genre" does indeed refer to a group of texts with a presumed homogeneity, that presumption has to be understood as one held by audiences rather than critics, who can and do vary in what they identify as appropriate distinguishing criteria – hence the need to examine how it is that *these* people like *this* horror in *this* place at *this* particular time.

Urbano proposes that "anxiety (understood in psychoanalytic terms)" is a central distinguishing feature of the experience of horror. Leaving aside his specification of "psychoanalytic terms," this may well be so in as much as many horror movie fans might offer the causing of (temporary) anxiety as part of the experience that they enjoy. But it is not a universal defining characteristic of the genre (non-horror texts can and do evoke "anxiety") but, rather, one specific feature which is variously understood and constructed in different times and places.

The third issue is raised by Levine and concerns my claims about "return of the repressed" analyses of horror. I have some difficulty here because at various points (for example, on "beast within" approaches, on "rottenness of humanity" claims) it seems to me that Levine misunderstands and therefore misrepresents my position. However, these minor matters aside, the heart of his apparent disagreement with me is clear enough. I suggest that "return of the repressed" arguments need to "pose supplementary mechanisms to bridge the gap between a general account of repression and the specific explanation of pleasure, and these supplementary mechanisms lead away from the pure form of the repression model." Levine makes two points in relation to this claim: that such supplements are available in the literature, and that I regard their use as "a kind of *ad hoc* maneuver."

On the first point I agree. Indeed, both Levine and I invoke Creed as one example of such theoretical elaboration, although I suspect that we may differ on how successful she is in so doing. On the second point, I am not sure why Levine has the impression that I consider posing additional mechanisms to be *ad hoc* maneuvers. I agree with his observation that "a more complete explanation requires additional theoretical detail." The questions then become, on what theoretical resources should we draw so that the basic repression model can be satisfactorily extended? Could or should such resources be drawn from non-psychoanalytic theories? And do they work? It is with that last question, of course, that we are returned full circle to the all-important epistemological issues with which this Afterword began.

Philosophical Problems Concerning the Concept of Pleasure in Psychoanalytical Theories of (the Horror) Film

I

Psychoanalysis, once the dominant theoretical paradigm in cinema studies, has not fared well since the mid-1980s. New theoretical paradigms have arisen, creating a pluralism in the field. More importantly, psychoanalytical film theory has been subjected to a trenchant critique by analytical philosophers as well as film theorists informed by contemporary scientific and philosophical theories of mind. Some have criticized its basic premises and methodology. Noël Carroll (1988), for example, has pointed to numerous flaws in its founding analogies between cinematic phenomena and the irrational phenomena (putatively) explained by psychoanalysis. David Bordwell (1989) has shown how psychoanalytical film theorists of the past failed to adhere to even the most basic empirical and logical protocols of theory-building and instead simply integrated psychoanalytic concepts into traditional humanistic interpretive practices. Others, such as Murray Smith (1995) and Jeff Smith (1996), have pointed to the considerable failings of psychoanalytical theories of specific cinematic phenomena, such as identification and film music. The silence of psychoanalytical film theorists in the face of this critique – the fact that they have not attempted to systematically refute it or to reconstruct their theories in a dialectical response to it – is, I think, ample testimony to its power.

Although devastating for psychoanalytical film theories of the past, nothing about this critique rules out the possibility that there might be more successful psychoanalytical film theories in the future, for this critique is aimed at the failure to date of film theorists to build rigorous, plausible psychoanalytical theories, not the scientific or philosophical legitimacy of psychoanalysis itself.[1] While this legitimacy has long been debated, and psychoanalysis is hardly a respectable theoretical paradigm in mainstream science and philosophy of mind, the resources are there for any enterprising theorist with an interest in reconstructing psychoanalytical film theory. For there have been a number of significant attempts over the past thirty years to mount defenses of psychoanalysis in response to the criticisms leveled at it by Wittgenstein, Sartre, Popper, Grünbaum, and others – criticisms responsible for widespread philosophical and scientific doubts about its legitimacy.[2]

Nevertheless, my view is that any film theorist undertaking such a reconstruction will face innumerable philosophical problems. One problem has to do with the concept of pleasure. This is a concept that psychoanalytical film theorists employ regularly, yet, like film theorists in general, they have devoted little time to clarifying its meaning. In this essay, I expose a basic confusion about this concept embedded in psychoanalytical film theory, a confusion exemplified by psychoanalytical theories of horror film enjoyment. This confusion, I conclude, leaves little room for optimism about the possibility of building more successful psychoanalytical film theories in the future. However, the real reason for pessimism, I argue, lies in a much more fundamental philosophical problem at the core of psychoanalysis, one that psychoanalysis shares with much psychological theorizing in general and that Wittgenstein repeatedly pointed to in his later writings on psychology – namely, reductionism. Although I see no way for psychoanalytical film theory to overcome this problem, and am pessimistic about its ability to overcome the confusion about the concept of pleasure that I expose, I offer the following in the spirit of dialectical theorizing. For if future psychoanalytical film theories can overcome these problems, I believe they will be all the more stronger for doing so.

II

Because psychoanalysis lacks a comprehensive account of the emotions, it is often dismissed by scholars of the arts as of little use in trying to explain emotional responses to art works.[3] As Carroll pointed out, "the garden-variety emotions – that is, the emotions marked in ordinary speech, like fear, awe, pity, admiration, anger, and so on . . . are what keep audiences engaged with art works" (1997: 191). Psychoanalysis has little to say about such "garden-variety emotions." Nevertheless, there are several emotions that receive extensive treatment in the psychoanalytical literature, including pleasure.[4] And psychoanalytical film theorists have generally assumed that pleasure is one emotion experienced by film viewers that psychoanalysis can explain.

Despite their considerable diversity, psychoanalytical theories of film enjoyment share a basic form of explanation, one which is, I take it, essential to psychoanalytical explanations in general.[5] They attempt to explain the viewer's enjoyment of film by postulating the existence of an unconscious wish of which viewers by definition are unaware, a wish that psychoanalytical theory brings to light. Although, as we shall see, psychoanalytical film theorists often disagree about what the content of this unconscious wish is, they nevertheless agree that it is the satisfaction of this unconscious wish by film, or indeed the cinema as an "apparatus," that is pleasurable for the viewer and that explains why the viewer enjoys film.

For example, Christian Metz, in his classic work of psychoanalytical film theory "The Imaginary Signifier, " argues that the modern, capitalist film industry has "filmic pleasure alone as its aim" (7). According to Metz, the cinema gives rise to pleasure because it satisfies – in a number of different ways – the viewer's unconscious wish to return to a "stage before the Oedipus complex" (4) among other forms of loss experienced as a child. For instance, Metz claims that the cinema is enjoyed partly because it is a "fetish. " Fiction films, he states, typically both acknowledge and disavow the various conditions of their production, such as the "equipment" used to make them, in the same way as a fetish object "disavows a lack and in doing so affirms it" (74–75) for the fetishist. Hence, the cinema fulfills the viewer's unconscious wish to return to a stage in life prior to the experience of loss – a wish that is, paradoxically, predicated on the now repressed experience of loss – in much the same way as a fetish does, thereby giving rise to pleasure: "Of course, this attitude [of fetishism] appears most clearly in a 'connoisseur,' the cinephile, but it also occurs, as a partial component of cinematic pleasure, in those who just go to the cinema" (75).

Another example of the use of the psychoanalytical form of explanation to account for the film viewer's pleasure can be found in psychoanalytical theories of horror film enjoyment. The enjoyment of horror films can seem to be a plausible candidate for a psychoanalytical account. For, as is often pointed out, enjoying horror films appears to entail a paradox, what Carroll has famously called "the paradox of horror": the defining feature of horror films seems to be the emotions they elicit in their viewers, emotions that are ostensibly unpleasurable, such as fear and disgust; yet viewers appear to enjoy horror films precisely because they are works of horror. Because it is hard to explain why viewers might enjoy films defined by their capacity to arouse ostensibly unpleasurable emotions, it is easy to leap to the conclusion that this enjoyment must be irrational and that its source lies hidden in the unconscious.

Yet, when one surveys explanations of this seemingly paradoxical phenomenon offered by psychoanalytical film theorists, one finds that they differ widely about what, precisely, is the unconscious source of the viewer's enjoyment.[6] One group of theorists argues that the viewer enjoys horror films because they satisfy the unconscious wish to regain pleasurable but repressed aspects of infancy. Barbara Creed, for example, suggests that the defining feature of the horror film is "bodily waste," which she believes is associated in the unconscious of human beings with the first period in infancy when there is supposedly a close, pleasurable bond with the mother prior to learning the social norms of physical cleanliness and autonomy. While the representation of bodily waste in the horror film fills the viewer with unpleasurable "disgust and loathing," it also gives rise to "a pleasure in returning to that time when the mother-child relationship was marked by an untrammeled pleasure in 'playing' with the body and its wastes" (1993: 13). For Creed, the viewer enjoys horror films because the representation of bodily waste in them satisfies the unconscious wish to return to a pleasurable period in infancy.

Robin Wood makes a similar argument, except that for him it is the wish to return to a pleasurable period prior to the learning of social norms in general – not just social norms governing bodily waste – that is satisfied by horror films. Wood argues that the defining feature of the horror film is that "normality is threatened by the Monster," and he defines normality as "conformity to . . . dominant social norms." Whereas human beings consciously "revere" dominant social norms and therefore find the monster's threat to them horrific and unpleasurable, unconsciously they "wish to smash" these norms because they are oppressive (1979: 175, 177).[7] The viewer therefore enjoys horror films, according to Wood, because the monster's threat to dominant social norms satisfies the unconscious wish to return to a pleasurable period in infancy free of those norms.

A second group of psychoanalytical film theorists, however, argues the exact opposite. The horror film represents unpleasurable, repressed aspects of infancy rather than pleasurable ones, and, far from wanting to regain these aspects, human beings unconsciously wish to overcome them. Horror films are enjoyable for viewers because they satisfy this unconscious wish. Krin Gabbard and Glen Gabbard (1987), for example, suggest that the defining feature of the horror film is the unpleasurable "repressed infantile anxieties" that it "evokes," at least in the case of the film *Alien*. While *Alien* gives rise to the unpleasurable emotion of horror by evoking these repressed anxieties, such as those "about nurturing figures that can turn against us," this evocation is also ultimately enjoyable for the viewer because of the "mastery" over and "relief" from these anxieties that it affords:

As Freud (1920) pointed out, there is a compulsion to repeat those traumatic events that were passively experienced [as infants] in an effort to gain mastery over them. People line up to see movies like *Alien* in order to reencounter powerful unconscious anxieties while retaining a sense that they have some control of an active nature the second time around. Moreover, the movie provides an aesthetic distance so that the audience knows that the terror on the screen is not actually happening to them, and they can experience relief along with their fright. (226, 230)

For Gabbard and Gabbard, while the horror film's evocation of repressed anxieties is unpleasurable for the viewer, ultimately it is also pleasurable because it satisfies the viewer's unconscious wish to gain mastery over and relief from these anxieties.

Finally, a third group of theorists has it both ways. According to Carol Clover, for example,

Our primary and acknowledged identification may be with the victim, the adumbration of our infantile fears and desires, our memory sense of ourselves as tiny and vulnerable in the face of the enormous Other; but the Other is also finally another part of ourself, the projection of our repressed infantile rage and desire . . . that we have had in the name of civilization to repudiate. (1987: 95)

For Clover, the horror film represents pleasurable and unpleasurable repressed aspects of infancy simultaneously. Viewers enjoy horror films because they satisfy the wish to regain the pleasurable aspects and overcome the unpleasurable ones at the same time.

Despite their divergent arguments, the theories I have just surveyed share the same basic psychoanalytical form of explanation. They all attempt to explain the viewer's enjoyment of horror films by postulating the existence of an unconscious wish, and arguing that horror films are pleasurable because they satisfy this unconscious wish – although they disagree about what the content of this unconscious wish is. What I want to do is show that this psychoanalytical form of explanation traffics in a major confusion about the meaning of the concept of pleasure.

III

Implicit in the use of the psychoanalytical form of explanation to account for the viewer's enjoyment of horror films are two basic assumptions concerning pleasure, assumptions so taken for granted by psychoanalytical film theorists that they are rarely explicitly articulated. Both can be found in Freud's writings.

(1) The satisfaction of an unconscious wish is pleasurable.
(2) Something is pleasurable because it satisfies an unconscious wish, for which satisfaction is pleasurable.

I will examine both of these assumptions and argue that each betrays a failure to grasp the same basic aspect of the meaning of the concept of pleasure.

Taking the second assumption first, psychoanalytical theories of horror film enjoyment assume that the pleasure of satisfying an unconscious wish explains why human beings enjoy what it is that satisfies the unconscious wish, namely, viewing horror films. But are they right to do so?

Certainly, we often invoke the pleasure of satisfying a wish to explain why we enjoy what satisfies it. For example, if I have a strong desire to eat a good meal because I have not eaten well for a long time, my pleasure in satisfying my wish by eating a good meal can explain why I enjoyed the meal. Similarly, if I have an intense urge to go for a long walk because I have been indoors for a lengthy period of time, the enjoyment of satisfying my wish by going for a long walk can explain why I took pleasure in the walk.

If we look closely at these two examples, however, we can see that the wish that is invoked to explain why we enjoy what satisfies it is of a certain kind. For in both cases, the act or activity that satisfies the wish is desired and enjoyed *as an end in itself.* It is not a means to something else that is desired and enjoyed. I do not go for a long walk because it is a means to something else that I wish for and whose attainment is pleasurable, say, seeing a friend who lives a long way away. Rather, I desire and enjoy a long walk for its own sake, because I have been indoors for a lengthy period of time. Similarly, I do not eat a good meal because it is a means to something else I desire and whose attainment is enjoyable, say, a stimulating conversation with my dinner partner. Rather, I wish for and take pleasure in a good meal for its own sake, because I have not eaten well for a long time. In both cases, the wish that is invoked to explain why we enjoy what satisfies it is of a certain kind. It is, to use the contemporary philosophical jargon, an "intrinsic" wish.[8] The act or activity that satisfies it, or a property of that act or activity,[9] is desired and enjoyed as an end in itself and not as a means to something else that is desired and enjoyed. Thus, as these two examples show, it can make sense to invoke the pleasure of satisfying a wish to explain why it is we enjoy what satisfies it, when the wish is an intrinsic one.

In psychoanalytical film theories, however, the kind of wish invoked to explain why we take pleasure in horror films is not an intrinsic one – for viewing a horror film, according to these theories, is not desired and enjoyed as an end in itself. Rather, it is a means to something else that is desired and enjoyed, namely, regaining or overcoming repressed aspects of infancy. The kind of wish invoked by these theories is, again to use contemporary philosophical jargon, "extrinsic." The act or activity that satisfies it – viewing a horror film – is not desired and enjoyed as an end in itself but as a means to something else that is desired and enjoyed: regaining or overcoming repressed aspects of infancy.

This difference between the intrinsic wishes of the first two examples and the extrinsic wish postulated by psychoanalytical theories of horror film enjoyment can be illustrated by pointing to the fact that, because it is not desired and enjoyed for its own sake, a different act or activity than viewing a horror film might bring about the satisfaction of the unconscious wish to regain or overcome repressed aspects of infancy. For example, the viewer might have a dream, daydream, or fantasy that satisfies this unconscious wish. (Indeed, psychoanalytical theory gives us reasons to think that these more "private" activities might satisfy this unconscious wish much better than viewing a horror film.) Satisfying the unconscious wish to regain or overcome repressed aspects of infancy by viewing a horror film is therefore like satisfying the wish to own new clothes by going to a clothes store to buy them, or satisfying the wish to get rich by investing in the stock market. In these two examples of extrinsic wishes, the act or activity that satisfies the wish is not desired and enjoyed as an end in itself, but as a means to something else that is desired and enjoyed. Hence, other acts and activities can satisfy these wishes equally well. For example, I might satisfy my wish to own new clothes by shopping for them online instead of going to a store, or I might steal to satisfy my wish to get rich, rather than invest in stocks. In the examples of taking a long walk and eating a good meal, however, no other act or activity will satisfy the intrinsic wishes that are invoked to explain why these activities are pleasurable, because they are desired and enjoyed for their own sake. If I desire a good meal because I have been deprived of fine food for a long time, for example, it is a good meal I desire and not, say, a bowl of porridge that will remove my hunger equally well.[10]

Psychoanalytical theories of horror film enjoyment, it might be remembered, assume that the pleasure of satisfying an unconscious wish explains why we enjoy what satisfies this wish. We have seen that invoking the pleasure of satisfying a wish can explain why we enjoy what satisfies it when the wish is an intrinsic one – when what satisfies it is desired and enjoyed as an end in itself. But what if an extrinsic wish is invoked, as in the case of psychoanalytical theories, and the act or activity that satisfies it is a means to something else that is desired and enjoyed? Are psychoanalytical film theorists, in other words, right to assume that the pleasure of satisfying the extrinsic wish to regain or overcome repressed aspects of infancy explains why we enjoy the means to its satisfaction, namely, viewing horror films?

I think not. For means and ends are separate and are therefore enjoyed (or not) separately. It is logically possible, for example, to enjoy the end, yet not enjoy the means. I might be indifferent to or not like shopping in clothes stores, even though I enjoy owning new clothes, or I might actively dislike investing in stocks, even though being rich is very pleasurable. It is also logically possible to enjoy the means regardless of whether I enjoy the end. I might, for example, enjoy going clothes shopping very much, regardless of whether I end up owning new clothes as a result. Similarly, I might take great pleasure in investing in the stock market, whether or not I end up making any money from it.

If this is the case, then the pleasure of satisfying the extrinsic wish to regain or overcome repressed aspects of infancy does not explain why we enjoy horror films. For even if we do possess this unconscious wish (a big if!), and even if viewing horror films does satisfy it, thereby giving us pleasure, this does not mean, as psychoanalytical film theorists assume, that we enjoy horror films themselves. For means and ends are separate and are enjoyed (or not) separately. Hence, just as we may not like investing in the stock market, even though we greatly enjoy being rich as a result, so we may actively dislike viewing horror films, even though we enjoy the satisfaction of the unconscious wish that this activity putatively brings about. Invoking the pleasure of satisfying a wish does not explain why we enjoy what satisfies it when the wish is an extrinsic one, as it is in the case of psychoanalytical theories of horror film enjoyment. Viewing horror films is not desired and enjoyed for its own sake in such theories, but as a means to something else that is desired and enjoyed. And means and ends are separate and are enjoyed (or not) separately.[11]

The fact that psychoanalytical theories confuse enjoyment of the end – the pleasure of satisfying the extrinsic wish to regain or overcome repressed aspects of infancy – with enjoyment of the means – viewing horror films – betrays a failure to grasp a basic aspect of the meaning of the concept of pleasure, which is that enjoyment cannot be separated from the thing that is enjoyed in the way that means and ends can be separated.[12] If I enjoy an act or activity, such as viewing films, then it is *that* act or activity I enjoy. My pleasure cannot, logically speaking, be separated from the thing that is pleasurable in the way that I can enjoy the means separately from the end. This is because, as Gilbert Ryle was the first to point out, "We cannot conceive of enjoyment occurring on its own. We could not make sense of the statement that someone had been just enjoying, any more than we could of the statement that he had been simply being interested or merely absorbed" (61).

Ryle clarifies this basic aspect of the meaning of pleasure by comparing pleasure to organic sensations such as pain. It is logically possible, for example, to have a headache on its own, and the same is true of organic sensations in general, such as tickles. Hence, it makes perfect sense to say, "I have a headache," or, "I have an itch on my leg," without reference to something that might be causing these sensations. But it is senseless to say "I have a pleasure," or "I am enjoying," without there being something to find pleasurable or enjoyable, just as it is unintelligible to say "I am interested," or "I am absorbed," without there being something to have an interest or absorption in. Another way of demonstrating this is by noting that, unlike an organic sensation, pleasure does not have a bodily location. While it makes perfect sense to say "I have a pain in my foot," or "My head is aching," it makes no sense to say "I have a pleasure in my foot," or "My head is enjoying."

David Perry usefully summarizes Ryle's clarification of this basic aspect of the meaning of pleasure in the following way: "One cannot just have pleasure as one logically could just have a pain, ache, or tickle; one must get pleasure from something, take pleasure in something, or feel pleasure [at] something. It is a part of the concept of pleasure that it have some object" (94). Psychoanalytical theories of horror film enjoyment, however, necessarily separate enjoyment from the thing enjoyed – horror films – by arguing that viewers enjoy an independent end to which horror films are the means: the satisfaction of the unconscious wish to regain or overcome repressed aspects of infancy. They thereby demonstrate their failure to grasp the basic aspect of the meaning of pleasure clarified by Ryle.[13]

Why is it that psychoanalytical theories separate enjoyment from horror films by confusing enjoyment of the end with enjoyment of the means? One reason, perhaps, is that in everyday life there is often no need to distinguish between whether we enjoy something for its own sake or whether it is merely a means to something else we enjoy. We therefore regularly use the concept of pleasure without being precise about what it is, exactly, we enjoy. G. H. Von Wright gives an example of a man who says he "likes" getting up early in the mornings:

Consider . . . the man who likes to get up early in the morning. Must he find early rising pleasant? *Some* men may rise early for "hedonic" reasons, i.e., in order to enjoy the morning; the freshness of the morning air, the beauty of the sunrise, etc. But rather few, I think, of those who say they "like" to get up early, would give such reasons for their liking. Someone may like to get up early because he has so many things to do that, if he stays in bed till [sic] late, he will not have time to do them at all, or his afternoon will be badly rushed or he will have to work at night. But he may be completely indifferent to the peculiar pleasures of the early morning hours. Should this man not rather then say that he *wants to* get up early than say that he *likes to* get up early? Or perhaps the suggestion will be that our man should say that he *has to* or *must* get up early, considering that this is not anything which he likes to or wants to do "for its own sake," but something that is forced upon him by the "practical necessities" of life. . . . The answer is that the uses of "like to do" and "want to do" and "have to do" shade into one another, and that we sometimes say that we like to do things, the doing of which is a source neither of passive nor of active pleasure to us. (78–79)

Thus, in everyday life, we often have no need to be precise about whether we enjoy an act or activity for its own sake, or whether it is a means to something else we enjoy. However, just because we often have no need to make this distinction does not mean that there is no distinction to be made. For if questioned, the man who says that he "likes" getting up early would, of course, be able to specify whether he enjoys "the peculiar pleasures of the early morning hours," or whether getting up early is a means to a separate end that he enjoys, such as completing his work.[14]

If the later Wittgenstein is right, however, there is another reason why psychoanalytical theories separate enjoyment from horror films by confusing enjoyment of the end with enjoyment of the means, which is that psychoanalysis is a reductionist theory. As others have noted, psychoanalysis shares with other philosophies and theories of mind numerous philosophical problems diagnosed by Wittgenstein in his later writings. This is because, as Jacques Bouveresse has pointed out, psychoanalysis is

in nearly all respects a thoroughly traditional theory of mind, regardless
of the standard clichés about Freud's "revolution":

> Freud has often been credited, if not with an actual "discovery" of the
> unconscious . . . at least with the introduction of a revolutionary idea of its
> nature and function. It is less frequently noticed, however, that his vision of
> consciousness remained utterly traditional and bound to the idea of con-
> sciousness as the internal perception of "objects" of a certain type – the
> paradigm of clear and immediate perception. . . . Freud's conception of the
> nature of consciousness conforms perfectly to the classical model . . . [except
> that] against the tendency of philosophers to identify the mental with the
> conscious, Freud maintains that the mental should rather be considered es-
> sentially unconscious, and only accidentally and occasionally endowed with
> the property we call consciousness; for a mental object, he contends, the fact
> of being perceived is nearly as contingent and secondary as it is for a physical
> one. (22–23)[15]

Because of what Bouveresse here calls its classical model of consciousness, psychoanalysis is just as vulnerable as other psychological theories
to Wittgenstein's philosophical arguments about private language, the
homunculus fallacy, and the distinction between reasons and causes.

   However, psychoanalysis also shares with psychological theories in general another, less noted but equally fundamental, feature: it assumes that
it can explain intentional mental states – states that are "about" something – by reducing or breaking them down into free-standing internal
states, processes, and mechanisms – such as an unconscious wish – of
which human beings have no necessary awareness and which therefore
need to be revealed by a theory. However, according to Wittgenstein, any
such theoretical reduction is doomed to failure from the start. As Tim
Thornton has recently put it,

> Wittgenstein argues that no substantial explanation of . . . mental content is
> possible. No account can be given that breaks [mental content] down into
> underlying mechanisms or processes. Any such attempt will either turn out
> to presuppose the very thing it attempts to explain, or it will fail to sustain the
> normativity of content. . . . Once mental states are construed as free-standing
> independent states, the question of what connects them to behavior and to
> the world becomes pressing. But, at the same time, it becomes unanswer-
> able. (27)

By "the normativity of content," Thornton means that an intentional
mental state prescribes what correctly fulfills it, just as a rule determines
what correctly accords with it. For example, if I wish to eat an apple, then

it is an apple I wish to eat, and not something else, such as a pear, which will stop me feeling hungry equally as well as an apple. Similarly, if I enjoy a horror film, it is the horror film that I enjoy, and not something else, such as the popcorn I am eating while watching the film, which may also be very pleasurable.

Reductionist theories attempt to explain intentional mental states such as enjoyment by breaking them down into free-standing internal states, processes, and mechanisms. But in doing so, according to Wittgenstein, they inevitably sever the normative connection between the intentional mental state and what it is about by postulating one or more theoretical intermediaries between the state and its object. As I have labored to show, it is precisely this latter failure that psychoanalytical theories of horror film enjoyment suffer from. By postulating the existence of an internal, free-standing mental state between enjoyment and the horror film – the unconscious wish to regain or overcome repressed aspects of infancy – these theories necessarily separate enjoyment from horror films themselves by arguing that it is the internal mental state (the satisfaction of an unconscious wish) that viewers enjoy. They therefore cannot explain what they set out to account for: why it is viewers enjoy horror films. In other words, to paraphrase Thornton, once it is argued that it is an internal mental state that is enjoyed, the question of what connects this state to the horror film becomes pressing but unanswerable.

This basic philosophical problem of failing to sustain the normative connection between enjoyment and the thing that is enjoyed due to theoretical reductionism is also evident in the first assumption implicit in the use of the psychoanalytical form of explanation to account for the viewer's enjoyment of horror films. This is the assumption that we can enjoy an internal state of which we have no necessary awareness and which therefore needs to be revealed by a theory, such as the satisfaction of an unconscious wish. This assumption is fundamental to psychoanalytical theory in general. But does it make sense?

According to this assumption, it is possible for a human being to enjoy something, such as the satisfaction of a wish, without being aware of what is enjoyable, because it is unconscious. In the case of horror films, the viewer enjoys the satisfaction of the wish to regain or overcome repressed aspects of infancy without being aware that this is what is enjoyable, because the wish is unconscious.[16] However, if this were the case, we would be able to conceive of someone experiencing pleasure without him being aware of what it is he is finding pleasurable. In other words, we would be able to conceive of pleasure as occurring independently of awareness of the thing that is pleasurable because that thing is unconscious. And, as we have already seen, this is senseless because it is part of the concept of pleasure that it have some object. As Ryle argues, we cannot experience pleasure independently of the thing that is pleasurable in the way that we can experience a pain, such as a headache, on its own. Thus, to find something pleasurable, it is logically necessary that we be aware of what that something is.[17] For we cannot, in the logical sense, find something enjoyable if we are not aware of what that something is, just as we cannot find something interesting or absorbing without being aware of what that something is. We have to, in other words, be aware of the thing that is enjoyable to find it enjoyable. For instance, to borrow an example from Ryle, if I find a joke amusing, then "the question 'What gave me that pleasure?' does not await an answer. For of course I already know that it was that joke, if it was that joke that had amused me" (59).

Of course, we may fail to know, or at least to acknowledge to ourselves, that something gives us pleasure. And we may not be able to say what it is about something, such as a joke, that we find enjoyable. But what we cannot do, if Ryle is right, is find something pleasurable without being aware of what that something is, as psychoanalytical theories of horror film enjoyment assume. Thus, not only do these theories fail to explain what they set out to account for because they confuse enjoyment of the end with enjoyment of the means, but the thing that they argue is enjoyed by horror film viewers – the satisfaction of the unconscious wish to regain or overcome repressed aspects of infancy – is one that it is logically impossible to enjoy. For by arguing that this wish is unconscious, psychoanalytical theories once again sever the normative connection between enjoyment and the thing enjoyed by assuming that pleasure can be experienced independently of awareness of the thing that is pleasurable.

In this essay, I have tried to show that there is a basic confusion about the meaning of the concept of pleasure embedded in psychoanalytical theories of horror film enjoyment. This confusion is revealed in two assumptions about pleasure implicit in the use of the psychoanalytical form of explanation by horror film theorists: that the satisfaction of an unconscious wish is pleasurable, and that something is pleasurable because it satisfies an unconscious wish for which satisfaction is pleasurable. Both of these assumptions, I have argued, in different ways betray a failure to grasp a basic aspect of the meaning of pleasure, one first clarified by Ryle: that it is part of the concept of pleasure that it have some object. To me, these assumptions seem so fundamental to the psychoanalytical form of explanation that it is hard to imagine psychoanalytical film theory without them. This is the reason I am pessimistic about the possibility of future psychoanalytical film theories overcoming this conceptual confusion about pleasure.

However, it is the reductionism of psychoanalysis, I believe, that is the real reason for pessimism about the future of psychoanalytical film theory. For if Wittgenstein is right, because psychoanalysis explains intentional mental states by reducing them to internal, free-standing states, processes, and mechanisms, it inevitably severs the normative connection between the mental state and its object. In the case of cinematic pleasure, by placing a theoretical intermediary between the viewer's enjoyment and the film he enjoys – namely, an unconscious wish – and arguing that it is the satisfaction of this wish that viewers enjoy, psychoanalysis can no longer explain what it sets out to explain: why the viewer enjoys film.

If Wittgenstein's critique of reductionism is correct, psychoanalysis is not the only theoretical paradigm in cinema studies that suffers from this basic philosophical problem. Any reductionist theory – including contemporary cognitivist theories that reduce intentional mental states to internal cognitive processes – will inevitably sever the normative connection between intentional mental states and what they are about by placing theoretical intermediaries between the state and its object. Normativity cannot be reduced, if the later Wittgenstein is right.[18]

NOTES

1. This failure is not surprising, given the fact that film theorists are for the most part humanistic scholars of the arts trained to interpret texts, not construct theories.
2. I am thinking of the work of philosophers and theorists of mind such as Richard Wollheim, James Hopkins, Sebastian Gardner, Roy Schafer, and Charles Elder.
3. See Hjort and Laver (5) and Plantinga and Smith (11).
4. Pleasure is an emotion only in the broadest sense of emotion as a feeling as opposed to a cognition. In the narrower sense of emotion as an "agitation" or "disturbance of mind," it is not an emotion, for one need not be moved in order to feel pleasure. See Perry (111).
5. I am using enjoyment as a synonym for pleasure. While the concepts of pleasure and enjoyment are not identical – unlike pleasure, enjoyment can be said to arise only when one is performing an act or activity, when something is done to one, or when one is experiencing something – wherever enjoyment is used, the same locution can be expressed using the concept of pleasure. For example: I get a lot of enjoyment (pleasure) out of watching horror films; *Alien* (1979) was a very pleasurable (enjoyable) film to watch. See Perry (61ff) and Von Wright (77ff).

6. The fact that psychoanalytical film theorists disagree about the unconscious source of the horror viewer's enjoyment could be seen as a sign of the health of the psychoanalytical paradigm, given that disagreement among practitioners of a theoretical paradigm is a necessary part of robust theorizing. From the point of view of critics of psychoanalytical film theory, however, there is no genuine disagreement among psychoanalytical theorists of the horror film – simply pluralism. In other words, typically such theorists do not dialectically engage with each others' theories by (a) showing why candidates for repressed mental content proposed by other theorists cannot explain the phenomenon they want to explain, or (b) showing why their candidate does explain the phenomenon better than others.

7. Wood does not, however, argue that all "social norms" are "oppressive." Some, he believes, are necessary for a civilized society to exist, and he refers to these as bringing about a "basic" – meaning "necessary for civilization to exist" – repression. "Oppressive" social norms are those he evaluates negatively from his political position, and he refers to these as bringing about a "surplus" – meaning unnecessary – repression. (Needless to say, this distinction is highly subjective.)

8. According to Robert Audi, "an *intrinsic want* . . . is a want for something simply for its own sake, i.e., roughly, a want such that either one has no belief to the effect that realizing it would bring about something further (particularly something to which it is a means), or, if one does have such a belief, one does not want the thing in question even in part on the *basis* of that belief. For instance, people often say, 'Do you really want to do that?' intending to ask whether one is looking forward to it for its own sake" (20–21).

9. My intrinsic desire to take a long walk, for example, may be an intrinsic desire for a specific property of taking a long walk, such as "stretching my legs," or "getting some fresh air."

10. Of course, if it is a specific, autonomous property of one of these acts or activities that I desire, then a different act or activity might satisfy the desire for this property. For example, if I wish to take a long walk because I desire to stretch my legs, then I may be able to satisfy my desire to stretch my legs by, for example, using an exercise bike or treadmill. In this case, the desire to stretch my legs is an intrinsic desire: it is something I desire for its own sake. Meanwhile, the wish to take a long walk is an extrinsic wish: taking a long walk is the means to the end of stretching my legs. Alternatively, my desire to stretch my legs may be a desire for the kind of leg stretching that only comes with taking a long walk. In this case, using an exercise bike or treadmill does not satisfy my desire to stretch my legs, and my wish to take a long walk remains an intrinsic wish.

11. A psychoanalytical theorist of the horror film might concede this point but argue that some kind of non-psychoanalytical explanation of why we enjoy horror films is needed to "supplement" his psychoanalytical account of the end – the enjoyment of the satisfaction of the unconscious wish to regain or overcome repressed aspects of infancy – to which horror films are the means. However, such a non-psychoanalytical explanation would not be a "supplement" to his psychoanalytical account, if this paper is right. Rather, it would

be an explanation of a wholly different phenomenon that psychoanalytical theory cannot explain, namely, why we enjoy horror films themselves.

12. See Perry (187–90).

13. Unsurprisingly, Ryle's arguments about pleasure have generated much debate. However, even those critical of Ryle's view that pleasure is not an organic sensation concede that he has demonstrated that "in normal circumstances, [pleasure] is only aroused by activities or events, and so is normally euphoria *at* or *in* something, and very hard to separate from attention to or engagement in that thing." See Lyons (168).

14. If psychoanalytical theories of horror film enjoyment were right, then the viewer who enjoys horror films would say that it is not "the peculiar pleasures" of horror films themselves that he likes, but an end to which viewing horror films is a means – even though he would not be able to say what this end is because it is unconscious.

15. As evidence for his claim, Bouveresse cites a passage from Freud (1915b: 104).

16. According to psychoanalytical film theorists, the viewer is, of course, aware of the means to satisfying the kinds of unconscious wishes postulated by psychoanalytical film theory. In other words, the viewer is aware of the horror film on the screen. But it is not the horror film on the screen that is pleasurable for the viewer, according to psychoanalytical film theorists, but the satisfaction of an unconscious wish.

17. See Perry (95–96).

18. Earlier versions of this essay were presented at the symposium "Problems of Representation in a Cognitive Theory of Moving Images" held in Pécs, Hungary, May 21–25, 2001, and at the University of Kent, Canterbury, June 1, 2002. I thank the respective audiences for their questions and comments. I also thank the students in my Fall 2000 horror film seminar at Sarah Lawrence College, as well as Steven Schneider for his editorial suggestions.

PART TWO

THEORIZING THE UNCANNY

Explaining the Uncanny in *The Double Life of Véronique*

It is only rarely that a psycho-analyst feels impelled to investigate the subject of aesthetics . . . But it does occasionally happen that he has to interest himself in some particular province of that subject; and this province usually proves to be a rather remote one, and one which has been neglected in the specialist literature of aesthetics. The subject of the "uncanny" is a province of this kind.

– Sigmund Freud

Krzysztof Kieslowski's 1991 film *The Double Life of Véronique* (*La Double Vie de Véronique,* hereafter *DLV*) is a gently tragic tale whose eerie tone merits the label "uncanny." Premised on the assumption that life itself may be uncanny, *DLV* tells the tale of two women in France and Poland who are somehow doubles – and who feel this about themselves. (Both are played by Irène Jacob, who won Best Actress at Cannes for her performance.) This premise is made plausible through a rich cinematic style, comparable to the paintings of Vermeer (we often see a woman standing in a room illuminated with side lighting from a window) and Rembrandt (the movie was shot with a filter that provided a golden tone).

Through strikingly composed sequences, *DLV* insists that unsettling structures of fate are at work in both art and life. For example, the Polish Veronika is singing an ethereal musical phrase on stage when she collapses from a weak heart and dies.[1] The screen is darkened as she is buried; then the viewer is suddenly transported into the world of Véronique, who senses her double's death. In the French scenes, this musical phrase recurs, but it is unclear whether a *character* is hearing it or it is film music that only *we* are hearing.

Véronique falls in love with a puppet artist, Alexandre (Philippe Volter), who performs at the school where she teaches music. When he

notices a photo she had accidentally taken of her double during a visit to
Poland, Véronique at last gains the proof she has sought that her feelings
were correct – but too late. She senses that the now-dead Veronika has
preceded her in a way that alerted her to certain dangers. For instance,
Véronique was warned off pursuing a high-stress singing career as she
became aware of her own heart problems.

Near the film's conclusion, Alexandre creates two new puppets depict-
ing Véronique, to use for a children's story. Though flattered, Véronique
becomes upset, and eerie aspects of the uncanny peak in this scene.
She asks why there are *two* puppets, and Alexandre explains that since
he "handles them a lot during performance" they are "easily damaged."
The hint of death is underscored as Véronique plays with one puppet
while the camera pans to show the other, lying limp on the table. Jacob's
luminous face is seen in close-up and her eyes fill with tears that spill
down her cheeks. She asks Alexandre the name of his story and he says
he will entitle it " 'The Double Life of' . . . I'm not sure what I'll call them."
This opens up what the French call a *mise-en-abyme*:[2] the puppeteer's story
turns out to be Véronique's *own* story – the story of this very film. This
scene has a subtle mystery and delicacy (and is not gimmicky, as it might
sound). Overcome with emotion, Véronique leaves Alexandre to return,
in the film's final scene, to find comfort at her father's house in the
country.

DLV is fascinating but puzzling. Is the puppeteer a metaphor for the
filmmaker – even for God? Does doubling in this film highlight fate or
contingency, salvation or loss, connection or disruption? Repeated viewing makes parts of the plot clearer, but leaves much ambiguity. The puppet scene takes this film into a Borges-like paradox. It becomes a fantastic
tale; in short, it is uncanny.

The uncanny is a broad notion that applies to phenomena, in both life
and artworks, that are eerie yet enticing, strange yet familiar, creepy yet
not horrific. The uncanny shows up in many artistic genres, e.g., in paintings by Magritte or Fuseli, or stories by Edgar Allan Poe. Uncanny films
can emerge in genres like horror, film noir, and melodrama – examples
include *The Birds* (1963), *The Shining* (1980), *Touch of Evil* (1958), and
The Piano (1993). Freud is probably right that the uncanny is not, even
now, the subject of intense study by aesthetics scholars. I hope this essay
will open up further discussions into how the uncanny relates to other
"uncomfortable" emotional responses to art, including horror, dread,
and the sublime.

FREUD AND THE UNCANNY

To explain the impact of a film like *DLV*, Freud's theory of the uncanny has initial appeal. Freud studied the uncanny from an interest in unusual psychological phenomena. His theory makes special reference to doubling, *DLV*'s main theme – and he uses as his key example a story that features a wooden doll who passes for human. Thus, links with *DLV* and its puppet theme are especially intriguing.

But I resist the appeal of Freud's account, partly because, like other writers in cognitive film studies, I reject psychoanalysis as a theory of the mind. Cognitivism employs newer theories of the mind and brain to explain how we perceive films and why we enjoy them.[3] (As Gregory Currie baldly states, "Psychoanalysis is false. If we use psychology to study film, we should use cognitive science" [xiii].) David Bordwell and Noël Carroll say that cognitivists seek "to understand human thought, emotion, and action by appeal to processes of mental representation, naturalistic processes, and (some sense of) rational agency" (1996: xvi).

"Rational" seems a troubling word here. Can cognitivists attend to subtle emotions to address the impact of uncanny artworks, with all their mystery and ambiguity? I think so, and that we can improve on what I see as another major problem with Freud's account. Attending to psychological nuances in life and art, Freud sought explanations of why we respond to certain fictions. He offered a "deep" explanation of the uncanny as grounded in more primitive and allegedly universal human motivations. But Freud neglected the very phenomenon he purported to be studying, namely an *aesthetic* one. Not only is it possible (and I think correct) to reject his deep explanations, we need a better alternative account of the aesthetics of the uncanny.

Freud dealt with the "uncanny" (*unheimlich*) in 1919, when he was working out the concept of the death instinct in *Beyond the Pleasure Principle*. Freud's essay begins with some etymological research, then focuses on the story, "The Sandman."[4] E.T.A. Hoffmann's tales, like Poe's, typically sustain a feverish atmosphere with mysterious, implied evil rather than monsters and outright gore and violence. "The Sandman" tells of a young man, Nathaniel, haunted by fear that an evil Sandman resembling a sinister visitor to his father's house will snatch out his eyes. Later in life, Nathaniel encounters this same evil man, who has used stolen eyes to adorn an artificial woman, Olympia, with whom the hero has fallen in love. Eventually, feeling deeply persecuted, Nathaniel tries to

murder his former sweetheart, Clara, then jumps to his death from a high
tower.

Freud argues that the uncanny involves something from ordinary life
that is familiar, yet alien and frightening. He interprets Hoffmann's story
as illustrating fear of castration due to Oedipal conflict and repression of
childhood libido. Nathaniel experiences the Sandman as uncanny, frightening yet familiar, and a block to his love. The uncanny involves a "repetition compulsion," the youth's need to repeat a critical early trauma:
"[W]hatever reminds us of this inner repetition-compulsion is perceived
as uncanny" (x).[5] Freud claims that something similar applies to *us* as
readers of the story: *we too* go through this repetition–compulsion and
experience the related, universal psychological anxiety. Freud apparently
believes this is connected to our pleasure in reading: we somehow enjoy
revisiting the threatening psychic arena of the Oedipal complex.

A second explanation is offered in Freud's essay for the specific phenomenon of uncanny doubling. Some types of the uncanny involve not
the castration complex, but feelings of magical power, doubling, or help-
lessness. Despite differences in origin, these cases manifest a similar mechanism. The story occasions not repetition of a repressed infantile *fear*, but
re-awakening and even confirmation of "an infantile wish or even only
an infantile belief" (140). Because such cases involve "effacing the distinction between imagination and reality" (152), Freud regards them as
more common in literature. A realistic story may re-awaken infantile beliefs that we have dismissed or, in Freud's words, "surmounted," like the
belief that the dead may return to life, that there are psychic powers, etc. –
or that we have a double. Not all such stories evoke the uncanny, but stories about such scenarios that convey them as vivid and realistic might.[6]
This is a condition that does seem to apply to *DLV*, but I still have doubts.

DOUBLING AND THE PSYCHOANALYTIC UNCANNY

For Freud, doubling involves the second, infantile belief, type of the uncanny. On this, he refers readers to an earlier (1914) essay by Otto Rank:

[Rank] has gone into the connections which the "double" has with reflections
in mirrors, with shadows, with guardian spirits, with the belief in the soul and
with the fear of death; but he also lets in a flood of light on the surprising evolution of the idea. For the "double" was originally an insurance against the destruction of the ego, an "energetic denial of the power of death," as Rank says;
and probably the "immortal" soul was the first "double" of the body. (141)

Freud construes the double as an idea an infant employs to ward off fear of death. This primitive or magical belief is overcome in adulthood, but literature (and presumably films) that make it believable can cause anxiety plus recognition. In art, a double is frightening because it brings to mind our fear of death – the fear we were originally trying to avoid. We can see how Freud's notion of repetition–compulsion in the uncanny links to his developing notion of the death instinct.

Freud's account seems to apply to *DLV*: in this film, a young woman facing a fear of death is protected and reassured by the existence of her double. Freud would say that Véronique's belief in her double reflects her infantile wish for a companion or guardian angel. We learn from the narrative that both girls' mothers died when they were very young. Véronique's double makes sacrifices for her and even dies, in a sense, to warn her against dangerous mistakes. Véronique, like us, gets reminded of the reality of death in the puppet scene by seeing the limp puppet on the table: hence the movie's power to disturb us.

This story supposedly works on viewers by reviving our *own* surmounted infantile beliefs. It makes the existence of the double seem very real: the narrative first sets out Veronika's story with concrete details of place and persons, so that we cannot deny her existence. Perhaps this seduces us into the infantile belief we once had but have now "surmounted" as we became adults. Strangely, it is not clear why Freud thinks such a story would be *enjoyable*; he never acknowledges that "The Sandman" might offer pleasure. Instead he implies that it is "compelling" – because of our own repetition–compulsion.

Freud's explanation of the uncanny in works of art invokes numerous postulates, including many not argued for in the essay itself. (Evidence was presumably supplied elsewhere, e.g., in Rank's article.) Such tenets include that certain kinds of infantile thoughts and fears exist and are universal; that among these thoughts are thoughts of a double; that such thoughts serve a particular aim, averting the fear of death; that certain processes of outgrowing or "surmounting" the relevant beliefs are a normal part of the maturation process; that an artwork can create or inspire (even if momentarily) the return of such a belief; and, finally, that should this happen, it will create a fairly specific emotional experience of what we call "the uncanny."

In sum, in the Freudian story about the uncanny, we can find a "deep" psychological account for certain conflicts of intriguing artworks. The conflicts supposedly occur between fairly universal and primitive emotions, desires, or libidinous feelings, and a more advanced and rational order of beliefs, recognition of laws, or convictions about reality. The depiction of certain scenarios is likely to evoke these emotional–cognitive conflicts.

Freud's explanation has many problems. It is a major step to accept all the tenets he presumes. I do not believe that these are well-supported views of the self, primitive thoughts, infantile thoughts, and so on.[7] Contemporary studies of the emotions do not support his view that all repressed emotion turns into anxiety.[8] And recent research into the neuropsychiatry of the doppelgänger phenomenon also casts doubt on Freud's approach. This phenomenon is a well-recognized effect of various disorders such as epilepsy and specific brain lesions and it can be treated with specific medications.[9] Its occurrence in authors like Dostoevsky might seem less surprising in this light, and it is also possible to explain its recurrence as a literary theme in terms of cultural familiarity rather than "deep" and "universal" psychic needs and beliefs.

But more problematic, and my real subject here, is Freud's inattention to the *aesthetic*. He relies upon identical causal hypotheses to explain uncanny emotions of the characters *in the story* and uncanny emotions experienced by readers (or viewers) *of the story*. But why must we explain the way *DLV* works by appeal to something "deep" and even "infantile" *within us* that makes us parallel to Véronique? I am not convinced that his account even works for her. When Véronique obtains the photographic "proof" of doubleness, it is both intensely pleasant (because it eases doubts about her conviction) and intensely painful (because she feels that this double is now dead). The uncanny as Freud analyzes it seems wholly one-sided; pleasure in particular is missing.

This problem worsens when we ask how *viewers* experience what is uncanny about Véronique's world. It is implausible that the film is uncanny because it re-awakens *in us* a conviction of some previously held belief in the existence of a double. True, the film depicts *a* double as plausible, but why must this relate to each viewer's *own* double? Why not say rather that viewers respond with varied thoughts and emotions to the very idea of a doubling of identity *as presented here* – just as to the presentation of Nathaniel's story in "The Sandman"? We need not fear that our own lovers are mere puppets to enjoy this fictional premise and play along with the storyteller's engaging world.

My point here is that Freud's treatment of the uncanny actually *ignores the aesthetic*. He writes, in the passage quoted at the start, as if psychoanalysis wanders unwillingly into terrain where it is competing with aesthetics professors.[10] Neil Hertz, in a brilliant discussion of Freud's essay, similarly criticizes Freud for finding "no literature there" in Hoffmann's story:

> Freud has overstabilized his first account of the story . . . there is, indeed, more cause for doubt and uncertainty as one moves through "The Sandman" than Freud allows. . . . What is remarkable is that everything he includes within quotation marks has already appeared within quotation marks in "The Sandman." . . . The words of the narrator have completely disappeared, replaced by Freud's own, and we have the illusion of watching Nathanael's actions through a medium considerably more transparent than Hoffmann's text. (105)

Hertz adds, "It may be that what is unsettling, if not uncanny, about 'The Sandman' is as much a function of its surface as of the depths it conceals" (105). "The Sandman" uses a complex narrative opening with a series of feverishly written letters. Its verbal descriptions are graphic and the narrator's increasing paranoia is evident to readers. The story is short and rapidly paced. Readers are led to question Olympia's "authenticity" by clues planted well before Nathaniel's own horrified recognition of her empty eye sockets and rattling wooden joints. Nathaniel occupies a paranoid position even in relation to his own readers.

I agree with Hertz, that Freud's search for "deep" emotions leads him to elide the surface of Hoffmann's story, ignoring how it creates and evokes *aesthetic* response. Similar problems arise when applying Freud's theory to a film like *DLV*. Not all stories about doubles are uncanny; some are amusing (*Twins* [1988]) and some horrific (*Sisters* [1973], *Dead Ringers* [1988]). We need more nuanced attention to this unique film's power *as an artwork* to see how it sustains an uncanny atmosphere – a more "textural" description of how its aesthetic surface prompts viewers' thoughts and feelings.

Cognitivists hold that reactions to a film like *DLV* are very complex and multifaceted. Many viewers are likely to enjoy the movie's visual beauty and its unusual music. Audience emotions are often cued by characters and situations: we may feel shocked and sad when Veronika dies; we may empathize with Véronique, while seeing her as unique and distinctive. No doubt many audience members feel desire for this beautiful young woman; similarly, people may sympathize when her lover turns out to be less than ideal. We must also employ cognitive abilities, for example, to follow the odd narrative and interpret its visual symbols. Some viewers may dislike the film because its plot has too many coincidences. Others, like myself, will suspend disbelief and relish the intellectual puzzles it raises about personal identity and fate.

Cognitivists do not deny that people have emotions, nor do we insist that they are aroused in ways that are always rational and predictable. Cognitivists aim to use the best available theories of the mind, whether from neuroscience, physiology, psychology, sociology, anthropology, or other fields. New research on the neuroscience of emotions has shown how humans have very complicated arrays of emotion systems. Scientists also emphasize the complex interactions among emotions, thoughts, and actions. We often need to allude to historical and social factors to account for specific emotions, say, those aroused by a religious ritual, a romantic scene, an advertisement, a horror tale, etc.

Diverse human abilities are brought to bear on the experience and interpretation of artworks like "The Sandman" or *DLV*. Kieslowski's film creates uncanny effects through a combination of beauty, surprise, confusion, and mystery, rewarding our active responses, both cognitive and emotional. The director both draws us into the story by its beauty and emotional power and forces us to see it *as* a story by deliberate devices.

For example, we are flung in a confusing cut from witnessing Veronika's sudden, shocking death and burial, to seeing her apparently "alive" again. After a fadeout in the Polish burial scene, the screen titles indicate we have changed scenes to Paris, and the characters are now speaking French. We must infer this is not Veronika but a mysterious redoubling of her. The same actress subtly imparts doubleness through enactment of the diegetic "reality" of a separate person, Véronique, who looks much the same but acts different. Also striking is the mood shift created by this disorienting cut. When we suddenly see Véronique after the sad burial scene, she is having sex with an old boyfriend. The switch from funeral lament to vivid eroticism is wrenching, allowing us no pause to catch our breath and regroup. The director heightens each scene's distinctive emotional power in various ways: he personalizes death in the burial scene by shooting from within the grave as clods fall down over the camera. He next films the sex scene in tight close-ups that show intimate images of lips, a breast, and tangled limbs.

This unsettling emotional roller-coaster ride, which calls for active viewing and imagining, is repeated in another scene juxtaposing eroticism with grief, after Véronique's crucial discovery of the photograph of her double she unwittingly took from a tour bus in Poland. In the picture, Veronika stares back, offering Véronique a look of recognition seen only too late, after her death. (Earlier, the film showed Veronika watching the tourist bus with the girl taking photographs, struck dumb by seeing her own double.) Véronique lingers over the photograph, then bursts into heart-rending tears. Her new lover, the puppet-master, strokes her face and kisses her, until comfort and consolation merge with arousal, and Veronique's sobs turn to sharp cries of pleasure. The camera creates viewer detachment and requires active interpretation, though, as it pans to show objects fallen out of her purse. It zeroes in on a crystal marble with silver stars. The alert viewer realizes it is just like one of Veronika's we saw earlier as she played with it. Now, Véronique's marble slowly rolls across a sheet of music and becomes a miniature globe encompassing the cosmos as the bed is jolted by the lovers' passion.

Beautiful small touches like these constitute what I am calling this film's aesthetic surface. Like the literary surface of Hoffmann's narrative style, this is crucial to making the work uncanny. Freud simply looks through a text's surface to its depths – repressed castration anxiety or reawakened infantile beliefs. There *are*, to be sure, depths in this movie. As a cognitivist I cannot ignore the emotions raised by its themes and subject matter. But a successful artwork's themes are inseparable from its style; both are needed to sustain the uncanny. I think the best account of what makes this particular film uncanny must cite many aspects of its style and plot, showing how it raises key puzzles of reflexivity and self-referentiality.

REFLEXIVITY

Much of what is puzzling and uncanny about *DLV* stems from its being, and being perceived as, a *reflexive* artwork. In this way too it resembles "The Sandman," which foregrounds the issue of how to tell Nathaniel's tale. *DLV* tacks between being a realistic film and being one with obvious reminders of its fictional status. The Borges-like twist at the end, through which this movie we are watching becomes "this movie we are watching," works as a labyrinthine device that requires reflection upon the filmmaker's storytelling art. This leads viewers to vacillate between the immediate power of emotions (like the sadness expressed by the actress/character) and a higher cognitive meditation on life and art. *DLV* raises multiple questions. Has Véronique simply made a mistake in choosing an insensitive lover, or have we made the mistake in finding her world convincing and enthralling?

Artworks since at least *The Iliad* have used life/art parallels to raise similar questions about human meaning and purpose: the horror Nathaniel feels upon realizing that Olympia is a puppet is not just repulsion at her, but a larger horror of being victimized by fate, as if there is an overwhelming plot against him; which there is, of course – Hoffmann's own! "The Sandman" is like *DLV* in that both works pile up coincidences that seem absurd but are shown so plausibly that they ultimately raise large questions about the role of art and creative choice in our lives.

DLV presents its emotional peak in the *mise-en-abyme* scene where Véronique's lover reveals the puppet-play that is the story of her life, and also of this very film. Our response to this scene does not end once we realize it is meta-cinematic, since we can remember and reflect on, or reinterpret, earlier scenes. The movie is permeated with metaphors for the doubling of art and life; it is a film about personal identity as an issue for art, and specifically for *film* art. *DLV* meditates on identity through many scenes of performance, acting, and (literal, visual) reflection that make us focus on doubling and authenticity. Let me just mention a few of these key scenes.

The film's opening sequence, marked "Poland 1968," shows a disorienting pattern of dark blues with bright white lights. We gradually read this as the globe of a night sky, and since we see a little girl whose face is upside down, it seems we are witnessing her point-of-view shot. A woman's voice, presumably her mother's, points out the infinitude of stars and how none of them are alike. This scene is visually beautiful, perceptually confusing, and intellectually challenging. It segués to a scene, marked "France 1968," of another little girl examining a leaf, as another mother's voice talks about the leaf's patterns and textures. The presence of patterns in nature, and of repeating items (stars, leaves), is thereby economically and seductively introduced.

Later sequences allude back to these opening scenes. When Veronika visits her aunt in Krakow, the landscape unfolds through a train window. She playfully views it through a small marble that acts as a lens, filtering her (and our) view. The clear glass marble has little silver stars floating around in it that "decorate" the scenery as we look. The girl/actress also looks directly at us (at the camera) and smiles, as if to ensure we have caught on to a point. Later, the puppeteer mischievously bounces light off a lens to cast dazzling reflections in Véronique's eyes. Such scenes imply various meanings and evoke complex thoughts: the light of the lens can dazzle as well as fascinate, hurt as well as please the eye, inform as well as seduce. Lenses cast multiple images, they mirror the multiplicity of the natural world, and so on. Even the final scene before the fadeout reinforces the doubling theme, as we see two images of Véronique embracing her father in the countryside, one real and the other reflected in a window.

Similarly, *DLV* presents messages about life and art, and evokes emotions, through its uses of music and performance. Both Véronique and Veronika are singers whom we see rehearsing, teaching, or performing. The lines on their musical scores are visually juxtaposed to the lines of their electrocardiograms. Veronika dies while straining to reach the high notes in her soprano solo, accompanied by full orchestra during a public performance. Both women's fathers are shown engaging in handiwork projects. We see the puppeteer's performance at the school, as well as his craft of making puppets. Alexandre courts Véronique with a sequence of clues drawn from his own children's stories.

Thus, one way this film is uncanny involves its complex use of cinematic means to juxtapose fate with contingency, and art with life. Movies, of course, are artifacts with constructed narratives, but *DLV*'s purposiveness is at odds with its emphasis on contingency. It was an accident that crushed Veronika's fingers in a car door, ending her career as a pianist. It was an accident that she sang while watching her friend's rehearsal, catching the attention of the committee and winning the competition to be soloist. Accidental encounters are rife here. These range from our quick glimpse of the man in an overcoat who flashes his genitals at Veronika as her head hangs down after she is stricken with heart pains, to the old lady she sees loaded with heavy shopping bags, to her aunt's lawyer who just happens to be a midget. The emotionally compelling encounter between the doubles, when Véronique visits Krakow on the tourist bus, is itself a matter of sheer contingency.

THE UNCANNY AND THE SUBLIME

For Freud, the uncanny is complex and self-referential because it brings to the fore our own psychic experiences or stages of development in previous desires and beliefs. This is why he says that the uncanny artwork is both familiar and alien. There is a similar duality and reflexiveness in the related aesthetic phenomenon of the sublime. Kant captures this feature of artistic reflexivity in his account of the sublime by describing the experience as involving our subjective feeling of reason's power. Reference to ourselves and to our nature, desires, feelings, and abilities becomes part of the overall experience of a sublime object like a mountain or ocean. The sublime has a particular appeal, Kant thinks, because through it we become aware of our own superior *moral* powers.[11] There are distinct echoes of all this in Freud's treatment of the uncanny: here we get another set of mental faculties, a new theory of pleasure and desire, a new hierarchy, and a new psychic conflict.[12]

DLV appears to meditate on or represent the conditions of its own creation. This kind of feature, concerning certain breakdowns of our conceptual and representational systems, has been at the center of analyses of the sublime by postmodern writers like Derrida and Lyotard. Derrida zeroes in on Kant's peculiar phrasing in saying that the sublime is "almost too great" to be presentable (125). The sublime is what a narrative shows without expressing, or what it indicates without spelling out – what is in the margins.

Various literary theorists have discussed a similar function of "excess" in works by authors of the uncanny. Psychoanalytic theory has blended together Freud's discussion of the uncanny with the Kantian notion of what is "almost too great" for expression, with some critics linking the sublime as an aesthetic category either to the Freudian pre-Oedipal or the Lacanian "Real."[13] Others relate this idea to Hertz's critical point about what Freud ignores in Hoffmann's style, his dazzling literary technique. Without endorsing either these Freud–Kant links or Derrida's reading of Kant, I do agree that the sort of feature that current literary critics are interested in *is* illustrated by *DLV*. It confronts us at moments with a breakdown of the medium of representation – here, of course, film.

I have argued elsewhere (partly following Burke), that one way to understand how an artwork like a movie may be sublime is to say that it arouses in the audience reflexive awareness of our human powers – not of the "Moral Law within," but of the power of the human artist to create.[14] Reflexivity is crucial to both the sublime and the uncanny to explain their combined effects of pleasure and pain. In both types of works, there is an ongoing tension in our experience between what may be painful *within* the story of artwork and what is pleasurable *about* its creation as a wonderful artifact. For Kieslowski the filmmaker to toy with us as viewers, as Alexandre toys with Véronique in his puppet-play, is painful, but also pleasant because the creation is marvelous and seductive.

So far, cognitivist studies of film emotions have focused primarily on what is involved in feeling emotions like empathy for characters or in imagining their worlds.[15] But some work has begun on this difficult issue of reflexivity. For example, in a 1996 book, Ed Tan outlines features of what he calls "artefact emotions" and calls for further empirical study of how certain film fans or "cinephiles" attend and react to movie genres, directors, special effects, and so on that they are passionate about.

Similarly, cognitivist accounts of how film *music* evoke emotions would also be relevant to understanding *DLV*. Such accounts recognize, for example, the ambiguity of "diegetic" versus "mood" music.[16] Cognitivist theories can describe both our ordinary abilities to think or feel and our more unusual and self-conscious abilities to process works that are self-referential. We can assess the work rationally as a kind of metaphor at the same time that we respond emotionally to whatever is within the metaphor.[17]

In Hoffman's story, as in plays by Shakespeare, Pirandello, Brecht, and many others, the characters are brought up short by thinking of themselves as that – only characters. *DLV* similarly highlights issues about art and representation. In its climactic scene of the two puppets of Véronique, the movie becomes a metaphor for itself. Véronique vacillates between being a "real" and sympathetic human being and a mere character. She is like the puppet figure, an image of a human created by a man who enjoys telling an artistic but sad story, premised upon a fiction. (This heightening of the fictional status of the story would also pose problems for Freud's account, which requires that we actually come to accept the hitherto-abandoned infantile belief in a double.) It is easy to link this man in the film, Alexandre the puppet-artist, to Kieslowski, the film-artist.

But it is uncanny to shift between seeing this movie as an engaging story and seeing it as "just a fairy-tale." (In another artwork the effect might be different: more horrific, uplifting, existential, or even humorous. I am again thinking of Shakespeare, Calderon, Beckett, Thornton Wilder, and others.) Watching this particular film is at once intriguing and frustrating. I feel resentment at being toyed with – the filmmaker has treated us, as viewers, as pawns in his little artistic game, much as Alexandre has treated Véronique. But both the film and the puppet-play are extraordinary works of art. The viewer must reach an independent decision concerning how to interpret and feel about the whole experience. Both the puppet-play and the film effectively express an idea that somehow breaks down when we examine it more closely; their "truth" or "reality" vanish into "it's just a story." Perhaps it stretches the point, but I would compare the shift that this movie effects at its ending to the one Wittgenstein describes at the close of the *Tractatus*: to see the truth of his claims about language and picturing, one must break through or out of the language he is using. Kieslowski seems to be doing something of this same sort in his film.

The uncanny here, I am suggesting, stems from our awareness of the undecidability of interpretations of *DLV*. The film draws us in enough to make us empathize, but then, in effect, pulls the rug out from under

us. A successful theory of the uncanny or the sublime, as a certain complex type or range of emotion relevant to film, would recognize this and
perhaps go further in describing or empirically studying how audiences
experience it. How do diverse people respond to a movie that breaks the
boundaries of what can be represented? Why is it effective and unsettling
here, but gimmicky, horrific, or comic elsewhere? I do not think the task
is insurmountably difficult; it would call for detailed attention to viewers'
ongoing interpretive strategies as we cope with difficult and confusing
material on screen. Such an account would resemble one that cognitivist
James Peterson (1996) has sketched to describe viewer strategies in con-
ceptualizing the equally difficult forms of avant-garde cinema.

PLAYS UPON GENDER

Another surface or textural feature of the uncanny as it emerges in *DLV*
involves the ways in which it *plays upon gender*. This is a film permeated
by sensibility and emotions. It is about a young woman's experiences of
love, the erotic, and her own sexuality. It begins with scenes of Veronika,
who seems to find joy and innocently lustful pleasure alike in singing, the
feel of rain on her face, and sex with her boyfriend. This same fusion of
emotions and sexuality recurs more quietly in the scene of Véronique's
devastation and sadness when her lover reveals how he has used her life
to create a tragic puppet tale. Kieslowski himself goes so far as to say
that *DLV* is a film of pure emotion, even that "[t]here's no action in
it" (189). But I do not mean to claim that this is a "woman's picture" in
the sense of being a melodrama fraught with emotions like sadness and
loss.[18]

Almost everyone who has reviewed *DLV* feels compelled to discuss the
beauty of its lead actress. Irène Jacob is so central to the film, and so
completely embodies this character who has a double, that it is impossible
to imagine its being made without her. It is also very difficult to conceive
of its being made as a film about a young man. Gender must therefore
be taken into account in proposing ways to explain *DLV*'s meaning and
impact.

Gender as an issue is often treated in psychoanalytic accounts, of
course, and less often so far by cognitivists. But this is not because it cannot be done. Again, as a cognitivist, I think we can use the best available
theories of the mind to interpret the role played by gender in this film.
Gender is related to emotions, social roles, and so on, in ways that many
contemporary scientists and social scientists are still exploring. To do this

it is obviously relevant to note that both Hoffmann and Kieslowski are male artists and that the theme of the male artist whose obsession leads to a muse or an artificially created woman is very common in art and literature. Gender is made relevant in *DLV* by its linkage to the broader themes of fate, life, and art. This film "genderizes" the relation between artist and artistic product because it concerns two women whose story turns out to be in the control of a male artist.

There have been many other cinematic stories of doubles or twinning. They are a frequent trope in the horror genre, e.g., in Brian De Palma's *Sisters*. It is also common for a single actor or actress to portray the twins in such films. The closest parallel to *DLV* that I can think of involving men is David Cronenberg's brilliant *Dead Ringers*, a film I also consider uncanny. But the doubling in *DLV* is not horrific, due to how the film's two primary characters experience their doubling. It is not, as in *Dead Ringers*, a sort of obsessive and ultimately destructive fusion of personalities.[19] Rather, it is comforting, although also eerie, and of course tragic for the one double left behind.

Gender is toyed with here in an interaction with the other key features I have described – the film's reflexiveness and its "excess," or depiction of the undepictable. This woman, an amalgam of Irène Jacob/ Veronika/Véronique, is a pawn masterfully manipulated by the intricate layerings of the movie. Jacob's role is very strenuous, because she is on-screen almost constantly. She, the physical woman, is in a sense the object of adoration here by the director and cinematographer (and perhaps by the audience) as she is studied, stretched, exhausted, and displayed naked in several scenes, even shown in excesses of sexual transport. Like Véronique, she is used by a male artist-director for the ends of *his* story. Véronique/Jacob has helped embody it, almost literally, but it is not after all *her* story. There is a tension here between activity and passivity that confounds simplistic feminist analysis. The actress's marvelous combination of sadness, beauty, and wondrousness help to turn her final scene of recognition into an indictment not just of her diegetic lover, but of the director-as-lover who has used and abused a woman in this story he has made up using her energy and life.

DLV's layered representation of woman as muse or pawn for the male artist(s) conveys a scenario that a feminist might criticize – except that it is also part of the very subject matter of *DLV* itself. The film builds in a kind of internal critique of the filmmaker and his attitudes by its reflexivity. Véronique responds angrily and abruptly when Alexandre confesses that his elaborate seduction with the mystery audiotape was just an experiment to test a plot device in his new novel – to "see if it could really be done." Later he admits he was lying when he said that. No wonder that Kieslowski has remarked that he doesn't see Véronique staying on and having a future with Alexandre after the last scene (182).

Yet the film also cannot be interpreted as conveying a simplistic condemnation of the power and manipulations of the male artist, because art is so celebrated within it. Alexandre's puppet artistry is marvelous, as shown by the way it profoundly moves an audience of small children at Véronique's school. This film does not present a simple anti-male message. Both the young women doubles have loving fathers they are close to and confide in. At the conclusion after she has left Alexandre, Véronique goes back home to the country to find solace in her father. In the final scene we hear her calling out to him as she reaches out to touch a large, symbolic, and beautiful tree in his yard.[20]

There are, of course, well-worked-out psychoanalytic approaches to film studies that highlight the role of gender in film spectatorship and enjoyment. Feminists have also applied psychoanalytic theories of the sublime to examples of women artists and writers[21] and have criticized historical theories of the sublime like Kant's.[22] There are few gender-sensitive studies of the emotions within contemporary brain-based cognitive science. What is presently offered about gender is often unacceptably essentializing or deterministic, focused on things like the role of hormones in establishing gender identity or in stimulating maternal affective behavior. Cognitive science tends to universalize the mind, and many books emerging in cognitive film studies pay little or no attention to issues of gender. The complexity of the social constructionist accounts of gender identity (versus sexual identity) is missing, but this situation can be amended and improved upon.

Again, I want to insist that cognitivists may employ diverse theories, including complex philosophical theories of the emotions. One of these would be Robert Solomon's theory of emotions as cognitive. (Actually this has old roots; a similar account by Aristotle may be found.) This theory fits well with the neuroscientific theories of someone like Antonio Damasio, and it also enables us to discuss sophisticated emotional responses to artworks like *DLV*. Another relevant and subtle philosophical theory of emotions, Ronald de Sousa's, fits with contemporary sociological accounts by recognizing the role of social learning in our own emotional repertoires and responses. This sort of theory lends itself well to gender analysis, because in most contemporary societies boys and girls are encouraged to express and even experience emotions differently. A boy who is "too scared" or a girl who is "too angry" receive social opprobrium to discourage these gender-inappropriate behaviors.

One attempt to adapt cognitive science to feminist literary theory is Ellen Spolsky's 1993 book, *Gaps in Nature.*[23] Spolsky cites Jerry Fodor's work on the modularity of mind, and generally on alternative human cognitive systems, to argue that there are various kinds of literary creation and interpretation reflecting these different cognitive systems. Translation between modules is difficult, and there are very different styles of interpretation, such as the "linear with propositional arguments" and the "analogy-based." Spolsky claims to find more manifestations of this latter style in feminist authors like Julia Kristeva. Spolsky thinks Kristeva and other feminists are writing from the visual module where metaphor is grounded.

This is perhaps a beginning toward discussing the sublime or uncanny within a new cognitivist and yet feminist framework. Spolsky recognizes the creative activity that the artist puts into expressing thoughts and ideas in a form in which they may be somehow alien, and the similar complexity of interpretive response to the reflexivity of artworks. However, her use of the modularity of mind theory is much too crude. And Spolsky's assignment of the various feminist theorists she discusses to the visual module, one that is non-linear and that uses metaphorical and analogical thinking, is dangerous for feminists. It invites the criticism that women are inherently less rational than men. (As she herself notes, many feminists have expressed similar doubts and criticisms of Cixous's and other's notions of *l'écriture féminine.*)

We must be reluctant to argue the unsavory option that structures of the mind and brain are themselves gendered (arousing specters of nineteenth-century social theory, or even that of contemporary sociobiology). Yet, obviously, if a cognitive or cognitive science-based approach aims to supplant psychoanalysis, it must offer a foothold for explanations that recognize how social dimensions of artistic creation and experience, like gender, interact with what seems to be hard-wired in the various emotion systems. While such gender-sensitive approaches are still forthcoming in the more brain-based cognitive sciences, there have been some significant suggestions about how to encompass gender within a broadly *cognitive* approach to film studies in work by Carroll, Leibowitz, and (elsewhere) myself.[24] And here also, I have suggested a cognitive reading that emphasizes what viewers may both think and feel in response to the depiction of gender in relation to *DLV*'s themes and style.

In suggesting that this film's particular power to evoke the uncanny arises in part from its play upon gender, what I mean is that audience thoughts and emotions are engaged by some very specific ways that *DLV* treats gender and sexuality. The theme of doubling occurs within the movie as a fact about its central *female* characters and also as a meta-filmic fact about the performance of the *actress*. Thus, the manipulation of Véronique by the puppet-artist Alexandre is paralleled by the manipulations the director Kieslowski makes of his actress Jacob. The movie involves us as viewers who empathize with Véronique's mystery and her sense of violation when Alexandre uses her unique tale to create a story. But it is unnerving or uncanny because we may also feel that we are participants in this violation because we too see her as "just a character in a story." Similarly, we may dwell with pleasure and desire upon this actress's beautiful face and body, even while intellectually regarding this as illicit voyeurism. The film creates an odd – an uncanny – mix of thoughts and feelings. Along with its intellectual puzzles of plot are puzzles about the director's meaning in telling the story. And along with its sheer beauty and pleasures of viewing there are pains about its treatment of both character and actress.

CONCLUSION

Freud's theory of the uncanny rests upon a host of disputable postulates, but at least he sought to take some complex psychological "data" seriously in an attempt to expand the field of aesthetic speculation into "remote" and "neglected" provinces like the uncanny. This is a reasonable aim and one I have also pursued here. A major reason I reject Freud's account of the uncanny is because he ended up ignoring the very aesthetic features he set out to explore, overlooking the aesthetic surface of artworks in his search for their alleged depths. There are new attempts underway in cognitive film studies to replace the psychological underpinnings given to aesthetic theory by Freud, and I have drawn on these newer methods to describe features of the uncanny that are central to this movie: its reflexivity, depiction of the undepictable, and play upon gender. More must be done to develop a subtler and more complete theory of the uncanny, to provide a better explanation of the unusual impact of films like *The Double Life of Véronique*.[25]

NOTES

1. The music was composed by Kieslowski's frequent collaborator, Zbigniew Preisner.
2. Neil Hertz uses the term to discuss a similar device in E.T.A. Hoffmann's "The Sandman" (112).

3. Also on cognitive science and film theory, see Anderson; Grodal; Plantinga and Smith; and Tan.

4. My reading of Freud is indebted to Schneider (2000) and also to Hertz (97–121).

5. Hertz asks whether Freud's view is that we are reminded of a process of repetition or of castration dread itself (102).

6. See Schneider (2000).

7. For criticism, see Grünbaum (1984); Sulloway; Cioffi (1970); Crews; and Torrey.

8. See Forgays et al. Recent psychoanalytic views of anxiety do refer to neuro-biological research; see Roose and Glick.

9. See Brugger et al. (1994; 1996); and Fasolo & Filidoro.

10. Freud writes, "We have drifted into this field of research half involuntarily," referring to literary effects that have "doubtless long been fully taken into account by professors of aesthetics" (160).

11. For further discussion and applications to film, see Freeland (1999b).

12. Critics have drawn links between the Freudian uncanny and the Kantian sublime; see Weiskel; and Hertz (40–60).

13. For an example of this Lacanian connection, see Mishra (16).

14. See Freeland (1999b).

15. For example, see Currie's (1995) treatment of empathy; some essays in Allen & Smith also adopt a cognitivist perspective.

16. See, e.g., Levinson; Smith (1996); and Kivy.

17. We need an account of how we humans consciously enjoy the manipulation of symbol systems, something more psychologically current but akin to the work of Nelson Goodman and Ernst Gombrich. Schneider (2000) also attends to the working of metaphors.

18. And such "women's pictures" should not be treated dismissively; see Leibowitz.

19. I discuss *Dead Ringers* in Chapter 4 of Freeland (1999a).

20. I don't feel impelled to interpret the tree as a phallic symbol but rather as simply a strongly rooted part of Véronique's home. Sometimes a tree is just a tree.

21. Yaeger uses the notion of the pre-Oedipal sublime to describe certain art-works by female authors.

22. See Battersby; and Gould.

23. Thanks to Alan Richardson for drawing this work to my attention.

24. See Leibowitz; Carroll (1995); and Freeland (1999a).

25. Thanks to Krist Bender and Lynne Brown, who watched and discussed *DLV* with me. In addition, my correspondence with Steven Schneider on Freud and the uncanny has been invaluable.

6 STEVEN JAY SCHNEIDER

Manifestations of the Literary Double in Modern Horror Cinema

It is . . . the relationship between normality and the Monster that constitutes the essential subject of the horror film. . . . The relationship has one privileged form: the figure of the doppelgänger, alter-ego, or double, a figure that has recurred constantly in western culture, especially during the past hundred years. . . . The doppelgänger motif reveals the Monster as normality's shadow.
– Robin Wood

According to Laurence Rickels, author of *The Vampire Lectures*, and a master of the catchy academic turn of phrase (yes, such a thing does exist),

Literature, which is where the phantasm of the double used to be at home . . . in the eighteenth and nineteenth centuries, during the opening era of the uncanny, suddenly released the double and no longer featured it. At the same time film and psychoanalysis were the two new institutions that began attending to the double feature. (90)

Of course, neither film nor psychoanalysis attended to this double feature in isolation from one another. Otto Rank, in a 1914 paper, claimed that "the uniqueness of cinematography in visibly portraying psychological events calls our attention, with exaggerated clarity, to the fact that the interesting and meaningful problems of man's relation to himself – and the fateful disturbance of this relation – finds . . . imaginative representation" (7). And after reading Rank's piece, Freud himself makes mention of Paul Wegener's German doppelgänger film, *The Student of Prague* (1913), in his seminal 1919 essay, "The 'Uncanny'." Going in the other direction, the sheer prevalence of doubles in horror cinema – whether in the form of murderous alter-egos, monstrous shape-shifters, maniacal twins, or malevolent clones – testifies to their psychic resonance, and dime-book Freudian explanations are often put forward by the films' smug therapists who may or may not be schizophrenic killers themselves (*Dressed To Kill* [1980], *Nightbreed* [1990], *Color of Night* [1994]).

It can hardly be denied that doubles often make for disturbing, uncanny, even horrifying presences – especially in horror films of the past forty years, where they really run rampant. The question is this: *In virtue of what do doubles engender such effects in viewers?* After all, we are not the ones getting doubled! My own answer to this question follows recent work on the literary double by such scholars as Carl Kepler, Robert Rogers, and Andrew Webber. After defining my subject matter more precisely, I will attempt to reconcile Rank's theory of the double with the apparently contradictory one put forward by Freud. I will then proceed to map the many varieties of the horror film double onto a hierarchical structure, tracing them to their literary prototypes along the way. Special emphasis will be placed on that distinctly modern doubling phenomenon I have elsewhere called "uncanny realism" (Schneider 1997). Finally, the psychoanalytic account of horror film doubles presented here will be defended in the face of cognitivist objections.

THEORIZING THE DOUBLE

Although consensus is by no means absolute, most theorists and psychologists define doubling as the experience of seeing or otherwise sensing, feeling, or believing that there exists another "you," from inside your own self. Possible causes of this experience include hallucination, illusion, delusion, vivid imagining, and (at least in fantasy and fiction) supernatural or alien forces, technological advances, or simply "that which cannot be explained by Reason." This definition is broader than the one typically given for "autoscopy," a documented psychopathological condition which is restricted to *visual* self-duplication. It is also to be distinguished from out-of-body experiences (whereby a disembodied self looks upon its physical body from the outside), Capgras' Syndrome (where the afflicted person asserts that friends or relatives are actually imposters),[1] Fregoli's Phenomenon (where patients hold that the appearance of someone has been intentionally altered to conceal their identity), and internal autoscopy (where subjects claim the ability to literally see inside their own bodies).

Where do the spectators of horror films in which doubles appear fit into this scheme? Unless we want to fall back on a thick notion of "identification," according to which viewers are held to undergo an illusion of identity with a specific character or else (less radically) an exact replication of that character's mental and emotional states, we need to widen the scope of our investigation to include third-person phenomenology.[2] And considering that even in reality people can be shocked and disturbed by the unexpected or inexplicable appearance of someone *else's* double, there seems no need to posit any such precise, uniform, and mysterious psychic connection between character and viewer. Let us define *cinematic doubling*, then, as the experience of seeing or otherwise coming to believe that an on-screen character has another self, whether or not this "other self" is actually observed by that character or is merely sensed, intuited, or empirically discovered by him or her. Note that, whatever is ultimately responsible for the double's existence within a particular filmic universe, by granting audiences visual access to him/her, the director gives the double an extra-diegetic reality. From *our* standpoint, the character's double is not a hallucination, illusion, delusion, etc., but a fact capable of independent confirmation – just pause the film in the appropriate places. And because, empirically speaking, we seem as capable of being disturbed, freaked out, or horrified by doubles as the characters who actually (think they) have them – though probably not to the same extent – any answer to the question of what accounts for the double's uncanny efficacy should extend from the first- to the third-person case.

In the paper mentioned above, and in a book published eleven years later, Rank sought to explain the doppelgänger's prominence in film and literature. His thesis was that this figure represents "the normally unconscious thought of the approaching destruction of the self" (77), i.e., that it signifies a return to consciousness – albeit in disguised, wish-fulfilling form – of the typically repressed fear of death. With reference to such texts as *The Student of Prague*, Hoffman's *The Devil's Elixirs*, Wilde's *The Picture of Dorian Gray*, and Dostoevsky's *The Double*, and citing now-dubious anthropological findings as evidence, Rank based his argument on the Freudian postulate that primary narcissism (a developmental stage during which the child takes himself or herself as love-object[3]) feels itself threatened by the inevitable destruction of the self: "this observation is supported by the choice, as the most primitive concept of the soul, of an image as similar as possible to the physical self." He concludes that "the idea of death . . . is denied by a duplication of the self incorporated in the shadow or in the reflected image" (83).

Although this account has a degree of *prima facie* plausibility, it remains to be shown why the presence of a double is so often accompanied by feelings of uncanniness or horror. If Rank is correct, shouldn't one's double be a source of psychological *security*? His answer to this question, though incomplete, is nevertheless provocative. "In the same phenomena of defense," he notes, "the threat also recurs, against which the individual wants to protect and assert himself... Originally created as a wish-defense against a dreaded eternal destruction, [the doppelgänger] reappears in superstition as the messenger of death" (86). This is reminiscent of Freud, who identifies the double as "the most prominent theme of uncanniness," one whose power of fright is due to its "being a creation dating back to a very early mental stage, long since surmounted... in which it wore a more friendly aspect" (1990: 358). Freud's thought, implicit in Rank, is that the threat of death or destruction of the ego experienced during primary narcissism is combated via the creation of a double, which in effect serves as a psychic insurance policy. When the stage of primary narcissism has been surpassed, however, and such insurance is no longer necessary, the presence of a double serves only as a reminder of what it once protected against: "From having been an assurance of immortality, [the double] becomes the uncanny harbinger of death" (357).

Freud's account differs from Rank's primarily in that it focuses less on the return to consciousness of repressed fears of death, and more on the idea of a long-since abandoned *belief* in the existence of a second self, a belief that is capable of being *reconfirmed* in either experienced or depicted reality. It is this reconfirmation, according to Freud, which produces uncanny feeling. Before proceeding, some additional explanation is in order here.

Elsewhere,[4] I have called attention to the widespread critical misunderstanding that Freud identifies repressed infantile fears and desires as the *sole* source of uncanny feelings. Strictly speaking, the Freudian "return of the repressed" formula, made famous in horror film studies by Robin Wood (1979) and subsequently picked up and run with by numerous others writing on the genre, constitutes only *one* class of the psychoanalytic uncanny. In his 1919 essay, Freud also identifies a *second* class of uncanny phenomena, which is constituted by surmounted infantile beliefs that gain some measure of validation in either reality or fiction. Thus, in response to something that seems to confirm our previously discarded (or so we thought) beliefs in the ability of the dead to return to life, the omnipotence of thoughts, or the existence of a double, feelings of uncanniness result: "we have *surmounted* these modes of thought; but we do not feel quite sure of our new beliefs, and the old ones still exist within us ready to seize upon any confirmation" (370–71). Here what has been relegated to the unconscious is a *belief in the reality* of a particular ideational content, rather than a particular ideational content *itself.*

So which of these psychoanalytic accounts of the double is preferable? Does the double signify a "return of the repressed" (Rank), where all that is necessary is the unearthing of a primitive fear embodied in human form, namely one's own self? Or does it signify instead a "reconfirmation of the surmounted" (Freud), where a previous commitment to the reality of doubles is required? The answer is most likely *both* to some extent, because all uncanny feeling ultimately has the same genesis. As Freud notes, "when we consider that primitive beliefs are most intimately connected with [repressed] infantile complexes, and are, in fact, based on them, we shall not be greatly astonished to find that the distinction is often a hazy one" (372). Briefly, it is a tenet of psychoanalytic theory that anxiety is the cause of repression; therefore, with the unexpected return to consciousness of some previously repressed ideational content comes all of the latent anxiety. The same holds for the reconfirmation of primitive beliefs "intimately connected with . . . , and . . . , in fact, based on" that content. So even if the double's uncanny efficacy stems from a renewing of our once-surmounted belief in its existence, this belief was *itself* formed as protection against the repressed fear of death.

MAPPING THE DOUBLE

Before defending the above psychoanalytic account of the double from possible cognitivist objections, it would be useful to sketch out a basic taxonomy of this figure as it gets manifested in the modern horror film.[5] Doubles may come in a variety of shapes, sizes, and numbers (because self-fragmentation can be multiple as well as dual), but they nevertheless fall pretty neatly into two basic categories: *doppelgängers* (physical doubles) and *alter-egos* (mental doubles). This distinction corresponds to one that Rogers makes between "doubling by multiplication" and "doubling by division." In the former category, a person's physical features are duplicated in another, whether through biological, technological, or supernatural means. In the latter, more complex case, there is "a splitting up of a recognizable, unified psychological entity into separate, complementary, distinguishable parts represented by seemingly autonomous characters" (5).

Physical doubles can themselves be divided into two types: *replicas* (natural doppelgängers) and *replicants* (non-natural doppelgängers). Replicas, which include primitive and alien life forms but not genetically or technologically engineered ones, fall into the following categories: *twins* and *chameleons*. One filmmaker fond of exploiting the uncanny potential of twins or, more precisely, of blurring the line between twins and schizophrenics, is Brian De Palma (*Sisters* [1973], *Raising Cain* [1992]). In David Cronenberg's *Dead Ringers* (1988), Jeremy Irons plays identical twin gynecologists whose sanity collapses as their identities merge. And who can forget the 1971 Hammer horror film *Twins of Evil*, featuring *Playboy* magazine's first identical twin centerfolds, Mary and Madeline Collinson?

Chameleons, not to be confused with shape-shifters (discussed below), are usually non-human life forms possessing the ability to take on the appearance of people or animals observed remotely. Probably the best-known chameleon in modern horror cinema is John Carpenter's eponymous *Thing* (1982), not to be confused with Christian Nyby's *Thing* (1951), which the film explains is "a highly intellectual carrot." More recently, in *Phantoms* (1998), a prehistoric creature that for centuries has been living underground comes up to wreak havoc on a small town and the obligatory Gen-X leads by temporarily adopting their identities (cf. *The Faculty* [1999]).

Replicants fall loosely into four groups: *robots, cyborgs, clones,* and *apparitions*. It is with respect to the first three of these that the cross-fertilization between horror and science-fiction cinema is most apparent. Robots – wholly mechanical doppelgängers – appear in *The Stepford Wives* (1975), *Westworld* (1973), *Crash and Burn* (1990), and of course *Metropolis* (1927), in which the angelic rebel leader Maria (Briggite Helm) is temporarily replaced by a debauched automaton, with catastrophic consequences.[6] Cyborgs (partial robots) turn up more often in straight science fiction, but to the extent that films like *Bladerunner* (1982), *The Terminator* (1984), *Hardware* (1990), and *Terminator 2* (1991) engender fear by dramatizing the interchangeability of man and machine – and the potential replaceability of man *by* machine – they find a place on this family tree of doubles.[7] Horrific clones (sometimes not so horrific) frequently appear in B-horror films, such as *The Manster* (1959), in which a patient injected with an experimental enzyme grows a head, then a whole new body, out of his shoulder, and *The Human Duplicators* (1964). Then there are the clones from *Invasion of the Body Snatchers* (1956, 1978, 1994), but these creatures are really alien life forms and so fall under the heading of natural doppelgängers... which just goes to show how permeable these categories can be (cf. *The Puppet Masters* [1994]).

Finally, among the many apparitions (supernatural replicants) to choose from, I will restrict myself to three: Asa (Barbara Steele), the vampy vampire who looks just like her virginal descendent Katia (also Steele) in Mario Bava's *La Maschera del Demonio* (aka *Black Sunday*, 1960);[8] the knife-wielding dwarf in a red raincoat who, from the back, is a ringer for Donald Sutherland's recently deceased child in *Don't Look Now* (1973); and the malevolent spirit child who so closely resembles Mia Farrow's dead daughter in *The Haunting of Julia* (aka *Full Circle*, 1976).[9] This is also the category of doubles explored most frequently in nineteenth-century literature, e.g., in Poe's *William Wilson* and James Hogg's *Confessions of a Justified Sinner*.

Alter-egos, or mental doubles, can also be divided up into four main groups: *schizos, shape-shifters, projections*, and *psychos*. Briefly, I will take each of these in turn.

Schizos are mental doubles who exhibit, as Rogers puts it, "behavioral dissociation in time" (15). Behavioral dissociation, a defining feature of multiple personality disorder, results from the fact that schizos possess one body but two or more temporally contiguous consciousnesses. Of course, the body in question can be made (up) to look like an entirely different one, even one of the opposite sex, as with Norman Bates (Anthony Perkins) in *Psycho* (1960), the killer priest in *Chi L'ha Vista Morire?* (*Who Saw Her Die?* 1971), and Dr. Robert Elliott (Michael Caine) in *Dressed to Kill* (1980). But it is to the extent that we can see, intuit, or otherwise discern that a unified physical entity underlies the various appearances and personalities that uncanny effects are engendered here.

Shape-shifters are mental doubles whose behavioral dissociation is accompanied by physical transformation. Paradigmatic examples include werewolves, the various Dr. Jekylls and Mr. Hydes (including Sister Hyde in the 1971 Hammer film, and Dr. Black in the 1975 blaxploitation vehicle), William Hurt's peyote-induced apeman in *Altered States* (1980), the cicada boy from *The Beast Within* (1982), and Natasha Henstridge's estrous alien–human hybrid in *Species* (1995). Certain vampires also find a place on this list, although in general vampire consciousness tends to be preserved through physical change: Dracula is still Dracula, even when he's a bat. The main reason shape-shifters are unlike chameleons is that their transformations do not so much *cause* the existence of a physical double as *manifest* the existence of a mental one.

Projections are similar to shape-shifters insofar as the split personalities are realized in different bodies. But in this case, the bodies are spatially as opposed to temporally distinct from one another.[10] In Robert Weine's

The Cabinet of Dr. Caligari (1920), as in James Whale's *Frankenstein* (1931), the somnambulistic monster can be interpreted as a nightmarish embodiment of his creator's repressed desires and, in this respect, stands as his double. According to Morton Kaplan, "one of the standard devices used in melodrama [is] the dramatization of conflicting motives which specifically belong to one individual by distributing them among a number of fictional characters. . . . These 'partial figures' who serve to compose one dramatic identity are doubles of each other" (135). I would only add that "partial figuring," or projecting, is a standard device of horror cinema as well as of melodramatic literature, as evidenced by such films as *It's Alive!* (1974), *The Brood* (1979), *The Dark Half* (1993),[11] and the "Barbara and Lucy" segment of *Asylum* (1972).[12]

Similar to projections, but more subtly realized, are psychos – admittedly the most speculative category of this taxonomy. For here, the sociopathic antagonist, almost always a serial killer, exhibits neither behavioral dissociation nor physical transformation. Yet it can still be argued that in many post-1960 horror films an effect is created whereby the murderer gets sets up as the double of the protagonist (typically a detective, policeman, or FBI profiler). At the center of such films as *White of the Eye* (1987), *Manhunter* (1986), *The Silence of the Lambs* (1991), *Se7en* (1995), and *Kiss the Girls* (1997) stands a psychopath who kills according to a more or less rigidly defined aesthetico-moral code (in *White of the Eye*, a police officer at the crime scene asks "Is it murder or is it art?"; in *Silence of the Lambs*, Hannibal Lecter's performance-art murder of a guard is set to classical music). In these films, the monsters are human rather than supernatural. What is more, they exhibit a high degree of thought, creativity, and skill; they are not mere slashers, which is precisely what distinguishes them from the indiscriminate stalkers of the Jason and Michael mode.[13] By creating "uncomfortable affinities" between these killers and their pursuers at the emotional, psychological, and symbolic levels, the films in question succesfully highlight "the links between normality and monstrosity" while simultaneously exposing the "[pronounced] dialectical tensions between binary oppositions" (Simpson 2000: 98).[14]

DEFENDING THE DOUBLE

In what remains, I will seek to defend the psychoanalytic account of the double presented above from possible (and actual) cognitivist objections. First, some general remarks: Cognitivist film theorists tend to argue their case by rehearsing familiar Popperian and Grünbaumian claims against

the legitimacy of psychoanalysis as a scientific discipline[15] or else by highlighting the numerous conceptual leaps and logical inconsistencies inherent in Metz and his followers' application of Lacanian ideas to the
cinema.[16] (Of course, these sorts of argument are by no means mutually exclusive.) With respect to the former, it should be noted that the
mere citing of such respected critics is as much an "appeal to authority"
as is a facile reliance on Freud, Rank, or Melanie Klein and is every bit
as egregious. In recent years, a number of philosophers – most notably
Richard Wollheim – have responded directly to the criticisms of Popper,
Grünbaum, and others and have argued fairly persuasively for a recon-
ception of psychoanalytic theory as an "interpretive science" (Hopkins
1992: 3), i.e., as a legitimate (systematic, cumulative, and sound) as well
as radical extension of commonsense psychology.[17] Until some kind of
consensus is reached, or a reasonable compromise worked out, writings
on film that employ psychoanalytic theory should be examined for flaws
(as well as merits) on a *case-by-case* basis – and this by Freudians and cognitivists alike.

I would also note the work of Clark Glymour, who has gone far to show
just how much psychoanalysis, at least as originally conceived, has *in common* with contemporary cognitive science: "Freud was reared to think that
psychology should be a neurophysiology of the mental in which the explanation
of capacities in terms of subcapacities proceeds in pace with the identification of parts of the brain essential for the component capacities"
(51). That Freud notoriously failed in this identification effort, in his
early *Project for a Scientific Psychology* and after, does not make this compar-
ison any less worthwhile. For as Glymour points out, "even when Freud
had the wrong answer to a question [about an issue in the philosophy of
mind], or refused to give an answer, he knew what the question was and
what was at stake in it. And when he was deeply wrong, it was often for
reasons that still make parts of cognitive psychology wrong" (46). Despite
the flaws and inconsistencies in his thinking at the level of detail, Freud –
like the vast majority of cognitive scientists today – held the brain to be
a machine, one whose computation processes explain our experience
and behavior; also like many contemporary cognitivists, he held there to
be a private, inner language of thought "in which propositions are expressed and which acts as the fundamental coding in the brain" (60). The
point to take from this too-brief discussion is simply that psychoanalysis,
in theory if not always in practice, is by no means antithetical to scientific
study of the cognitive faculties, and that looking for similarities between
these paradigms may be a great deal more productive for film studies
today than constantly reiterating the differences. (Supporters of Freud

must be wary of falling into the opposite trap of claiming scientific status for psychoanalytic theory at all costs. Something that is not recognized often enough – except superficially – is that even if psychoanalysis is *not* scientific, it may nevertheless be *true* and justifiably believed to be true.[18])

With respect to the latter type of argument, directed against psycho-analytic film theory based on Lacan's, and later Kristeva's, revision of Freud – that is to say, *most* psychoanalytic film theory – I would just note that the account of the double presented above makes no reference to Lacan or his successors and, in fact, stands as a self-conscious effort to make new use of an essay of Freud's, "The 'Uncanny',", which has to date generated significant interest among literary scholars but very little interest in film studies.[19] Certainly, Rank has not yet been given his due in the latter field. None of this is to claim that either Freud's or Rank's theory of the double is beyond criticism – far from it (see below) – but I believe these theories are less suspect, and more open to empirical testing, than most if not all of the Lacanian ones appealed to by Baudry, Metz, Mulvey, and others (including, e.g., the association of the "Law of the Father" with such traditional filmic elements as narrative sequence).

Specific objections to Freud's theory of the uncanny, and in particular to his treatment of the double, have been proffered by cognitivist film philosopher Cynthia Freeland. In her essay on Krzysztof Kieslowski's *The Double Life of Véronique* (1991) in this volume, Freeland argues that the film's uncanny elements can be described within a cognitivist framework without overly rationalizing our responses, yet also without resorting to unconscious motivations or repressed beliefs. *Véronique* is a film about two young women, one Polish, the other French (both played by Irène Jacob), who never actually meet, but who look exactly alike, share the same name, and possess a vague sense of the other's existence. Freeland acknowledges that a Freudian reading of this film in terms of uncanniness possesses "initial appeal," but goes on to raise a number of difficulties for such a reading. She begins by pointing out that Freud's explanation of the power of uncanniness

invokes numerous postulates, including many not argued for in the essay itself.... Such tenets include that certain kinds of infantile thoughts and fears exist and are universal; that among these thoughts are thoughts of a double; that such thoughts serve a particular aim, averting the fear of death; that certain processes of outgrowing or "surmounting" the relevant beliefs are a normal part of the maturation process; that an artwork can create or inspire ... the return of such a belief; and finally, that should this happen, it will create a fairly specific emotional experience of what we call "the uncanny." (198–99)

Freeland's objections are basically threefold: first, she challenges Freud's claims concerning primitive thoughts, infantile beliefs, and the developmental process of "surmounting." Second, she questions whether works of art are truly capable of reconfirming such primitive/infantile thoughts and beliefs in depicted reality, with the result that feelings of uncanniness are produced. And third, elsewhere in her essay, she cites "recent research into the neuropsychiatry of the doppelgänger phenomenon [which] casts doubt on Freud's approach" by showing that it is a "well-recognized effect of various disorders such as epilepsy and specific brain lesions and it can be treated with medications." An additional objection, implicit in Freeland's discussion, might be stated as follows: Considering its relative lack of theoretical economy, what is so fruitful about reading the uncanny dimension of this film (and others of its ilk) in specifically psychoanalytic terms?[20]

Needless to say, these criticisms are intelligent, powerful, and not to be cast aside completely in the space of a few paragraphs. Nevertheless, sufficient room is left to show how a more considered response might proceed. And so, in order, whereas one might agree with Freeland that Freud's claims in favor of primitive thoughts, infantile beliefs, etc., have yet to be proven true, neither have they been proven *false*. (Then again, has the unconscious been "proven" to exist? For varying reasons, including inference to the best explanation, one could plausibly argue that indeed it has.[21]) If this objection is to have any force, it must fall back on the Popperian argument alluded to above: that psychoanalytic theory – specifically, Freud's theory of the uncanny – is in fact *unfalsifiable* and, therefore, unscientific. Because there is no way of demonstrating that infantile thoughts, beliefs, or complexes do *not* exist, the argument goes, their purported existence cannot be subject to empirical confirmation or disconfirmation. Therefore, Freud's theory of the uncanny, including his account of the double, is "metaphysical" (because untestable) rather than genuinely scientific in nature.

I have already mentioned the existence of considerable scholarship that tackles this sort of criticism head-on. At the very least, it must be acknowledged that the scientific status of psychoanalysis, including its postulates and fundamental tenets, has always been more of a problem for philosophy of science *in general*, "rather than having any intrinsic connection to psychoanalysis." After all, "what constitutes a scientific theory? What are appropriate scientific inductivist canons" (Levine 2000a: 3)? More importantly, James Hopkins has shown how Popper's reliance on the notion of predictive power – one consequence of falsifiability – as the essential indicator of a theory's scientific status is *itself* methodologically suspect (1992: 24–26).

Even leaving aside Hopkins's sophisticated and fairly complicated counterargument, however, it seems that with sufficient ingenuity one could devise empirical means of testing the validity of Freud's theory. Consider, for instance, the following hypothetical study, one which *prima facie* appears capable of helping dis/confirm his account of the double. Start with a group of people who, for whatever reason, currently evince the belief that they possess a doppelgänger or "second self." Now test to see whether or not these people experience uncanniness or fright to anywhere near the same degree as "normal" subjects (those lacking such a belief, at least consciously) when watching the portrayal of doubles in selected horror films. To do this, one might observe the subjects' responses (linguistic, physical, behavioral, etc.), ask for self-evaluations, check for pulse-rate and heart-rate increases, etc. The Freudian prediction would be that the first group of subjects will prove *less* susceptible to uncanny feelings than the second group because these are people who have never completely surmounted their infantile belief in the existence of a double. Therefore, a double's appearance (on screen or off, in fiction or reality) does not constitute a return to consciousness of something long-forgotten and, therefore, its original life-sustaining aspect remains unchanged.

In another essay, Freud calls attention to the fact that "the omnipotence of thoughts [another surmounted belief capable of generating feelings of uncanniness when reconfirmed] is seen to have unrestricted play in the emotional life of neurotic patients" (1989: 108). This raises the question of whether neurotics experience a sense of uncanniness/horror when their beliefs in the omnipotence of thought, the prompt fulfillment of wishes, etc., are reconfirmed. Once again, the Freudian prediction would be no, at least not to the same degree as non-neurotics. By way of anecdotal support in favor of this prediction, consider the "frank incomprehension" expressed by Denis Nilsen, a London serial killer who operated during the 1970s and 1980s, in response to the outrage people felt when they learned how he disposed of the bodies: "I can never quite understand a traditional and largely superstitious fear of the dead and corpses" (Masters: 160). At the other extreme, but employing similar reasoning, Freud claims that "anyone who has completely and finally rid himself of animistic beliefs will be insensible to this type of the uncanny" (1990: 371). And so we find even in Freud's own writings the empirically verifiable assertion that certain types of people – those who have *never* surmounted their infantile beliefs, those who have surmounted such beliefs "completely and finally" – will prove considerably more or less immune (respectively) to uncanny effects.

Freeland's doubts concerning the aesthetic dimension of the uncanny can be dealt with more straightforwardly. At one point, she notes that Freud "relies upon identical causal hypotheses to the uncanny emotions of the characters *in the story* and uncanny emotions experienced by readers (or viewers) *of the story*." "But why," she asks, "must we explain the way *DLV* works by appeal to something 'deep' and even 'infantile' *within us* that makes us parallel to Véronique?" This is really just a rephrasing of the question raised earlier of why the double's uncanny efficacy should be extended from the first- to the third-person case. Freeland continues: "It is implausible to require that each viewer who finds the film uncanny does so because it re-awakens a conviction of some previously held but abandoned belief in the existence of a double. Perhaps the film depicts *a* double as plausible, but how does this relate to each viewer's *own* double?" Our initial response to this question was to note that filmmakers are able to provide cinematic doubles such as Véronique/Veronika with an extra-diegetic reality by making them audiovisually accessible to viewers. But clearly this response is not sufficient. For while it helps to account for the viewer's presently held belief in the existence of a double,[22] it does *not* account for the sense of uncanniness/horror that apparently results even when one recognizes full well that the double in question is not one's own.

Turning things around, why does Freeland assume that on Freud's account viewers who find *Véronique* and other doppelgänger films uncanny must somehow be convinced, even momentarily, that their *own* doubles exist? According to Freud (even if he does not make this sufficiently clear in his paper), all that is necessary for a feeling of uncanniness to result is that one's belief in the existence of *a* double be reconfirmed. *Whose* double it is makes little difference, save for determining the *intensity* of uncanny affect: If you are led to believe in the existence of your *own* double, you will almost certainly be more creeped out than if you are led to believe in the existence of someone *else's*. *Contra* Freeland, then, there is no real "problem" needing a solution here at all; under the right conditions,[23] the appearance of a double – whether in reality or fiction, whether one's own or someone else's – is capable of reconfirming previously surmounted beliefs in their existence and is therefore capable of generating feelings of uncanniness and horror.

As for Freeland's objection that the anatomical basis of the doppelgänger phenomenon undermines Freud's account of the double, I return to a point made previously (and note, the studies Freeland cites only concern cases of *first-person* doubling, and are in no sense conclusive): after Glymour, it would seem we have good reason to suppose that a Freudian explanation of the phenomenon in question is ultimately *compatible* with one framed in neuropsychiatric terms. For instance, it may turn out that autoscopic experiences are correlated not just with "epilepsy and specific brain lesions," but with the possession of certain uncommon beliefs of the kind identified by Freud, a discovery which may in turn lead to some interesting hypotheses concerning the neurophysiological basis of such beliefs. Once again, the crucial point is that such a discovery certainly looks like an empirical possibility, even if the necessary experiments have not yet been performed.

Finally, with respect to the last objection raised above, concerning the rationale for adopting a psychoanalytic account of the double despite its lack of theoretical simplicity or obviousness, it is my hope that essays such as this one might be seen as contributing to an answer. What Freud, Rank, Jung (whose related writings on the "Shadow" self could not be taken up here for reasons of space[24]), and their more recent followers have sought to provide is an explanation of the doubling phenomenon that can account for its widespread familiarity, its apparent timelessness, and its archaic basis in human experience.[25] By connecting the double's undeniable uncanniness to primitive fears of, and beliefs in, one's own impending death, this explanation – abstracted, and thus taken collectively – goes a long way toward accomplishing these critical goals.

...And so it seems that the literary double as manifested in modern horror cinema remains susceptible to psychoanalytic explanation and cannot be explained *away* by cognitivist film theorists as easily as they would have us believe.[26]

NOTES

1. A paradigmatic case of Capgras' Syndrome appears in *The Curse of the Cat People* (1944), where an elderly woman stubbornly refuses to believe, without any apparent justification, that her daughter is in fact her daughter.
2. For powerful criticisms of the notion of identification as employed in contemporary film theory, see Carroll (1990: 88–96); Smith (1997); and Gaut (1999). For a qualified defense, see Perez (2000).
3. See Freud (1957).

4. Schneider (1997; 2000). This paragraph and the next rework claims made by Schneider (2000: 172–73).
5. This builds on the taxonomy of Schneider (2000).
6. As Chris Hassold notes, "Maria is not simply duplicated in the film as the robot on whom human features have been imposed, but toward the end of the film the robot is momentarily pluralized as well. In the concluding scenes..., as the false Maria is being burned at the stake as a witch by the angry populace, she undergoes several transformations.... This collapsing double reflects the implicit tendency of any doubling to pluralize personas beyond the initial two" (255).
7. In *Terminator 2*, as opposed to its predecessor, the malevolent cyborg is also a chameleon. See Telotte (1994: 248) and Harvey Greenberg's essay in this volume.
8. Bava returned to the supernatural replicant theme in *Kill, Baby, Kill* (1960).
9. For discussion of *The Haunting of Julia*, see Schneider (2002).
10. Cf. Jung on the phenomenon of "synchronicity," which he defines as "the coincidence of a psychic state with a corresponding (more or less simultaneous) external event taking place outside the observer's field of perception, i.e., at a distance, and only verifiable afterward" (1981: 511).
11. *The Dark Half*'s narrative ambiguity allows it to be placed just as easily in the twin or schizo categories.
12. For discussion of this segment of *Asylum*, see Schneider (2002).
13. See Schneider (2001; 2003a) for extended discussion of the murderer-*artiste* in modern horror cinema.
14. Simpson (47–57) traces this species of doubling back to the Gothic literary tradition.
15. E.g., Prince (1996: 73–76); Freeland (1996: 198–99).
16. E.g., Allen (1995: ch. 1); Carroll (1988: chs. 1–2); Gaut (1994); Freeland (1996: 199).
17. E.g., Cavell (1993); Gardner (1993); Hopkins (1988; 1992; 1996); Wollheim (1991).
18. Thanks to Michael Levine for emphasizing this point. See his essay in this volume.
19. This may be changing; see Arnzen (1997).
20. Thanks to Daniel Shaw for articulating this objection.
21. This point is due to Michael Levine.
22. Admittedly, such beliefs may conflict with various pieces of background knowledge (e.g., that Véronique/Veronika is played by the same actress) – but I take it this is part of a more general problem in aesthetics, the so-called "paradox of emotional response to fiction," which asks how we can be moved by fictional objects and events considering that we "know" such objects and events do not really exist.
23. For more on these "conditions" (a reference to that "conflict of judgment" necessary for feelings of uncanniness to arise) see Schneider (1997: 422–23).
24. See Jung (1959).

25. For a response to the charge that the universalizing implications of psycho-analytic theories of the uncanny, including the phenomenon of the dou-ble, necessarily fail to account for individual difference and sociohistorical change, see Schneider (2000).
26. Thanks to Michael Levine, Tamas Pataki, and Daniel Shaw for helpful feed-back on earlier versions of this essay.

Heimlich Maneuvres: On A Certain Tendency of Horror and Speculative Cinema

> I've seen things you people wouldn't believe – attack ships on fire off the shore of Orion . . . sea beams glittering in the dark at the Tannhauser Gate . . . All those moments will be gone in time – like tears in rain . . .
> – Roy Batty (Rutger Hauer) in *Blade Runner*

The present volume emerges out of an ongoing, sometimes acrimonious, debate over the viability of psychoanalytic theory to explicate horror and speculative cinema.[1] The doubtfulness of influential critics like Noël Carroll on this score is indicative of a general skepticism about the worthiness of "applied analysis" in cinema and other critical studies, which has escalated over the past decade. One notes that not a few spear-carriers for the current eruption of anti-Freudianism have been former true believers themselves (e.g., Frederick Crews, *generalissimo* of the famous *New York Review of Books* "Freud Wars," who in a previous incarnation authored a workmanlike analytical study of Hawthorne).

The analytic enterprise – notably the idiosyncratic Freudianism of Lacan – dominated film theory for several decades, variably conflated with semiotics, Marxism, feminism, deconstructionism, etc. But even as psychoanalytic practice withers under the lash of managed care, and the Founding Father is everywhere denigrated by clinicians and scholars alike, "Lacanalysis" along with less arcane analytic tactics have lost much of their luster for the Academy. In the quest for genuine relevance or mere tenure, the rubrics of applied analysis have been ditched for archival investigation, or other *a la page* endeavors.

Indeed, some former enthusiasts now claim that psychoanalysis has wielded a disproportionate, even toxic, influence upon film studies. Gross oversimplification, woeful ignorance about industry practice, and cinema aesthetics are cited among the reasons for disaffection. *Mutatis mutandis,* staunch adherents of the analytic project grumble about the superficiality of archival research. The deal of sour invective on both sides reminds one of the former rants hurled at each other by adherents of opposing schools of clinical psychoanalysis who, one imagines, would gladly have consigned dissenters to rack, thumbscrew, and flame. (The slash-and-burn tactics of HMO therapeutics has since converted these bitter adversaries to uneasy colleagues, but that is another story. . . .)

Criticism levied against the analytic investigation of horror cinema – and cinema entire – is far from baseless, echoing earlier complaints about the naïve presumptuousness and simplistic reductionism of psychoanalysts who have tread heavily in the halls of art (e.g., Princess Marie Bonaparte's fatuous botch-up of Poe). If Lacanalysis is not solely responsible for film scholars' disaffection, it surely warrants a great deal of the blame because of its often frustrating obscurantism and elitist contempt for other projects.

Critics like Norman Holland, however, have brought to literary studies a felicitous blend of strong scholarship and solid grounding in analytic methodology.[2] Today, similarly versed film scholars continue to pursue their craft with dedication, *sans* fanfare. I have elsewhere stated that analytically oriented film criticism ideally should encompass knowledge of industry business and aesthetic practice, mastery of other critical strategies, and renunciation of the illusion that definitive interpretation is achievable through psychoanalytic means alone.[3] The psychoanalytic film scholar does best illuminating "the text, the characters, and the subtext of a film as well as the way in which an audience experiences it. . . . *our aims are to be psychoanalytically valid and internally consistent*" (Gabbard & Gabbard: 187; emphasis added). This genuinely "applied" analysis enriches rather than vitiates appreciation of the horror film's often oneiric beauty. For instance, an abundant analytic literature has usefully probed horror cinema's evocation of those mysterious creeps prized by hopeless buffs who do not hesitate to disrupt hectic schedules to catch a Corman cheapie at some distant fleapit, or awaken a dismayed spouse to the dubious pleasures of an hour-of-the-wolf TV viewing of *Caltiki, the Immortal Monster* (1959).[4]

The stuff that spurs the idiosyncratic frissons of the uncanny is conventionally perceived as gothic – nocturnal graveyards, haunted castles, and so forth. However, the genre is especially adept at exploiting a latent eeriness residing in prosaic locales and objects (the huge carnivorous ants of *Them!* [1954]; the homicidal roadster of *Christine* [1983]; the demonically possessed Chucky doll of the *Child's Play* films). The dread lurking within the quotidian calls to mind Freud's well-known observation that intimations of the uncanny (derived from the German "unheimlich," translated more precisely as "unhomely") always arise from known quanta (1919: 399, 401). Without assuming the legitimacy of psychoanalytic theory *tout court*, and by deploying other complementary theoretical paradigms, this essay "analytically applies" Freud's *aperçu*: I will interrogate an intriguing reversal, whereby movie monsters are transformed into (1) figures of fun; (2) friends and/or protectors of children, their relatives, friends, etc.; (3) recipients of concern or protection by children, to whom monsters relate in a mascot-like fashion; or (4) omnipotent protectors/rescuers of humanity at large. The rehabilitated creature may reflect one, some, or all of these "heimlich maneuvres."

Jeffrey Cohen states that "the monster is a genus too large to be encapsulated in any conceptual system" (2–3). Monsters are *sui generis* polysemic, ambivalent figures: liminal, defying boundaries and categories, generating an infinite regress of contestation and interpretation – e.g., the creature as agent of social oppression (*THX 1138*'s [1971] Oscarlike robocops); the creature as Byronic rebel against tyrannical authority (*Blade Runner*'s defiant replicants). One is thus even warier of simplistic hypotheses about the highly overdetermined psychological and cultural underpinnings of the monster's heimlich transformations. My references to Freudian notions of the uncanny, the unconscious, etc. are not tendered toward the application and confirmation (even worse, self-confirmation) of some essentialist, monolithic psychoanalytic theory. Instead, *pace* Carroll et al., I hope to demonstrate the abiding suitability and adaptability of analytic instruments for dynamic textual elucidation.

EXAMPLES

The following summaries recount benchmark recuperations of the monster in mainstream film and television over the past sixty years. Readers doubtless will free-associate to others.

Classic Universal Studios Monsters

Frankenstein's Monster. Abbott and Costello Meet Frankenstein (1948) is seminal to the movie monster's rehabilitation. After the independently produced *The Noose Hangs High* (1948) did poorly at box offices, the slapstick duo returned to Universal Studios, site of their greatest hits. Searching for new material, producer Robert Arthur realized that Universal still owned rights to the Frankenstein story and set about reinventing the 1931 gothic classic in a comedic vein. Dracula and the Wolf Man were added later to the plotline, because the studio also held rights to these creatures. A convoluted screenplay devolves around the unwitting resurrection of Dracula (Bela Lugosi) and the Frankenstein monster (Glenn Strange) by a pair of nitwit shipping clerks played by Bud and Lou, despite warnings from incipient wolfman Lawrence Talbot (Lon Chaney, Jr.). Because the creature can no longer be easily manipulated by Dracula, the Count conspires to transplant Lou's more biddable brain. He uses a seductive accomplice to lure Lou to his castle. The operation is kiboshed when a transformed Talbot attacks Dracula at full moon, Frankenstein joins the fray, and all the monsters are eventually eliminated.

Abbott and Costello Meet Frankenstein cleverly articulates signature tropes of Universal's three renowned bogeymen with signature shticks of the day's most popular film funnymen. No significant bloodshed occurs. Set against the comic duo's clowning, the monsters' usual depredations register as more antic than terrifying. The film was a tremendous hit, and several profitable re-releases followed. Universal replicated the lucrative blend of comedy and horror using its other familiars in *Abbott and Costello Meet the Invisible Man* (1951), *Abbot and Costello Meet Dr. Jekyll and Mr. Hyde* (1954), and *Abbott and Costello Meet the Mummy* (1955). The series' success, while not consistent, nevertheless underscored the commercial and aesthetic viability of a monstrous *mise-en-scène* that encouraged viewers to laugh even as they shuddered. Mel Brooks's hilarious and unexpectedly poignant *Young Frankenstein* (1974) cleverly recapitulates the monster's trajectory from uncanny fearfulness to uxorious domesticity. The film sends up memorable scenes of the original, while touching upon major psychological themes related to monstrosity.

The popularity of *My Favorite Martian* (1963) prompted a migration of the major networks into stranger sitcom territory. In 1964, CBS presented *The Munsters* and a major heimlich maneuvre: an attractive monster family, living comfortably in a generic suburbia. Father Herman (Fred Gwynne), Dr. Frankenstein's last model, works at the local mortuary. His wife Lily (Yvonne De Carlo) is a four-hundred-year-old Dracula clan member. Their part-werewolf son sleeps in a casket. Other relations include Lily's Draculoid Grandpa (Al Lewis) and Uncle Gilbert (Richard Hale), arguably the resurrected Creature from the Black Lagoon. Much of the series' pleasures derive from the characters' unwavering inability – Fred especially – to view themselves as particularly different from their neighbors.

Dracula. Dracula has proven more resistant to rehabilitation than the Frankenstein monster. The vampire is spawned by the powers of evil, rather than scientific hubris, and glories in his foul deeds. Contrasted with the Frankenstein monster's few impulsive, chiefly off-camera murders during its short life, Dracula slays incessantly and remorselessly over centuries, while dominating the undead lives of chosen victims toward the propagation of his unwholesome kind. His sexual sizzle is substantial. However, the Count's availability for domesticity is compromised by peculiar nutritional requirements and excruciating photophobia: both dictate a *modus vivendi* only a partner working a blood-bank nightshift could tolerate.

Mel Brooks's *Dracula: Dead and Loving It* (1995) performs a satiric close reading of Tod Browning's 1932 classic, in which the essential storyline and Dracula's corruption remain unchanged. For the delightful humanization of the *Dracula* mythos Brooks practiced upon the Frankenstein narrative, one turns to Stan Dragoti's *Love at First Bite* (1979) and George Hamilton's marvelous impersonation of the Count as a Carpathian lounge lizard. Here Dracula is driven from his castle because of his dynastic politics rather than oral sadism. After settling into Manhattan's Hotel Plaza, he visits a disco and charms Cindy (Susan Saint James), a pixilated model, to the strains of "I Love the Night Life." His opponent for Cindy's hand is her feckless psychoanalyst (Richard Benjamin), a Van Helsing descendant who changed his name to Rosenberg "for professional reasons." Pursued by Dr. Rosenberg and the police to Kennedy Airport, the lovers change into bats. As they wing it towards Bermuda, the Count explains that henceforth Cindy must sleep during the day. "That's okay," she replies, "I never could get my shit together before seven anyhow."

The Werewolf. The Werewolf's recuperation is rather problematic, because his human half is *already* heimlich. The hapless hero/victims of the Universal original (1941), *An American Werewolf in London* (1981), and *An American Werewolf in Paris* (1997) remain thoroughly decent between monstrous metamorphoses – likewise the mildly rebellious adolescent treated by mad school doctor Whit Bissell in *I Was a Teenage Werewolf* (1957), whose "regression therapy" with wolf serum produces predictably hairy results.

Teen Wolf (1985) elegantly devises a completely heimlich Wolfman, the hero's (Michael J. Fox) lupine metamorphosis producing an improved version of his attractive, if conflicted, adolescent humanity. His self-confidence blossoms as a teenage wolf. And his enhanced athletic ability combine with his weirdly attractive hairstyling to make him the school idol.

The Godzilla Canon

Godzilla debuted in 1954 as *Gojira* (the name is a portmanteau meld of "gorilla" and "whale"). The gigantic prehistoric creature, mutated by hydrogen bomb testing in the Pacific, reduces Tokyo to rubble. A reclusive scientist whose body and mind are scarred from World War II service invents an "Oxygen Destroyer," then fears his discovery will be as dangerous to the world as Godzilla. In a somber conclusion, the scientist descends to Godzilla's ocean lair, annihilates the creature, his device, and himself.

Gojira became world renowned through its 1956 Hollywood revision, *Godzilla, King of the Monsters!* The original film possesses a stark documentary power and has acquired the status of a genre masterpiece. Its allusions to nuclear holocaust and the depravity of war are unmistakable. But, like many genre classics, it stirs more profound primal echoes. *Gojira*'s essential thrust is tragic: the brilliant Dr. Serizawa's (Akihiko Hirata) desolate alienation resonates with the monster's "outsider" identity.

When *Godzilla* was first released, atomic horror, the shame of national defeat, and occupation were unknown to many Japanese children, or else were dim memories. Youngsters were even more captivated by Godzilla than their parents; Toho Studios was quick to exploit this appeal. Over the next fifty years, the Toho team and its successors produced more than a score of highly profitable Godzilla features. Godzilla grew less frightful in form, becoming *primus inter pares* of a bizarrely engaging monster pantheon – Mothra, Rodan, Ghidra, etc. In diversity of powers, if not in sentience, the Toho creature clan intriguingly mirrored superhero and supervillain cadres that proliferated in American comic books during the 1950s and 1960s.[5]

Over the years, the Japanese have come to view Godzilla as a curious national treasure, admired by intellectuals like Yukio Mishima – a protector of the environment and symbolic defender of the nation against Western encroachment. Godzilla pictures also regularly matched up the colossal hero with children as a shambling buddy, tutor...and unlikely family guy. Godzilla became a father in *Son of Godzilla* (1967). His son, Minya, hatched with no Mrs. G. in sight, is a winsome teddy-bear/saurian hybrid who blows smoke rings when he attempts to belch fire. Godzilla repeatedly comes to his rescue, until the ultimate sacrifice of *Godzilla versus*

Destoroyah (1995). Junior is killed by a frightening recombinant of other monsters. Godzilla dispatches it, then is vaporized into a radioactive mist that eventually reanimates the dead lad into a new, full-grown Godzilla.

Jaws of the James Bond Cycle

As the Bond movies evolved, their arch villains acquired sidekicks with invincible physical prowess. Bond's terminal battle with hypertrophied yeggs and yobbos like Oddjob (Harold Sakata in *Goldfinger* [1964]) became a much anticipated set-piece. The most unheimlich of these formidable opponents – "Jaws" – is also the only one to survive combat with 007, appear in a subsequent Bond picture, and undergo a heimlich transformation.

In *The Spy Who Loved Me* (1977), Bond's nemesis is Karl Stromberg (Curt Jurgens), a wealthy marine biologist who plans to incite nuclear global war with kidnapped missiles, then construct an undersea habitat for the surviving elite. His hitman is Jaws, played by 7′4″ actor Richard Kiel. A none-too-bright giant with an unmistakable resemblance to the Frankenstein monster, Jaws sports repellant metal death, tearing out his victims' throats in a vampire-like embrace. In their final set-to, Bond uses an overhead magnet to snatch Jaws up by his gleaming dentures and drop him into a pool of killer sharks. Whether the sharks devour Jaws or vice versa is left unclear.

In the next Bond movie, *Moonraker* (1979), Jaws reappears, this time employed by Hugo Drax (Michel Lonsdale), a Stromberg clone who wants to replace humanity with a genetically engineered super-race after bombarding Earth with nerve gas. Bond and a lovely CIA scientist are caught trying to foil Drax's scheme. Drax launches the Moonraker orbiters, then commands Jaws to kill the captives. But Jaws has become smitten with Dolly (Blanche Ravalec), a diminutive blonde Drax employee. Bond mordantly suggests that Drax's brave new eugenic order is unlikely to hold a place for Jaws' questionable genetics. Jaws abruptly shifts sides, liberates Bond, Drax is destroyed, and Jaws and Dolly are last seen waving happily at 007 and his latest amour.

Terminators

In *The Terminator*'s (1984) dystopian near future, a ragged resistance army has stymied a machine race's attempts to stamp out humanity. The machines dispatch a murderous cyborg into our present. It is tasked to kill

Sarah Connors (Linda Hamilton), a young woman destined to bear a son, John, who will become the resistance's resourceful leader. John sends back Kyle (Michael Biehn), an elite trooper, to protect Sarah. Kyle dies after a night in her arms. She destroys the Terminator, then leaves Los Angeles for rugged mountain territory, where she will presumably deliver Kyle's baby and prepare him for battle in the coming armageddon.

The Terminator comprised a hallmark role for Arnold Schwarzenegger, conflating the former bodybuilder's already robotic persona with a motorcycle bar's icy homoeroticism. Encased in studded leather, his voice a guttural snarl, Schwarzenegger was a nightmarish icon of remorseless, relentless violence. Grim humor, inflected by his character's utter lack of emotion, informed Schwarzenegger's deadpan ripostes ("Ah'll pee pack."). But no true sympathy was possible for this postmodern child of the night. The Terminator's uncanniness was cleverly enhanced by burning away what little of the heimlich the creature possessed, revealing an exquisite technological incarnation of the medieval dance of death: titanium skull beneath synthetic skin.

The Terminator II's (1991) deft inversion of *The Terminator*'s sinister mission virtually facilitates the entire repertoire of heimlich recuperation. Sarah, now a pumped-up adept at survivalist terrorism, has been institutionalized. Her rebellious pre-adolescent son (Edward Furlong) has been taken from her and placed in a repressive suburban foster home. Unaware of his future, he deems Sarah mad. The machine tyrants construct a new Terminator (played by Robert Patrick) – a liquid-metal shape-shifter – this time dispatching it to kill young John. Future John counters by sending an old Schwarzenegger model T-800, stolen by the resistance and reprogrammed to protect John as tenaciously as its clone once pursued Sarah's destruction. To facilitate its mission, the T-800 has been given the ability to learn about humanity and to progress toward humanity itself.

From John and the audience's as yet uninformed perspective, Schwarzenegger's hulking figure remains grotesquely unheimlich. But his spectacular rescue of John from the shape-shifter's first attack recalls Kyle's rescue of Sarah at the disco, forcefully challenging his prior menace. The sequence is followed by other "matching" rescues, beginning with Sarah's liberation from the asylum by her son and his unlikely sidekick. An unlikely parallel is gradually forged between Kyle and his former nemesis; between the dead, unknown parent and the grim cyborg who – as Sarah muses – ironically has become the only competent father John has ever known. Schwarzenegger's physical appearance remains consonant with his newfound sensibility. Although savagely battered by the liquid T-1000, his deaths-head armature is never unmasked.

Animated Heimlich Maneuvres

From the late 1930s to the 1980s, the comic potential of Universal's gothic monsters was exploited in the lunatic cosmos of Warner Brothers' *Merrie Melodies* and *Loony Toons*, though Warner's worry over possible copyright litigation may have dictated the Universal creatures' animated depiction as generic stereotypes in brief, peripheral appearances.[6] For instance, in *Porky's Road Race* (1937), the stuttering pig competes with cars driven by Hollywood stars. Boris Karloff and his Frankenstein alter-ego are momentarily glimpsed behind the wheel of a passing auto. A Draculoid vampire appears at greater length in *Transylvania 6–5000* (1963). Fortunately, Bugs Bunny discovers a magical word that defuses the vampire's menace by turning him into a bumbling bat. Always enchanted by wretched excess, Bugs experiments with ever-weirder abracadabras, resulting in ever-more-extravagant vampiric incarnations.

In addition to their free adaptation of Universal's creatures, Fritz Freling, Chuck Jones, and their madcap colleagues drew up their own risible creatures; mad doctors particularly flourished at WarnerWorld. In *Hair Raising Hare* (1946), Bugs is lured by a robotic lady rabbit into the lab of a Peter Lorre-like scientist who wants to perform the usual brain transplant. Bugs masquerades as a drag-queen beautician and neutralizes the loony surgeon's Igor, a giant hairball, with a manicure. And in *Hyde and Hare* (1955), Bugs is transformed into a hulking monstrous version of himself by Mr. Hyde – alter-ego of a kindly doctor who has just adopted him (Loony Toon's creators frequently capitalized on the Jekyll/Hyde duality's comic potential).

Beginning in the mid-1960s, heimlich characterizations of other familiar monsters were substantially elaborated in children's television programming. Child-friendly versions of the Frankenstein creature appear in *Milton the Monster* (1965) and *Frankenstein Jr. and the Impossibles* (1966); the latter depicts the creature as a giant robot backing up a team of maladroit adolescent superheroes. During the 1980 season of *The Flintstones*, the stone-age family's jovial new neighbors were The Frankenstones – obvious animated cousins of *The Munsters*.

The Hanna-Barbera production company ceaselessly recirculated the Godzilla mythos on children's television throughout the 1970s and 1980s, commencing with *The Godzilla Power Hour* (1978), followed by *The*

Godzilla–Dynomutt Hour and *The Godzilla–Globetrotters Hour.* Paralleling heimlich revisions in the Toho films of that period, the animated Godzilla served as companion/defender to an intrepid band of globetrotting scientists; he also cherished his nephew/sidekick, Godzooky.[7]

Heimlich Maneuvres in Myth, Folklore, and Literature

The movie monster is only the latest in the long procession of ogres, demons, werewolves, vampires, and other children of the night who have haunted oral and written tales from every tribe and nation, time and place. Chronicles of monstrosity are countered by the fewer stories in which the creature is neutralized or converted to respectable behavior.

In most heimlich transformations of folklore, an unredeemed monster is rendered impotent and ridiculous through bluff, boast, deception, or magic. Adult heroes of these narratives possess scant power or prestige; alternately, the protagonist is a child or youth, usually of poor degree.

In a Baltic variant of numerous "stupid ogre" tales, the hero tells an ogre that gilding his beard will make him irresistibly beautiful. After the hero gives his name as "nobody," "anybody," or "such-a-one," he dips the creature's beard in tar and escapes, leaving his opponent glued to the tar-kettle. The enraged ogre wanders the land, stuck to his kettle, provoking derision when he asks the whereabouts of "nobody."

In other stories, the villain is Death, the Devil, or a similar demonic figure. He is as obtuse as the ogre and is likewise gulled to general merriment. A common tale of this type describes a blacksmith who sells his soul in return for becoming a master at his trade. A heavenly character (Jesus, Gabriel, etc.) gives the smith a magic tree or bench to which people will stick, or a knapsack that swallows up anyone in the vicinity. The smith persuades his demonic adversary to sit on the bench or touch the tree, then flees. Alternately the magic knapsack swallows up the demon – the smith pounds the sack on an anvil until his howling opponent promises to void their contract.

Tales in which monstrous beings permanently surrender their evil powers in favor of doing good are uncommon. The Devil is sometimes a cunning helper or ally, but his evil nature remains unchanged. A witchlike figure of Teutonic mythology travels the night punishing lazy women. In Grimm's version she becomes an ugly crone, "Frau Holle," who rewards a scapegoated stepchild with a shower of gold after the girl industriously cares for her house. The heroine's indolent sister, dispatched by an envious mother to duplicate the "good" stepsister's fortune, shirks her domestic chores. Frau Holle rewards her with a shower of pitch, which clings to her forever.[8]

A demon's unambivalent heimlich transformation occurs in various *Robert the Devil* narratives popular during the medieval period. In the basic tale, a woman appeals to Satan after petition to heaven brings no relief from her barrenness. The Devil impregnates her with a monstrous infant, Robert, who upon being born promptly slays his nurses. After numerous nefarious adult crimes, he is finally freed from his father's evil influence by conversion to Christianity, accompanied by stringent acts of repentance.

The "Wild Man," another staple character of eldritch folklore and subsequent written tales, is the ogre's worthier cousin. Enkidu of the Gilgamesh ur-myth is a prototype, a savage berserker who befriends Gilgamesh after a titanic battle. The Wild Man's appearance is frightening, feral hairiness being a stigmata of his quasi-human condition. His speech is as uncouth as his demeanor; he may be incapable of language. Although his actions can be threatening, dangerous, even lethal, he is not fundamentally evil – merely untutored in civilized deportment like Frankenstein's creature.

The Wild Man may be delineated as an unrepentant Caliban. But his terrifying exterior more often conceals a sensitive, compassionate disposition, especially in "Beauty and the Beast" narratives of Indo-European origin, as popular today as they were centuries ago (e.g., the underground beast-man of the 1976 TV series; James Bond's Jaws [see above]). The Beast's noble nature is matched by his high birth and handsome form, both constrained by enchantment. A pure maiden's love is required to break the spell and liberate the heimlich inner man.

A friendship between monster and child is rare in folklore and traditional fairytales. *Hansel and Gretel*'s Wicked Witch and *Jack and the Beanstalk*'s giant treat youngsters as fodder rather than friend. One of the few mutually beneficial child/monster affiliations, involving another Wild Man, occurs in an *Iron Hans* body of tales from German and Slavic folklore. Grimms' Iron Hans story curiously echoes the plot of *Terminator II*:

For years, huntsmen and dogs vanish from the forest near a king's castle. The king discovers they are being slaughtered by a Wild Man living at the bottom of a pond. He is captured; taken to the castle and confined in an iron cage. The king's small son liberates him and the two leave. "Iron Hans" promises to be the prince's surrogate parent and omnipotent benefactor. The grown Prince survives a series of picaresque adventures with Iron Hans' secret

help; wins the hand of a lovely princess. The wedding festivities are inter-
rupted by the arrival of a mighty monarch with his retinue. He embraces the
prince, reveals he was transformed into Iron Hans through an evil spell. Now
released from enchantment, he pledges to give the Prince "all the treasures
that I possess."[9]

Compared with their predecessors, monsters of contemporary fairytales
are more likely to be loving toward children. Their heimlich behavior
betokens the modern writer's rejection of that summary cruelty constantly
encountered in narratives from the oral tradition, arguably reflecting
actual harsh treatment meted out to children within and outside their
families centuries ago. An egregious sadism toward the vulnerable young
also pervades numerous cautionary stories by Grimm, Anderson, and
subsequent Victorian authors concerned with constructing what Maria
Tatar calls "a pedagogy of fear" (30).

Maurice Sendak's oeuvre is informed by profound psychological
shrewdness about the vicissitudes of childhood aggression and the heal-
ing power of fantasy, his *Where the Wild Things Are* (1963) definitively
repudiating the monster as a punitive figure. Little Max, sent to his room
because of his "wild" deeds, is identified with the goofy ogres of his imaginary island, whom he tames with a piercing glance and an arresting
demand to "Be Still!" He is immediately appointed chief and leads them
in an uproarious "wild rumpus." They are prostrate with grief when he
sails back to the recuperated comforts of his bedroom, reassured that
being "bad" isn't so bad after all.[10]

The gruesome families of myth and folklore are no more friendly to
child or mankind than the solo monsters of yore; *Beowulf*'s Grendel and
his merciless beldam are as devoted to each other as the cannibal clan of
The Texas Chainsaw Massacre (1974) or the murdering mutant family of *The
Hills Have Eyes* (1978). However, their involvement with humans always
remains utterly malignant. Unlike the Munsters, *Goldilocks*' bear family
has no desire to share food, home, or lifestyle with the human community.
One of the few monstrous families of earlier fiction to have friendly,
although occasionally disastrous, commerce with humanity because of
their Brobdignagian stature is the Gargantuas of Rabelais' satire.

HUMOR AND THE HEIMLICH MANEUVRE

Like their fairytale predecessors, many movie monsters possess innate humorous capability because of a generic *excessiveness*. Heimlich or unreha-
bilitated, their extravagant size, grotesqueness of shape, awesome energy,

and freedom from social constraint energize that anarchic, Rabelasian spirit of playfulness which Bakhtin theorized was central to the rituals of Carnival.

Humor Related to Unheimlich Monsters

Freud argued that humor functions as a reverse zoom from harsh reality, enabling the mind to master sundry mishaps and misfortunes by facilitating healthy objectivity (1905: 370–84). One suggests that the humor in an unheimlich monster movie, as well as humor paradoxically kindled in receptive viewers by the monster's onslaught, helps master inner psychological trauma. One further conjectures that the spectator's traumatic anxiety is related to the arousal of those once-surmounted early beliefs which, according to Freud, underpins intimations of the uncanny.[11] Thus, from a comfortable seat one mocks and gibes in an illusory triumph, a dubious victory over whatever distorted infantile/primitive/collective concept – frequently about the origins of life and death, ultimately over the grim truth of mortality itself – is being "processed" by the horror scenario. And one laughs at screened atrocities inflicted by the monster upon others, not oneself.[12]

Besides betokening the endeavor to master resurrected fears, the peculiar mirth-amidst-screaming of horror film viewers may also arise from satisfaction of the audience's childhood delight in wreaking pure havoc,[13] as well as gratification of darker unconscious desires. The horror film's boisterous, grotesque Bakhtinian thrust (e.g., the hilarious, lethal hijinks of the eponymous *Gremlins* [1984]) is raised exponentially by the "gross-out" film so favored by teenage audiences, with its bloody celebration of perverse fantasy (e.g., the oral-cannibalistic urges gaggingly evoked in George Romero's *Dead* Trilogy).[14]

A common type of wit expressed by characters of films with unheimlich creatures is ironic, essentially peripheral to the chief business of exhibiting the monster's threat and eventual elimination. The protagonists' humor allows them (and viewers by proxy) to step back from the horrors at hand, mitigating fear before the creature's attack – consider the pervasive banter of the intrepid airmen while fighting off the vampiristic carrot-man of *The Thing from Another World* (1951).

Humor Related to Heimlich Monsters

As Freud observes, "[e]ven a 'real' ghost, as in Oscar Wilde's *Canterville Ghost*, loses all power at arousing . . . any uncanny horror in us as soon as the author begins to amuse himself at its expense and allows liberties to be taken with it" (1919: 407). In the elementary heimlich maneuvre of folklore monster movies (the most prevalent heimlich trope of monster folklore generally), amusement is generated at the creature's expense by its defeat or stalemate. Degraded into an object of ridicule, the monster is rendered as powerless as it once was powerful. Its evil or destructive purposes remain unchanged: it simply can no longer accomplish them. The peasant protagonist of folk or fairytales who renders ogres impotent and laughable reads as the audience's stand-in, owning no special skill beyond pluck and quickness of wit. Much folklore, monster tales included, was improvised by just such ordinary people – laborers at rest in the field; women spinning.

Setting aside unconscious fears symbolized by the ogres of folk narratives, these creatures arguably also personified realistic destructive agencies, natural or human[15] – flood, plague, famine; the menace of capricious human oppressors, cruel rulers, or warlords who conscripted, taxed, or crushed the lowly according to their whims. How entertaining and gratifying must have been stories in which fantastic stand-ins for these real-life "giants" were brought low ... and turned fool in the bargain!

The earliest heimlich maneuvre of the horror film similarly depicts the monster's hilarious defeat without altering its sinister or destructive intent. The humble tailor, the indigent orphan hero of folklore, are reincarnated as bumbling, feckless Bud and Lou; or there is sassy Bugs Bunny, perennial gadfly of authority. The victory of these "little guy" heroes over the movie monster, beyond amusing us as it quells unconscious fears, may also indulge our fantasies that we, too, can yet defeat contemporary persecutors less lethal than a warlord, but sufficient unto the day – a new boss showering the office with pink slips; the faceless, relentless IRS.

The pleasure of "elementary" heimlich scenarios is enhanced when a familiar monstrous attack is reprised, then satirically defused. One experiences a frisson of recognition, as well as a relief of tension attendant upon the ridiculous failure of the monster's assault the second time around. For example, in a particularly eerie sequence from Browning's *Dracula*, the Count (Lugosi) transforms into a bat, then morphs back to his elegant vampire persona after flapping through his lovely victim's bedroom window. In the send-up scene from *Dracula: Dead and Loving It*, Dracula (Leslie Nielsen) mutates into a wacky chimera, with the Count's head pasted onto a bat's body. Just as the Count is about to sail into the heroine's bedroom, French windows are slammed shut: one hears a ludicrous "*plonk!*" and sees Nielsen's tiny face, scrunched excruciatingly against the windowpane, sliding slowly to the ground.

The heimlich transformation of the movie monster's evil or destructive nature goes beyond merely neutralizing the creature: it spurs strong viewer sympathy and produces a radical shift in humorous response. Now one no longer laughs derisively, or takes sadistic satisfaction, at the monster's expense. The monster has become endearing, rather than traumatizing, and provokes affectionate empathy rather than dreadful repulsion.

When the congenial monster is animal-like, one is diverted by "cute" anthropomorphisms, much as one is entertained by pets who we believe are aping human behavior – e.g., the exuberant victory dance of Godzilla's son at his father's triumph over "bad" monster adversaries. When the heimlich monster is humanoid, one smiles at its clumsy attempts to learn human ways. And so in *Terminator II*, the hulking Schwarzenegger is drolly shown how to do a proper "high-five" by his preadolescent charge. One is pleasured by the category collisions implicit in the heimlich monster's disingenuousness during interaction with alarmed "normals" – in the glaring contradictions between the creature's human sensibility, relatedness, or observance of human custom, as opposed to its inhuman appearance, physical attributes, or monstrous mores. And so, for instance, Herman and Lilly Munster become entangled in a convoluted O. Henryish scheme to secretly earn money for each other's 100th anniversary present.

THE HEIMLICH MONSTER AS RECUPERATED CHILD, ADOLESCENT, PARENT . . . AND DIVINITY

Psychoanalytic critics have elucidated the movie monster's unheimlich representations of childhood, adolescence, and parenthood (any or all identities may be dissected out of the same entity). Child or adolescent traits embodied hyperbolically by the creature include clumsiness, messiness, low frustration tolerance, impulsivity, disregard or disdain for rules, joy in mischief and disorder, and that curious "unknownness," so unsettling to adults, about what the young are really up to.[16]

During the horror genre's early decades, filmmakers shied away from portraying actual children or adolescents as monsters, fearing that audiences might be repelled by the repudiation of youthful innocence. The popularity of *The Bad Seed* (1956), which featured a psychopathic killer child audiences loved to loathe, encouraged the portrayal of monstrous youngsters in mainstream cinema, including *Village of the Damned* (1960),

It's Alive! (1969), *The Exorcist* (1973), *Carrie* (1976), and *Firestarter* (1984). The trend remains highly bankable – consider, e.g., the aforementioned Chucky of the *Child's Play* movies, and the carnivorous cyborg waifs of *Screamers* (1997).[17]

The monster's heimlich transformation restores the attractive side of its child or pubescent persona while maintaining a now unthreatening excessiveness. The original unheimlich Godzilla spurred that fascination with dinosaurs which, in my clinical experience, is more prevalent among little boys and is partly based on the projection of a youngster's aggression upon the giant lizards. Girls and boys alike were subsequently enchanted by kinder, gentler Godzillas, as well as by Toho's loopy monster peer group. The creatures offered children multiple points of identification because of their many kid- and pet-like qualities. As noted, mascot/pal attributes were later developed at length in the Hanna-Barbera animated television series.

Besides eliminating the catastrophic potential of the creature's youthful wretched excess, heimlich transformation also heals the traumata wrought by abusive adults or peers upon the vulnerable monster-as-child/-adolescent. I have elsewhere addressed the Universal *Frankenstein* as an essay on warped pedagogy.[18] Under this rubric, the creature is a battered child who identifies with his oppressors, returning in kind the uncharitable treatment first meted out by his laboratory "parents" – especially Henry's stand-in, Igor – and then by society at large.

The monster can also be construed as a typical early adolescent, both alarmed and exhilarated by his burgeoning biology, who confronts the resurrected Oedipal strivings of childhood in a strapping new physique (one notes that Karloff looks like a teenager bursting out of his clothes). A model for future beasts in the boudoir, the creature snatches Henry's fiancée from her bedroom the night before her marriage. What he would do with her is obscure, reflecting the pubescent male's anxiety about the mechanics of sexuality as well as the Oedipal taboo. The monster's execution by the townspeople interprets as retribution for his illicit Oedipality.[19]

In *Young Frankenstein*, Henry's descendent Frederick (Gene Wilder) explicitly addresses his creation (Peter Boyle) as an abused, misunderstood "good boy." The doctor heals his surrogate son's psychic wounds with unstinting compassion, then boosts his IQ – and socialization – with a literal implant of his human identity. In return, he receives an infusion of the monster's exuberant virility – thereby actualizing a common "exchange" fantasy many parents have involving their adolescent children. Victor cheerfully disavows his corner of the Oedipal triangle by giving his fiancée (Madeline Kahn) to the civilized monster, then bedding his sexy lab assistant (Teri Garr). Everyone is happy with *jouissance* aplenty to go around.

Tatar observes that fairytale monsters often bear the imprint of traumatizing parental authority. While "children need monsters . . . to conserve idealized images of their parents, . . . it is coercive sadism on the one hand and forbidding hostility on the other that produce many of the monsters that haunt children's imaginations. And in each case it is parental behavior that creates the "monster crowd" (31). William Paul discerns an analogous encryption of hurtful parental authority in the movie monster (233). The literal depiction of monstrous parenthood has escalated since *Psycho* (1960), e.g., in *The Texas Chainsaw Massacre, The Brood* (1979), *The Shining* (1980), *The Hills Have Eyes, Aliens* (1986), *Dead Alive* (1992), and *The People Under the Stairs* (1991).

The monster's heimlich conversion from "forbidding hostility" to a benevolent parental role constitutes a winning thrust – especially for young viewers – in the evolution of the Godzilla canon beyond the creature's original insensate savagery. In *Godzilla's Revenge* (1972), Godzilla nurtures a human child by proxy. The film's vulnerable young hero is Ichiro (Tomonori Yazaki), a lonely latch-key kid living in a bleak Tokyo suburb. Harassed by local bullies, Ichiro creates a fantasy of "Monster Island," where Godzilla teaches his son how to combat assorted monster tormentors. By drawing upon Godzilla's tutelage, Ichiro acquires new self-respect and vanquishes his own playground persecutors.[20]

Another rehabilitated monstrous parent rescues a surrogate child from mortal danger at the end of *Terminator II*. By now nearly human in sensibility, Schwarzenegger's T-800 saves John (and mother Sarah) Connor from the shape-shifting T-1000 by hurling it into a furnace of super-molten metal. The T-800 then realizes his brain contains the advanced microchip which – according to one of those tortuous loops of time travel – will be used by contemporary scientists to inadvertently create prototypes of the future machine tyrants. And so he proceeds to lower himself into the fiery pool, his hand raised in poignant farewell to the grieving John and Sarah, melting away like Grimm's Loyal Tin Soldier.

The T-800's rescue of humanity entire touches upon an immense, ambivalent power latent within the monster film, infinitely exceeding the narrow confines of a Freudian parental paradigm. The creature customarily wields it in his guise of Pope's Great Anarch, toward uncreation and universal darkness. It is occasionally manifested by the heimlich creature through acts of deliverance and redemption, which transcend familiar generic tropes, intimating an ineffable grace. The most moving of these strange theophanies occurs at the end of *Blade Runner* (1982), when replicant Roy Batty suddenly hauls fallible Rick Deckard (Harrison Ford) from the abyss, then receives his own death with Christ-like serenity:

DECKARD: I don't know why he saved my life. Maybe in those last moments he loved life more than he ever had before. Not just his life. Anybody's life. My life. All it[21] wanted was the same answers the rest of us want – Where do I come from? Where am I going? How long have I got? . . . All I could do was sit there and watch him die.

One recalls S. S. Prawer's superb characterization of the horror movie as "spilt religion" (125).

IN SUM

The unconscious is never visible through the ego's eye; it is recoverable only through its enigmatic conscious residues. From obscure traces – particularly from dreams – one gleans that the unconscious thrives on radical reversals and oppositions. Its polarized binaries coexist unproblematically according to the peculiar logic of the primary process.

Freud's 1919 essay, "The 'Uncanny'," famously focuses on an eerie interpenetration, an intimate opposition between heimlich and unheimlich. Beyond the "logical," psychological, sociohistorical grounds one adduces for monstrous rehabilitation looms the mysterious – indeed, uncanny – mutual attraction inherent in the heimlich/unheimlich binary, drawing each category to its obverse, to become the other's Other, infinitely generative of heimlich and unheimlich maneuvres. In horror cinema or folklore, the heimlich's very existence invokes the desire for its transformation into richer, stranger, numinous, yet often terrible stuff. *Mutatis mutandis*, the unheimlich instantiates ineffable melancholy and hope.

Once upon a time there was a home – an Eden, a womb – from which one was compelled to journey toward terra incognita (arguably, in psychoanalytic terms, toward necessary but vulnerable individuation). Once there was a way back home, back to the common joys and comforts of a blessed ordinary. Reminiscent of those other anguished eternal voyagers, The Flying Dutchman and The Wandering Jew, movie monsters are compelled to wander ceaselessly between each contested site, to our enduring fascination and delight.[22]

NOTES

1. For simplicity, horror, science-fiction, and speculative cinema will hereafter be distinguished under the single category of "horror."
2. See Holland (1992; 2000).
3. Greenberg and Gabbard.
4. See, e.g., Arnzen.
5. Attempts at resurrecting Godzilla in his original *unheimlich* corpus (*Godzilla 1985* [1984]; *Godzilla* [1998]) have proven curiously unsatisfactory, never achieved the enduring popularity of child-oriented Godzilla movies, and are considered outside the canon by many fans.
6. Richard Leskosky, private communication.
7. For a reprise of monster series in children's television programming, see Woolery.
8. "Mother Holle," *The Complete Fairy Tales of the Brothers Grimm* (96–99).
9. "Iron Hans," *ibid.* (482–88).
10. Spitz eloquently elucidates the therapeutic value of modern "heimlich" children's stories, arguing that they affirm children's right to exercise their native playfulness, exuberance, and self-assertiveness, so regularly and gruesomely chastised in the seventeenth- and eighteenth-centuries' "pedagogy of fear." Tales like Sendak's privilege the child's need for mischief and disobedience as parameters to test and expand its world – to revise social and family boundaries without fear of sadistic retaliation by adults.
11. Schneider (2000) anatomizes the horror creature's concretization of "earlier surmounted beliefs" into *reincarnated monsters* (the dead return to life), *psychic monsters* (omnipotence of thought), and *dyadic monsters* (existence of a double). He then subdivides these categories further.
12. Adolescents are perpetual fans of horror movies and are especially prone to hilarity while watching them – taking ever-greater delight in ever-more egregious, repellant displays of gore. Their shrieks and howls in the theater have even been incorporated into self-reflexive pictures such as those of the *Scream* (1996) cycle. Study of adolescent psychological development shows that, during puberty, youngsters are first truly able to grasp death as a certain, personal reality. This recognition paradoxically provokes a wide range of counterphobic, even death-defying behavior. Testing one's ability to survive a stalker movie while hooting at its fictive nemesis is clearly less perilous than a helmetless race on a broken-down Harley.
13. Susan Sontag (209–25) elegantly discourses on the yen for pure havoc gratified by the monster film, notably Japanese monster cinema.
14. See Paul (409–30) for more on the comic dimensions of "gross-out" cinema.
15. Folklore scholars observe that the cruelty and violence endemic to folklore/fairytales probably reflected brute circumstances of earlier times: war, famine, child abuse, and abandonment. Tatar, for instance, views Beauty and the Beast narratives as fantastic elaborations on the vicissitudes of arranged marriages (141). It can be imagined that many "actual" arrangements did not have nearly as felicitous an outcome as Beauty's triumph.
16. See Paul (273).

17. Paul addresses the psychosocial grounding of the post–World War II "evil child" phenomenon (260–86).
18. See Greenberg (1970b).
19. For further discussion of the monster as love-struck adolescent, see Greenberg (1970a).
20. Many scholars have emphasized the importance of illuminating the specific cultural stresses and historical contingencies surrounding the movie monster's creation (see, e.g., Andrew Tudor's essay in this volume). Heimlich, no less than unheimlich, monsters are inflected by the vicissitudes of their particular time and place. *Godzilla's Revenge,* for instance, was produced when the Japanese were concerned with the threat posed by nascent industrialization to the nuclear family. Ichiro's plight as a latchkey child of working parents mirrored the depressing isolation of many real-life youngsters, Godzilla's proxy parenting thus offering a magical solution to a major social problem. As well, *Terminator II*'s heimlich cyberparent – with his potentially dangerous cerebral computer chip – redresses young John Connor's lack of a reliable father at a time when America was encountering both a rise in single-parent households and burgeoning computer technologies.
21. During his meditation on Batty's death, Deckard calls the replicant leader both "he" and "it." This locution reflects Deckard's persistent, albeit radically diminished, ambivalence about the replicant's humanity. One further construes the "he/it" opposition as a figuration of the unconscious heimlich/unheimlich binary elucidated in this essay's conclusion.
22. Sincere thanks to Ellen Handler Spitz, Alan Dundes, Richard Leskosky, Christopher Sharrett, Steven Jay Schneider, Linda Deigh, Moira Smith, and Fujami Ogi for their kind assistance in developing this essay.

"It was a dark and stormy night . . .": Horror Films and the Problem of Irony

I

John Carpenter's f/x heavy remake of *The Thing* (1982) contains a brief interaction between man and monster that graphically foregrounds the chief problematic of the horror film. Under attack from a shape-shifting parasite that readily jumps from species to species and host to host, the members of an Arctic research team attempt to hold their own. In a rare moment of human advantage, the beleaguered company manages to temporarily isolate the chameleon invader. Sequestered in the host head of a decapitated human, the parasite seeks escape by morphing into a hermit-crab-and-skull combination that scuttles to freedom on scaly legs. As the beast of fusion skitters away, a gape-jawed, goggle-eyed technician exclaims, "You gotta be fucking kidding!"

Composed in equal measure of ontological and epistemological bewilderment, this profane cry exactly delimits the boundaries of the genre. Bound between what can and cannot be, the astonished prole must decide between exclusive options. Is the crab head that once crowned a colleague's body a macabre joke, eyes playing tricks, or is the foul crustacean an oracle? Cast between the antipodes of raillery and revelation, the lab tech and his double, the protagonist and the audience must decide if seeing is truly believing. Over and again, *The Thing* and others of its ilk call for a response. Horror is then an interrogative genre that demands of its subjects, on screen and off, a reply. Is this some kind of joke? In formulating an answer, in defining those subject to horror as victims, either of practical jokes or something more serious, the audience enters into a dialogue.[1]

There are, of course, a multitude of alternate readings of horror that do not consider the genre a mercurial construction oscillating between the

jest and its sober antithesis. When surveying the range of alternative interpretations for horrible entertainment, however, it is worth underscoring
just how often a *question* is central to explaining the genre's operations.
Tzevetan Todorov, for example, offers a tripartite definition that hinges
on the type of answer readers give to the question of the text. In his
schema, eerie fictions are best defined by what answer we submit to explain strange goings-on. Can the odd events of the fiction be explained
by appeal to coincidence or other natural explanation? Or, conversely,
can we assert the undeniable presence of the supernatural when sizing
up a cryptic story? Finally, some strange fictions refuse a straightforward
answer and the reader must allow for an ambivalent response. There is
no compelling reason to opt for either the hand of the supernatural or
the operation of chance. In this sort of weird tale, as Freud notes in his
remarks on the uncanny, the author "cunningly and ingeniously avoid[s]
any definite information on the point to the last" (1990: 251). Rendered
dumb, the narrative's power is contingent upon our inability to fashion a
certain reply. Nevertheless, across all three variations, the marvels of the
text are only limned when a questioning call is met by a response.

   Noël Carroll too defines art-horror – his preferred term to demarcate
fictions from real terrors – as contingent upon the question. In contrast
to Todorov, Carroll cedes the audience pride of place in beginning the dialogue. The audience clearly initiates the exchange because horror tales
are manufactured in response to the need that some audiences have for
their "curiosity [to be] stimulated and rewarded" (1990: 193). In this
view, horror gratifies the questionable appetites of those who dream of
what lies beyond. Unrestrained by the dictates of stultifying reason, dark
tales offer free range to audiences with active imaginations and inquisitive natures. Here then, as with Todorov's structuralist account, horror
comes into being after a question has been posed. The only difference, in
regard to the central role of the query, is that the problem is forwarded,
for Todorov, by the text. For Carroll, art-horror is summoned when the
audience calls into doubt the limits of what can be known. In either case,
horror cannot be until the audience has spoken.

   Cynthia Freeland, in conjunction with Carroll and Todorov, also considers the genre an arena open to question. Freeland, however, argues
for a very specific type of question. In her analysis, the genre is a space
constructed for reflection on the nature and meaning of evil. In combination with scaring us, "the genre also stimulate[s] *thoughts* about evil in
its many varieties and degrees: internal or external, limited or profound,
physical or mental, natural or supernatural, conquerable or triumphant"

(1999a: 3). A grotesque theodicy, with evil graphically embodied in the flesh of the monster, the genre provides a ready outlet for contemplating the terrible scourge of sin and other heinous wrongs.

From the most abstract of considerations – "what can be known" – to the concrete study of base behavior – "what can evil do" – the genre summons responses for pressing queries. And while all narratives pose questions, if only to ask what happens next, the horror genre seems, from a variety of theoretical perspectives, to be particularly inquisitorial. In this space, with the audience functioning as prosecutor and judge, charged with interpreting evidence and apportioning blame, the genre is a trial. Horror demands that the audience come to terms with the truth and assay what stirs beneath the surface. As a trial, horror is also an endurance event. The audience is called to withstand a fearsome assault of threats, shocks, and terrible visions before rendering a verdict. Without these threats, without the shock to the senses, without the noxious irruption of the monstrous, the questions put to the audience would be of no particular moment. Under violent pressure, however, even the most abstruse queries become of considerable import.

If the question and horror are common companions, and the probing cry is to be expected whenever the horrible is encountered, then we must ask, following Todorov, Freeland, et al., why text and readers alike are so very inquisitive.[2] In *The Thing*, as in most initial meetings between the monster and the audience, the opening question initially takes the verbal form of a double take. Is the protagonist really seeing what she or he thinks she is seeing? Has the head of my co-worker atop a scrambling tangle of king-crab legs really just broken across the laboratory floor? Consider the visual feints found early in most horror films wherein brief glimpses of what may be a monster are specifically edited into the tale for the benefit of a suspect audience. These brief hints allow spectators to ask the same question forwarded by astonished actors: "Is this real or is this some kind of joke?"[3]

As the tale pitches between these poles, the law of the excluded middle regulates horror cinema.[4] Either there is nothing to worry about or the dead walk. What the audience needs is confirmation. Has something wicked this way come or are we, viewers and players alike, being had? This is a question of irony. Can the world of the film be believed, or are the goings on-screen not to be trusted? Put simply, the audience must decide whether to trust their eyes or assume the filmmaker is a confidence artist. For example, like most contemporary woman-in-peril films, *Scary Movie* (2000) opens with a lissome twenty-something harassed by an unidentified male caller. As soon, a millisecond or two, as the audience recognizes Carmen Electra, *Baywatch* ingénue, vamping through a reprise of Drew Barrymore's cameo in *Scream* (1996), the film surrenders the ability to evoke any affective resemblance to the horror film. The Wayan brothers do not mean what they say and, insofar as horror is concerned, the film cannot be trusted.

The question of right intentions and irony in the horror film is often-times not resolved early on in the narrative. The tension between faith and distrust may be maintained until quite late in the film when, finally, the reality of the supernatural becomes a given. In these straits, forced to endure radical doubt for much of the narrative, the audience reasonably adopts a paranoid relation to the world on screen. When it is simply im-possible to discern, long into the narrative, whether or not things are what they seem, as in *Rosemary's Baby* (1968) and *The Birds* (1963), everything on screen, all interiors, exteriors, characters, and their interactions, are imbued with dread import.[5] In this world there is too much meaning, and confirmation of the supernatural comes as a relief.[6]

Whereas confirmation can relieve the audience of a significant burden, there is no guarantee of similar relief for characters whose worst fears have been, at last, confirmed. Often confirmation, succor for the audience, turns out to be an actant's death knell. In addition, as in many horror films from the 1950s, confirmation comes only to transcendent spectators allied with one or two hardy protagonists. The rest of the cast doubts either the ethos or the sanity of those who scream wolf. In this elastic confirmation scenario, the horror film becomes a dual struggle to defeat obdurate skeptics and the monster. Typically, in films like *Invasion of the Body Snatchers* (1956), erstwhile compatriots prove more unyielding than the most intransigent monster. In films with an extended confirmation plot, the problem of irony does not disappear once the audience can trust their senses. Instead, the question of irony is transformed into the sad irony of fate as the film resolves audience apprehensions at the expense of doubly persecuted protagonists. At odds with friends and foes, delayed confirmation plots offer impotent protagonists the cold comfort of being right in a sea of doubt.

When the horror film is not meant to be taken seriously, or in the case of inept filmmaking *cannot* be taken seriously, irony becomes a parodic attack. This attack can take at least two different forms. When the au-dience takes the lead in assuming an ironic attitude, poorly made films are celebrated for their absolute indifference to technique and genre convention. Alongside the work of other uniquely gifted directors, the enduring cult cinema of Ed Wood, Hershell Gordon Lewis, and Andy Milligan represents the unalloyed triumph of the learned audience over primitive or truant technique. As the work of these directors departs further and further from the minimum threshold of credulity, the decadent audience, whose pleasures are informed by a remarkably refined "supra-formal appetite" (Booth: 176), inverts the ironic question delivered in competent horrorshows. Instead of certifying their trust in the filmmaker – "you've convinced me" – the ironic audience now celebrates every moment where a director, crew, and cast went wrong. Reworking the unspoken dialogue between filmmaker and spectator the knowing audience is free to ask, "What were you thinking?" Superior in the knowledge that the filmmaker cannot offer a worthy reply, the audience has license to revel.

The good horror film, the film that follows the rules, assures spectators, through exact obedience to convention, that it deserves to be taken seriously. Impossible visions can only be taken as "true" when filmmakers frame them within otherwise solidly constructed and decorous narratives. There is a strong positive correlation between the degree of obedience to convention exhibited by the well-executed horror picture and the apparent verisimilitude of the impossible narrative. A bad genre picture, a film lensed in apparent ignorance of form and convention, disabuses spectators and invites nomination as a terrific failure – the film is so bad you cannot believe it. At this point, when a film reaches low enough, sinking well beyond the limits of imagination, the audience is at liberty to make movie-going an act of alchemy. The bad is magically transformed into the good.

Generally, parody is considered an ironic exaggeration of style or manner intended to send up an unworthy original. In the case of bad horror films, hyperbolic style is not a consideration. Even a lackluster, run-of-the-mill horror film evidences an admirable stylistic flair that is forever beyond the capacity of an inept effort. Parody cannot exist apart from style and the bad genre film is a style lacuna. Instead, when a film is void of conventional style, an exile from vogue, the audience is free to parody a receptive public. A warm reception establishes the audience's bad faith, not their good intentions. Applause and appreciation for the virtues of a junk horror film are acts of perverse will and insider's delight.

The audience is not the only group free to parody the genre. Starting in the silent film era, the horror film has been readily and regularly corrupted in horror-comedy. Here, unlike the films celebrated by the ironic audience, which have worth because the audience deigns to adore them, the horror-comedy is intended to evoke laughs.[7] This time the filmmaker is in on the joke. What is interesting about horror comedy is that the same characters, the entire Universal studio ensemble, the slasher, and the zombie can easily move back and forth between straight films and burlesque. As George Romero was concluding his sober zombie trilogy with *Day of the Dead* (1985), his original production partner on *Night of the Living Dead* (1968) was making a competing sequel from the same source material. Romero's film was a relatively straight-ahead gorefest, whereas John Russo's *Return of the Living Dead* (1985) emphasized the broad humor in undead cannibalism. Contemporaneously, tan meister George Hamilton played the urbane Count for laughs in *Love at First Bite* (1979), while the equally photogenic Frank Langella played the role straight in *Dracula* (1979). Both were big hits. Similarly, Abbott and Costello met Frankenstein, the Wolfman, the Invisible Man, and the Bride of Frankenstein without making it impossible for these icons to find work in roles demanding monsters with gravitas. Unlike most other forms of parody that work to denigrate their source material, horror parody seems to provoke laughter without acidulous, fatal ridicule.

These assorted variants might best be conceptualized as parallel universes or wonderlands running alongside but never overlapping the world belonging to the horror genre proper. In these other regimes, the laws common to convention are suspended, rewritten, or otherwise altered. In the wonderlands, Dr. Frankenstein and his monster may prove to be a talented song-and-dance team celebrated for their rendition of "Puttin' on the Ritz" (*Young Frankenstein* [1974]). Here, the phallic knives of the slasher may be stripped of symbolic sheaths as mad killers penetrate the ears of their prey with real penises sprung from deadly glory holes (*Scary Movie*). And in these magic alternate hinterlands, dread ghosts may even become capable guardian angels who can navigate the New York subway system saving loved ones ensnared in perilous jams (*Ghost* [1990]). Regardless of how far such variant universes depart from the domain of right horror, there is never any danger that we will forget the rules appropriate to the principal strain of the genre. Bizarre funhouse distortions of prime horror may be produced only by manipulating the rules of right fright; consequently, the central standing of canonical horror is regularly underscored with each and every laughable departure from convention.

There is also a fourth course between these alternatives. The postmodern horror film, as in the *Scream* and *I Know What You Did Last Summer* series, drifts back and forth between scares and laughs without warning. Sick humor and sickening violence, coupled with narrative and affective incoherence, define the horror film's final incarnation. These films are both serious – they can be very threatening – and they jest. Oftentimes trading on "insider knowledge," a fan's familiarity with the rules of the game, these efforts underline their status as neither genre creations nor genre malcontents.[8] Obeying some conventions and shattering others, the most successful of these bipolar amalgamations manage to be both funny and scary simultaneously.

The multiple options for the horror film foregrounds the genre's striking ability to endure and outlast even the fiercest mockery. It may be that a genre, ironic at heart, is resistant to its own venom. In addition, as the genre works by inviting the spectator to play along, and as a good genre film must explicitly promise to play by the rules, these productions may be so openly self-conscious about their status as productions that they cannot be sent up. For this genre, all parody is homage and imitation (even skewed imitation) flatters the self-conscious production.

II

The pleasure we have so far ascribed to the horror film and its deviant cousins – the badly drawn effort, horror-comedy, and the postmodern chiller – has been explained through an analysis of technique. It may also be possible to ground the indomitable irony of the horror film in a source other than conscious delight in wicked play. As Freud notes in *Jokes and their Relation to the Unconscious* (1905),

> we are aware that we may be deceived into confusing our enjoyment of the intellectual content of what is stated with the pleasure proper to jokes; but we know that that pleasure itself has at bottom two sources – the technique and the purposes of jokes. (117)

No matter how well technique accounts for what makes a successful horror film, Freud's important consideration has not been addressed. Explaining worthy technique is not the same thing as explaining the purpose or ends to which technique is marshaled. For Freud, a creditable exegesis must distinguish between means and ends. Confusing *how* something is done with the reasons *why* something is done is to mistakenly conflate method and motive.

If the good horror film works by convincing the audience to believe their lying eyes, then the crucial operation for horror entails getting an audience to entertain that which they know is not true. Freud addressed this process in his 1919 essay, "The 'Uncanny'." First, the writer, like the filmmaker, "deceives us by promising to give us the sober truth, and then after all overstepping it" (250).[9] In this fashion, by couching the uncanny within an otherwise realistic setting, we are more likely to assent to the possible existence of that which cannot be.

The Sixth Sense (1999) is a fine example of a film tailor-made to Freud's specifications. Although it opens with the supernatural complaint of a boy who claims kinship with the dead, his dreadful encounters are treated, for almost the entire film, as the symptoms of a tortured hebephrenic. Until very late in the movie the supernatural is treated as nothing more than the *idée fixe* of a broken psyche. Once the secret is revealed, and the audience reviews the entire story in light of the uncanny truth, the narrative is so scrupulously plotted that all actions are consistent, for nearly the entire length of the film, with both a psychological and a supernatural explanation. The film never missteps, never prematurely betrays its supernatural core, and as such is genuinely disarming when the truth is unveiled.

Such films, which slyly make this world strange, allow us to entertain that which we have long since left behind. Under the influence of a tale that appears to esteem verisimilitude, surmounted beliefs are made tenable and ridiculous superstitions become plausible. A successful encounter with the uncanny undermines years of reality testing and allows us to reconsider the possibility that we actually could enjoy magic powers longed for in childhood. On the other hand, a film or story couched far in the past (e.g., Hamlet's ghost-plagued Denmark) or stories from other realms (e.g., *The Wizard of Oz*) are so transparently not of this world that they can have no uncanny effect even when "peopled" with hydrophobic witches, aeronautic monkeys, and spectral papas (Freud 1990: 250).

Along with the retreat into childish superstition there is another vector for Freud's uncanny. The uncanny can also facilitate a re-emergence of repressed complexes (248). Going well beyond a reconsideration of magic powers and necromancy, a return to benign animism, the uncanny at this deeper level serves to release normally repressed "infantile complexes." Fear comes, at this juncture, from the inimical depths of the psyche and not from a fleeting return to childish fancies.

As opposed to merely allowing the thrilled viewer to trifle a moment or two with omnipotent thoughts, this considerably more serious engagement with the uncanny threatens to undo the constitutive ego supports of the subject. The horror tale endangers the sovereignty of the symbolic order via a return of the repressed. The spectacle of horror – the singing blade that cleaves the flesh, the carnivorous monster that devours the body with relish – re-awakens deeply seated and long-buried fantasies of castration, abjection, and the like.[10] In so doing, in compromising the ego's hard-won autonomy, the uncanny casts us back to some traumatic point in infancy or childhood that we had, mercifully, long since forgotten. If we trace some neuroses to an unsuccessful mastery of these sorts of primal chimeras, as does Freud, then the horror film is a symptomatic expression of an unresolved psychic conflict.

Repressed and surmounted beliefs are not, by their very nature, readily or commonly encountered. This is particularly true for the experience of the uncanny in everyday life. Striking coincidences and conscious wishes that come true are among the few quotidian experiences likely to lead to an uncanny shiver. The uncanny is more frequently encountered in the realm of fiction, where the attenuation of disbelief, vital to the uncanny effect of fascinating imagery, is more easily achieved (249). Under the shadow of story, where nothing is real, censorship is relaxed and it becomes possible to entertain the impossible. However, if authors and directors are not careful, if they ask too much of the audience, moving too far from the quotidian, all affect is lost – hence, the failure of horror-comedy or bad horror films to provoke or invoke chills. Through the good offices of sober authors taking special care not to betray the allure of siren fiction, the good horror film and the uncanny tale successfully marshal, cultivate, and maintain chary disbelief.

The problem with this proviso is that horror films are generally not as circumspect about maintaining the reality effect as Freud would like. In spite of his cautionary advice, few works can keep from going too far. Furthermore, despite failing to follow Freud's direction, these impure efforts *do* seem to give audiences the creeps. Near any epoch in the history of the horror film, from the silent era to the present, has signal films that, however diligent in their pursuit of fear, take time to play.[11] From moments of cinematic caprice in F. W. Murnau's *Nosferatu* (1921), offering respite from the horrible suffering inflicted by Orlok (Max Schreck), to the ghoulish double-entendres of Pinhead in the *Hellraiser* series and the convoluted postmodern machinations of *Scream*, the genre has always offered some space where fear and arch whimsy coexist. Horror films have long since found a way of making irony work: it is the *uncanny* that stands in need of alteration. The uncanny needs to make room for the ironic play ingrained in horror cinema.

Freud would not perform this labor himself. In both his essay on the uncanny and his monograph on the joke, Freud disavows irony. In "The 'Uncanny'," he states, referring to an Oscar Wilde ghost story, that the tale "loses all power... as soon as the author begins to amuse himself by being ironical about it and allows liberties to be taken with it" (252). In *Jokes and Their Relation to the Unconscious*, Freud writes: "representation by the opposite... can be understood without any need for bringing in the unconscious" (1905: 174). For Freud, the successful performance of an ironic gesture or statement requires conscious, advance preparation. The ironic source must make sure that the audience grasps his or her real intent. Saying one thing and meaning another is a deliberate act of conscious consideration. The unconscious does not work to these specifications.

While Freud was not willing to theorize a working relationship between the unconscious and irony, there may in fact be grounds for allowing the unconscious to employ irony. As Frank Stringfellow argues, Freud was too precipitous in dismissing irony as merely a conscious, rhetorical flourish. Certainly, irony does function as a conscious defense mechanism. The canny rhetor is shielded from censure because the author always says the opposite of whatever substance the audience makes of his or her remarks. This is the refuge of plausible deniability (Stringfellow: 24). With latent and manifest content at odds, ironic statements are always unclear; it is this ambiguity that saves the ironist from condemnation. But ambiguous utterances fashioned to elude censure are also an ideal avenue for the unconscious to have its say. Seen from this perspective, irony serves for an even *craftier* act of subterfuge. As a confused admixture, anaclitic irony allows *other* unspoken meanings to percolate to the surface.

An ironically reformed account of the uncanny would not immediately dismiss horrible tales that are flagrantly preposterous. The impossible, not-to-be-believed crab–head that dances across the floor is deserving of a second look because irony is an ideal vehicle for escaping censorship. Irony allows repressed traumas free play while permitting audiences and filmmakers to maintain the fiction that the genre is really nothing more than a cinematic funhouse. The perceptible wink, the knowledge that no harm is really meant, catches consciousness off-guard and serves the ends of irrepressible complexes. In this way, irony may be reconceived as a vital part of the arsenal that gives authors and directors their "*peculiarly directive power*" (Freud 1990: 251).

As a form of psychic double-cross, ironic tales proclaim their duplicity to mask their true intent. In betraying itself from the start, the ironic production dons negation as deep cover. Because negation is "irrelevant to the unconscious," the absolute meaning of an utterance is independent of either a positive or negative valence (Stringfellow: 6). Contrary to Freud's preference for upright eerie fictions, a scrupulously earnest discourse may not always be required of the circumspect uncanny.

An impure uncanny would go a long way toward making sense of the horror genre's long history of incongruous play. It would include films with no room for humor, the grave tragedies of David Cronenberg, and the disingenuous, but still potent, eviscerations of *Andy Warhol's Frankenstein* (1974). Unlike other realms, where irony and parody can have devastating consequences, ironic horror does no irreparable harm to less-compromised creations. The genre has happily coexisted with comedies and parodies that do not seem to have any negative impact on an audience's ability to enjoy more restrained efforts. It would thus be appropriate for the uncanny to welcome irony's assistance.

Spotting irony always involves a moment of hesitation (Stringfellow: 17). As the ironic utterance unfolds, there is a moment of doubt when we ask, "Can this be serious?" Depending on the answer, the utterance will be taken either as ironic or in earnest. If a horror film elicits this question, spectators decide whether or not a horror film is to be taken straight or in jest. Returning to this question in light of a revised uncanny, however, the distinction between jest and sobriety is moot. The uncanny can be experienced under cover of irony *and* in Freud's preferred straight mode. Consider Hannibal Lecter's delicious remarks on savoring an internal organ with fava beans and a good bottle of red. Only a reformed treatment of the uncanny would rightly deem this horrible witticism a legitimate extension of Freud's original formulation. Clearly, there will be some efforts that cannot evoke the uncanny, e.g., some horror-comedies absent anything but calculated humor, but doubt and humor can also be allied on behalf of an unconscious unwilling to forgo any effective persuasive appeal.

III

Readings of the horror film from any theoretical perspective, psychoanalytic or otherwise, must address irony's function. Irony is now so well woven into the horror genre that it cannot go overlooked. As yet undecided is how to best register irony's effect. Is a retrofitted uncanny incorporating irony as a mechanism for abetting the release of bridled complexes the best account of irony? What are the consequences of an unconscious that avails itself of all available means of persuasion? Apart from psychoanalytically informed criticism, what is a horror film that says one thing but means another? Finally, what function(s) might horrible irony have for filmmakers and audiences absent the unconscious?

By most accounts, modern horror arose as a consequence of, and a form of resistance to, the all-encompassing empiricism of the Enlightenment.[12] As Carroll notes, "the scientific world view of the Enlightenment... supplies a norm of nature that affords the conceptual space necessary for the supernatural, even if it regards that space as one of superstition" (1990: 57). In offering an explanation for all the things of this world, the empirical enlightenment stripped mystery and awe from experience. Horror attempts to restore a measure of enigmatic frisson to a denatured world shorn of dark secrets.

No matter how efficacious scientific praxis may be, a world without mystery is an altogether dull place. As a rejoinder to omnipotent method, horror offers a world where there are more things in heaven and earth than science may dream of. From its gothic foundations to the latest neo–stalker flick, horror proffers a hyperbolic fantasia beyond the reach of dry, bloodless science. In everting the explained universe, horror manufactures an ironic world in place of a sterile vacuum where all is rationally ordered. In this new creation, empirical reality must contend with irrational subversion.

This transubstantiation is particularly obvious in the realm of the senses. Horror, especially filmed horror, achieves its greatest effects through a marked distortion of empirical reality. If science privileges sense data across observers, then the horror film trumps science by offering indelible sounds and memorable images that would rattle even the most dispassionate of research fellows. The malevolent soughing that runs through the *Friday the 13th* series, Bernard Herrmann's electric psychostrings, the two-note riff of the great shark, Dr. Frankenstein's grand electrical machinery, Lon Chaney's warped make-up, Rick Baker's spasmodic gore effects, and Cronenberg's revolting bodies – among a thousand other examples – are some of the effects filmed horror employs to turn the senses against the body. In a world where imperious sense data rule, the horror film is king.

In revivifying desiccated reality, horror almost always overplays its antipathy to empirical analysis. The mordant reality of the horror film is never merely dark, but always dark and stormy. Regan (Linda Blair) in *The Exorcist* (1973) is not just possessed: her head spins 360 degrees, she vomits gallons, and we hear the piss hit the floor as the Devil's work begins.[13] Repudiating science necessitates the invention of irony. If this world, the world enervated by science, is not to be believed, then the horror film must offer extravagant fantasy that is at once over the top and just right. Not surprisingly, this is a difficult balance to maintain, and horror easily tumbles across the line into horror-comedy and parody.

Finding irony in mutiny against the tyranny of science does not render it unfit for a role in conjuring the uncanny. Because the job of horrific irony is to disavow too great a reliance on arid reality testing, it would be useful in scorning an overly rational *mentalite*. In so doing, the psychic conflicts common to infancy and early childhood might also prove more readily recovered. Of course, should irony go too far and descend into unruly farce then it will be unsuitable for calling up the uncanny.

The more difficult problem in addressing irony, inside and outside psychoanalytic criticism, entails a discussion of irony's orientation. Allied with the uncanny, irony's orientation is *centripetal*: it serves to bring the audience back to the traumas of the psyche; in so doing, unconscious irony is open to the usual litany of complaints directed against psychoanalysis. It negates the agency of individual viewers, for example, through the creation of a universal model of the subject. Furthermore, not only are all subjects alike, sharing the same basic intrastructure, but they are also similarly liable to be taken in by the phantasms of the unconscious. In addition, if it is possible to enhance the powers of the unconscious by allowing it more rhetorical liberty, we come very close to arguing not that the unconscious is structured *like* a language, but rather that it *is* a language.

Outside of psychoanalytic criticism, irony has a *centrifugal* force: it frees horror to embrace a wide range of affects that take it well beyond the usual limits ceded to the genre. Most accounts of horror do not address the ease with which horrible texts and their audiences move readily across different horror modalities. Ironic horror frees the genre to shift across registers, from horror to comedy and back again, without alienating or losing an audience with a taste for irrational entertainment.

In addition, the centrifugal force of ironic horror allows individual texts to address issues that go well beyond conventional form. Ironic, doubting horror opens the genre to knowing revision. When the genre threatens to become stale, the past can be easily sloughed off, ironically dismissed, and horror is free to adopt aggressively up-to-date visions of the monstrous. Only a slippery genre with the capacity to remake itself via irony could move from Bela Lugosi to George Hamilton to Lestat.

And only an ironic genre would number Van Helsing, Buffy, and Clarice Starling as collective agents of all that is good and true.

Finally, a centrifugal irony is an *explosive* irony, available to filmmakers and spectators alike. As a consequence, horrible fictions are indeterminate texts that can be taken either in jest or as dead serious. Centrifugal irony has, by definition, a center that cannot hold. In contrast, centripetal irony, the irony of the uncanny, is an implosive, centered irony in the service of one master.

NOTES

1. Witness the recent furor that accompanied the Nike slasher ad run briefly, on U.S. television, during the 2000 Olympics. The ad featured a dogged slasher chasing Olympic runner Suzy Favor Hamilton. Eventually the winded slasher cedes the contest, being in no shape to compete with a champion athlete. Quickly pulled, in response to a tremendous number of complaints, discussion of the ad broke down into two antithetical camps. Some called it a joke, whereas others bemoaned it as yet another instance of vicious corporate misogyny.
2. It must be emphasized that the terms Carroll, Freud, Freeland, and Todorov employ to discuss horrific texts are not in any way interchangeable. These different terms do, however, serve to map a shared territory.
3. The same types of sequences are also commonly inserted at the end of the horror film. This time these sequences lead the viewer to doubt the efficacy of the measures taken against the monstrous. Think too of the foreboding question mark that appears on screen in 1950s monster movies after the end titles roll. Finally, the question mark that stands in place of Boris Karloff's name in the credits for *Frankenstein* (1931) works to similar effect.
4. The rare ambiguous horror film, best exemplified in the original *Cat People* (1942) and other Val Lewton projects, represents an absent exception to this observation.
5. For a fuller treatment of the cognitive and emotive affects common to the paranoiac horror film, see Grodal (245–52).
6. Carroll (1990: 97–119) discusses the importance of confirmation at great length. In his analysis, the confirmation plot in its many variations makes up a considerable portion of the genre.
7. The last independent gore studio in the States, Troma Entertainment, has adopted this style as its house brand. In its own productions and the films it distributes, e.g., *Rockabilly Vampire* (1997), *Chopper Chicks in Zombie Town* (1989), *Dead Dudes in the House* (1991), and *Terror Firmer* (1999), Troma treats the genre as if it has always comfortably nested "between Benny Hill and Luis Buñuel" (O'Hehir).
8. See Pinedo (44).
9. Freud concludes these remarks by arguing that we aren't generally pleased to be deceived in this fashion. Even if his account of the uncanny is compelling,

there is little evidence we harbor any resentment toward those who take us for a ride.

10. See Kristeva (1982); and Creed (1986).
11. This paragraph reworks an observation made by Crane (62–63).
12. See also Kendrick; and Twitchell.
13. I am borrowing here from remarks made by Clive Barker discussed in Tyson (248).

PART THREE

REPRESENTING PSYCHOANALYSIS

9 WILLIAM PAUL

What Does Dr. Judd Want? Transformation, Transference, and Divided Selves in *Cat People*

I

Why should we take psychoanalysis seriously in thinking about Hollywood movies? Let me propose the simplest answer: because Hollywood took psychoanalysis seriously. In claiming this, I don't want to overlook doubts about the depth of psychoanalytic understanding in Hollywood films, since such doubts are in fact commonplace. Still, as Nathan G. Hale has noted in *The Rise and Crisis of Psychoanalysis in the United States*, "The number of Hollywood movie stars, directors, and producers who were 'in analysis' was legion" (289). Taking this fact into account should lead us at the least to posit that psychoanalytic theory is not necessarily external, something that we as critics and scholars might wish to impose on texts, but, rather, that it is possibly immanent in the texts themselves. Furthermore, it may be present in varying degrees with varying degrees of sophistication and variously articulated.

If we question the level of sophistication in films dealing explicitly or implicitly with psychiatry of any kind, we might in part be questioning the use of generic conventions. The issue here should be how the formal constraints of Hollywood filmmaking – demands of characterization and dramatic structure – in effect become filters through which psychoanalytic thought might be expressed. In trying to determine how conventions might shape articulation of thought, I want to focus on horror films in this essay for two reasons: the conventions of the horror film are much more formulaic than those of realistic drama; furthermore, the fantastic material of the horror film seems particularly suited to psychoanalytic interpretation. Because fantasy is itself a product of the mind's capacity for *imagining*, creating images rooted in, but departing from, reality, it is perhaps inevitable *in a psychoanalytic age* that the metaphoric displacements of fantasy would be understood by its practitioners psychoanalytically. Overlooking the psychoanalytic dimension of many horror films, then, is something like deliberately ignoring any element of the text that can't be assimilated to a pre-existing theoretical approach. So, say, a cognitivist approach to *Cat People* (1942) that ignores the psychoanalytic aspects of a film which explicitly invoke psychoanalytic thought would be as self-limiting as an approach that ignored its generic inheritance as a horror film.[1]

I bring up *Cat People* here because it has already figured prominently in debates on the value of psychoanalytic approaches to cinema. In a review of the academic writing on the film, John Berks has found two opposing approaches: "To psychoanalyze or not to psychoanalyze, that seems to be the question in criticism addressing Jacques Tourneur's and Val Lewton's *The* [*sic*] *Cat People.* . . . Something in the film's narrative or imagery seems to activate a dazzling hermeneutic force-field that ineluctably shapes subsequent readings by compelling either acquiescence or active (though not necessarily acknowledged) resistance to a psychoanalytic method" (26). Rather than try to settle this debate, I would like to shift its terms by noting one incontrovertible fact: the film gives an unusually prominent role to a psychiatrist, a character who, generically, could and perhaps should be quite minor. Furthermore, the conflicting approaches to the film that Berks finds derive in part from this character's generic inheritance.

II

Whether or not we consider a psychoanalytic hermeneutic appropriate to an interpretation of Hollywood movies, it is incontestable that some concern with psychoanalytic thought, simplified or not, must play a role in films that feature psychoanalysts in prominent roles. Although *Cat People* appeared before the period that Hale has dubbed "The 'Golden Age' of Popularization, 1945–1965," the prominence of its psychoanalyst is particularly striking because he is a relatively new dramatic character in the history of Hollywood film – the *AFI Catalog to Feature Films 1931–1940* has only eleven listings of significant parts for psychiatrists or psychologists. Furthermore, his characterization is unique for the time. "After years of showing psychiatrists as absurd or sinister," Hale writes, "for a short period, from the late 1950s to the mid-1960s, coinciding precisely with the high point of psychoanalytic influence, psychiatrists were presented as humane and effective" (289). Hale's periodization is neat and tidy, but

Cat People certainly confounds it by making its psychiatrist, Dr. Judd (Tom Conway), both sinister *and* humane.

As novel as this character might be, we might best understand his appearance in *Cat People* by considering how Hollywood integrates new materials by working them through existing conventions.[2] If *Cat People* confounds Hale's categories of sinister and humane therapists, some of the reasons for this are in fact generic. The character of Dr. Judd draws on conventions already established by a small number of films about psychiatrists and psychoanalysts: they are most often foreign-born and, perhaps in a conflation with mad doctor traditions, they always have trouble keeping a proper psychoanalytic distance from their patients. Glen and Krin Gabbard see him as the possible prototype for the skeptical shrink of later horror films (23), but two important differences should be noted. First, in terms of later films, Judd occupies an unusually salient position in the plot: although he enters the film relatively late, he nevertheless becomes one point on the two romantic triangles structuring the film and, furthermore, he impels the narrative toward its violent denouement. Second, a generic prototype for this character exists in early horror films, but it's a character who should be a straw man.

Compare *Cat People* to *The Wolf Man*, which appeared the year before and is the most likely immediate influence on the production of the film.[3] There is nary a psychoanalyst, psychiatrist, or psychotherapist in sight, but Warren William, in a small part, plays Dr. Lloyd, a medical doctor who assures Larry Talbot (Lon Chaney Jr.) there are no werewolves in the following manner: "Why, I believe that a man lost in the mazes of his mind may imagine that he's anything. Science has found many examples of the mind's power over the body." *The Wolf Man* presents the standard horror film all-in-the-mind explanation that would continue to be heard up through and beyond *The Exorcist* (1973) and would continue to be just as wrong. In *The Wolf Man*, we never take the explanation seriously for two reasons: Dr. Lloyd doesn't figure directly in the plot; furthermore, we possess contrary empirical knowledge to his claims, having already seen Talbot's lupine transformation. If *Cat People* has instigated an opposition of critical approaches between psychoanalyzing and not psychoanalyzing, this might in part derive from a conflict between Judd's manifest role as a motivating force in the plot and the film's generic inheritance, which demands that the scientific *raissoneur* in horror films be proven wrong.

An important source of vacillation derives from a double role granted Judd by virtue of an opening title that complicates his generic inheritance. Long before he enters the film as a character within the diegesis, this title effectively grants Judd the first word and, consequently, a prominence in the film before the onset of the narrative: "Even as fog continues to lie in the valleys, so does ancient sin cling to the low places, the depressions in the world consciousness." Although seeming to echo the Freud of *Civilization and Its Discontents,* the quotation is attributed to a Dr. Lewis Judd.[4] Retroactively, we might want to claim this introductory title is already part of the diegesis because it is attributed to a character from within the world of the film, but more than a third of the narrative must pass (approximately twenty-seven minutes into a seventy-three-minute film) before we could even make that ascription.

What, then, is gained by the odd rhetorical strategy of beginning with a quotation from a fictional character that the fiction does not allow us to know is fictional? First of all, the quotation appears prior to plot conventions that would establish Judd as a character whose pronouncements we are likely dismiss. Furthermore, because the quotation seems to appear extra-diegetically and also attempts to appear "real," right down to the made-up book title that completes the citation, the authority of the film seems to grant Judd literal authority here, as if he were indeed the film's *raissoneur.* In effect, by the time Judd appears as a character *within* the diegesis, at the least the potential for a conflicted response has been introduced into his conventional role as someone who must be disproved.

Precisely because the film takes so long to credit the quote to a specific character within the diegesis, we can ascribe the delay to the film's rhetorical strategies: the quote serves the purpose of conditioning the way we understand narrative events prior to Judd's actual appearance. Most of all, the seemingly independent authority of the opening title inevitably authorizes an initial psychological understanding of the film's central character. Long before there is any evidence of supernatural occurrences, the narrative encourages an understanding of Irena's (Simone Simon) problems as sexual and with a possible psychoanalytic etiology. Ordinarily, horror films will offer at least one seemingly supernatural event before anyone raises a rational interpretation of strange events, much as *The Wolf Man* showed the werewolf transformation *prior* to the all-in-the-mind explanation. *Cat People,* on the contrary, seems to take a psychological approach initially by highlighting disturbing aspects about Irena's psychology from the first scene on and greatly delaying any supernatural explanation.

Consider, for example, the film's first genuine *frisson,* which comes at the close of the opening scene: it is entirely based in character psychology.

The meeting between Oliver (Kent Smith) and Irena plays as a conventional Hollywood cute meet: in a small urban zoo, Ollie watches Irena standing in front of a panther's cage sketching in a sketch pad, then crumpling up the sketch and tossing it on the ground. As she creates litter, he directs her attention to a sign, which cautions, "Do not let it be said, and said to your shame, that all was beauty here before you came." Her continuing to litter he takes as an invitation to come over and introduce himself. While Ollie talks rapidly and glibly throughout the scene, Irena says very little in reply. There is, nevertheless, a startling moment at the end when the camera in effect suddenly allows her to speak – and to speak directly to us. Throughout the scene, Irena has shielded her drawings from Ollie, with the *mise-en-scène* shielding them from us as well. But, at the end of the scene, just as Irena and Ollie walk away, the camera dollies over to a discarded sketch to show us what Irena has carefully concealed: the panther impaled on a sword. The sketch grants a direct access to Irena's innermost subjectivity, a subjectivity that must appear disturbed because of the disturbing way it is presented to us. How can we understand the surprising content of the sketch as anything other than an expression of *her* desire to destroy the panther? This would seem confirmed by an object that will provide the transition to the interior of her apartment: the statue of King John impaling a cat.

Given the kind of perverse psychology the film alerts us to in the opening scene, it is then striking that, the first time the narrative provides a supernatural explanation for Irena's behavior, it comes not from Irena herself, the believer in ancient tales, but rather from the representative of modern scientific understanding, the psychiatrist Dr. Judd. In a shot that positions Irena under a cross-like lighting fixture, echoing the cross formed by King John's upended sword with impaled cat and possibly suggesting the extent to which Irena is dominated by her superstitions, Judd reads from his session notes about Irena's belief in women who transform themselves into cats. The supernatural explanation effectively loses the priority it normally has in horror films by occurring simultaneously with the psychoanalytic one and, furthermore, by receiving voice from a skeptical psychiatrist.

As a character in the fiction, Judd is in part defined by his pronouncements. There are three specific moments in the narrative when Judd explicitly tries to explain mental functioning, with each explanation sufficiently different to warrant a separate scene. Together, they create a progression that moves from a possibly Americanized and optimistic view of psychoanalysis to a darker vision and, finally, in the face of a

stubbornly resistant patient, to a seeming abandonment of psychoanalysis. As a counterforce to the supernatural explanation, each new psychiatric explanation provides us with a different way of looking at Irena that
can cast previous events in a new light.

In his first appearance, Judd offers an explanation for Irena's trou-
bles that reinforce the popular American understanding of psychoanalysis as a kind of engineering of the mind. The mechanistic dimension
(already present in Freud, to be sure) is inevitably foregrounded in popular representations, no doubt in part because it can be most easily amal-
gamated with the cause-and-effect dramatic conventions of Hollywood
film – hence, the familiar emphasis on trauma creating blockages to the
perfect functioning of the mind. If you locate the trauma and remove
the blockage – one inevitably leads to the other in popular fictions – the
mind will resume running like a well-oiled machine:

These things are very simple to a psychiatrist. You told me about your childhood. Perhaps we'll find that this trouble stems from some early experience.
You said you didn't know your father, that he died in some mysterious accident in the forest before your birth. And because of that, the children teased
you and called your mother a witch, a cat woman. These childhood tragedies
are inclined to corrode the soul, leave a canker in the mind. But, we'll try to
repair the damage. You're not to worry.

The bleaker and more pessimistic side of Freud is always missing from
this overly mechanistic model. One of the most striking features of *Cat
People*, however, is the extent to which it departs from this model and
moves into darker regions.[5]

Part of that sense of a darker region derives from the fact that the
treatment is troubled in ways familiar to actual psychoanalytic treatment.
At their last interview, when Irena finally returns to his office to ask for
help, Judd explains the resistance to her. The intervening scene at the zoo
by the panther's cage is itself a consequence of her resistance; he comes
to see her there since she has stopped coming to his office. It is here that
Judd moves the film into Freudian regions rarely touched by Hollywood
movies: the death instinct. After praising her for resisting temptation by
not using a left-behind key to let the panther escape, Judd offers this
generalizing explanation: "There is in some cases a psychic need to loose
evil upon the world. And, well, all of us carry within us a desire for death."
We could initially read this desire as directed at others, but the aggression
can also turn inward, much as Irena's dream condenses the phrase to "a
psychic need . . . a desire for death." What might initially appear as sadistic

is reduced to a masochistic formulation, appropriate for the latter part of the film which will move toward the peculiar dance of death between Irena and Judd.

The second interview recasts the initial etiology of childhood trauma in the context of troubled instinctual drives. Judd's opposition of sadistic and masochistic impulses points to the unexpectedly fraught identification Irena has with the panther. Because Irena's identification with the cat has been at the center of much writing on the film, I do need to emphasize that it is in fact a fraught identification. At first, the film works to ally Irena with King John, the man who *slays* cats. There is Irena's sketch of the impaled panther, but also throughout the film she is visually associated with King John by being framed with his statue in her apartment. On the other hand, she also sees herself as the panther. The conflicted identification signals Irena as neurotic, torn between conflicting impulses of superego (King John) and id (panther). This conflict is dramatized throughout the film by an elaborate play of life against death, a play that finds an echo in the ending of *The Seventh Victim* (1943), the other Val Lewton–produced film in which the character of Judd (also played by Tom Conway) plays a prominent role. In the latter film, a character who has insistently sought to embrace life in the face of death walks off to her own suicide at the very same time a tubercular woman leaves the apartment house for the first time to rejoin the world of the living. A similar contrary movement takes place at the end of *Cat People* when a dying Irena finally releases the panther from its cage.

While Judd's acknowledgment of the death instinct seems to be moving him toward a more tragic acknowledgment of Irena's illness, in the final interview he pulls back from this, almost as if it would be too much for the film to bear. In his last attempt to explain the workings of Irena's mind to her, he openly rejects her fantasies in a manner that suggests she could cure herself by doing the same:

I can't help you. But I can warn you. These hallucinations approach insanity. . . . I can't help you. You can only help yourself. You keep going back to the mad legends of your birthplace. Forget them! You surround yourself with cat objects, pictures. Get rid of them! Lead a normal life!

Oddly, these exhortations to get over it succeed where the talking cure failed. Irena replies, "You know, for the first time, you've really helped me." Judd is not so much abandoning the talking cure as acknowledging that Irena's potential psychosis moves her beyond the realm of psychoanalysis. In adopting an exhortatory mode, he effectively reverts

to earlier forms of treatment, where positive suggestions from the psychiatrist should be sufficient to counter the noxious notions in the mind.
This does seem to move back to a more optimistic view, but the options
are stark and unbridgeable: either sanity or psychosis and institutional-
ization.

Judd is granted a kind of double articulation in the film. As the extra-
diegetic spokesman of the opening title, he has the authority to explain
psychological motivation. But as a character within the fiction, he himself
may be subject to similar analysis. Furthermore, in neither articulation
is Judd static. The shifting psychological explanations are mirrored by
shifts in our sense of his character. Part of this is determined by genre: if
stages of the narrative may be marked by individual characters accepting
Irena's supernatural status as a cat woman, generically Judd must be the
last to succumb. As a rationalist who looks at the architecture of the mind
rather than (like Oliver and Alice [Jane Randolph]) the architecture
of ships, Judd must be the last one to fall prey to Irena's fantasies. By
the end, Judd will become mesmerized by Irena and, consequently, by
her fantasies, either in effect acknowledging their reality or, perhaps,
becoming consumed by them. No one can escape the power of the mind
to transform the world, least of all the man who analyzes the mind.

What does Dr. Judd want?[6] In his first interview with Irena, he seems
smug and complacent, as if treating her problems were routine and she
interests him no more than any other patient. By the second interview, we
can no longer take this smug manner as a sign of indifference, because
he has gone to the trouble of seeking her out when she failed to turn
up for her appointment. Furthermore, when he talks about the desire
for death, he does so in a way that includes himself: "... all of us carry
within us a desire for death." This will serve later in the film to make
sense of his desire to see her alone even after he has been given evidence
that she is dangerous, evidence he apparently accepts because he arrives
at her apartment with a sword. Driven by both Eros and Thanatos, his
attraction to Irena establishes Judd as conflicted in a way that parallels
her own inner conflict.

Judd's complexity is most fully realized in the final interview, which
has him occupy an extraordinary number of conflicting positions in one
scene. In his exhortatory speech that tries to shake her from her obses-
sions, he is both punitive and supportive. Moving in a radically different
direction, he then directly expresses his own desire for her, asking what
would happen if he were to kiss her. She expresses revulsion, but, remarkably, this is the scene that will conclude with Irena thanking him

for helping her. Just as remarkable is his response to her gratitude: for once dropping the ironic and slightly bemused tone that he normally uses in addressing her, he says, with real feeling, "Maybe it is because you interest me." Supporting the truthfulness of this line, for the first time in the scene non-diegetic music is heard, beginning in the middle of his statement, validating its emotionality. Judd is an unstable subject, vacillating between polarities of engaged and indifferent, nurturing and seductive, sexually attracted and ultimately murderous.

If my description makes it sound as if Judd himself could therapy, that is because he anticipates the many film psychiatrists who have trouble with countertransference, the emotions the psychiatrist brings to his relationship with the patient. Judd's emotional response to Irena is in part conditioned by her emotional response to him. This effectively complicates our view of Judd as a character within the fiction: not only is he an independent character – we see him in scenes apart from Irena – but he also exists in Irena's imagination, a creation of her transference. Appropriately, Irena's dream, one of the rare moments in the film that allow us to see things precisely as Irena sees them, presents transformation – a trope central to the film's horror – as a form of transference, making Judd appear as King John and casting him in contradictory roles as both savior and avenger.

Another transformation from the dream, this time around an object, figures in an uncanny countertransference for Judd: King John's sword becomes a key. In the narrative proper, but specifically echoing Irena's dream, Judd makes his cane/sword (itself a transforming object) work as a key by using it to gain access to Irena's apartment. Because his actions seem to follow from Irena's dream, the full emergence of Judd's desires in effect becomes the overt manifestation of his countertransference. Accordingly, the countertransference manifests itself with Judd's entry into the world of her fantasy, his final recognition of Irena as a dangerous cat woman. It is at this moment that he perversely unites with Irena; like her, Judd is a character with a divided self.

III

In the final scene between Judd and Irena, when Irena transforms into a panther before his very eyes, *Cat People* seems to be following a conventional horror film's progression from obscurity to visibility, paralleling the usual progression from rational to supernatural explanations. Still, we never actually see what Judd sees here; the moment of transformation remains maddeningly obscure. Further, although at the very end of the sequence there is one brief (perhaps studio-imposed) shot of an actual leopard, the action following Judd's reaction to the transformation is shown entirely through a series of shadows. A shadowy presentation of the monster is conventional, but *Cat People* becomes unconventional in sticking with the convention even after the cat is literally out of the bag. By this point in the film, why not show the action directly?

A possible answer lies in Tourneur's remark that he tried to deal with the studio-imposed panther by shooting it in such a way that we could still doubt its existence.[7] The only way we could see the panther and still doubt that it might be there would be to take it as a character's delusional vision. This is why the film's slow and progressive revelation of supernatural elements is tied to the characters' psychological states. Alice is the first to believe in Irena's possible transformation because she is the character who has the strongest *psychological* reasons for doing so. If it dawns on Alice that Irena may well possess supernatural powers, the belief operates as a projection of guilt over her increasingly successful attempts to break up Irena's marriage to Oliver. Oliver will eventually join Alice in accepting the possibility of Irena's transformations, but only *after* he has joined her romantically and told Irena he wants to end their marriage, thus instigating his own guilty feelings.

The timing of the panther's first actual appearance is crucial because it allows for the possibility of a joint delusion for Oliver and Alice, united by this time in the guilt of their betrayal. Up to this point, as ship-building architects and engineers the pair represents a world of clarity and geometric forms: appropriately, the scene in which they will see an actual panther begins with Ollie dictating measurements to Alice. This is a world of rational understanding, where love can be described as friendship, by Alice, and happiness is regarded simply as an absence of unhappiness, by Ollie. Correspondingly, the architect's office where they work together is the most open and brightly lit interior space in the film. The possibility that the panther might be a delusion is signaled by the changed appearance of this set: it is thrust into darkness with only an eerie light coming from below the frame line.

All shots of the panther in this scene are eyeline matches, which effectively restrict the panther's "actuality" to Alice and Ollie's vision. The scene's eerie lighting furthers the sense of a joint delusion: when Ollie transforms a tool of his trade, a t-square, into a cross by pleading with the panther, "In the name of God," an unmotivated cut to the wall behind Oliver and Alice shows their shadows and makes the t-square look even more like a cross. The cut's lack of internal motivation makes it seem as if Oliver and Alice have *themselves* transformed, as if they have entered into another world and another belief system, the darkly insubstantial world of metaphor. This transformation may be understood as a consequence of their own guilt, which leads them fully into Irena's delusional fantasy much as Judd's countertransference will eventually lead him. By contrast, the first stalking sequence of Alice comes close to offering empirical evidence of Irena's transformation or, at the least, a trace of empirical evidence. The sequence's remarkable stylistic strategies encapsulate what the entire film accomplishes and underscore how much *Cat People*'s aesthetic is rooted in character psychology. Furthermore, following my argument that genre shapes expression, I want to note how the film employs differing generic traditions in this sequence to create conflicting responses to the characters and suggest divisions within each character. In terms of the horror film, Alice is a potential victim, but in terms of the woman's film, explicitly invoked at the beginning of the sequence, Alice is the "other woman" and, as such, something of a predator herself; in terms of the horror film, Irena is a possible predator, but in terms of the woman's film, she is a victim.

This divided response is reflected in the very structure of the stalking sequence: although the middle concentrates on Alice's emotions, the entire sequence begins and ends with a focus on Irena's state of mind. Things are set in motion by Irena's phone call to Ollie's office, where he is supposed to be working late. When Alice answers, Irena hangs up without a word and leaves. The respective shots of Irena and Alice on the phone echo each other: Irena is standing next to the statue of King John spearing the cat, which fills out the right side of the image, while John Paul Jones, the office cat, sits on the table in front of the phone where Alice is talking. After Irena hangs up, Alice addresses the cat as if he were an understanding confederate: "John Paul Jones, don't you hate people who do that?" Although the subsequent sequence would seem to suggest Irena is the cat, in terms of the conflicted identifications the film sets up, Irena here is once again allied with King John, while treacherous Alice is allied with the cat.

The stalking begins with Irena's reaction at seeing Alice and Oliver together. Outside an office building, Irena spies the couple in a nearby restaurant. The shots of Alice and Oliver as they get up and walk out the restaurant are all eyeline matches reflecting Irena's view. It isn't clear if Irena can hear Alice's response to Oliver's thanking her for listening to him: "That's what makes me dangerous. I'm a new type of other woman."

But she can clearly see their body language, which expresses shared intimacy. The eyeline match, then, serves to foreground Irena's pain and jealousy, making them the keynote of what follows. Similarly, the eyeline match introducing the actual stalking places all the shots of Alice within the context of Irena's emotional state.

Yet, at a striking point, Irena seems to drop out of the sequence, which allows Alice's subjectivity to take over. This happens first on the soundtrack, with the sudden cessation of Irena's clicking high heels: as Alice walks past the camera in a side view, the other footsteps stop abruptly while the camera seemingly waits for Irena – who does not appear. Without shots of Irena, shots of Alice can no longer function as eyeline matches, and we can no longer speculate about what Irena might be thinking, as we could up to this point. The central concern now becomes what Alice sees and hears. A frontal shot shows Alice looking behind herself and seeing nothing. Her anxiety increasing, she now begins to walk more briskly, as if trying to get away from something she cannot see. As she stops once more to look around, a full eyeline match shows what she sees, or more precisely, what she doesn't see. The nothingness is crucial here because it emphasizes the subjectivity of her response: it is grounded in absence, not presence, suggesting that her anxiety is based in a fantasy of what she projects onto the outside world.

The emphasis on Alice's subjectivity reaches an aural and visual climax at one of the film's most celebrated moments. After seeing nothing, Alice, in a closer shot that tracks with her, begins to run, stopping only as she reaches the light of a street lamp. As she looks about in fear, a mysterious, low growling sound begins on the soundtrack. With the cut back to a longer shot, the sound suddenly becomes much louder and is clearly identified with a bus – a burst of air brakes? – suddenly driving into the image from the right. (This strange sound will subsequently be echoed in the scene at the office discussed above precisely when the panther mysteriously leaves, thus underscoring the possibility that the panther is delusional there as well.) The camera looks through the driver-side window with the driver in the foreground and Alice toward the back of the image, framed through the door. In a closer shot, Alice looks up, and a full point-of-view shot shows us a low angle of a tree with rustling branches. On a cut back to the shot through the window, the driver says to the hesitating Alice, "Climb on, sister. Are you riding with me or aintcha?" As Alice climbs aboard, he remarks, "You look as if you'd seen a ghost." Alice anxiously seeks confirmation: "Did you see it?" But the driver snaps his head back as if surprised by her question, then decisively shakes his head no as he drives the bus away.

If the bus driver couldn't substantiate Alice's fears, the ensuing shots seem to offer us possibly objective confirmation that she had something to fear, but presented in a way that actually confounds their objectivity. After the bus leaves, we again see the rustling branches, but in precisely the same point-of-view shot that has been granted Alice, now seemingly untethered from any subjectivity. Can we fully understand the shot as independent and objective if we had initially seen it as specifically Alice's point of view? This shot appears to offer independent confirmation, but its empirical status is compromised by its initial subjectivity. The subjectivity of the audience is invoked as well: the growl/air brake transformation is not just an external reflection of Alice's anxiety; it also plays with *our* perception (perhaps our *mis*perception) and in a visceral way because the abruptness of the image and sound startles us as well as Alice.

The shots that follow further the play with subjectivity via off-screen sound. Sound serves to anchor, seemingly, shots that are spatially distinct and have no apparent motivation for their sequencing – a clear break with the film's stylistic procedure up to this point. After the untethered point-of-view shot of the branches, there is a shot of a panther in a cage pacing; with this shot begins the off-screen sounds of bleating. The panther turns its head to the right, as if hearing the off-screen sound. Next there is a shot of a caged leopard, who takes a step forward and looks to the left, again as if in response to the off-screen sound. The off-screen bleating then leads to a high-angle long shot of sheep in a field, with a fence barely visible in the back left of the image; as we note four sheep dead on the ground, the camera pans a brief distance to the right with the flock as a caretaker with a lantern enters from the right. The camera pans left with him back to the dead sheep; he kicks at the head of one with his foot, bends down to examine another, then looks at the ground. At this point there is an insert of a point-of-view shot to show what he sees: with the camera moving slightly to the right following the circle of light cast by his lantern, we see animal tracks in the mud. Strikingly, at this point, the sound of the bleating stops abruptly. The image itself offers no justification for the cessation of sound. The justification, rather, is poetic: the tread of the animal must be associated in our minds with silence.

Sound nevertheless continues to unify shots that otherwise, as before, have a mysterious spatial connection. Silence continues with a return to the shot of the caretaker, who takes out a whistle and brings it to his mouth. We actually hear nothing until the next shot, when a shrill blast of the off-screen whistle accompanies a tracking insert shot of muddy paw prints. This shot itself is a bit odd because it seems to have a light at the center that moves with the camera, illuminating the prints within a shadowy field of vision.[8] Like the second shot of the tree branches, it echoes a previous point-of-view shot, but it is now untethered from any specific point of view. As the camera continues tracking to the right, we see the paw prints stop and high heel prints take over, the clicking sound of heels finally returning to the sequence. Just before the end of the shot, we hear a second blast of the whistle.

The end of this sequence echoes Alice's departure, both visually and aurally. A medium shot with a lamp post on the left shows Irena entering the image from the left and moving to the center. She holds a handkerchief to her mouth and looks down as if lost in a reverie, silence dominating the soundtrack. A third off-screen blast of the whistle causes her to look up, breaking off from her thoughts. The angle is somewhat oblique, partly obscuring our vision, but we see enough to note that both handkerchief and Irena's face are spotless. A fourth, seemingly more urgent blast serves as a sound bridge as it segues into a motor sound, which takes over and grows louder. A cut back to a full shot shows a cab pulling into the foreground of the image and coming to a stop so that we see Irena behind it. The motor sound continues through the shot, but no more whistle blasts are heard. The cab driver asks Irena, "Taxi, lady?" Irena gets in, the driver starts his meter, and drives off to the right.

This sequence offers us the temptation of accepting seemingly empirical evidence that Irena, once provoked, has the supernatural power of turning into a large cat. Yet troubling that temptation is the indirect presentation of the evidence – the trace of something, not the thing itself. Can we finally be sure of the evidentiary status of what we see? There are other reasons for raising this question. First of all, the sequence begins clearly centered on Irena's subjectivity, then lets Alice's emotional responses dominate before returning to Irena. Complicating this scheme is the fact that the sequence begins and ends with visual tropes that actually serve to ally Irena and Alice: at the beginning, following the phone call, a shot of Alice exiting a door is immediately followed by a shot of Irena exiting a door; at the end, we have the parallel motor vehicles suddenly moving into a shot of each character, overcome with emotion, standing by a street lamp, in each instance accompanied by a sound transformation – a growl becoming air brakes, a whistle becoming a car motor.

Finally, the sequence that offers the most apparent factual evidence is spatially incoherent, unified by sounds that have an ambiguous status or even lose their reference to the image. By daylight, the zoo we have seen is a fairly conventional urban zoo of the time, likely Central Park Zoo, with animals kept in small cages. A reminder of these small cages precedes the shot of the sheep in an open meadow spatially unrelated to the zoo. Furthermore, there is no cry in the night, but rather just quiet bleating that has the magical power of instantly summoning a caretaker. And the bleating itself magically disappears over the shot of the animal tracks. In similar fashion, the shrill whistle of the caretaker, becoming more and more insistent, abruptly disappears when the taxi wakens Irena from her reverie.

My description is intended to suggest that the empirical evidence can function contrarily as a projection of Irena's delusional beliefs. A zoo with big cats could presumably offer more appropriate prey like antelope. Sheep, on the other hand, suggest we have moved into the realm of metaphor because they adhere more to the religious imagery that crops up around King John as well a the t-square/cross, making sheep more appropriate as victims for the "wicked" cat woman that Irena here imagines herself to be. The profoundly psychological quality of the sequence derives from nesting Alice's subjectivity within Irena's. This merging of subjectivities is central to the sequence because Alice, as the first character to believe Irena has supernatural powers, here begins to take over Irena's delusional set of beliefs: the seemingly normal Alice merges with abnormal Irena. The sequence begins by opposing Irena/King John to Alice/cat; yet, as Alice and Irena merge, the opposition in retrospect seems to parallel King John *with* the cat as punishing figures.

One of the film's most insistent strategies is the pairing off of unexpected parallels *between* opposing characters with unexpected oppositions *within* individuals. In the whole host of oppositions that surface around characters in *Cat People*, I want to single out one that will foreground how much a sense of divided self figures in the film's methods of characterization. Two triangles underlying the film's drama – Irena, Oliver, and Alice in one; Irena, Oliver, and Judd in the other – suggests an opposition between American and European. Judd's psychoanalysis comes from Europe, but so do Irena's folk beliefs, and both must remain foreign to Alice and Ollie's matter-of-fact world. Furthermore, conflicts quickly surface with Irena and Judd, whereas Alice and Oliver always retreat from their own conflicts. The instabilities of the two triangles finally resolve themselves into two couples – one American, one European – the former presumably stable, the latter engaged in a highly sexualized *danse macabre*.

The opposition of the two couples also points to a parallel, however, because Alice and Ollie are not without their own conflicts. Alice helps to arrange for Irena and Ollie's wedding, then does everything possible to destroy the marriage – all the while claiming, quite sincerely, that she only wants to help Irena. And while Ollie subscribes to Alice's untroubled definition of love, he can't dismiss his attraction to Irena: "I'm drawn to her. There's a warmth from her that...pulls at me. I have to watch her when she's in the room. I have to touch her when she's near." Judd later echoes Ollie when he explains his attraction to Irena: "There's a warm perfume in your hair...your body." Whereas the resulting parallel seems to collapse the European-American opposition, Oliver's language in asking Irena to marry him had earlier hinted at this collapse: "You're with me. You're here in America. You're so normal, you're even in love with me, Oliver Reed, a good, plain Americano." America is the land of normality, but, in describing himself, Oliver splits in two what should have been a simple taxonomy. Oliver is more like Judd than he himself might know, but the parallel is built on the fact that he himself is equally conflicted. The film further foregrounds the divided self by giving him two names: Alice always calls him Ollie, while Irena always calls him Oliver. If like pairs off with like, and American Ollie is drawn to American Alice, then it is the Americano Oliver who is inexplicably drawn to the foreign Irena. The quote from John Donne that ends the film and parallels the opening quote from Judd applies to all the central characters: "But black sin hath betrayed to endless night / My world, both parts, and both parts must dies."9 All four characters are divided, all are sinful to the extent that divisions cover over guilty desires, and only in death may opposing halves be reconciled.

IV

It is difficult to know what Dr. Judd wants because he is as much defined by conflicted desires as the other characters in the film, which makes it difficult to know what *any* of them want. For example, hints of lesbianism in Irena's character have been noted in the film from early on.10 Yet, in the scene that concludes with Oliver's proposal, she confesses with sensual pleasure that she was watching Oliver as he slept, a remark that seems intended chiefly to define the depth of her attraction. On the other hand, later in the scene, as if to foreground her own conflict, she says ruefully, "I've never wanted to love you." This sense of characters driven by conflicting desires is finally what makes this film so deeply psychoanalytic in its conception. Moreover, this sense of conflict extends to our own experience of the film, because its method effectively makes us ask what *we* want. Do we want to accept rational explanations for irrational behavior, or do we want to accept fantastic conceits we know empirically are wrong? *Cat People*'s aesthetic method, its strategy of tempting us with belief in Irena's delusions, then pulling back from fully certifying such belief, in effect foments something like a neurotic response in the audience.

Roughly contemporary, the David O. Selznick–Ben Hecht–Alfred Hitchcock film *Spellbound* (1945) begins with the introductory title, "Our story deals with psychoanalysis, the method by which modern science treats the emotional problems of the sane." An important distinction is being made here for a popular audience at the time. How important it is may be seen by comparing *Spellbound* to its source novel, *The House of Dr. Edwardes* (1927). Although Freud is invoked a number of times throughout the novel, the patients there are for the most part psychotic, which should place them beyond the help of Freudian psychoanalysis. This is, as we have seen, a distinction Judd makes in the more sophisticated *Cat People*. Past portrayals of mental disorders made it necessary to instruct a mass audience away from understanding mental disorder as a sign of insanity. By its insistence on conflicted desires, *Cat People* also deals with "the emotional problems of the sane." *Cat People* does not employ what would become common approaches to psychoanalysis in Hollywood film. Most often, psychoanalysis seems to occasion a kind of mystery narrative whose solution is occasioned by a sudden understanding of character motivation, which is what happens in *Spellbound*.[11] *Cat People*, on the other hand, never allows us any such certainty about what we are seeing. Rather, its psychoanalytic approach is more radical, pervading its very aesthetic strategies. The odd breaks in continuity the film resorts to at moments when we seem to have the most definite evidence of the panther's existence suggests that an empirical world offering evidence of fantastic beings cannot itself stand up to scrutiny. By maintaining an aura of uncertainty long after other horror films would have resolved it, *Cat People* induces in us the kind of sensation we might have upon waking from a dream of apprehending that which we can't quite remember. By means of blocking vision, a parallelism in character alignments that is almost geometrical, an insistent repetition in narrative events and visual strategies, and an emphasis on conflicting impulses within all its central characters, the film instances an extraordinary economy and density approaching the condensation of the Freudian dreamwork.

NOTES

1. In support of his cognitivist approach to the horror film, Carroll cites *Cat People* for its "categorically contradictory" monster (1990: 48). Although he rejects psychoanalysis, Carroll's cognitive definition of the monster nicely complements Freud's notion of the uncanny.
2. This parallels a point made by David Bordwell, although I see less containment of the new material than Bordwell does. See Bordwell, Staiger, and Thompson (21–22; 72ff).
3. This and other influences are traced out by Bansak (117).
4. J.P. Telotte disputes Joel Siegel's claim that the quote is from Freud, noting "Freud seldom uses the key term here, 'sin'. . ." (1985: 197). Telotte suggests possible parallels in a passage on religion from *Civilization and Its Discontents*, but a closer parallel may be found earlier in the same volume, when Freud explains psychological processes by a topographical simile (likening the mind to historical Rome), as does *Cat People* (likening the mind to valleys and low places).
5. Director Jacques Tourneur has said his father Maurice was one of the first people in Hollywood to be psychoanalyzed. Through his father's influence, he "discovered Freud, Jung, Adler, Havelock Ellis" (Fujiwara: 16).
6. Feminist discourse that allegorizes Irena's position in society has paid attention to Judd, but solely for what Deborah Linderman calls "his gaze, a classifying, taxonomizing gaze" (81), while specifics of his characterization are left unexamined. Others have generally dismissed him as, in Tom Gunning's words, "unethical and sexist" (1988: 32), a villain who deserves his fate.
7. Siegel (24).
8. Fujiwara, also recognizing that the shot is divorced from the watchman's point of view, describes the light as "a nondiegetic component of the search by the *camera*" (76).
9. Mary Ann Doane (1987: 49) stresses an opposition between the two quotations, thus ignoring their striking similarities – the invocation of "sin," the figurative language (albeit not of comparable poetic accomplishment), and the sense of a divided mind.
10. According to screenwriter DeWitt Bodeen, "Val [Lewton] got several letters after *Cat People* was released, congratulating him for his boldness in introducing lesbiana to films in Hollywood . . ." Quoted in Mank (222).
11. Bordwell sees this as an example of Hollywood's reductive approach to psychoanalysis. See Bordwell, Staiger, and Thompson (21).

"Ultimate Formlessness": Cinema, Horror, and the Limits of Meaning

I

An approach to some of the questions posed by the relation between popular culture and psychoanalysis is suggested by Barbara Creed's 1986 essay, "Horror and the Monstrous-Feminine: An Imaginary Abjection." Creed turns to Ridley Scott's 1979 film *Alien* in an attempt to clarify issues of otherness and the monstrous-feminine. By "monstrous-feminine" she refers to woman seen from the point of view of Freud's understanding of castration – as shocking, terrifying, horrific – as the site of abjection. Her theoretical underpinnings derive from Julia Kristeva's *Powers of Horror*, a book whose project is to establish the abject as a new theoretical entity beyond meaning – beyond the confines of the human (as understood within patriarchal society) – but which nonetheless can be given significance within a psychoanalytic understanding of the formation of the subject. Creed's aim is to show the inescapable relevance of this to an analysis of dominant culture and the subordination of women within that culture.

Kristeva pictures the abject as a place where meaning collapses, where I, the subject, am not. The abject is thus to be identified with what threatens life, and it must, therefore, be radically excluded from the place of the living subject. The abject, in other words, is all that the subject excludes in order to be what it is, to have the identity that it does. The abject is, for Kristeva, what in Judaism is characterized as "abomination": sexual perversion, murder, the corpse, incest, and the feminine body. In effect, the abject concerns everything that figures in the archaic relation to the mother; hence, the equation between what is abject and the monstrous-feminine. It is, in fact, this equation between the abject and the feminine body that points most clearly to the source of Kristeva's concept, Lacan's interpretation of Freud's account of his dream of Irma's injection. Just as the abject is a horrific expression of the monstrous-feminine, so the vision that Freud has in his dream, a vision of Irma's turbinate bones covered with a whitish membrane is, according to Lacan, "a horrendous sight."

There's a horrendous discovery here, that of the flesh one never sees, the foundation of things, the other side of the head, of the face, the secretory glands *par excellence*, the flesh from which everything exudes, at the very heart of the mystery, the flesh in as much as it is suffering, is formless, in as much as its form in itself is something which provokes anxiety. (1988: 154)

This is the final revelation of what "you" are – "*You are this, which is so far from you, this which is the ultimate formlessness.*" The origin is the formless which in turn is the body of the woman. Insofar as this structure embodies the threat of castration, it provokes anxiety.

Given this context, it is hardly surprising that Kristeva considers the ultimate in abjection to be the corpse. The body expels from itself wastes such as feces and urine and by so doing continues to live:

Such wastes drop so that I might live, until, from loss to loss, nothing remains in me and my entire body falls beyond the limit – cadere, cadaver. If dung signifies the other side of the border, the place where I am not and which permits me to be, the corpse, the most sickening of wastes, is a border that has encroached upon everything. It is no longer I who expel. "I" is expelled. (3–4)

The corpse – at least within the Old Testament tradition – is wholly abject. It constitutes a basic form of pollution, a body without a soul. It is this notion that Creed applies to the horror film. Bodies without souls, such as vampires and zombies, and corpse-eaters such as ghouls comprise the basic iconography of the horror film, an iconography of abjection. Creed carries this further when she argues that the central work of the horror film is the construction of the maternal figure as abject. She considers that, within our culture, central images of pollution are related to the mother – in particular, images of menstrual blood. These images of pollution are horrific because images of this kind – of blood, pus, shit, vomit, and so on – signify a split between two orders: the maternal authority and the law of the father. These images of waste threaten a subject that is constructed within the Lacanian symbolic as whole and proper and, as a result, they induce loathing and disgust. At the same time, these images hark back to an archaic period when the child's relation to its mother was such that it did not experience embarrassment and shame at the emergence of its bodily wastes. Thus, images of filth give rise not only to fear and loathing but also to pleasure, a perverse pleasure deriving from the archaic mother–child relation that was marked by untrammeled playing with the body and its wastes. The menstrual blood in *Carrie* (1976) is taken by Creed to give significant backing to this argument.

This approach allows Creed her fundamental point, that "the central ideological project of the popular horror film" is "purification of the abject" through what Kristeva calls a "descent into the foundations of the symbolic construct" (18). This means that the horror film brings about a confrontation with the abject such that the abject (the zombie, the vampire, etc.) is finally ejected and the boundaries of the symbolic, of the human, are re-established. Horror films are a kind of modern defilement rite in which all that threatens the symbolic, all that is of the Other, is separated out and subordinated to the paternal law. This can be seen in Lacanian terms as the subordination of the desire of the mother to the Name of the Father, the paternal prohibition, the Father's "Non."

This project is, for Creed, fundamentally reactionary, and she finds it in *Alien*, which represents "the monstrous-feminine in terms of the maternal figure as perceived within a patriarchal ideology" (54). The archaic mother, the monstrous-feminine, is present in the film as primordial abyss, manifest in the alien spacecraft, as well as in the images of blood and the all-devouring, toothed vagina. The same presence is also embodied in the monstrous figure of the alien born from the rupturing of Kane's (John Hurt) chest, and in the *Nostromo*'s computer, Mother, whose children, born from the sleeper-pods of the spaceship at the opening of the film, are devoured by the toothed alien during the course of the narrative. The archaic mother is not represented as such in these scenes, nor indeed does she appear at any point in the film's subsequent development. She is, however, present in the film's *mise-en-scène*, in the womb-like imagery of the alien craft, its tunnels leading to the rows of hatching eggs, and in the body of the *Nostromo*, the mother-ship. Present in the voice of the controlling computer, she is also present in the birth of the alien, who is her representative, and in its destruction of the *Nostromo*'s crew. For Creed, the archaic mother informs all things though she is localized in none of them.

It is the underlying strategy of *Alien* to contain this pervasive alterity, this radically ungraspable and unrepresentable Other, within a structure of female fetishism that makes of the alien the mother's fetish. That the alien is the mother's phallus is made perfectly clear when it arises from Kane's body:

But the alien is more than a fetish; it is also coded as a toothed vagina, the monstrous-feminine as the cannibalistic mother. A large part of the ideological project of *Alien* is the representation of the maternal fetish object as an 'alien' or foreign shape. (68)

The film finally signals the accomplishment of its phallocentric project in its presentation of Ripley's (Sigourney Weaver) body as she undresses just before her final confrontation with the alien in the escape capsule. We have here a reassuring and pleasurable image of the "normal" woman, the humanity of whose maternal feelings are expressed in her stroking the cat as if it were her baby. The final sequence not only disposes of the alien, but also represses "the nightmare image of the monstrous-feminine," which has been constructed in the film "as a sign of abjection" (69). Thus, the abject is literally expelled from the image in a restoration of the symbolic order.

II

Creed's approach exemplifies the use standardly made of psychoanalysis in theoretical studies of Hollywood cinema. First, concepts are taken over from an approved source – in this case, Kristeva's theories of abjection – and applied directly to the film in question. No criticism or evaluation of the concepts involved is considered necessary, so notions such as abjection are taken as given. This procedure follows the model laid down by *Screen* in the 1970s, where the theories of Lacan were taken to be self-evidently beyond criticism and were applied to films as though no problems were attached to Lacan's concepts in themselves. However, all theories of the kind Kristeva puts forward run into difficulties that derive from the attempt to explain the origin of meaning in terms of non-meaning. Not only do such theories necessarily presuppose the very condition they are trying to explain, but, because they are unable to conceptualize that which lies beyond concept, they themselves can be given no coherent expression. The result is that, insofar as one can understand what is meant by the notion of the abject, that notion cannot be the one at issue.

In effect, the assumption underlying Kristeva's argument is that what the discourse of psychoanalysis represents is the "unrepresentable." Once this idea of representation has been displaced onto art, any given work can be taken to exemplify it: the "logic" of the signifier is that which subsequently and inevitably must be discovered in it. The view implicit in a position of this kind is that human psychology is constituted by the impersonal reality of language. Hence, language becomes the theoretically "impossible" object whose otherness the language of a theory like Kristeva's seeks not only to unveil but also to re-enact. Aporia is taken to be the self-authenticating mark of truth – a truth manifest in self-contradiction.

Second, the conclusion to which Creed finally comes – namely, that in *Alien* and films similar to it, the Other (the monstrous-feminine) is subordinated to the phallic order of the symbolic – is presupposed by the very concepts from which the argument is derived. The monstrous-feminine, as defined by Kristeva, can be ascribed to the film only insofar as Creed can show that the repression postulated by Kristeva's theory is an effect of the film text. Given the nature of Kristeva's ideas, and Creed's use of them, no such demonstration is, or could be, forthcoming. No questions of fact arise, and there is nothing to be confirmed or falsified, because the whole argument is circular.

A further difficulty derives from the fact that Creed is concerned not with narrative but with *mise-en-scène*. The *mise-en-scène* model tends to imply a static relation between subject and object that is difficult to connect with narrative development. The *mise-en-scène* picture allows one to envisage the monstrous-feminine, the Other, as vaguely object-like. As a result, its relation to the film's action remains obscure. One consequence of this picture is that it induces Creed to base her interpretation of *Alien* on the set and production design. The vaginal openings and the maternal aspect of the alien spacecraft, as well as the phallic appearance of the monster that bursts forth from Kane's body, are part of the film's overall design and are clearly conscious elements in that design. The maternal/phallic elements in the film's organization are – as elements of the *mise-en-scène* – self-consciously part of what makes the film the kind of film it is.

This means that the supposedly unconscious structures, the latent meanings that, on the model of dream interpretation, are teased out by the interpreter, are in fact present in the manifest organization of the film. Indeed, in the case of *Alien* the maternal/phallic elements are not simply manifest, they are blatantly obvious. Psychoanalytic material, as Creed and many other film analysts understand it, is part of the film's consciously organized rhetoric. Like *Carrie, Psycho* (1960), *The Texas Chainsaw Massacre* (1974), and many other modern horror films, *Alien* is at all levels of its construction informed by psychoanalytic presuppositions, which both motivate and justify the narrative. If this is so, then the use of a

psychoanalytically derived analysis to found an ideological critique of
modern Hollywood horror films is on difficult ground. To criticize ideology from a secured theoretical position above the ideological struggle, a
position secured by the application of psychoanalytic notions of the unconscious, the subject, or the monstrous-feminine, is itself ideologically
suspect. Furthermore, not only is psychoanalysis required to provide a secured meta-language, but, as Creed's account shows, it is also inseparable
from the material it is being used to analyze.

Difficulties of another kind arise from the fact that psychoanalytic readings in film theory tend toward the ahistorical, inasmuch as the psychic
structures, discerned within a given film, are taken to be operative independently of either the spectator's or the film's historical circumstances.
Thus, for Creed, *Alien* exists in an eternal present, determined by the
unchanging structures of "patriarchy" and the archaic mother. There
are obvious problems, ideologically speaking, with such a refusal of the
historical.

The difficulties – the circularities and incoherences – that underlie the
psychoanalytic analysis of cinema undoubtedly derive from the nature of
Lacanian and post-Lacanian thought. Lacan's account of the dream of
Irma's injection can be taken to exemplify his position more generally.
In his interpretation, Lacan writes out the formula for trimethylamine,
which Freud tells us appeared to him during the course of his dream.
In Lacan's graphic presentation of the formula, the nitrogen atom is
linked to three carbon atoms, each of which in turn is linked to three
hydrogen atoms. As John Forrester has pointed out, in French chemical
nomenclature the symbol for nitrogen is AZ, so that for Lacan the place
of the nitrogen atom in the formula represents the subject outside the
subject, the alpha and omega "who designates the whole structure of the
dream" (1988: 159).

Similarly, if one were to take nitrogen as N, this can read as *nemo*, no
one, which can also be allegorized as the subject beyond the subject,
the subject who articulates the formula itself. Since Lacan has already
argued that the dream is constructed out of triadic elements – three
women, three men, and so on – the formula in effect comes to represent
the dream's dreaming of its own genesis. For Lacan, the formula is like
the enigmatic writing on the wall at Belshazzar's feast, or the Islamic
formula: "There is no other God but God." The formula is the answer
to the question of the meaning of the dream. "There is no other word,
no other solution, to your problem, than the word" (158). Meaning and
word are one and the same. This, however, is unclear. The meaning of

a word and the word itself are not the same thing. Words can be split up, cut into stone, pronounced loudly or softly, and so on. Words are physical things – and can be found in dictionaries. However, meanings cannot be contained, divided, redesigned, or uttered in the way words can. Meanings are neither entities nor processes. It might be argued that, for Lacan, dreams represent the lack of the function that engenders them. This lack of meaning *is* their meaning, inasmuch as the unconscious is the discourse of the Other. Arguments of this kind, however, once more dissolve the theory into *aporia*.

There are, therefore, certain ineradicable problems with the application of Lacanian and post-Lacanian concepts to cinema. These problems derive from the attempt to provide a theory that encompasses subjective experience as a whole and are internal to the mode of thought itself. The question remains, then, of the significance of intellectual undertakings of the kind Creed offers. There are other readings of *Alien* (e.g., Neale 1989; Kavanaugh) which are based on non-psychoanalytic premises and which, it can be argued, attend more interestingly to the specific detail in the film's narrative. One difficulty with Creed's approach is that the conclusions of the analysis are presupposed in its premises. A second is that the film itself is already organized around the kind of interpretation she seeks to discover in it. The concepts she takes over from Kristeva allow her to elaborate variant descriptions of the generic elements present in the film by virtue of its being the film it is, but in no sense does she reveal for the film an unconscious significance that, without her analysis, would have remained hidden.

It is true that no other analyst of the horror film has applied Kristeva's categories in the manner that Creed has chosen to do. But this of itself does not constitute a new understanding of the film *Alien*, and furthermore, as I have argued, the logic of Kristeva's theoretical position is such that arguments derived from it are highly problematic. I would suggest, then, that the force and purpose of Creed's arguments lie elsewhere, in areas whose significance can be merely suggested.

Kristeva's account of abjection attempts to offer a totalizing understanding of feminine sexuality in relation to the religion of the Old Testament. The impulse of *Powers of Horror* is, therefore, to place its own understanding of the human subject beyond the understanding that traditionally would have been thought to follow from an adherence to, and understanding of, the laws of God. These very laws themselves are now to be understood in ways that allow the theorist to explain why the concepts that they embody are the concepts that they are. Kristeva (like Lacan before her) is therefore driven beyond the conceptual as such. For Creed to read *Alien* in terms of this totalizing project of transvaluation is to speak out of, and as, the Other. One can, in speaking in accordance with the logic of a theory whose meaning is elsewhere, speaking oneself as abject, as oneself the monstrous-feminine, as the alien. If this is the appeal, within our culture, of this order of theoretical enterprise (and of the aporetic logic that goes with it), then it may be that arguments like Creed's point to something of what constitutes the more general appeal of a film such as *Alien*. The film allows at least certain of its spectators a vicarious participation in an alterity that partakes of death. In other words, films like *Alien*, in allowing us to exist beyond ourselves, also allow us to live through our own deaths.

III

Stephen Mulhall's recent discussion of the *Alien* series also emphasizes the question of what constitutes horror, a question that is inseparable from an understanding of the nature and meaning of the alien itself. Mulhall begins from some thoughts of Stanley Cavell's concerning what it is that makes for an experience of the horrific:

Horror is the title I am giving to the perception of the precariousness of human identity, to the perception that it may be lost or invaded, that we may be, or may become, something other than we are, or take ourselves for; that our origins as human beings need accounting for, and are unaccountable. (Cavell 1979: 419; cited in Mulhall: 17–18)

This explains, for Mulhall, why the monster in horror films is frequently a zombie or a vampire, one of the living dead: such beings are at once human and not human. But what has this to do with Ridley Scott's alien? What is it that we see of our human "precariousness" in the monstrosity of this monster? To begin with, the alien threatens to inflict a particularly rending violence on human flesh. Beyond this threat, however, a threat inducive of terror rather than horror is what we might call the threat posed by the alien's mode of being. The alien has no general or specific animus against the members of the *Nostromo*'s crew. It attacks the crew because they threaten its survival and because they provide the means for its continued survival. It is, as Mulhall has it, simply following the imperatives of nature. Nonetheless, there seems to be something *essentially* alien attaching to Scott's alien, as though it were possessed of something more than mere natural existence. It is not simply one creature among many, one monster amongst others. Mulhall writes: "The alien's form of life is (just, merely, simply) life, life as such. . . . [I]t is Nature incarnate or sublimed, a nightmare embodiment of the natural realm" (19).

This view of horror links up again with Lacan. Slavoj Zizek argues that, for Lacan, the source of horror is what embodies the pure life instinct, and he sees the idea exemplified by *Alien*. The libido, as pure life instinct, is irrepressible life, "life that has need of no organ"; it is "simplified, indestructible life." It exists as what is "subtracted from the living being by virtue of the fact that it is subject to the cycle of sexed reproduction" (Lacan 1979: 198; cited in Zizek 1993: 181). The element subtracted from the living is what Lacan calls the "lamella," a thin strip or plate, such as the placenta, that part of the child's body lost by the child and by the mother, which, Lacan imagines, might come to envelop one's face while one is asleep. The lamella is an otherness prior to subjectivity and, as Zizek has it, "[a]re not all the elements of Lacan's myth contained in the first truly horrifying scene of [*Alien*] when, in the womblike cave of the unknown planet, the 'alien' leaps from the egg-like globe when its lid splits off and sticks to John Hurt's face?" (181). The flattened amoeba-like form, the lamella, stands for – indeed, embodies in the film – an irrepressible life that is beyond that of any of the finite forms that merely represent it. It is in this sense that it stands beyond or outside subjectivity and meaning. It exists between what Lacan calls the "two deaths," between the death inflicted by language (the symbolic) on the uniqueness of things and the death that is, at the same time, paradoxically, the life of what is utterly alien to the symbolic order.

Seen in this light, the alien is evidently an image of the precariousness of human life and identity. Mulhall points, however, to a further aspect of the alien's alterity, deriving from the fact that its mode of reproduction is parasitic. The alien – at the "lamella" stage of its life-cycle – forces part of itself down into the body of its host and deposits a version of itself there, within the host, from which it must in due time force its way to the outside: "The alien's parasitism exemplifies the essential parasitism of Nature; it represents the radical lack of autonomy that is of the essence of creaturehood" (Mulhall: 20). For Mulhall, this is a procedure of penetration and parasitism that threatens the whole of the human species with feminization. Haunting the ducts and passages of the *Nostromo* is a being that embodies sexual difference as monstrous. And yet, one might say, what is monstrous here is not only, or even primarily, the threatened feminization of humanity, but rather the doubled character of the alien itself. It appears as nothing less than an embodied or incarnate

articulation of the impossible – of a spatiotemporal differing that, as
Derrida would put it, prevents being or subjectivity being thought except
as an impure *différance*, inseparable from radical finitude. Derrida has addressed the issue of parasitism in relation to *différance* during the course
of his discussions of Austin, bringing together the parasite, writing, and
a general logic of "supplementarity." To attend to the alien in the light of
this intervention, inseparable from an articulation of the quasi-concept
of iterability, is to attend to something that, as the film presents it, is both
in and beyond the film, in and beyond representation as such.

The figure of the alien is a figure of catastrophe. In the moment of
the creature's "birth" from Kane's chest, we are confronted by a moment
of collapse, of the abyss. It is as though the film were seeking to void
or reduce or hollow out the image. Inasmuch as representation pertains
only to what is present, what is in the process of appearing is not in that
sense to be represented. As the alien bursts forth from the man's flesh and
bones it thrusts off-screen into the dystopic space it has thereby opened
up in a movement that is essentially projective, futural. The alien is a
being of the future, a being that, in Lacan's expression, is what it will
have been for what it is in the process of becoming: immeasurably old, it
bespeaks a future which it is itself in the process of bringing into being
and from which it reinvests the "here" and "now" of the present. As the
members of the crew seek for it in the body of the ship in the aftermath of
Kane's death, they come across a discarded epithelium, mark of the alien's
transformations and of what it has become and is becoming. The alien
appears less as a creature than an *event*, an event oriented toward a future
of its own elaboration; by virtue of a series of repetitions that project it
toward that future it constitutes for the crew a complex intertwining of
anticipation and retroaction. The alien is thus not a thing to be known
or understood: the space it opens up is one in which identification and
exchange are contaminated by the alterity the anticipation of its irruption
introduces into them.

The alien irrupts into the film, an event of caesura or spasm. It signifies,
without signifying – it says nothing. One may consider in relation to it
the Neckar cube, as it flip-flops back and forth. Like Wittgenstein's duck–
rabbit, one aspect of the figure obscures the other, so that it is not, and
never can be, present in its totality. The alien may be said to inhabit a space
similar in its sheer incomprehension (imbecility) to that which exists,
and does not exist, that *is* under erasure, between the two projections
of the cube: the "in-between," where no meaning is. It may be said that
language use itself (the following of a rule, such as Wittgenstein's "+2,"

for example) is likewise abyssal – meaning is set up retroactively, but the act of speech or writing is in itself without meaning. What I mean and *that* I mean what I mean are internally related, but there is always a delay such that the one is always deferred in relation to the other. The act of following the rule constitutes or grounds what I do in the very rule my application of it has sprung away from. As Cavell has it, the step I take in following the path is an act of relinquishing the path that in the same act creates that very path as the path I am following. It follows that the Company can no more possess or own the alien than science can comprehend it.

This complex knotting can be further exemplified within the film's temporal singularity inasmuch as the relation between Ripley and the alien is configured as a disruption of any mediation between opposing poles. As Mulhall has noted, it is as though Ripley and her opponent had been "somehow made for another" (25), as though they were gathered into a structure where there is identification without identity, where each is the wound of the other. That is, the irruptive and undecidable shifting between human and alien, centered on Ripley, which generates all four films of the series, is not that of a unique identity, a unique "I," confronting another such identity. It is, rather, a question of an indefinite "who?" affirmed through an interrogation that yields no answer even as it supports the insane dialogue that inscribes it.

Freud's Worst Nightmare: Dining with Dr. Hannibal Lecter

Castration, sexual abuse, hysteria, perversity, excrement, bestiality, animal phobias – Freud's case histories read like horror movies. They are alive with fears – fear of being bitten by a horse, fear of wolves, fear of having one's bowels gnawed by a rat. His famous *Interpretation of Dreams* is permeated with anxieties and phobias of a similarly horrific nature – nightmares of falling, suffocation, ghosts, dead children, burning skin, urine and feces, people with bird's heads, snakes, men with hatchets, decapitations. In Freud's view, nightmares were the result of wish fulfillments from the unconscious, deadly dreamscapes of sexual origin in which he included murder and cannibalism (Freud 1975: 723–39). Samuel Goldwyn once offered Freud a lucrative contract to write a script for a movie about great lovers of history. Goldwyn could see how the screenwriter might benefit from an understanding of Freud's theories: "How much more forceful will be their creations if they know how to express genuine emotional motivation and suppressed desires" (Gay: 454). Freud refused outright. Goldwyn might have had more success if he had suggested a horror story.

Much of Freud's writings, in fact, contain the elements one might expect, not from the pen of a respectable, middle class doctor from *fin de siècle* Vienna, but from the laptop of contemporary masters of horror such as Stephen King or Thomas Harris. Freud's worst nightmare? How to select one dream of untold terror from such a macabre collection? To underscore the horror, one could imagine Freud's worst nightmare in a more whimsical vein. Perhaps it might have been the specter of finding himself the subject of a furious debate by opposing camps of film theorists. Or imagining himself signing a Hollywood contract to direct a film on psychoanalysis, which starred Jung in the leading role. Freud we know did not actually see an example of the modern world's newest art form until 1909, when he, Ferenczi, and Jung (before his bitter falling out with the latter) embarked upon their famous trip to New York. On the third day, after the group dined in Hammerstein's Roof Garden, they all went to the cinema "to see one of the primitive films of those days with plenty of wild chasing." Ferenczi was "very excited" but Freud "was only quietly amused" (Jones 1957, 1955: 56).

Born in 1856, Freud would have been forty years old when the first movies were screened to an astonished public. Perhaps Freud's worst nightmare might have been being observed, "caught out," in the late 1890s in one of modernity's new picture houses, watching an early short film, a romance, or a horror-fantasy – Edison's *The Kiss* (1896), maybe, or Méliès' *Le Manoir du Diable* (1896), in which the devil plays a vampire bat. I have suggested Freud might consider being "caught out" at the movies a nightmare not because of a secret aversion to being observed, but because Freud held the cinema – considered a mass form of entertainment – in some disdain. Opera, painting, sculpture, literature – these were more to his liking. His writings on scopophilia, however, suggest he understood full well the kinds of pleasures to be derived from the act of looking. Freud was certainly not impervious to the attraction of the new phenomenon of the film star. Paul Ferris tells us that, in a letter to Max Schiller, Freud wrote that he nearly saw Charles Chaplin in the streets of Vienna. He added that the famous actor "invariably plays only himself as he was in his grim youth" (Ferris: 374). Freud could not resist the urge to psychoanalyze, to comment on the relationship between the actor's real life and his role on the screen. He himself did not like being the object of the camera's gaze. The home movie of Freud, which screens at the Freud Institute (London) and which was taken by his daughter, Anna, reveals him carefully avoiding the eye of the camera.

By the time of Freud's death in England, in 1939, the cinema of horror had developed into a sophisticated and popular form of entertainment. By the early 1920s many of the traditional monsters had already made their first appearances – werewolf, vampire, doppelgänger, ape-man, ghost-woman, lunatic, and hellhound. Masterpieces of early cinematic horror such as *Frankenstein* (1910), *The Cabinet of Dr. Caligari* (1919), *Nosferatu* (1922), and *The Phantom of the Opera* (1924) were followed in the early sound era by *Dracula* (1931), *Vampyr* (1931), *White Zombie* (1932), and *King Kong* (1933). Like Freud's dreams and case histories, the horror film was quick to explore the nature of perversity. Themes of castration, bestiality, masochism, sexual abuse, and animal phobias all made early appearances.

FREUD, FILM, AND MODERNITY

Although Freud does not appear to have used film as a cultural reference point in his writings, his revolutionary ideas share a parallel history with the world's newest art form. In some instances, Freud's psychoanalytic theories and critical writings drew upon terminology central to the cinema, such as "screen," "projection," "identification," and "censorship." In his essay on William Jensen's popular novel of the day, *Gradiva*, Freud developed a theory about the gaze in which pleasure in looking becomes pathologically voyeuristic. Theories of looking – so central to an understanding of the new mobile gaze of modernity – became, at the other end of the century, the inspiration for a new form of feminist film theory based on the importance of the male gaze, fetishism, and screen–spectator relationships.

There are other connections. Freud described his manuscript for *The Interpretation of Dreams* as a "dream-book" (Freud 1975: 257), a concept that is echoed in the popular description of the cinema as a "dream factory." Freud's theory of "screen memories" is difficult to read without immediately thinking of the mechanisms of film projection and the workings of cinematic memory. In his 1915 "A Case of Paranoia Running Counter to the Psychoanalytic Theory of the Disease," the photographic camera plays a central role. Freud's interpretation of the "click" of the camera shutter as the "sound" or "feel" of a clitoral orgasm anticipates debates about the phallic power of the camera and the pleasure involved in posing as the erotic object of the voyeuristic camera.

Freud also refused to take part in a German film illustrating his psychoanalytic concepts. Entitled *Secrets of a Soul* (1926), it was eventually directed by G. W. Pabst and became a classic of the silent cinema. Freud's *Three Essays on Sexuality* inspired another German script, *Sensational Revelations from the Night Life of the Human Soul.* Apparently it was to star the boy wonder, "Jackie Coogan as Young Oedipus and the Tiller Girls as erotic dancers" (Ferris: 332). One can see why Freud, whose professional reputation was constantly under attack for overemphasizing the role of sexuality in human development, refused to have anything to do with modernity's newest art form, which was bent on exploring and exploiting the universal appeal of narratives of sex, desire, and eroticism. The parallels between aspects of psychoanalytic theory and the cinema were brought about in part by the way the two responded to and were shaped by the new forces of modernity. There are a number of areas in which we can see these parallels at work. They include the modern view of the "self", the structures or workings of memory, the prominent role given to the emotion of shock in both discourses, and the presence of an optical unconscious.

THE MODERN SELF

In *Freud and His Critics*, Paul Robinson draws attention to the view, held in the 1960s by a number of important intellectuals (Lionel Trilling, Philip Rieff, and Steven Marcus), that Freud was "the virtual creator of the modern conception of the self" (3). Writing in 1993, after Freud's fall from grace, Robinson continues to support this view:

Above all, the modern self is a site of internal tension and conflict. This new conception made Freud the central figure in the emergence of the modernist sensibility in the early twentieth century. (116–17)

In his counterattack on Jeffrey Masson, Robinson argues that, when Freud abandoned his theory of seduction and spoke out about his views on childhood sexuality and the unconscious, "he made himself the foremost spokesman for a new way of thinking about the subject" (117). Freud argued against traditional notions: the self was not some pre-given divine essence implanted in the body at birth, nor was it a superior, transparent entity which simply interpreted the world around it. Rather, Freud saw the self as an evolving, active force, a participant, interacting with people and events in the outside world in ways that it did not necessarily understand or even condone. Influenced by irrational forces, unconscious desires, secret wishes, hidden jealousies, and events beyond its comprehension, the self, Freud argued, was actively implicated in its own decisions even if it did not always understand their rationale.

The strains of modern life, the fast pace of living, the bustling crowd, the emergence of more democratic politics, the emancipation of women, new modes of travel, communication, consumerism, and entertainment – all of these factors and more have been cited by historians and cultural theorists as grounds for giving rise to the emergence of a new type of modern individual. Freud's attempt to define the individual as a part of this new state of flux, mobility, stress, and change, as a being not necessarily in control of – even able to comprehend her or his desires, placed him at odds with those who espoused a view of the self as rational, superior, and fully cognizant of thoughts and actions. The titles he gave to his case histories ("The Rat Man," "The Wolf Man") emphasize the concept of the divided self, a theme that was also basic to the emerging genre of horror.

Freud theorized the concept of the repressed, conflicted individual: the horror film made the repressed, divided self the subject of its narratives. Freudian theory and the early horror film both responded to the forces of modernity through a re-examination of subjectivity. Both set out to explore beneath the surface, to look into the self, to determine the extent to which the modern subject was able to embrace or recognize the dark, non-human, animal self. As Elizabeth Wright argues, Freud's theory of the unconscious and repression are his most radical:

Author and reader are both subject to the laws of the unconscious. To concentrate on "mechanisms" without taking account of the energies with which they are charged is to ignore Freud's most radical discoveries: it is precisely the shifts of energies brought about by unconscious desire that allow a new meaning to emerge. (1984: 4)

Freud's theory of the unconscious and repression is revolutionary precisely because it offers a basis from which we might question the workings of conscious desire, and the role of the unconscious, to understand the workings of the creative process in horror – from the perspective of both author and reader. The horror genre is also radical in that it explores the formation of human subjectivity, the conditions under which subjectivity disintegrates, and the subject's fascination for and dread of sexual difference and death. *The Student of Prague* (1913) examined the divided self in relation to the double; *Nosferatu* explored the connections between sex, death, and the perverse self; *King Kong* and *Cat People* (1942) opened up the controversial area of the bestial self and the extent to which the human subject defines itself in relation to the animal. Psychoanalytic theory offers the most relevant body of work to employ as a basis for the interpretation of horror, particularly given Freud's emphasis on sexual difference in the formation of subjectivity.

Freud introduced gender into debates about the formation of the self. Despite the misogynistic nature of a number of Freud's theories and utterances, he was, in a sense, the first modern male thinker to "listen to women." Through his famous "talking cure," Freud paid close attention to what women said. Even though, at the end of his life, he pronounced in some desperation that he did not know what women wanted, he listened nonetheless. It could also be argued that the horror film, despite its misogynistic themes, has from its beginnings "listened" to women. The horror genre created a space in which woman could take the active terrifying role of the monster (e.g., *Cat People, Dracula's Daughter* [1936], *Trader Horn* [1931], *Island of Lost Souls* [1933]). Gothic horror (e.g., *The Secret Beyond the Door* [1948], *Dragonwyck* [1946], *Gaslight* [1944]) explored women's anxieties about the mysterious desires of their husbands. The heroines of these dark narratives eventually found a voice, taking control of their own fate.

At the other end of the century, female academics have in turn "listened to Freud." Commencing with Laura Mulvey's famous essay on visual pleasure, feminist film debates of the 1970s and 1980s represented "a return to Freud." These theorists re-interpreted and re-read, listened for other meanings, and drew unexpected conclusions from Freud's original writings. This is why, Wright argues, psychoanalysis is crucial for feminists. It is "the only discourse offering a theory of the subject of the unconscious" and as such is relevant to "all those wanting to situate themselves outside a rigid definition of sexual difference" (1998: 173).

SCREEN MEMORIES

The role of memory, and its mechanisms, is central to psychoanalytic theory and to an understanding of the screen–spectator relationship. Freud placed crucial emphasis on the part played by memory in the formation of the modern self. The idea that the self was constructed in and through memories – conscious and unconscious – was central to emerging concepts of the modern self as a site of tension and conflict (Charney). The power of film to encourage spectators to identify closely with the main character, to experience their feelings and emotions intimately, was created by a number of factors; memory, in particular, played a key role. Memory was central not just in assisting the spectator in constructing a coherent story, but also in keeping the spectator in a constant state of fear as the horror unfolded.

In *The Interpretation of Dreams*, Freud discussed his preference for only learning things out of monographs and spoke of his fascination for the photographic image: "I . . . was enthralled by their *coloured plates*" (257). When publishing his own papers, he explained that because of his fascination for the image, he drew his own illustrations. When a friend "jeered" at his "wretched" attempt, he experienced what he later described as a "screen memory" from his early youth. In this memory, Freud's father had given his five-year-old son, and Freud's younger sister, a book with colored plates about a journey through Persia.

[T]he picture of the two of us blissfully pulling the book to pieces (leaf by leaf, like an artichoke, I found myself saying) was almost the only plastic memory that I retained from that period of my life. (258)

His "plastic memory" seems related to the colored plates as if the latter imbued his recollection with the physical quality of plastic like the coating over a strip of film. Freud carefully distinguished his "plastic memory" of tearing apart the book and its colored plates from other kinds of memories. In so doing, he emphasized that this particular memory was somehow charged with a different emphasis; his "plastic memory" had the power to enthrall like a "coloured plate." Memory is linked to color, plasticity, pleasure, and the image. Freud adds that he "recognised that the childhood scene was a 'screen memory' for [his] later bibliophile propensities" (258).

Freud's use of the term "plastic" occurs in another context, this time in relation to the cinema, when he said he did not believe his "abstract theories" could be adequately presented in "the plastic manner of a film" (Jones 1957: 114). Freud might have consciously regarded film as a superficial medium, but the associations he drew (although in differ-ent contexts) between the plasticity of memory, the movement of sepa-rated pages and memory, film as a plastic art, and the power of the plas-tic image suggest the opposite. It could be argued that Freud's theory of screen memories owed much to the influence of modernity's image-making machines: photography (to which Freud specifically refers), the diorama, panorama, flip books, and magic lantern shows, which were so much a part of the everyday entertainment of the period. His theory of screen memories anticipates the power and role of the moving image in the construction and repression of memories. Perhaps Freud might have agreed with Dominique Païni's much-later observation, delivered in her analysis of Hitchcock's use of rear projection: "The screen could be seen as a page on which images are inscribed. In this context, cinema is like an imprint of reality, a flat mould, a bottomless abyss, as Jacques Derrida has said" (69).

In 1899, Freud published a paper on "Screen Memories" which is of particular relevance to an understanding of the role of memory and the *associative* power of the image in horror films. Freud defined screen memories in three contexts. First, screen memories can be those that the adult recalls from earliest childhood, but which are really a cover for memories that have been repressed. Freud argued that "a person's earliest childhood memories seem frequently to have preserved what is indifferent and unimportant." The explanation was that the "indifferent memories" of the child's early years are "substitutes, in [mnemic] repro-duction, for other impressions which are really significant. This process is 'retroactive' or 'retrogressive'." He concluded that

As the indifferent memories of childhood owe their preservation not to their own content but to an associative relation between their content and another which is repressed, they have some claim to be called "screen memories," the name by which I have described them. (1975: 83)

Freud also argued that the "opposite relation" exists and is more frequent:

an indifferent impression of recent date establishes itself in the memory as a screen memory, although it owes that privilege merely to its connection with an earlier experience which resistances prevent from being reproduced directly. These would be screen memories which have been *pushed ahead* or been *displaced forward*. Here the essential thing with which the memory is occupied *precedes* the screen memory in time. (84)

Third, a screen memory is related to the "impression that it screens not only by its content but also by contiguity in time: these are "*contemporary* or *contiguous* screen memories" (84). Screen memories can be retroactive; that is, they originate in the far distant past where they are associated with the essential event. Screen memories can also be displaced forward; situated in the present, they can be based on an event that has taken place long after the essential event which they screen. And screen memories can be contiguous as well. Retroactive, displaced forward, contiguous – in all three instances Freud is describing a relationship between the screen memory and the essential event it covers in the context of a relationship in time. Through the power of editing, film similarly has the ability to move freely from past to present and future.

SCREEN MEMORIES AND THE HORROR FILM

Never did Covent Garden present such a picture of agitation and dismay. Ladies bathed in tears – others fainting – and some shrieking with terror – while such of the audience who were able to avoid such demonstrations as these sat aghast with pale horror painted on their countenances. (Hardy: viii)

The horror film also adopts a process, not unlike that of Freud's screen memories, to maximize its power to disorient and shock the viewer. A

horror film can present a relatively disturbing image (*truly* horrific or
abject images are withheld) that has the power to activate the viewer's
worst fears, and then can screen or protect the viewer from that fear by
offering a more palatable one in its place. The latter images are ones that
would be more acceptable to the culture and the censorship restrictions
of the period. Viewers are encouraged to imagine or conjure up other
horrific images – invoked by the image that has been screened. The
imagined images would not necessarily be identical for each viewer. On
the contrary, the barely tolerable images that are screened are most likely
to uncover, or hint at, other more horrific images and scenes that remain
only partially glimpsed, if at all.

The horror film plays on a range of fears and phobias that have the
power to affect the viewer individually and as part of a group. Freud's
theory of screen memory explains the enormous power that the flickering
images of horror can assume in relation to the spectator and his/her
specific fears and phobias. It should be noted that films which set out to
upset the viewer by a process of direct confrontation are often referred
to as splatter, or schlock. These films do not horrify through a process of
"screening"; their aim is to disgust.

Walter Benjamin observed that modernity was characterized by the
experience of shock. Looking back over the century, we can see that the
history of modernity – played out by the horror film – has been that of
exposing the audience to images which are more shocking than those
of the previous decade; this, in turn, has created in audiences a desire,
perhaps insatiable, to be shocked even more deeply and disturbingly
than on the previous occasion. Shock feeds upon itself, cannibalistically
creating its own dynamic and appetites.

The moral history of the horror film has been marked by a gradual
relaxation of censorship laws over the century that has led – years or
decades later – to the eventual screening of images once considered too
abject for popular consumption. The images screen out or censor other
images, yet it is impossible not to imagine what the latter might have been
when watching a horror film. The slightest suggestion of more horror
beneath the visible horror is exactly what disturbs yet entices viewers.
The displacement and projection of images in time, between past and
future, also works to enhance horror in relation to the unsettling effect
of such movement on the spectator.

In 1929, audiences viewing *Pandora's Box* saw, in a rapid, half-glimpsed
shot, Lulu (Louise Brooks) being knifed by Jack the Ripper (Gustav
Diessl). By 1960, the knife in *Psycho* enters the naked woman's body;

we see her wounds and the blood splattering across her flesh. The entire narrative movement of *Psycho* relies on the process of revelation. As we travel further into the depths (blood swirling down the plug hole, the body sucked into the bog, the body buried in the cemetery, the abject horror lying in wait at the bottom of the cellar), each scene carefully peels back another layer (like Freud's artichoke) to reveal something even more shocking. In *Psycho*, the layers are peeled away to reveal new scenes which shock more than the previous ones. However, the scenes of ultimate horror (matricide, removing the mother's internal organs and entrails, bodily decay) are withheld. Truly horrific images always threaten to exceed the frame: the unspeakable thing lurking off-screen. Kristeva has suggested that "represented horror is the specular par excellence"; that the "specular is fascinating because it bears the trace in the visible, of the aggressivity" of the unsymbolized drive (1979: 44).

The horror film has always demanded an emotional gut response rather than the "detached" approach (the assumption that detachment is possible is itself questionable) stemming from the logical categories and precise formulations of positivism and formalism. A theoretical approach to the horror film based on theories of the unconscious (a murky realm), repression (never successful), abjection (the crossing of borders), and screen memories (a covering over of past anxieties) offers a way into the horror film which best suits its macabre intention and form. If employed with careful consideration, psychoanalytic theory offers a means of exploring fantasy, repression, disruption, excess, slippages, borders – all of those elements that escape a detached, formalistic critical approach (e.g., Tudor 1989; Carroll 1990). Unlike a psychoanalytic critique, a formalist approach is not primarily concerned with the roles played by consciousness, desire, and ideology in the dual acts of representation and interpretation.

THE OPTICAL UNCONSCIOUS

In the photographic camera [man] has created an instrument which retains the fleeting visual impressions ... (Freud 1930: 279)

In his 1931 essay "A Short History of Photography," Walter Benjamin discusses a series of photographs and offers reasons why he finds the photograph so much more compelling as an aesthetic form than painting. He marvels at the way in which a photograph, no matter how carefully the subject has been posed, can capture "the tiny spark of chance, of the here

and now," that moment which Freud described as "the fleeting visual impressions." Benjamin's urge is to "find that imperceptible point at which,
in the immediacy of that long-past moment, the future so persuasively
inserts itself that, looking back, we may rediscover it" (7). Benjamin is
fascinated by the way a photograph can capture an action or facial expression that has taken place "in a fraction of a second." This moment
is not planned or arranged but spontaneous; it may even be disruptive.
"Photography makes aware for the first time the optical unconscious, just
as psychoanalysis discloses the instinctual unconscious" (7).

The concept of the "optical unconscious" points to a visuality which
offers a different and deeper kind of richness and pleasure, one which
belongs to the moment and to chance. With its flickering images, primitive tricks, and images of the everyday, early cinema also possessed the
disruptive quality that Benjamin, drawing on Freud, terms "the optical
unconscious." Rosalind Krauss suggests that Benjamin's concept of "unconscious optics" would have been "simply incomprehensible" (179) to
Freud. I am not so sure. Freud is clear, Krauss argues, that the world of
technology "is not one that could, itself, have an unconscious" (179). Not
even photographic images of mass movement (even if the latter in reality
possessed a "collective unconscious") could be said to possess an optical
unconscious.

My interpretation of Freud's theory of screen memories, and their
relation to the screening of the image in the horror film (a screening
over/censoring of the truly horrific or abject), suggests that the workings
of an optical unconscious are evoked by the workings of the film text,
staged in the flow of the relationship between the images selected and
the images discarded/rejected/repressed. A horror film draws on the
imagination of the viewer to help create its effects while simultaneously
creating a memory bank of images not screened, an optical unconscious.
Images of horror horrify not simply because of what they reveal but also
because of what they do not reveal.

Movement, fluidity, flux – the tempo and pace of modern life was
echoed in the movie camera which, through the speed of projection,
was able to join still images into a flow of images. The optical unconscious refers to those fleeting visual moments in a film text which invite
us to pause and reconsider representation itself – the camera's power
to construct or create a screen memory, open up a gap not previously
comprehended, gesture toward the horror that resides in the shadows
of off-screen space. It is the flickering, unstable nature of such moments
that has assumed such a central place in discussions of modernity. Such

moments seem to destabilize the separation of reality and representation, creating what Margaret Cohen in her discussion of the "everyday genres" of modernity has described as "an epistemological twilight zone" (247).

It might be argued that feminist psychoanalytic film criticism (although not a unified discourse) has played a key role in the development of post-structuralist theory and has paid too much attention to the interpretation of such moments of textual rupture (in terms of gender, ideology, specta-torship in horror) and not enough to the abstract aesthetic play of sounds and images or to the epistemological twilight zone. There is no reason why such approaches should be seen as mutually exclusive. The main problem occurs when other critical approaches (structuralist, formalist, phenomenological) tend toward a neutrality, as if all experiences of hor-ror were genderless, which is incompatible with feminist critical practice. The reason feminist writings on the horror film have drawn on psycho-analytic theory is that it enables a discussion of the text in relation to gender, fantasy, and desire. It encourages a discussion of how meaning is produced in horror in relation to the text, as well as the screen/spectator relationship. Problems arise when psychoanalytic theory is adopted un-critically or when it is employed reductively or in a manner that is too abstract. The existence of such problems, which apply to all theoretical approaches, does not mean the methodology should therefore be re-jected out of hand; it should be utilized more carefully by those of us who believe that interpretation should lead eventually to more fluid, less phallocentric, less colonizing modes of representation.

HANNIBAL LECTER: THE CANNIBAL MONSTER

Dr. Hannibal Lecter, star of three blockbuster horror films – *The Silence of the Lambs* (1991), *Hannibal* (2001), and *Red Dragon* (2002) – owes much to the founder of his profession, Dr. Sigmund Freud. Played to perfection in all three by Anthony Hopkins, his deeds are monstrous yet parodic. They play with the images of horror that are suggested but not represented; in a sense, they play with "nothing." Lecter, the brilliant psy-chiatrist turned cannibal, the sophisticated insidious man of words who eats his own patients, is the postmodern monster *par excellence.* Parallels between Freud and Lecter offer some insights into the nature of Thomas Harris's monster. The aim of this brief discussion is not to engage in a psy-choanalytic reading of *Hannibal,* but to explore some ways in which the ghost of Freud haunts the text of *Hannibal,* just as the ruins of modernity haunt the discourses of psychoanalysis and the cinema. A parallel aim is to suggest that the very existence, the very possibility, of a Dr. Hannibal Lecter might well constitute Freud's worst nightmare.

The monster of *Hannibal* is named after Freud's hero. Freud identified passionately with Hannibal, the famous Semitic conqueror who crossed the Alps and took Rome, "the 'Mother of Cities'" (Jones 1955: 21) In addition, Freud was one of the first psychoanalysts to offer a theory of cannibalism. Freud associated cannibalism, which he linked to the "*oral phase of the organisation of the libido*," with the act of identification, which he regarded as inherently ambivalent. The subject desires to incorporate, to consume, those with whom he identifies. "The cannibal, as we know, has remained at this standpoint: he has a devouring affection for his enemies and only devours people of whom he is fond" (1995: 135).

Freud also joked about the psychoanalyst as cannibal. Apparently, in 1886 Freud was struck by a cartoon in the *Fliegende Blatter* that showed a hungry lion "muttering 'Twelve o'clock and no negro'" (Jones 1953: 166). According to Jones, in the mid-1920s Freud took to seeing his patients at noon and for some time referred to them as "negroes" (1953: 166; 1957: 110). At that time, Freud was also in great discomfort because of the tumor on his soft palette. In the telling of this racist joke, Freud identifies with the hungry lion, but the act of identification transforms him into the role of cannibal, waiting for his patient/food ("food for thought") to arrive. Thomas Harris seems to have known exactly what he was doing when he named his nightmare monster Dr. Hannibal Lecter, gave him the profession of psychiatrist, and turned him into a cannibal with a sense of humor and a persuasive way with words. The significant thing, in the tradition of all great horror films, is that his monster is a deeply sympathetic, and in this case attractive and mesmerizing, figure.

Perhaps Freud's worst nightmare might have been a dream in which he dined at a cannibal feast with Hannibal Lecter, the psychiatrist whose appetite for counter-transference was so insatiable he took to devouring the "other" literally and with the appropriate garnishes. "I ate his liver with some fava beans and a nice Chianti." Freud was fascinated by the cannibal feast in which the sons of the primal horde rebel and devour the father. The twist in *Hannibal* seems to be that the father, so enraged by the century's lack of manners, has returned; Lecter, self-appointed guardian of the Symbolic order (signified by his insistence that codes of civil society, good manners, should always be observed), has taken it upon himself to eat up the unruly, impolite offspring, sending them hurtling back into the semiotic realm.

For a fuller understanding of Hannibal Lecter, we need to go to Freud's writings on the relationship between jokes and the unconscious. Part of Lecter's enormous appeal to audiences is his ability to make jokes, to pun and play with the victim/viewer. To one of his intended victims he says, playfully, "I'm giving serious consideration to eating your wife." Eating is, of course, a metaphor for oral sex – a meaning not lost on *Hannibal*'s audiences. David Thompson suggests that Clarice Starling (Jodie Foster), the heroine of *Silence of the Lambs,* understood perfectly: "The rest of the world dreamed of cannibalism, but Foster's eyes widened with the sudden vision of cunnilingus. No, not even the vision – the sensation" (20). What we are screened from is the image of Lecter and Clarice as a couple, making love, having oral sex. Like Freud, Lecter also takes up a traditionally oedipal position relative to the daughter, Clarice, whom he desires (openly in the novel) and wants to devour in an erotic/sexual manner.

The final sequence of *Hannibal* treats us to a proper cannibal feast. In the gracious manner of *Babette's Feast* (1987), in which dining is symbolic of communion and regeneration, we see the doctor-as-chef dining on the brains of a victim who is still alive, trussed up, and being spoon-fed, with loving attention to detail and etiquette from his cannibal host. Lecter delicately fills the serving spoon from his guest's exposed cranium, whose top he has carefully sawed off. Lecter is literally "picking his brains." The scene, of course, created a censorship controversy. Despite the absence of blood and gore, Hannibal's excessive attention to good manners, and the general tone of camp parody, it was considered too explicit, too nauseating, too abject. There is no attempt to screen the spectator from the shocking images that relate to violence – only the sexual, as discussed above.

Lecter is very much center stage in the sequel – "in the flesh," so to speak. The joke whose humor is based on conflicting interpretations is embodied in Lecter, whose verbal play with metaphors for "eating" also makes him a perfect representative for the cannibalistic practice of critics trying to trap others into "eating their own words." The trademark of the cannibalistic *serial* killer is consumption – of people and the words they utter. Hannibal Lecter straddles the ancient world (by virtue of his name), the modern world (by virtue of his profession), and the postmodern (by virtue of his olfactory jokes). A hybrid, abject figure, he both repels and fascinates.

In the novel, Lecter and Clarice are a couple; she does not balk at the cannibal feast. Unfortunately the film resists the novel's logical ending, retaining Clarice in the role of law enforcer, the heroic woman who refuses to be devoured by Hannibal or his sumptuous lifestyle. While this ending might offer a more "positive" heroine to female viewers, it closes down the possibility of exploring the nature of perverse female desire.

Unlike the modern censor, Freud himself may not have viewed the father/daughter couple as monstrous. A stickler for the bourgeoisie lifestyle, Freud would, most likely, have approved of Lecter's good manners, culinary skills, and meticulous attention to language, enunciation, and jokes. I am not sure, however, if Freud would have similarly endorsed Lecter's efforts to rescue the "dutiful" daughter (professional law enforcer) from the clutches of the FBI; that is, from the civilizing/feminizing ritual of symbolic castration. In contrast to Dr. Freud, Dr. Lecter seems to have a more finely developed grasp of the perverse.

PART FOUR

NEW DIRECTIONS

Doing Things with Theory: From Freud's Worst Nightmare to (Disciplinary) Dreams of Horror's Cultural Value

As a genre, horror has provoked a range of theoretical work from academic audiences, work which seeks to make sense of horror's affective powers. In this essay, I want to resituate the theoretical debates that have circulated around horror. By way of pursuing an "alternative paradigm," I will discuss theoretical work as performative rather than constative. My interest lies not so much in what theories of horror *say* (i.e., whether they are true or false, metaphysical or falsifiable), but rather in what such theories *do*. I borrow this distinction from "speech act" theorist J. L. Austin:

> The constative utterance, under the name, so dear to philosophers, of statement, has the property of being true or false. The performative utterance, by contrast, can never be either: it has its own special job, it is used to perform an action. (13)

Austin accepts that the "Performative–Constative" antithesis is never absolute, and that the purely "constative" can rarely be disengaged from aspects of performativity (16–17). Even from the constative "side of truth and falsehood," Austin concludes, "we feel ourselves driven to think again about the Performative–Constative antithesis" (22).

Theoretical work on horror has typically been addressed through a constative lens. This is unsurprising, because it is the habitual orientation of the truth-seeking theorist; a given theory should be, either scientifically or hermeneutically, more adequate than its rivals and should, thus, refer to a state of affairs outside its own model of these affairs. And yet, even while pursuing a constative or referential view of theoretical work, theorists continue to do things with theory; that is, they continue to perform cultural identities, (de)value objects of study and disciplinary approaches to these objects. Thinking about theories of horror as performative does not mean entirely bracketing off all questions of truth; this would mean accepting the Peformative–Constative antithesis as absolute, something that Austin warns us not to do. It does, however, mean (temporarily) shifting our focus away from the referential claims of different theories.

Performative theorization is the cultural work that theory performs as a persuasive, legitimating, affective, and valorizing form. I do not intend to examine all aspects of performative theorization here. Instead, I will focus on the way that theories of horror bid for horror's increased cultural value. In the next section I will consider several models of theoretical and disciplinary distinction that I will relate to work on horror, demonstrating that issues of disciplinary value and identity are never far from the scene of horror's theorization. I will then focus on the organizing role of concepts of *time* in competing (psychoanalytic and sociological) disciplinary theories of horror. In conclusion, I will draw briefly on the work of Pierre Bourdieu, arguing that theories of horror bid for cultural value in distinct ways according to the different disciplinary norms that they occupy. A "psychoanalytic habitus" (Winter) and a "sociological habitus" (Flanagan), which inform different strands of work on horror, can thus be discerned.

Attempts to analyze theories of horror as performative cannot fully break with the disciplinary norms that they investigate. My work is therefore open to a charge of logical regression. If psychoanalytic or sociological theories of horror can themselves be studied sociologically or psychoanalytically, then any "alternative" view of theory as performative must fail to dislodge the disciplinary norms at work. Quite the reverse, any such approach becomes ensnared in the very disciplinary assumptions and bids for cultural value that it seeks to analyze. I will return to this objection at the end of my discussion.

"FRACTAL DISTINCTIONS"

Andrew Abbott offers an intriguing explanation for the way specific binary oppositions circulate within the social sciences. He suggests that there are a number of oppositions (e.g., quantitative/qualitative) that structure disciplinary fields via a type of "fractal" activity. Such oppositions are fractal because they are repeated at lower (i.e., increasingly situated) levels of "indexicality." This principle of "self-similarity" means that "fractal distinctions" are recurrently nested within one another. Such distinctions are fractal precisely because they repeat within themselves; as you zoom in on one side of a distinction (e.g., "psychoanalysis" from a "sociology/psychoanalysis" distinction) you find that this supposedly singular term breaks down into a version of the same distinction that you started with ("ego psychology/Lacanian psychoanalysis"), and so on (Lacanian "followers"/Lacanian "revisionists"). Each different subdivision (i.e., each self-similarity) introduces a different level of indexicality. Abbott relates these levels to the struggles for distinction that go on *between* schools of thought ("level 1 indexicality," if you like) and *within* schools of thought ("level 2," or "next-level-down indexicality"). However, Abbott himself discusses these ideas specifically in relation to social science:

Synchronically, this means that if we use any one [distinction] . . . to distinguish groups of social scientists, we will then find these groups internally divided by the same distinction. Diachronically . . . [,] fractal distinctions cause a perpetual slippage of the concepts and language of social science. (10)

I will argue that key distinctions that operate within theories of horror can also be analyzed as fractal distinctions. The principle of self-similarity suggests, for example, that the distinction between "psychoanalytic" and "sociological" readings of horror can be replayed at different levels of indexicality. This situation suggests that no substantive opposition between the two approaches is ultimately sustainable; instead, this opposition can only function within a cultural context and at a given moment in theoretical debate in order to mark out the opponents' mutual exclusivity and cultural "distinctiveness." However, constative approaches to theories of horror assume that substantive argument between approaches is the norm.

As Abbott notes, fractal distinctions provide "an extraordinarily powerful element for both offense and defense in academic discourse" (27). They mark out theoretical "differences" while also allowing theoretical similarities to be constructed by changing one's frame of reference or level of indexicality:

Indexicality . . . provides a general means for rejecting any assertion about a fractal dichotomy by changing the frame of reference. For example, it enables one to reduce an opponent's position to a version of one's own simply by changing the frame of reference. (12)

This ability to characterize alternative positions as a version of one's own, this "slipperiness" of fractal distinctions, has the potential to generate "endless misunderstanding and provides a disturbingly powerful tool for non-substantive argument" (13).

Abbott refutes the position that binary oppositions are fixed and referential, and thus that academic work "progresses" via the scientific disproving of rival positions. What is important about fractal distinctions is that they provide cultural maps for theorists and, thus, ways of separating and valuing their cultural identities via theoretical allegiances. On this basis, we might suggest that what is important to sociologists of horror is primarily that they are *not* psychoanalytic theorists of horror; fractal distinctions always possess a relational quality. However, sociological critiques of psychoanalysis that are assumed to secure the "identity" of sociology and sociologist are subject to fractal self-similarity, this problem being repeated within thought that identifies itself as "psychoanalytic." Thus, it is perfectly possible for a leading psychoanalytic scholar, Jean Laplanche, to agree with Andrew Tudor's (1989; 1997 [reprinted this volume]) critiques of psychoanalytic readings:

"What is known as a 'psychoanalytical reading', whose banality we are sick and tired of, is a direct means of repression" (Laplanche: 112) . . . "Psychoanalytical readings" are a means of repression to the extent that they shield the reader from the productive enigma of the text/object/practice by imposing a standardised narrative interpretation: the Oedipal reading, the "depressive position" reading, the real reading. (Osborne: 114–115)

This is one "return of the repressed" argument that critics such as Tudor would heartily endorse! Repression is returned to "psychoanalytic readings" by a psychoanalytic scholar. According to constative models of theory, this makes little sense. However, using the concept of fractal distinction to consider theoretical work as a performative claim to cultural identity and distinction, it can be explained. Laplanche uses a fractal distinction to create new differences *within* a discipline by replaying a distinction already operating across psychoanalysis and sociology.

Randall Collins's work shares a number of points with Abbott's approach. Collins emphasizes that theorists can, at different moments, seek to split apart or reunite disciplinary lines of distinction. "There are two polar types of creativity: the creativity of fractionation as thinkers maximise their distinctiveness, and the creativity of synthesis as intellectuals make alliances among weakening positions . . . " (131). Types of creativity identified by Collins are evident in recent work on horror; Steven Schneider (2000) attempts to bring together "universalizing" and "particularistic" theories of the horror film monster, whereas Janet Staiger proceeds as if psychoanalytic and sociological accounts can be unproblematically used side-by-side. Meanwhile, the position adopted by

Laplanche displays a tendency to "fractionation," marking out the distinctiveness of his work.

This type of approach – the "maximising of distinctiveness" – also plays out fractally, because it allows those defending psychoanalysis to point out that their critics have mistakenly attacked "psychoanalysis" *tout court*, while actually only attacking one school of psychoanalytic thought: "Creed [has] rightly criticis[ed] my own inclination to construe all psychoanalytic perspectives in terms of the repression model" (Tudor, this volume). Where work on the horror film is concerned (Tudor 1989; Carroll 1990; Creed 1993), it seems that David Bordwell's emphasis on a "strategy of exclusion" (1989: 39) is misplaced. Bordwell has suggested that "[t]he history of film criticism is largely that of . . . ships passing in the night . . . more than most of his peers in philosophy or psychology or art history, the academic film interpreter avoids dialectical confrontation with alternative positions" (39) This is far from the case in horror film criticism; theorists expend considerable energy staking out their own terrain.

Although psychoanalytic and sociological critics spend much time addressing one another's concerns, perhaps they are still "ships passing in the night." It seems that no one within this debate is about to be converted; instead, positions are reiterated and defended. And yet academic debate is, one might suppose constatively, a matter of proof, evidence, and rationality. After all, academic debate deals with statement or assertion in which pursuit of the "truth" is the highest moral virtue.[1]

Performatively, however, we need not idealize academic discussion in this way. Starting from Occam's Razor, and acting as a theoretical slasher,[2] it seems that performative investigation is called for where the fractal distinctions of horror theory are concerned. Constative approaches cannot account economically for the interminable nature of theoretical debate, for the problematic status of "evidence" in this debate, or for the fact that seemingly nobody is ever persuaded that their disciplinary approach is inadequate. These mysteries are neglected in work which continues to treat theories as referential, and any account of them usually invokes the "nonfalsifiability" of an opponents' position. This is a typical accusation made against psychoanalytic theories of horror. But the "nonfalsifiability" argument also works against sociological theories; what would it take for a sociologist to accept that their concept of "zeitgeist" had been falsified?[3]

Despite recurrent problems with the notion of falsifiability for all schools of thought in horror theory, sociological critics have continued to imply that psychoanalytic work is distinct from sociology on this basis:

> [T]here is a sense in which all explanation is reductive, at least inasmuch as we try to explain things by mapping them onto a pre-existing framework. But the distinctive feature of psychoanalytic reduction, when applied to cultural artefacts, is that the terms of the explanatory theory are also the terms in which the analyst's interpretative readings are constructed. . . . [T]he approach . . . requires esoteric readings of the texts it seeks to analyze, readings which definitionally could not be part of any audience's conscious interpretative apparatus. (Tudor 1989: 3)

Tudor's argument appears to accept that sociological explanations of horror might be construed as "reductive," but then goes on to create a separation that values sociology and concomitantly devalues psychoanalysis as guilty of excessive reductionism. Tudor's notion of "any audience" must be rhetorical, since it is immediately empirically falsifiable. This is true given that, if we divide cultural experience into two levels – where level 1 is the reception of media texts and level 2 is the theoretical analysis of these same texts – then "the cultural analyst is him- or herself an interpreter of cultural messages at Level 1" (Osborne: 116). But Tudor implies that academic audiences, or audiences composed of psychoanalytic critics (or audience members familiar with a range of tenets of psychoanalysis), cannot exist within "any audience" for horror.[4]

It could be suggested that the widest implication of Tudor's point is that even psychoanalytic critics could not (or should not, according to psychoanalytic logic) have conscious access to the "interpretative apparatus" of psychoanalysis. But this seems logically nonsensical. And even if one argued that the unconscious of a psychoanalytic critic would cause them to interpret horror films in a specific and personalized way, this argument would still be forced to accept that the critic's "esoteric" reading would be mediated through the interpretative apparatus of psychoanalysis.

It could also be argued that Tudor's point was never meant to apply to academic audiences, only to "general" audiences, but, if so, this remains a conceptual separation which cannot be empirically sustainable and, thus, cannot make sense within Tudor's sociological stance. The use of the phrase "any audience" is really the root of all these problems; perhaps Tudor simply exaggerated his point. But polemical exaggeration surely opens up the charge that Tudor is universalizing without warrant rather than being specific, which is exactly what he would accuse psychoanalytic work of doing. . . .

Lied Scottsbluff
Public Library
1809 3rd Avenue
Scottsbluff, NE 69361
Ph: 308-630-6250
www.scottsbluff.org/
departments/library/

User ID: 23193000001384

Item ID: 33193002192486
Title: SCOTTILL/Horror film and
psychoanalysis
Date charged: 6/10/2013,12:57

Date due: 7/7/2013,23:59

Wednesdays and
Saturdays are Fine Free

Furthermore, in what sense do sociohistorical "readings" of horror not replay a situation whereby "the terms of the explanatory theory are also the terms in which the analyst's interpretative readings are constructed"? Reading horror films in terms of a zeitgeist (where this term is likely to be understood by fewer audience members than basic tenets of psychoanalysis, or will at least be understood by a similarly restricted section of educated audience members) accounts for the meaning of horror by constructing an explanatory framework (an enclosed and enclosing "cultural context") which then constructs the terms of the analyst's reading.

It is worth recalling that I am not here defending psychoanalysis against Tudor's critique. My interest lies in emphasizing Tudor's recognition that "all explanation is reductive" and thus pointing out that psychoanalysis and sociology are caught up in similar "substantive" theoretical problems. And this is so despite the fact that psychoanalytic and sociological critics offer insistent and mutual attempts at "non-substantive" argument, constantly implying that the other discipline is subject to distinctive and irresolvable logical problems, whereas the critic's own disciplinary position is performatively valued and exempted from these problems.

In short, Tudor's statement here only makes sense if we view it performatively. It makes little sense if inspected "logically" as a series of statements, but it *is* readily understandable as a performance of "sociological reduction" which acts as a marker of disciplinary affiliation and implies the cultural value of sociology:

[T]actics of sociological reduction are directly analogous to Freud's own strategy of psychological reduction. . . . While neither Durkheim nor Freud directly challenges the others' work, their theoretical reductions are mirror images of each other: sociology reduces psychological explanations to "more scientific" sociological ones, and psychoanalysis reduces sociological explanations to "more basic" psychological ones. These are also both epistemological reductions that function strategically to *constitute the identity* of the discipline rhetorically positioned as dominant. (Winter: 238; emphasis added)

If theories of horror have predominantly operated within disciplinary conflicts, then it is instructive to consider approaches to horror that have failed to fit into this contest of the disciplines. Robin Wood's work immediately suggests itself. Wood (1986) has explored a distinctive approach to horror that combines aspects of psychoanalytic and cultural-ideological perspectives. But, as he himself discusses in the Preface to this volume, his work has been viewed by sociological critics of horror as if it replicates the "faults" of psychoanalysis. Adopting a liminal position in relation to disciplinary norms, Wood's work is doubly damned. Not only is he criticized for being *too* psychoanalytic by sociological theorists, his work is also criticized for being *insufficiently* psychoanalytic by psychoanalytically inclined critics:

I have called attention to the widespread critical misunderstanding that Freud identifies repressed infantile fears and desires as the *sole* source of uncanny feelings. Strictly speaking, the "return of the repressed" formula innocently attributed to Freud by horror film theorist Robin Wood (1979) and subsequently picked up (and run with) by others writing on the genre, constitutes only *one* class of the Freudian uncanny. (Schneider, this volume)

The academic reception of Wood's work on horror demonstrates the dangers that are opened up by the construction of a liminal disciplinary identity. Wood's innovative use of "basic" and "surplus" repression is all too often reframed and recontained within disciplinary reductions. His work is thus subjected to the different "interpretive communities" (Stanley Fish's phrase) of sociological and psychoanalytic theorists.[5]

This indicates that when seeking to transcend the epistemological reductions that are in force, horror theorists need to be self-reflexively aware of the ways in which theoretical liminalities could be broken down into cruder disciplinary components. In any such reduction, we "lose a concept which, however contradictory, goes some way towards indicating a complex and possibly contradictory reality and replace ... it with a fairly simple idea that is clearly inadequate" (Craib: 151). This interpretive process cannot, of course, be stalled purely by the efficacy of textual or constative statements, but it can be proleptically countered and thus built into the "implied reader" constructed by a theorist.

By focusing on the way that psychoanalytic and sociological reductions mirror one another, Sarah Winter's study of the cultural circulation and legitimation of psychoanalysis presents an exemplary emphasis on theory as performative. Winter focuses on the ways in which psychoanalysis has sought to accrue cultural value. She suggests that a number of "institutionalizing strategies" were pursued by Freud, one of which was the use of Greek tragedy as an intertext to lend "universality" to psychoanalytic theory (8). Winter also addresses the use of "applied" psychoanalysis (psychoanalysis as a form of cultural theory), which acts to extend psychoanalysis beyond the status of "profession" and into the realms of disciplinary knowledge rather than professional expertise.[6]

Freud's worst nightmare was perhaps that psychoanalysis itself would perish. In an attempt to secure a wide cultural circulation for psychoanalysis, Freud used strategies of popularization at the same time as attempting to "authorize" psychoanalysis in his own name (Winter: 148–49). Despite Freud's attempts to align psychoanalysis with literary value, such that "[a]mbivalence can only become 'Oedipal' historically when it is codified and endowed with cultural significance through its affiliation with classical education in its function as cultural capital" (47), Winter argues that psychoanalysis never succeeded in absorbing the cultural value of its literary antecedents. She concludes that "psychoanalysis itself still lacks the transcendent cultural value of classical literature and its almost unquestioned capacity to confer legitimacy" (280). Whether or not psychoanalysis has succeeded in devouring the cultural value of classical literature, or appropriating the conventions of gothic fiction,[7] Winter's approach can tell us something about theories of horror as well as illuminating the cultural career of psychoanalysis. Winter draws attention to the intertextual mechanisms through which cultural value can be transferred from object to object or through which such parasitic transfers of cultural value can be attempted. The transference of cultural value is clearly not a context-neutral exercise; as well as an invoked intertext, the differing (though perhaps not semiotically stable) cultural contexts of text and intertext should also be considered.

We can therefore examine horror theory not simply as a performance of disciplinary affiliation but also as a simultaneous attempt to valorize/revalue horror as an object of study. In the next section, I will argue that it is not only in terms of disciplinary reductions, and shared logical problems, that the sociology and psychoanalysis of horror performatively mirror one another. Both also bid for an increase in horror's cultural value, albeit in rather different (disciplinary) ways.

THE TIMELESS TERRORS OF PSYCHOANALYSIS AND THE TIMELY SPIRITS OF SOCIOLOGY

The importance of this form of criticism [post-structural psychoanalysis; Jancovich cites work by Barbara Creed and Clare Hanson] was, at least in part, that it attempted to take cultural forms such as horror seriously, rather than simply dismissing them as had been the tendency in previous forms of criticism. (Jancovich 1992: 11)

Mark Jancovich, despite his opposition to psychoanalytic theories of horror, recognizes in passing that these approaches do something *to*

horror. As an instance of performative theorization, psychoanalytic work
(re)positions horror as culturally significant and valued. Just as psychoanalysis avoided Freud's worst nightmare by drawing on intertexts that
could sustain its bid for cultural value, then so too do theories of horror draw on psychoanalysis as an intertext aimed at bolstering horror's
cultural value.

Against this view, Tudor – perhaps prioritizing disciplinary value and
cultural identity above his object of study – has suggested that "psychoanalytic theories of horror gain credibility from the widespread belief that
horror fans are a peculiar bunch who share a perverse predilection" (this
volume). This argument links psychoanalysis to devaluations of horror
and its fans, implying that its deployment supports a wider cultural view
of horror's disreputable and "low cultural" nature. However, it seems to
me that Jancovich's basic point is rather more convincing, especially if –
unlike Tudor – one stops to empirically consider the range of intertexts
that are invoked in psychoanalytic work on horror:

Barbara Creed has long passages in her [1990a] article on Sigmund Freud,
Egyptian art, Elaine Showalter and Julia Kristeva, while also including references to Jacques Lacan and Greek tragedy.... [T]hese other writings are
crucial to the ... critical perspective." (Klevan: 160)

Greek tragedy appears once again, reactivating those points raised by
Winter in relation to the intertexts used by psychoanalyis. This illustrates
a kind of supersession in bids for cultural value. Having already fought
disciplinary and institutionalizing battles, and circulating across a wide
range of cultural sites (Winter: 279–80), psychoanalysis may not possess
the "transcendent" cultural value of classical literature, but it nevertheless
possesses multiple forms of cultural authority. It can thus be used itself
(alongside the original intertexts through which it secured respectabil-
ity) to intertextually validate horror. This is one of the functions of intertextuality recently discussed by Janet Staiger: "Intertextuality ... permits
scholars to align texts with other texts for the purposes of praising them
as art or denigrating them as trash" (186).

Creed's intertextual use of Freud, Kristeva, Lacan, Egyptian art, and
Greek tragedy would not seem to support the latter strategy. Horror is
"praised" and positioned as artistic.[8] Creed's use of Kristeva's work is particularly notable in this respect, given that Kristeva's *Powers of Horror*, despite its title, is not concerned with the horror genre but deals instead with
"[g]reat modern literature ... Dostoyevsky, Lautreamont, Proust, Artaud,
Kafka, Celine" (Kristeva 1982: 18). Creed's appropriation of this work,

and her argument that it illuminates horror as much as it illuminates the collapse of "subject and object" in Proust or Dostoyevsky, is thus a marked intertextual bid for horror's cultural value.

Creed's use of psychoanalysis is premised not on the pathologization of horror fans *per se*, but rather on the claim that horror engages centrally with crucial (and non-pathological) processes of subjectivity set out by psychoanalytic theory: "The horror film also provides a rich source for constructing the settings upon which phantasy is attendant. It continually draws upon the three primal phantasies . . . – birth, seduction, castration – in order to construct its scenarios of horror" (1993: 153). The relationship of "drawing upon" is reversed in this statement, however; Creed's *reading* of horror draws upon psychoanalytic concepts, while *stating that it is the horror text itself that "draws upon" psychoanalytic "primal phantasies."* Constatively, this is undoubtedly open to critique,[9] but its performative reversal of roles indicates very clearly what is at stake for Creed. The horror text under analysis is constructed as indebted to psychoanalysis. This causes the analyst's mediating role to magically disappear, at the same time suggesting that the relationship between popular culture and psychoanalytic theory is rather more direct than it might otherwise appear to be. Such a construction posits popular culture as a reflection of theory and, hence, implies that the cultural value of (psychoanalytic) theory can be transferred directly to the object of study.

The way in which psychoanalytic horror theory bids for horror's cultural value cannot be separated out from the disciplinary norms that structure such work. While defending its own cultural distinctiveness – and its own psychoanalytic reduction – such theory produces horror as culturally valued by positioning it as transhistorical. It is the posited "timelessness" of horror that seeks to raise its cultural value, an affiliation that also makes sense of the constant and concomitant invoking of classical literature and mythology as intertexts, given that these are cultural forms that are more readily (or ideologically) accepted as "timeless."

It is worth noting here that, despite a pronounced opposition to psychoanalytic theories, philosophical approaches to "art-horror" replay a *performative* emphasis on horror's "timelessness": Noël Carroll (1990: 7–8, 10) intertextually invokes Aristotle and the eighteenth-century writers John Aikin and Anna Laetitia Aikin by way of legitimating his "philosophy of horror." This performative bid for horror's cultural value allows Carroll to do something with theory – to elevate horror's cultural status by implying its timelessness – even while constatively arguing against psychoanalysis (168–78). By constructing theoretical debate as a matter of adequacy and detailed argument, Carroll – much like Creed – brackets off consideration of the performative aspects of horror theory. Significantly, this "bracketing off" neglects the fact that both cognitive-aesthetic critics opposed to psychoanalysis *and* champions of psychoanalysis are involved in very similar bids for horror's increased cultural value.

If aesthetic/philosophical and psychoanalytic theories of horror both performatively value horror as timeless, then it must be said that sociological theories do not fit this pattern. The "sociological reduction" commits its practitioners to a disciplinary valorization of the "timeliness" of social agency and structure. As the mirror image of "psychoanalytic reduction," timelessness is always/already a marker of ideology or falsehood within sociological systems of cultural distinctiveness, identity, and value. This is plain enough when one considers Jonathan Lake Crane's dismissal of Walter Evans's 1984 essay, "Monster Movies: A Sexual Theory": "[W]hat exactly is the rhetorical space and time continuum where 'has ever been the case'?" (26). For Crane, as for other sociohistorical theorists of horror, any description of horror as "timeless" is interpreted as a lack rather than a source of value; timelessness is "ahistorical" (29). In his response to Evans's essay, Crane shifts from a constative to performative approach, but only in order to allege that Evans's work is undeserving of serious (i.e., constative) consideration, being viewed as "rhetorical" rather than as a series of true/false statements.

Although sociological theories of horror are committed to a valorization of historicity rather than timelessness, this is not to say that they do not *also* seek to elevate horror's cultural value. However, this process occurs by linking horror to its zeitgeist, or to crucially significant elements of cultural context: "In all these cases [Tudor, Carroll, Dika, Jancovich] . . . the appeal of particular features of the genre is understood in relation to specified aspects of their socio-historical context" (Tudor 1997: 445). As Crane puts it, by relying on psychoanalytic models, critics "dismiss, all too hastily, the possibility that horror films have something to say about popular epistemology" (29).

Sociological horror theory bids for horror's cultural value in its own disciplinary form. Here, horror is culturally valued because it fantastically encodes the social knowledge circulating at a given moment. This is a theoretical account that focuses on the cognitive and symbolic dimensions of horror, attempting to rescue it as a cultural form by downplaying its affective, "gut-level" aspects. It is a performative bid for horror's cultural value that is shared – again across lines of constative debate and disagreement – with some cognitivist theorists (see, e.g., Freeland 1999a: 274–75).

CONCLUSION

Viewing disciplinary approaches performatively demonstrates that specific objectives, for instance the cultural valorization of horror, cut across disciplinary debates in horror theory. Might it then be possible to construct *subject-led coalitions* across interpretive communities rather than remaining within *discipline-led oppositions*? By subject-led coalitions I mean something slightly different from the "synthetic" arguments presented by Staiger (2000) and Schneider (2000). Creatively synthetic positions typically present their hybridization of psychoanalysis and sociology as a matter of adequacy to "the truth." They thereby remain staunchly constative rather than self-reflexively performative and focused on disciplinary "reductions." This leaves such work readily open to recontainment within disciplinary interpretive communities. By contrast, the subject-led coalitions I am calling for here would require theorists to self-reflexively acknowledge:

(i) the *common* performative ground that their different disciplinary approaches occupy and
(ii) the *common* extra-disciplinary affects and fandoms that underpin their theoretical valorizations of horror.

Such acknowledgments, I am arguing, would significantly disrupt the disciplinary norms that currently guide work on horror. In fact, it may well be for precisely this reason – their disruptive potential – that performative theorization and the fandom of horror's professors are so infrequently acknowledged in any substantive form.

Placing horror's valorization explicitly on the theoretical agenda, rather than allowing this to function as a tacit, unspoken, and "bracketed off" aspect of horror theorization, may open up an alternative paradigm whereby horror theory is no longer habitually addressed as only constative. As long as theories of horror are addressed as constative, and thereby as statements that are true or false, then the cultural distinctions performed by and through theoretical work remain invisible.

And yet, the situation cannot be as clear as a simple "move" from constative to performative aspects of theory. While shifting out of constative gear, I have shown that psychoanalytic and sociological theories tend to bid for horror's cultural value in line with their disciplinary commitments: what can be *done with* theory is dependent, to an extent, on what can be said or *stated within* theory. It is thus possible to observe a "sociological habitus" (Flanagan: xiii; see also Brubaker) and a "psychoanalytic habitus" (Winter: 276) at work in related theories of horror. The term "habitus" is taken from the work of Pierre Bourdieu, and it indicates a disposition that is both "structuring and structured," being transposable from one area of the subject's experience to another.[10] The habitus indicates the habitual and generative value judgments and discriminations that a subject is liable to make.

A dispositional habitus can be formed in relation to a specific field – e.g., the discipline of sociology or psychoanalysis. The concept provides a way of tracing how the "sociological reduction" and the "psychoanalytic reduction" are used by sociological and psychoanalytic theorists, and how these reductions can be transferred from object of study to object of study, and transferred – as structured and structuring dispositions – from constative discussion to performative theorization. The "sociological habitus" brackets off issues of psychology and the "knowing of the self in terms of sensitivity and availability to a topic [that] ... requires systematic cultivation" (Flanagan: 25). The "psychoanalytic habitus," by contrast, focuses on the individual's interiority and their cultivation of self-knowledge (Winter: 276).

However, falling back on Bourdieu's work to meta-theorize theories of horror runs the risk of reinstating a disciplinary logic, relying on "a sociological critique of sociological reasoning" (Bourdieu 1993: xii). This introduces the problem of logical regression – namely, that attempts to transcend discipline-led approaches to horror nevertheless remain placed within the disciplinary norms that they seek to interrogate. Calling up the notion of the habitus to embody sociological and psychoanalytic reductions has precisely this effect, although one could argue that, even without such a concept, the same problem remains implicit in any attempt to "break" with theory-as-constative.

How, then, can horror as a subject displace theoretical paradigms? – perhaps by reintroducing the possibility, closed down by Tudor, that horror's professors are also horror's fans and audiences. It could be suggested that extra-disciplinary affects underpin each different theoretical reduction/habitus, and that theories of horror are thus not only ways of bidding publicly (but tacitly) for horror's cultural seriousness and cultural value, but are also ways of coding the writer's pretheoretical "love" for horror:

Prefaces to professors' books on horror have ... common refrains, so I'll get straight to those. Yes, I've been an almost lifelong fan of horror – ever since my parents refused to let me see *Psycho*. ... I decided to write in this book only about movies I love. (Freeland 1999a: xiii)

Joan Hawkins has recently studied the cultural value of horror, finding that the usual categories of "high" and "low" horror are confused within "paracinema" fan cultures. Hawkins attributes this confusion of cultural value and hierarchy to the fact that the "operative criteria here is *affect*: the ability of a film to thrill, frighten, gross out, arouse, or otherwise directly engage the spectator's body" (4). By placing the same emphasis on horror's *affective aims* – outside of disciplinary concepts of affect, and in terms of academics' lived experiences of horror texts (biographically both before and after entering the academy) – it may be possible to construct subject-led rather than discipline-led approaches to horror.

Horror's (and horror theory's) intertextualities are not only about valuing or devaluing texts as art or trash; they also simultaneously serve affective functions.[11] But horror's affects remain an embarrassment to horror theorists, even as they offer a focal point for the categorizations of paracinema fans. By "embarrassment," I don't mean to suggest that horror theorists are unwilling to admit their status as horror fans. Indeed, as my quotation of Cynthia Freeland's preface to *The Naked and the Undead* above implies, the "I am a horror fan" acknowledgment is a "common refrain" for horror theorists. My point, more specifically, is that by confining such acknowledgments to prefaces and the like, theorists safely separate out their horror fandom from their disciplinary commitments. Academic work on horror thus appears to be carried out in the shadow of fandom while never being substantially touched or affected by it. This "splitting" causes the extra-disciplinary nature of horror's affects – the fact that psychoanalytic and sociological theorists of horror are themselves *similarly fascinated by horror texts* – to be suppressed. Instead, horror fandom and its extra-disciplinary affects are typically avowed only to be thereafter disavowed and subordinated to disciplinary models of horror's affects and cultural value. And as long as constative and disciplinary approaches to horror theory predominate, then the twin facts that otherwise opposed critics share a project to revalue/valorize horror, as well as sharing an affective engagement with horror, will remain radically underexplored.

One horror theorist who has focused on the interplay of academic theorization and fandom is Mark Jancovich:

I have to be critical of my own work in the field which has frequently criticized other academic accounts of horror on the basis that they do not share the competences and dispositions of the popular audiences by whom horror films are "ordinarily" consumed. This strategy has required me to speak *as* a horror fan rather than *for* the horror fan. But it has also led me to make an implicit distinction between the *real* horror fan, and the usurpation of horror by "inauthentic others" (2000: 30–31).

Jancovich usefully brings fan distinctions self-reflexively into focus within his own academic work. However, this move is legitimated by the fact that Jancovich *theorizes fandom sociologically at the same time* by drawing on the work of Bourdieu. Thus, a self-reflexive move that might appear to disrupt disciplinary norms is, ultimately, played out entirely within disciplinary boundaries. It is this type of interpretive containment, this discipline-led approach, that I have sought to challenge here by calling for a performative focus on horror theory.

Freud's worst nightmare – the cultural demise of psychoanalysis – has not yet come to pass, but disciplinary dreams of horror's cultural value remain alive and well.

NOTES

1. See Collins.
2. See Craib (150–51).
3. Other than a series of competing interpretations of the same cycle of horror films, which might be taken to imply that no singular or fixed "cultural context" can be identified such that films could have been read – actively or otherwise – through this "context."
4. See Wells (21) for a spirited counterargument.
5. This argument should not be taken to imply that *all* sociological theorists of horror will inevitably read Wood's work as excessively "psychoanalytic" and hence reductive. The concept of "interpretive community" allows for dissent and difference across interpretations, but nevertheless indicates that readings will tend to cluster around specific issues and interpretations within a given community. This interpretive clustering is evident when one surveys the responses to Wood's work that have been set out by sociologists of horror such as Tudor (1989: 3), Jancovich (1992: 16), and Dika (57). Carroll (1990: 160) also criticizes Wood by seizing on the phrase "return of the repressed."
6. See Parker on the cultural circulation of "psychoanalytic discourse."
7. See Young.
8. This process need not only occur within the *theoretical* valorization of horror. It can also arise as an internal, textual bid for cultural distinction on the part of specific horror films. Schneider (2003a) discusses what he terms the "*monster as corrupt artist* metaphor" in horror film whereby murder is aestheticized. Several of the films referred to by Schneider, particularly *The Silence of the Lambs* (1991) and *Se7en* (1995), self-consciously articulate the horror genre with "high cultural/art" intertexts. We might well expect academic critics to render such films canonical, a process that I would suggest is already under way (see Staiger 2000; Freeland 1999a; Dyer; Simpson 1999).

9. And just such a critique is offered by Michael Grant in this volume. However, where Grant constatively and critically views Creed's Kristevan arguments as "circular," my own emphasis falls on the performative "reversal" that is embedded in Creed's argument.
10. See Jenkins (74–84).
11. See Staiger (2000: 186).

The Darker Side of Genius: The (Horror) Auteur
Meets Freud's Theory

Once discredited, the auteur theory has come around again. After haunting "the stately castles of film theory and criticism" (Levy 2001: xi) for more than a quarter century, it has been recovered in a number of unlikely contexts – from structuralism to feminism, queer theory, identity politics, and star theory – and is today a major marketing strategy (Saper 2001: 35). With it comes a core of assumptions based in psychoanalysis. But where discussion of film spectatorship has been dominated by Freud and Lacan, discourses surrounding film authorship have shown little interest in psychoanalysis. I will examine the phenomenon of the horror auteur as an exception to this rule. As recognized in recent meta-films – films about the filmmaking process itself – and in popular and academic culture, the horror auteur exposes the theory's psychoanalytic and gothic assumptions, thus interrogating auteurism while lending it levels of mystique.

Reviewer Jan Stuart has stated my first premise, more or less, in a comment about E. Elias Merhige's *Shadow of the Vampire* (2000) having the same non-news "*The Blair Witch Project* had up its threadbare sleeve" – that "there is no greater horror than the making of a horror movie: the terror wrought by an insecure actor, a monomaniacal director, a stalking camera." However, Stuart disparages a cliché I propose to take seriously as an idea and extend to the making of movies in general: that there is something uncanny about whatever drives the "true" auteur. The popularity of this trope suggests how auteurism is thriving and also rather gothic.

The film about the filmmaker has often been a horror movie of sorts, a biography/psychodrama grounded in the filmmaker's existential dread, symptomology, and socio- or psychopathic gaze, underscoring (as in Donald Spoto's definitive biography of Hitchcock [1983/1999]) the "dark side" of his genius. One reason for this "tendency" is an association between art and decadence, monstrousness, madness, and violence that goes back to Romanticism and, as pointed out by Steven Jay Schneider, became widespread as modern and contemporary art came to be associated with "'shock,' transgression and offensiveness, with the violation of standing cultural and conceptual categories . . . and with incongruity" (2003b: 191). More broadly, in the past two decades, an understanding of psychopathic violence as artistic spectacle (and vice versa) has emerged in everything from a public fascination with the forensic reading of serial killers' signatures to Cindy Sherman's blend of splatterpunk, feminism, and postmodern performance art. In film, the association goes back to German Expressionism where, e.g., in *The Cabinet of Dr. Caligari* (1919) and *Nosferatu*, a *mise-en-scène* of elaborate artifice expressed the trauma or insanity of the protagonist or anti-hero (Schneider 2003b: 175). In films such as Michael Powell's *Peeping Tom* (1960), where the serial killer is a sort of deranged performance artist, it is epitomized. And in the psychotically self-reflexive violence of the horror cycles of the 1980s and 1990s (Dario Argento's *gialli*, most of Brian De Palma, Wes Craven's entire post-*Nightmare on Elm Street* [1984] oeuvre, and serial killer films from *Manhunter* [1986] through *The Silence of the Lambs* [1991], *Se7en* [1995], and *The Cell* [2000]), this motif is treated to baroque variations.[1]

The trend I am concerned with represents yet another level of horrific self-awareness. My pretexts are four recent, highly acclaimed, and elaborately packaged independent (or quasi-independent) films about horror directors and the making of their "signature" films: Merhige's *Shadow of the Vampire*, on F. W. Murnau and the making of *Nosferatu* (1922); Bill Condon's *Gods and Monsters* (1998), about James Whale, "father" of the Universal Frankenstein films (1931, 1935); Tim Burton's *Ed Wood* (1994), about the reputedly "worst" director of all time (most notably due to *Plan 9 from Outer Space* [1956]); and Chris Smith's *American Movie* (1999), a documentary about subindependent filmmaker Mark Borchardt and the downsizing of his aspiration – that of making the Great American Movie – to the completion of a $3,000, thirty-five-minute direct-market "thriller" entitled *Coven* (1997). *American Movie*, which won a Sundance Grand Jury Prize and was Facets Choice for Best Picture over the Academy-chosen *American Beauty* (Foley: 76), slyly hints that the Great American Movie is a film about Everyman making a movie, or a cheap horror video, or both. The near-equation is no fluke. These films – each about the "horror auteur" and the making of his (it is usually *his*) signature movie(s) – provide a spectrum of views about horror, auteurism, and the relationships between them. Together they reflect the evolution of auteurism from Andrew Sarris's pantheon to the present and, in so doing, expose the psychoanalytic and gothic discourses underlying it.

While representing several genres – biopic, "making-of" documentary, docudrama, black comedy, queer romance, and horror – these films are all essentially psychodramas that expose the auteur theory's deep structure. They literalize a view of the auteur as overreaching scientist (Murnau), artist (Whale), would-be or anti-artist (Wood, Borchardt), and the making of a signature film as a transgressive act with a pathological origin and subtext. They say in effect that the auteur's signature or "soul" (Sarris 1962: 587) is little more or less than his (again it is usually *his*) trauma, which his films revisit and re-project in cinematic nightmares and monstrous doubles, as the auteur imposes his "vision" on cast and crew. In the reductive logic of stereotypes, the (meta)horror auteur film exposes the Gothic ideologies underlying expressionism, surrealism, and, most recently, postmodern "indie" auteurism, in which the truest auteur is the least "healthy" and sometimes least technically competent – hence the least likely to be co-opted.

"A CERTAIN TENDENCY" AND THE MURDEROUS GAZE: HORROR AND THE AUTEUR

This group of films is part of a more general trend. Where there are countless "Hollywood" films (from *Sunset Boulevard* [1950] to *The Day of the Locust* [1975] and *The Player* [1992]) and fictional autobiographies (e.g., Woody Allen's *Stardust Memories* [1980]), feature-length director biopics are rare. Those that exist tend to be darkly romantic psychodramas or close to it – partly ironic, self-reflexive tales of vision triumphant over "the system" and nature defeated by tragic hubris – or vice versa – e.g., Les Blank's *Burden of Dreams* (1982), Fax Bahr and George Hickenlooper's (and Eleanor Coppola's) *Hearts of Darkness: A Filmmaker's Apocalypse* (1991), and Clint Eastwood's *White Hunter, Black Heart* (1990). Interrogating the pathology of the director's psyche, these films are based on Joseph Conrad's *Heart of Darkness* (1899) and a vision of reality as an act of "overwhelming and collective murder" topped only by the filmmaker's act of chronicling "what we are" (Werner Herzog in *Burden*). They are all but (or all-too-real) horror films themselves.

In this context, let us look at that minor phenomenon of the "horror auteur," by which term I mean the large number of notable recent directors whose films are recognized as employing, throughout a body of work, horror film syntax and themes to express, often self-reflexively and "subversively," their "visions": Michael Almereyda, Dario Argento, Clive Barker, Mario Bava, Tim Burton, John Carpenter, Wes Craven, David Cronenberg, Larry Cohen, Brian DePalma, Abel Ferrara, Larry Fessenden, Jesus Franco, Lucio Fulci, Stuart Gordon, Tobe Hooper, David Lynch, Roman Polanski, Sam Raimi, Jean Rollin, George Romero, and Ken Russell. Ranging from indie exploitation (Romero) to arthouse (Lynch) and international (Argento) to blockbuster (Burton), these directors have used horror discourses consistently to express a "personal" aesthetic (e.g., Burton, Argento, Lynch, Raimi, Carpenter, Jackson) or a sociocultural worldview (e.g., Cohen, Romero, Cronenberg, Barker, Craven).[2] Even so, it is relevant that an additional number of distinguished auteurs (as opposed to horror directors) typically deploy a range of "dark" genres, from dark fantasy to noir and thriller and even animation – e.g., Donald Cammell, Peter Jackson, Neil Jordan, Ulli Lommell, David Lynch, Jan Vankmajer.[3]

I should admit at this point that my argument risks slipping into a tautology – one in which proportionally far too many horror directors are called auteurs and far too many auteurs, on the other hand, demonstrate a proclivity for the horrific. But a brief review of the origins of auteurism brings light to this apparent paradox and suggests that perhaps, in some broad sense, the auteur (theory) is a horror (story).

In their revolt against genteel European cinema and their shared affinity for "B" genres, the *Cahiers* writers reduced cinema to a "pure," non-discursive, non-literary, and inherently masculinist "art of action" (Hillier 1985: 74). In Alfred Hitchcock, they found the "quintessential" auteur (Spoto 1983/1999: 495). As Robert Kapsis (1992) argues, the master of suspense and the auteurists filled each other's needs, with François Truffaut's *Hitchcock* (1967) and Andrew Sarris's *American Cinema* (1968) forming the seminal documents of American auteurism. Evoking "a self-contained world with its own laws and landscapes" (Sarris 1968: 39), Hitchcock fit neatly into Sarris's "pantheon" and subsequently into countless theorizing essays, monographs, and film school courses. Forged out of the "lowest" materials – the thriller, exploitation/horror, and even television – the Hitchcock film lacked social context or content other than a self-implicating exchange of looks between characters, audience, and camera.[4] It helped that Hitchcock's aesthetic equated "the medium of pure cinema" with fear cinema, with the "assembling of pieces of film to create fright" (quoted in *Dial H for Hitchcock* [1999]), just as Poe reduced beauty to vicarious melancholy and terror. Thus the definitive auteur is recognized less readily today for the testamental *Rear Window* (1954) and *Vertigo* (1958) as for the definitive modern horror film, *Psycho* (1960).

Hitchcock's elevation from schlock theater host to auteur exemplary in turn gave the horror film a pedigree as, throughout the 1980s, stalker films took shelter under the master's aegis by calling themselves "suspense thrillers" (Kapsis: 158–216). The mainstreaming of horror and related genres continued as the first generation of film-school-educated (and therefore self-consciously auteurist) directors, many of whom apprenticed under Roger Corman and the horror/exploitation industry of the early 1960s, emerged at the head of the 1970s New Hollywood cinema, in which aestheticized violence became a kind of group signature.[5]

Outside of Kapsis's study, these links between auteurism and horror have gone nearly unnoticed. One reason is that until recently film authorship was rarely discussed outside of who or what had creative control – the individual or the collaboration, the "artist" or the conditions of Hollywood commodity production.[6] After Barthes pronounced the death of the author, discussion of auteurism was diverted into the more legitimate channels of spectatorship and ideological theory, what Craig Saper terms "neo-auteurism," making the auteur "a marker for sociopolitical processes and structures" (35).[7] As consciously practiced by the New Hollywood directors, it flourished as a myth of creative autonomy and as a marketing strategy leading to today's auteur superstar (Corrigan) – to whose state everyone from producer and cinematographer to star actor aspires. In an era of director's cuts, "special" and "collector's" editions (with director's commentaries, outtakes, and scene dissections), widespread university-level film education, and the Independent Film and Sundance channels and websites, our culture now mass produces auteurs. A "rare instance of a critical mode that has totally reorganized the public imagination" (Braddock and Hock 2000b: 7), the auteur theory is now a "necessary fiction," says Thomas Elsaesser, "for the name of a pleasure that seems to have no substitute in the sobered-up deconstructions of the authorless voice of ideology" (11). To refer to this seemingly ineradicable desire *for* the auteur, Dana Polan proposes the term "auteur desire." Repression, it seems, has made the collective heart grow fonder. From whence came this auteur desire? Thanks to *la politique des auteurs*, Andrew Sarris, and Freud's well-known fascination with creativity, we don't have to dig far.

"AUTEUR DESIRE" AND THE PSYCHOPATHOLOGY OF GENIUS

Nouvelle vague auteurism was a young, romantic concoction of impressionism, existentialism, and surrealism (Ray: 62–66). Identifying creativity with access to the unconscious, surrealism suggested that the "truest" auteur was often the "darkest" auteur. But when introduced to Americans by Sarris, the auteur theory became a blend of André Bazin and simplified or "Hollywood" Freud: it unearthed "inner meaning" via "certain recurrent characteristics of style, which serve as [the auteur's] signature" (Sarris 1968/1996: 586) that Sarris eventually called "subtext." Interpretation of representative works replicated the analysis Freud performed on patients' dreams, recovering the deep structure of the director's psyche by "reading" films for themes – indicating condensations and displacements symptomatic of latent wishes and complexes. A pop-Freudian case whose neurotic symptoms were sublimated through craft into art, Sarris's auteur contested the prefabricated productions of the *metteur-en-scene*.[8]

Auteur theory allowed the auteurist to experience the film through the intimate level of subtext, where the originating impulse, the authorial dream, was located. Indeed, what Polan calls "auteur desire" makes too-perfect sense in terms of Freud's suggestion that all of us dream and project fantasies. We desire the auteur (theory) because we fancy ourselves the authors of our very own home movies – our personal worlds of gods and monsters.

Underpinning popular auteurism are Freud's statements about creative writing, which reduced art to symptom, sublimation, and (therefore) psychodrama. In "The Paths to the Formation of Symptoms," Freud defines the creative personality as a case of arrested development, an introvert "oppressed by excessively powerful instinctual needs" (1917c: 376). In "Creative Writers and Day-Dreaming," his subject is the similarity between creative writers, daydreamers, and "victims of nervous illness . . . obliged to tell their phantasies . . . to the doctor by whom they expect to be cured by mental treatment" (1908: 146). Yet art was also the introvert's path "back to reality": winning admiration and creating something permanent, he "achieve[d] through his phantasy what originally he had achieved only *in* his phantasy" (1917c: 377). In turning his fantasies into sites for identification and vicarious experience, the artist enabled others to bring repressions to the surface and could be therapeutic, Freud deduced after Aristotle (1917c: 376). His function was much like that of Freud himself, whose talking cure provoked neurotics to reconnect with their repressed past, releasing them from its grip.

Freud finally identified with the creative writer in many ways, using the latter's methods in the case histories and throughout his self-analysis. He increasingly found literary examples (such as Oedipus and the Sandman) to corroborate his clinical findings and insisted on using them despite their threat to his work's status as science (Marcus; Trosman: 70–88). As early as May 1897, he was interested in the link between displacement, projection, and creative writing. At that time, Harry Trosman notes, he referred to how Goethe, writing *The Sorrows of Young Werther*, displaced onto his hero the suicide he had contemplated for himself, creating a "hedge against suicidal wishes" and adding to the novel's power (70–72). "Shakespeare was right in his juxtaposition of poetry and madness (the fine frenzy)," Freud concluded (1954: 208).

Yet in so pathologizing the creative process, Freud inadvertently paid it his highest compliment. In "Creative Writers and Day-dreaming," he showed a keen interest in the self-analysis of the modern "psychological" novel (e.g., Zola) in which the author (not unlike the analyst) "sits inside his [the hero's] mind . . . and looks at the other characters from outside"

in a fantasy of omnipotent voyeurism, able to split up his ego, by self-observation, into many part-egos, and, in consequence, to personify the conflicting currents of his own mental life in several heroes. Certain novels . . . stand in quite special contrast to the type of the day-dream. In these, the . . . hero plays only a very small active part; he sees the actions and sufferings of other people pass before him like a spectator. (1908: 151)

In becoming conscious of its own processes, Freud *almost* says, the modern novel mimicked the analyst's consciousness of consciousness and exposed the narcissism inherent in the meta-fictional – or the meta-cinematic.

Similarly, and particularly in our post-Lacanian era, "The 'Uncanny'," Freud's 1919 reading of E.T.A. Hoffmann's story "The Sand-man" as a case of castration anxiety, seems to be about scopophilia and the doubling that is the product of the gaze. Nathaniel, the protagonist, slips into a surreal space signified by doubles and optical instruments: spectacles, illusions, blindness, unseeing eyes, and "living dolls" or automatons. Caught looking, he discovers doubles of his act of looking and is punished, in one final sight of Coppelius, with death. Seeing and incorporating knowledge is here *identified* with the process that produces the uncanny, deadly double. Moreover, Hoffman, Freud tells us, "intend[ed] to make us, too, look through the demon optician's spectacles or spy-glass – perhaps, indeed, that the author in his very own person once peered through such an instrument. For . . . Coppola the optician really is the lawyer Coppelius and also, therefore, the Sand-man" (1919b: 230). To-day, as Polan's catchphrase suggests, we desire and fear the auteur, much as Nathaniel desires and fears Coppelius's visual technology, for its power to plunge us into the postmodern fantastic where we can be overwhelmed with doubles. The horror-auteur film also represents our desire to *be* the Sandman.

As an auteurist's fantasy, the horror auteur meta-film is a similar wish fulfillment and nightmare. It depicts the auteur as a conflicted mind that turns a powerful, forbidden, or frightening idea into a fantasy (per Otto Rank), projects the early oral-aggressive instincts and/or death drive on a monstrous effigy or double (per Melanie Klein), which stands for the film as a world with laws of his own making. The spectator or auteurist, moreover, is invited to share this auteurial gaze; s/he identifies with the auteur's pleasure in observing himself doubling the self in his "world of gods and monsters," even while analyzing that pleasure's pathology.

The horror auteur film portrays the pleasurable act of doubling oneself through fantasy as forbidden and uncanny, as in the Promethean myth. In realizing his vision – or "soul" – the auteur creates an illusionary integrated and permanent image that repels the threat of annihilation, only to have the doppelgänger return, as in Freud and Rank, a "harbinger of death," as the *un*dead. Cinephilia becomes necrophilia. In each of these films, auteur desire is identified with a star actor or "monster": in *Shadow of the Vampire*, Schreck/Orlok/Nosferatu; in *Gods and Monsters*, Clay Boone/the Frankenstein monster; in *Ed Wood*, the wraithlike Bela Lugosi; in *American Movie*, Mark Borchardt. Ultimately the undead doppelgänger is identified with cinema itself. These four films reflect the evolution of auteurism from Sarris's pantheon on down to the post-Tarrantino era and the "end of cinema." In the process, they expose the psychoanalytic/gothic ideologies (the two inseparable) that are the theory's intellectual baggage, historicize them, and deconstruct the auteur.

FILM THEORY'S WORST NIGHTMARE: THE HORROR AUTEUR FILM

Shadow of the Vampire: *Post-Lacanian Snuff*

A "deconstruction of the mythology surrounding [Wilhelm Friedrich Murnau] and the making of *Nosferatu*," according to director E. Elias Merhige ("Interview" 2000), *Shadow of the Vampire* exposes the auteur's "murderous" gaze. The film's Murnau (John Malkovich) is an auteur in the Grand Romantic sense, the Promethean "maker" of the new century, and a Faust who has made a pact with the Devil himself. Set in the Weimar period, the film prefigures World War II, noting German Expressionism's links to Nazi-style documentary and the war machine. Playing out an analogy between weaponry, science, filmmaking, and progress, the film's production design and iconography explore the sinister implications of Murnau's genius, which turned the "pestilence of World War I into an effigy" ("Interview" 2000). In the opening title sequence, the camera penetrates the labial layers of the center design on an Art-Deco frieze to reveal, in a survey of Modernist art styles, battle scenes from the Greeks to Dracula's armies to Murnau's present, indicating the march of technological change. This motif is linked with the cinematic territorialism of the opening shot – an extreme close-up of a lens cuts to Murnau's eye, followed by contrasting low- and high-angle shots, one of the "Great Murnau" on high and another from his point of view as he directs *Nosferatu*'s opening scene. Another low angle displays the filmmakers (in white lab coats and goggles) lined on a platform high above the actors, a "pantheon" of demi-gods. Addressed as "Herr Doktor," Murnau dictates what his actors are doing and feeling, stentoriously imposing his "vision" on the proceedings.

In Merhige's film, Murnau's Expressionistic naturalism, associated through hindsight with film-as-technology, German nationalist ideology, and two world wars, becomes Gothic and oppressive. Over the roar of the train into Czechoslovakia, Murnau's voiceover proclaims that "we are scientists in search of memory . . . that will neither blur nor fade." He coerces peasants at a country inn into acting as unpaid extras, yet removes their crucifixes when they "overwhelm" his composition and screams at an unplanned intrusion. He forges a route into territory untouched by technology and unearths "Schreck," a real vampire, to be his star.

Schreck, Murnau's double as method actor as vampire, demonstrates an auteur's instincts and competes for control of the shoot, viewing dailies, demanding make-up and relocations, and consuming "dispensable" crew members. His final consummation of the leading lady is followed by Murnau's camera, which thus out-consumes Schreck. In so doing, Murnau, the Pantheon auteur that he represents, and also, by implication, Merhige, are all linked through Schreck to basic oral–sadistic–territorial drives. The film, moreover, demonstrates how these are sublimated through cinema technology and in turn projected via the shoot. In a pivotal scene, Schreck/Orlok tinkers with the projector and discovers the cinema's undead world for himself: he stares in fascination at the shadow of his hand, extending and retracting his talons in the light, and gazes, for the first time in centuries, at the flickering image of the sunrise. The image is repeated in the final sequence, which duplicates the real Murnau's signature as the shadow of Schreck/Orlok's hand grasps and snuffs out Greta's (Catherine McCormack) beating heart. The vampire's signature simultaneously carries out the (murderous) vision of the historical Murnau, the character Murnau (Malkovich) as a caricature of the Pantheon auteur, and Merhige himself.

The vampire's lethal/auteurial desire, as Schreck explains it, originates in pre-Oedipal separation, loss, and projection. The producer and writer, drinking into the night, query him about how he became a vampire. "It vas vooman," he grunts, telling the Ur-story of his separation from the archaic Mother. Driven by his memory of loss, he attempted to recover her by projecting his desire in undead fetish images – the same desire as the courtly lover, the painter, the auteur. Unable to reproduce (as paternity is indicated through name only), he created language, art, and culture. Thus the artist's/auteur's vision Schreck reduces to a Lacanian–Freudian formula that refers back through the history of psychoanalytic theory, to desire/bloodlust (or primitive drives), thereby vindicating Mulvey's theory of the "male gaze."

By the conclusion, we have flashed back (or forward?) to *Psycho, Peeping Tom*, the slasher film, and the snuff film, whose distinction is its incorporation of the life and death it also represents. Schreck/Orlok is lured into feeding on the drugged, then dying, Greta, and dozes satiated until dawn when, rising stuporously under the inpouring light, he incinerates in an image of celluloid dissolving under a heat lamp. The auteur's "soul" is revealed as his drive empowered by the technologies of vision, which Schreck's method-style vamping acts out. In the final scene, Murnau is sociopathically one with his camera as it upstages and consumes the vampire, its lens glowing preternaturally to suggest cinema's absorption of the history and monstrosity of its desire. The final shot repeats the first, as Murnau looks through the lens, then lines up the camera with the endboard: "There. I think we have it." With a camp-sinister flourish, Merhige imposes his signature upon the real Murnau's incorporation of Bram Stoker's novel *Dracula* (1897) via Dafoe's virtuoso performance (as Tithonus doomed to a decrepit immortality, eternal life without eternal youth; as Dracula, the now servantless prince; as the decline and fall of empires). Ultimately, perhaps, the film sends up Merhige's own late-postmodern, postmillennial gesture.

Gods and Monsters *and Classical Auteurism*

Gods and Monsters uses the same concept of projection but to opposite purposes – to remythologize Hollywood, cinema, horror, and James Whale.

Based on Christopher Bram's 1994 novel *Father of Frankenstein,* which hypothesizes about Whale's final days some fifteen years after his last film, James Whale (Ian McKellen) goes on directing, transforming those closest to him into projections of his personal nightmares, turning their lives into the performance that will be his life's final picture. Thus *Gods and Monsters* is projected expressionistically "from the inside out" (Condon). The poster reinforced this perspective, showing McKellen's blue gaze piercing a film strip containing inserts of Hannah, Boone, and Whale.

1930s Hollywood provided Whale, who grew up a "freak of nature" in an English factory town, with a medium for remaking himself, and he polished off the picture with a set of elegant mannerisms and a fake biography. Hollywood was also a safe space for homosexuals, where Whale would project, as did Ed Wood later, "complex aspects of his sexuality and his relation to class into [his] films" (Wells: 46). *Gods and Monsters* is about how these have been absorbed into the *Frankenstein* films and our collective consciousness. As in *Shadow of the Vampire,* directors (gods) and monsters exchange roles in a story of a queer couple, an uneasy friendship between Whale and his new gardener, Clay Boone (Brendan Fraser), an angry washout ex-Marine, the embodiment of Frankenstein's monster. Boone's uncanny resemblance triggers associations from the pictures that imprinted Shelley's monster on popular imagination.

The film begins as, after a stroke, Whale undergoes a delayed form of shell shock, a psychic fragmentation that leads to reintegration. Plagued by an electrical storm of images shut off by years of disavowal, he is forced to revisit his memories of World War I, particularly his feeling for a young soldier who was shot down and left hanging on the wire demarking no-man's land, decomposing into an effigy of desire, grief, and horror – and finally a grotesque joke. With Boone and Whale we see how these trauma memories condensed into the *Frankenstein* film settings, images, and themes: the stark, "telephone pole" forest through which the terrorized monster escapes, the expressionistic cemetery landscape, the body in pieces.

As the Murnau and Whale films tell us, the Great War – the first in which thousands of mutilated men survived – was the backdrop for German Expressionism and the Universal horror cycle, and the monster embodies Whale's interior scars. His darkest films, he explains to Boone, were "comedies about death" that used humor as a coping mechanism. "The real monsters are here," he concludes, referring to emotional and physical trauma. In contrast to Murnau, who seeks immortality through the "science" of cinema, Whale disvalues the "art" of horror/filmmaking even as he directs his own death – casting Clay Boone as a enraged homophobe whom he plans to seduce into killing him ("clay" suggesting the *golem*-derived Frankenstein monster, Whale's death wish, and his all-too-human flesh). Like Goethe in Freud's 1897 reading, he creates a double that functions simultaneously as a death wish and as a "hedge against suicidal wishes." But Boone recognizes the plot and refuses this role at the crucial moment – sobbing "I am not your monster!" – thus forcing Whale to take responsibility for his life and death. Before drowning himself like the real Whale, in his swimming pool, he acknowledges his hideous progeny – his monsters/his movies/his life devoted to making movies, this including, in some sense, the man he has made of Clay – and sends them on their way, having empowered them to authorize themselves.

Earlier, Whale surprises himself with a confession that "[m]aking movies . . . was the most wonderful thing in the world." And in *Gods and Monsters*, the horror film, as our collective nightmare, can be a humanizing experience. As Bruce Kawin explains, a "good" horror film "takes you down into the depths and shows you . . . the landscape" of the unconscious: "it might be compared to Charon, and the horror experience to a visit to the land of the dead. . . . The seeker . . . confronts his or her own fallibility, vulnerability, and culpability as an aspect of confronting the horror object, and either matures or dies" (309–10).

Through the flashbacks to the war atrocities, the trench/mass grave, and the *Frankenstein* films, Condon segues between memory, filmmaking, and the present, between personal and collective, Freudian and Jungian perspectives, to speak about the way "authored" films communicate to spectators. Three dream sequences explore connections between the psychic processes of the auteur's "vision" and the psychic processes of spectatorship. The blue-filtered sequence that opens and closes the film shows Boone silhouetted as Boris Karloff leading Whale across a blasted landscape to a deep trench. In the concluding sequence, Boone directs Whale to look down where former comrades sleep in death. Finding his lover, Whale lies down next to him. This sequence connects with a wishful dream of Boone as Frankenstein removing Whale's damaged brain and replacing it with a new one. Referring to how Boone "opens" Whale's mind to trauma memories, the sequence also prefigures his archetypal role as Charon-like deliverer. In the end, Condon's, Bram's, and McKellen's auteur is an unlikely ideal father – giver of life, identity, and "war stories" – to an inarticulate Boone, veteran of a private battle with his father. Auteurism is associated with Frankenstein's "unnatural" paternity in all its transgressive and transcendent possibilities. If Whale projects his desires – for youth, sex, intimacy, and death – onto his surrogate monster (as he has projected them in his films), Boone learns that everyone has war stories to tell (movies to make).

Through the common language of *Bride of Frankenstein* (1935), which *Gods and Monsters* makes its primary intertext through embedded scenes, reenactments, and fantasy sequences, we see (as Whale sees) where his "vision" came from and its value to succeeding generations. The auteur achieves immortality by giving his vision over to spectators (via Jung, reception theory, and postmodernism) and lending the film diverse sub-texts, moods, and audiences. In the middle of *Gods and Monsters*, the major characters screen the film on television, each finding something different: camp humor for Betty (Lolita Davidovich); "terrible" horror mitigated by poetic justice for Whale's prune-faced housekeeper Hanna (Lynn Redgrave); a queer romance with a message – "We belong dead" – for a ruefully smiling Whale. Thus perspective gradually shifts to the spectator as author of the film. This shift becomes overt in the epilogue, where Boone (smoking Whale's trademark cigar) and his young son watch the scene between Karloff and the blind hermit, marking the son's (and that generation's) initiation into the mysteries of monstrosity, male bonding, and auteur desire. In the film's eloquent final images, where, silhouetted in the slanting rain, he shambles and lurches into the blue darkness, Boone has assumed the mantle of the monster archetype.

Ed Wood, Identity Politics, and the Anti-Auteur

Preceded by studies by Vito Russell (1981) and Harry Benshoff (1997), *Gods and Monsters* also reflects horror auteurism's historical intersections with queer theory and identity politics. Mary Russo traces the latter to the 1960's identification of and with the "'freak',," with the "otherness within the secret self" (1994/2000: 90). Even the middle-class conservative or his wife could "freak out," and "narratives of their rage and mental illnesses were often allegories of conversion to new, better families or communities" (2000: 90).

Tim Burton's *Ed Wood* is such an allegory: a buddy film (the story of Eddie and Bela) and an alternative family romance. Rather than recovering traumas (he rather fondly recalls his mother dressing him as a girl and his single war story – of parachuting with pink bra and panties under his fatigues), Wood (Johnny Depp) projects the Oedipal family romance outward, building an alternative family Warhol Factory-style. Burton celebrates and identifies with Wood's auteurism as postmodern identity politics, much as Wood celebrated freakishness through his entourage. Wood's films are motley masterpieces in making do. Far from the pantheon director's control over materials, resulting in the projection of a self-contained world (Routt), he "found" his "vision" in his cast's monstrous, incontrovertibly self-authored acts – Bunny Breckenridge, the Great Criswell, Tor Johnson, Vampira, Lugosi. In *Bride of the Monster* (1955), we watch "the great ham," Wood's double, Lugosi, alchemize Wood's gibberish "into something genuinely eerie" (Travers) – into something personal: "Home. I have no home. Hunted . . . despised . . . living like an animal – the jungle is my home! But I will show the world that I can be its master. I shall perfect my own race of people – a race of atomic supermen that will conquer the world!"

Wood is the auteur as child. He enjoys his drives, exercising – as opposed to exorcising – his inner demons. Projecting his "vision" simply means acting out his/her desired ("real") selves. For Burton's Wood, the monsters are "here" in a completely reversed sense than for Condon's Whale. Far from repressed, condensed, and sublimated, they are flamboyantly confessed – in *Glen or Glenda* (aka *I Led 2 Lives*; *I Changed My Sex*, 1953), in which he acts out his angora fetish, and even more joyously performed in the sci-fi/horror extravaganzas *Bride of the Monster* and *Plan 9 from Outer Space*. *Ed Wood* is psychodrama projected outward and shared in the spirit of Carnival.

Where *Shadow of the Vampire* and *Gods and Monsters* lent the auteur a dark mystique, *Wood* both validates and makes nonsense of the classic theory and the Freudian hypothesis that underlies it. When there is no repression, the auteur's subtext becomes text, craft becomes straightforward or irrelevant, and anyone with a desire or a trauma and a camera is potentially an auteur. For Burton's Eddie, "genius isn't the point. Vision is, along with a gusto to communicate that seems to have vanished in the age of merchandising" (Morris). Indeed, even for Sarris in 1962, genius – as technique – wasn't the point. "Buñuel was an auteur even before he had assembled . . . technique," which is "simply the ability to put a film together with some clarity and coherence," Sarris notes, adding that an "expert production crew could probably cover up for a chimpanzee in the director's chair" (587).

For the Ed Wood cult, the least "competent" auteur is the least compromised, reducing classical auteurism to hash. Andrew Hultkrans notes how a "tongue-in-cheek" film theorist might argue "that Wood was a true surrealist (in his ability to deliver the . . . unconscious to the screen with a directness that an intellectual like Louis Buñuel could never manage)."

And so, in Burton's daydream, Orson Welles and Ed Wood haunt the same Hollywood bar. In this context, Freud tells us what we knew already: that horror auteurs are "purer" auteurs whose nightmares emerge nearly uncensored.

Perhaps finally, Wood has become the "punk" auteurist's ideal: the anti-auteur. As the same tongue-in-cheek theorist could argue, "he was a radical-avant-garde filmmaker, unpacking the hidden ideology of film by revealing its apparatus" (Hultkrans). The intentional fallacy, together with a number of reception-oriented and poststructuralist theories, makes moot the issue of whether Wood was incompetent or whether, like Godard, he deliberately placed felicitous incongruities in his films. To his defenders, Wood's films are entertaining and full of life, albeit life given over to them by his audiences. The technical errors, non-special effects, and inept acting are part of his vision, whose naïveté is its essence. Or as Dolores Fuller, Wood's one-time girlfriend and *Glen or Glenda* costar, explains, Eddie has empowered other filmmakers: "People say, 'If he could do it, I could do it'" (*Flying Saucers* 2000). If Wood's anti-auteurism reduced classic auteurism to a joke, it preached a populist auteurism available to anyone. The latter has inspired a "legal" religion – "Woodism" – which finds in the director's films a "vivifying" energy given "to teach us how to live our lives" and practices auteurist exegesis to recover "hidden" truths (Galindo). In Woodism, where everyone lives out his or her desire(s), the repressive hypothesis has become self-expressive utopia.

Woodist anti-auteurism, the celebration of "trash" films as "classic outsider art" (Morris), was part of a 1990s neopunk revolt against Hollywood that followed Malcolm McLaren in the fashion of advocating purposely failed products (Saper: 43) and is perhaps epitomized in the celebration/creation of the "artificial auteurism" of Allen Smithee (Saper). This revolt contributed to a general overhauling of auteurism, one that halted the quest for subtexts and attended instead to materials and craft. Far more visible than any of these recent trends, however, are the legendary success stories of Quentin Tarantino and Kevin Smith, giving rise to the self-made auteur.

Psychology Today: American Movie, Trauma Culture,
and the Self-Made Auteur

In the 1990s, independent filmmakers reclaimed auteurism with the twist exploited by *The Blair Witch Project* (1999) that left Hollywood trembling: with the digital era upon us, virtually anyone can become an auteur –

at the very least, of his or her home movies. As Paul Arthur contends, such home-schooled auteurism is the new American Dream. Whereas during the 1940s and 1950s the western embodied our "cherished cultural myths," today "as close as we get is the shimmering belief that every one of us, regardless of race, creed, or creative ability, is destined to make a movie – or at least be endlessly conversant with the intimate details of the moviemaking process." This "postmodern fable," Arthur concludes, is the core of Chris Smith's *American Movie: The Making of Northwestern*, and represents a recent intersection of horror, psychoanalysis, and auteurism.

Northwestern, explains Borchardt, is to be about "a writer drinking in a junkyard and dreaming the American Dream." Locations will include a rural gas station, an abandoned farmhouse (to be transformed into a Halloween haunted house), a deserted drive-in theater, and a cemetery. *Coven* (1997), the short film he actually finishes, is about an alcoholic writer coerced to join a support group that turns out to be, or whom the protagonist hallucinates to be, a (Satanic?) cult. The remarkable thing about this devolution is that neither the setting nor the story changes much. *Northwestern*, *Coven*, and *American Movie* are all so informed by Borchardt's "vision" as to double one another, collapsing into the same Gothic psychodrama of dysfunction, poverty, dreaming, drinking, writing, and attempting to make movies.

American Movie's thirty-two-year-old Borchardt, who has been making films since he was twelve, lives in his mother's basement, has three children, pitches newspapers, and works at a cemetery. His goal, as his latest girlfriend puts it, is to live "the good life": "to be someone that he's not." Indeed, *American Movie*'s subjects lack a language for their subjectivities other than the Horatio Alger story, the discourses of pop psychology, and horror as performance. Bolstering (and dunning) his frail eighty-two-year-old Executive Producer and Uncle Bill, Mark urges: "When you go in the grave . . . , what're you gonna' think about. . . . You gotta' assert yourself, man. You gotta' say 'I am here because . . .'." " 'I am here because . . .'," Bill repeats, trailing off, the point being that neither can finish the sentence. Yet in his film's litany of rusted dreams, "dilapidated duplexes, worn trailer courts," as Borchardt describes them, "You're gonna' see Americans in American dreams and you won't go away depressed, I promise."

The truly dark side of this story is what Mark Seltzer calls "wound culture." Or, as Mark Edmundson has noted, postmodern America is fundamentally Gothic, haunted through the discourses of pop psychology, academic theory, and an iconography of violence that lives out our myths.

We are a "hysterical" culture (Showalter) obsessed with recovering (or projecting) past seductions, abductions, and atrocities to exorcise our sense of violation in a mediated world. In wound culture, Freud is turned inside out; trauma becomes a discourse, whether in the public display of "torn and open bodies" (Seltzer: 1) or through the confession of psychological damage on *Oprah* or *Jerry Springer*. Lacking subjectivity in an information culture that measures success in wealth and celebrity, we seek our "selves" in what pop psychology and sociology identify (and track, through symptoms such as addiction) as our traumas. In displaying them, we achieve signification/healing.

Thus Seltzer argues that serial killers, one product of wound culture, practice a kind of sadistic performance art, "making something of themselves" in the pathology of the public sphere. As Borchardt's disgruntled brother Alex opines, "[Mark] was always talking about becoming a millionaire," but "I always thought he [would be] a serial killer or one of those people who plans someone's death, and unfortunately I sometimes think that might be true," adding, "he's just best suited for work in a factory maybe." Alex has stated two sides of a conundrum in which the mass production of dreams is "murder by numbers."

Therapy, or "the group thing," is much the same. "You know about the group thing, man?" Mark rhetorically asks his catatonic friend (and double) Mike Shank, who endlessly narrates his trauma of overdosing on LSD and vodka and subsequent addiction to addiction support groups. *Coven*, Borchardt's surprisingly evocative *film-a-clef*, takes up the analysis where *American Movie* leaves off: the protagonist, a writer and addict named Mike (Mark), is forced by his one friend to attend a group meeting. As the sessions turn from increasingly strange confessionals into hallucinogenic indoctrination rituals, Mike/Mark ceases writing, turns to drink, "bottoms out," and kills his friend. The film ends as Mike stares vacantly at the screen.

The only true option, as *Coven*'s existence proves, is to become an auteur. Borchardt is the filmmaker-as-Everyman who, lacking identity other than the "burden of the dream" and his failure to achieve it, finds success through confession of trauma (about the confession of trauma) in his films.

Like *Shadow of the Vampire, Gods and Monsters,* and *Ed Wood, Coven* and *American Movie* can be fully understood only in a context that acknowledges the impact of psychoanalysis on classical and contemporary auteurism. In *American Movie* and, in particular, *Coven* (where psychoanalysis is absorbed and reprojected as dark pop psychology), as in films from

M (1931) to *Psycho* to *Hannibal* (2001), psychotherapy has become the
horror, and it haunts the cultural landscape of contemporary life. More-
over, *American Movie* suggests that the drive to make one's movie has become fundamental to the impulse to construct a self. Mark often refers to
an idyllic childhood memory of making super-8 movies in the cemetery:
"At home, your parents were telling you what to do," but "out in the
cemetery with your beer and your movie camera...you are one with
the world and equal with the world. It was a vast work field." The graveyard "is a stage" in some existential sense. Asked about influences, he
quickly names Romero's *Living Dead* trilogy and Hooper's *Texas Chainsaw
Massacre* (1974) for their "gray sky and dead trees and the National Guard
and all," *mise-en-scène*s that make them "real" and "alive" as opposed to
"something dead like a Hollywood film."

Another auteur who haunts *American Movie* is Francis Ford Coppola.
Smith asks Mark's three young children what film their dad had them
watch the previous night. "*Apocalypse Now!*" squeals the boy, about 6. "Did
you like it?" asks Smith. "Uh huh. When he keeps on saying 'The horror'."
"The hooorror!" the girls scream, giggling. "*Who* said that?" asks Smith.
"The guy on *Apocalypse Now!*" the boy shrieks, obviously delighted with
himself.

In today's trauma culture, and as we enter the digital millennium, six-
year-olds understand Brando, Kurtz, and "the horror" (with or without
reading Conrad) – the world is a vast psychodrama, and everyone is an
auteur.

NOTES

1. See Brophy; Black; Simpson (2000); and Schneider (2003b).
2. By auteur, I mean a filmmaker whose body of work demonstrates a
   consistency – to use Wollen's key terms – of "style" or "basic motifs." This
   is manifested, as Steven Jay Schneider, drawing on Thomas Elsaesser, usefully
   puts it, "in both content and form (better: content through form)" and in
   spite of "significant countervailing forces" (2001–02: x).
3. This list does not begin to cover the classics or the earliest horror auteurs
   of silent cinema, Scandinavians Benjamin Christiansen and Carl Dreyer,
   German Expressionism, Universal's Tod Browning and James Whale, or the
   subindie movements of the 1950s and 1960s in which Herschell Gordon Lewis
   and William Castle found their callings, inspiring filmmakers as different as
   George Romero and David Lynch.
4. In the 1970s, through Laura Mulvey's application of Lacan and Freud to
   Hitchcock's signature films, and the subsequent work of Linda Williams,
   Barbara Creed, and Carol Clover, the equation of the camera's oppressive

"male" gaze with the auteur's "vision" became an assumption of psychoanalytic feminism.

5. See Cook (1998); and King. In an influential 1979 essay, Hitchcock critic Robin Wood lent independent horror/exploitation auteurs a trendy political edge. Applying a Marcusean spin on Freud's concept of the "return of the repressed," Wood argued that directors such as Romero, Cohen, and Hooper expressed not mere personal neuroses but the pathological symptoms of Western culture, thereby subverting Hollywood hegemony.

6. See Gaut (1997); Cook (1999); Gerstner; and Staiger (2003). The Smithee collection (Braddock and Hock (2000a)) poses as an homage to the pseudonym legally reserved for directors who wish to disown their mediocre, codirected, or otherwise compromised films. The editors "out" Smithee as a pretext for analyzing the director's *artificial* importance, deconstructing the auteur and announcing a "crisis" in film studies.

7. Saper divides neoauteurism into four types: one, influenced by Peter Wollen and structuralism, emphasized coherence across a series of films; a second, which included feminist criticism, gender and cultural studies, and identity politics, used auteurs as markers when analyzing power politics and social processes; a third was used by Hollywood as a marketing tool for film-literate audiences and festivals; and the fourth marketed the star or celebrity as self-invented auteur (37).

8. On psychoanalysis's influence on Sarris, see Haskell; Lopate (58); and Levy (2001).

Violence and Psychophysiology in Horror Cinema

I

Film studies is, and has been, deeply involved with cultural categories of explanation. Features of cinema, such as the shot/reverse-shot series, are explicated in terms of ideology and the propagation of a socially determined dominant discourse. The viewer's involvement with cinema has also tended to be framed in terms of culturally construed models of psychology, such as psychoanalysis. I refer to psychoanalysis as culturally construed for two reasons. The first involves the conditions of its origin: Freud as a late Romantic philosopher/scientist whose brilliant work is not separable from the parameters of the bourgeois, patriarchal era in which he lived, and whose project was to substitute a new paradigmatic ideal – the self, the psyche – for those previously holding sway in Western culture. Philip Rieff describes this as the replacement of religion, politics, and economics by "psychological man" (356–57).

Psychoanalysis has also operated within the arena of film studies to advance certain large-scale analyses of cinema's cultural impact, viewed in terms of the mobilization of desire within the medium's mass audiences. Since the 1970s, film studies' appropriation of psychoanalysis has been tied to the efforts of film scholars to explain how cinema connects desire (at the level of individual viewers) to ideology (at the level of social discourse). Allied with the ideological study of cinema found in Marxist or feminist approaches, psychoanalysis has provided film scholars with a method for connecting cinema's operations to the individual spectator as well as to social formations. Psychoanalysis has provided the categories that mediate these two levels of analysis and has thereby become a widely used component in psychologically based social analyses of cinema.

However, as I have discussed elsewhere (Prince 1996), the use of psychoanalysis by film studies is an exercise in theoretical speculation that is disconnected from the study of actual viewers. I have called this "the problem of the missing spectator." Note that this situation is unlike the therapeutic context in which a psychoanalyst works, where the life history of an actual person furnishes the object of analysis. The psychoanalytic study of film focuses on features of the medium or of particular films (e.g., horror films) that are said to induce psychic processes, but the analyses never get around to looking at the responses of real viewers. Thus, psychoanalytic film theory amounts to a meta-psychology of the sort that Freud practiced when he shifted his psychological categories onto the large-scale domains of culture and society in such works as *Civilization and Its Discontents* and *Totem and Taboo*.

My goal here is not to offer a critique of psychoanalytic film theory or to advance an alternative to it that would be as totalizing in its sweeping explanatory claims.[1] I would like, instead, to suggest a different approach to the psychology of film viewing than the terms proposed by psychoanalytic film theory and show how it may help us to think about some of the appeals of violence in the horror genre. Rather than making totalizing claims about invariant psychic laws in relation to which cinema necessarily operates, I will be examining dispositional differences among film viewers and the relative impact of certain kinds of film content and style on these dispositions. Cinema is a rich and multifaceted medium, as are its appeals and modes of operation. As such, it is reasonable to examine cinema not just in terms of culture (e.g., the meta-psychology of psychoanalytic film theory) but also in terms of the biology or physiology of viewer response. Cinema scholars in the area of "cognitive psychology" have examined how cinema builds on a viewer's biologically based perceptual processes and habits, and visual perception is not the only area in which biologically based questions might be asked of cinema. They may also be posed with reference to certain aspects of screen violence and the appeals that violent film genres may hold for their viewers. In this essay, I examine such questions with reference to the horror film.

II

Along with westerns, war films, and gangster films, horror is one of the main repositories of screen violence. Each of these genres was implicated in the explosion of a much harder screen violence that occurred in 1967–68 when the last vestiges of the old Production Code were scrapped in favor of a new content ratings system (G-M-R-X). *The Wild Bunch* (western), *The Dirty Dozen* (war), *Bonnie and Clyde* (gangster), and *Night of the Living Dead* (horror) collectively announced the onset of a new era of graphic bloodshed, with greatly expanded boundaries governing what would henceforth be permissible.

But it would be the horror genre, at least in its modern incarnation relative to the pictures of earlier decades, that would become synonymous with a detailed visual attention to the mechanics of violent death and graphic mutilation, to the point where this imagery and the emotional responses it elicits in viewers would become the very style and subject matter of the films. The genre's remarkable resurgence beginning in the 1980s was tied to this investment in graphic violence. The production of horror films climbed dramatically as the decade began, from thirty-five pictures produced in 1979 to 70 in 1980 and 93 in 1981.[2] Many of these pictures were famously violent, e.g., *Dressed to Kill, Friday the 13th, Prom Night* (all 1980), and *Maniac* (1981). Another production boom occurred in 1986–87, peaking at 105 pictures in 1987. By mid-decade, the video market was thriving, and many of these pictures, especially the most violent ones, were low-budget entries that bypassed theatrical release, aiming for the ancillary markets.

The genre's turn to graphic violence in this period was predicated on innovations in special effects make-up and the arrival of a new generation of make-up artists. These included Tom Savini (*Dawn of the Dead* [1978], *Friday the 13th, Maniac*), Rick Baker (*It's Alive* [1973], *Squirm* [1976], *The Funhouse* [1981]), and Rob Bottin (*The Howling* [1980], *Piranha* [1978], *The Thing* [1982]). New make-up tools enabled these artists to picture grievous physical wounds and mutilations in greater, more lurid, and convincing detail than ever before. They employed prosthetic limbs and latex (as a convincing stand-in for human skin) to simulate detailed violence. Limbs were hacked off with a convincing show of bone and gristle, and skin (latex) could be ripped, scored, punctured, and peeled away.

Among the most controversial of the new horror pictures were the slasher films about serial killers slaughtering promiscuous teenagers, films whose production disturbed many observers inside and outside the industry. Bloody horror films were present in big numbers at the international film markets in 1980, and they revolted many distributors and studio sales reps. "All they want is blood pouring off the screen. I question the mental balance of the people making and buying this stuff," noted a Carolco executive (Watkins: 3). The imagery of victims run through meat grinders or dismembered by spikes, axes, chainsaws, or power drills swiftly evoked a critical backlash, and while teenagers continue to be enthusiastic consumers, slasher films have remained controversial and somewhat disreputable cultural artifacts.

Relative to other screen genres, horror was better equipped to explore and exploit these new thresholds for showing graphically detailed mutilation. Violence in the western was always limited and contained by that genre's archaic weaponry and the codes of restraint and reluctance that governed displays of violence. In war films, narratives of heroism and sacrifice recuperate the genre's violence, and in gangster films it is absorbed into the terms of a large-scale social critique. These other genres sublimate their violence into larger moral, cultural, and narrative frameworks. By contrast, graphic violence is a more central preoccupation of contemporary horror. It is a necessary component in the genre's appeal for viewers and an essential means of inducing the intense emotional experiences that viewers seek from contemporary horror. I will have more to say about these emotional experiences momentarily. Here I wish merely to emphasize something that is fairly obvious, that the representation of graphic violence is a normative feature of contemporary horror and that the genre's fans are drawn to the films for their transgressive power, their ability to visualize wounding and violent death in novel and imaginative ways.

Violence within a context of fright and terror has not always been so central to the genre, as a look at the relatively genteel productions of earlier decades demonstrates. Accompanying the escalation of violence has been a shift in the nature of the form's fright-inducing elements. One could write a stylistic history of the genre focusing on changes in the distribution of fright elements in horror films, and it would reveal a striking shift. In what follows, I do not wish to deny areas of continuity in the genre, namely, a continuing interest in the psychological dimensions of horror as manifest recently in such films as *The Sixth Sense* and *The Blair Witch Project* (both 1999). Instead, I am interested in the general shift toward graphic violence that has characterized mainstream horror since the 1970s.

Discussing the ways that children and adolescents respond to horror films, social scientists Joanne Cantor and Mary Beth Oliver have identified three categories that are frequently depicted in fear-inducing media and that frighten because they are sources of fear in the real (non-media) world. These are (1) distortions of natural forms; (2) depictions of physical injury, victimization, and death; and (3) a focus on the experience of endangerment and fear by others.[3] Deformities or injuries that alter the shape or appearance of natural forms can be inherently frightening, and Donald Hebb has pointed to a biological basis of such fears by observing them in baby primates, who exhibit fear reactions to physical deformities. Hebb suggests that such responses are spontaneous and unlearned. To the extent that horror films traffic in deformity and distorted physical shapes, they may evoke primitive, instinctual fear responses in viewers.

The graphic violence of contemporary horror has given the depiction of physical injury, victimization, and death considerable focus, emphasis, and screen time. These depictions induce anxiety because of the perceived dangers to characters in the enacted scenes. Slasher films, which typically feature lengthy stalking sequences, devote extensive attention to the spectacle of fear and physical endangerment. With respect to this category, Cantor and Oliver note that viewers experience fear in response to the fear expressed by others – in this case, by characters within a film. Portrayals of fear on screen are thus an excellent means of evoking fear responses in viewers, and the design of contemporary horror films is such as to maximize this stimulus potential. A content analysis of fifty-six slasher films, for instance, found that 474 characters were shown in fear of being killed, and 86 percent of these characters did not survive their terror ordeal (Cowan and O'Brien).

Whereas the three categories mentioned by Cantor and Oliver have been present in horror films throughout the genre's history, the balance among the three has shifted in recent decades. The distortion of natural forms evident in the genre's monsters (vampires, dwarves, hunchbacks, werewolves) is essential in much early horror, where it is the confrontation with such beastly characters by normal humans and by the films' viewers that provides for the experience of "horror." Depictions of the other two categories – injury and death, and fear and endangerment – were constrained in earlier periods, inhibited by the conditions of film production in those eras. The injunctions of the industry's Production Code prevented filmmakers from dwelling on the infliction of injury or the endangerment and terrorizing of others. As a result, older horror films do not have the same repertoire of fright-inducing elements, or their intensity and duration, as contemporary examples. The Wolf Man would invariably sink out of the frame with his victim at the height of attack. Even films deemed unacceptably gruesome at the time – Florey's *Murders in the Rue Morgue* (1932), Ulmer's *The Black Cat* (1934) – play their moments of atrocity quickly or in the shadows.[4]

By contrast, while many of the genre's monsters – Freddy Krueger, the aliens in the *Alien* series – continue to exhibit a fear-inducing distortion of natural forms,[5] contemporary horror has greatly expanded the time and visual attention devoted to the other two categories identified by Cantor and Oliver: the infliction of grievous injury and the endangerment of characters. Indeed, the terminology by which modern horror films are described – "slasher" and "stalker" films – denotes this expansion of attention. The narratives are extended episodes of terror devoted to prolonged rituals of stalking and murder or mutilation, which the film's viewer is invited to witness at length. As Cantor and Oliver note, "this genre, perhaps more than any other, provides abundant opportunity for viewers to experience fear in response to injury and danger, as one of the defining characteristics is the portrayal of victimization and death" (65).

In a content analysis of the ten biggest-grossing slasher films, James Weaver found that the average length of scenes showing the death of male characters was just under two minutes and those showing the death of female characters was just under four minutes, and that these lengthy intervals were accompanied by expressions of fear, terror, and pain. In a content analysis of thirty slasher films from 1980, 1985, and 1989, Fred Molitor and Barry Sapolsky found "extreme" forms of violence (burning, dismemberment, beheading, bludgeoning, stabbing) in more than a quarter (28 percent) of all violence coded across the sample.[6] They also measured the duration of expressed fear of violence by victims and found, on average, that eleven minutes per film were devoted to the spectacle of victims in fear.

In this respect, then, the balance of fear-inducing factors has shifted over the genre's history in a way that, arguably, has produced an intensification of the fright experience for viewers. Thus, one might chart a partial history of the horror film in terms of its overall level of violence and the intensity of its fright-inducing ingredients, and in both cases the resulting graph would show a relatively steep rise. Why has this genre evolved in the general direction of intensifying the negative affect (fear, anxiety, disgust) evoked in viewers? Is there something peculiar to the horror film, or to the gratifications sought by its viewers, that would require that the history of its evolving forms move in the general direction of intensified affect?

The causes of the efflorescence of graphic violence in contemporary cinema are clearly multifactorial: no one explanation, or single set of variables, is likely to offer a full or complete accounting. At a minimum, a comprehensive explanation would need to incorporate frameworks drawn from individual and group psychology, institutional factors within the film industry, and sociological trends at large within the culture. Elsewhere (Prince 1998; 2000), I have examined some of the institutional and sociological factors that coalesced in the late 1960s to nudge American film onto the path of graphic violence. Here I would like to concentrate on some factors that seem relatively genre-specific, i.e., that may be operative in horror films more than in the industry's other genres. These factors involve the nature of the relationship prevailing between horror filmmakers and members of the genre's core audience. In my view, this relationship has likely operated to exert an upward pressure on the degree of explicitness embraced by the genre in its presentation of violence. In short, horror cinema's movement in recent decades toward greater quantities of ever-more-graphic violence and fear-inducing spectacle may partially reflect an ongoing transaction between the genre's filmmakers and its audience, a transaction rooted in one of the genre's key appeals: an appeal to sensation.

III

As Cantor has noted (114), it is likely that screen violence holds different appeals for different sets of viewers. One viewer may watch violence to experience aggression vicariously, whereas another finds that it calms fears about a world perceived as dangerous. In either case, personality variables intersect with film content in ways that produce differential sets of appeals. This way of regarding the relationship between viewers and films is somewhat akin to what is known in the humanities as "reader-response" theory, but the superficial similarity conceals a more substantive difference between the explanatory paradigms used in psychology and communication and those used in film studies. Whereas these disciplines have all been concerned with studying viewer responses to film and other visual media, psychology and communication have regarded the audience as being stratified by sociological variables (e.g., gender, age, race) *as well as* by personality variables. Film studies, by contrast, has tended to look primarily at the sociological variables and has treated these as being internally homogeneous. Within the gender category, for instance, the critical distinction is drawn between male and female spectatorship, with the categories being not further divisible. "Male" spectatorship is a unified phenomenon or "viewing position," as is female spectatorship. Individual personality variables do not enter the picture. When film studies has considered personality, it has tended to do so in terms of the explanatory categories furnished by psychoanalysis.

Thus, film studies has scrutinized the horror genre, at great length, in terms of hypothesized gender dynamics that are said to prevail among the genre's viewers and to constitute some of its primary appeals. Indeed, gender – often within a psychoanalytic framework – is probably the interpretive framework applied most frequently to horror movies by contemporary film studies.[7] The most detailed and perceptive study of slasher films is Carol Clover's *Men, Women and Chain Saws*, in which she suggests that the essential viewing dynamic that these films instigate in viewers is one marked by an oscillation between subjectivities marked as "male" (active, aggressive, empowered) and "female" (passive, unempowered, victimized) in terms of their cultural coding. These "positions," according to Clover, do not correspond in any fixed way with the gender of the viewer, in part because the films in question collapse and combine gender categories by featuring a killer who is a feminine male and a main character (the "Final Girl") who is a masculine female.

As a genre, horror movies produce intense emotional responses in viewers. Whereas film studies has tended to frame these responses in psychoanalytic terms – seeing the films over and over again as evocative of Oedipal anxieties, seeing the viewer's response as a displacement of these anxieties onto the filmic materials – psychology and communication have been concerned with "effects," in terms of the biology and cognitive framing of emotional response, and the duration of the response, because these issues are mediated by personality traits.

Within film studies, Linda Williams has termed the horror movie a "body genre" – like pornography or melodrama – because the viewer's emotional and physical responses mimic those of the characters. In horror, we scream or feel terror with the on-screen victims: "it seems to be the case that the success of these genres is often measured by the degree to which the audience sensation mimics what is seen on the screen . . . the success of these genres seems a self-evident matter of measuring bodily response" (1999: 704). But, rather than pursuing the implications of this insight – measuring response – she proceeds to explicate horror in terms of the gender and psychoanalytic issues raised by screen spectacles that place suffering women at their center. Those who are committed to psychoanalytic modes of explication are well represented throughout this volume, and it is not my purpose here to critique that approach.[8] Instead, I would like to suggest how a different approach to personality might help us to understand some dimensions of the shift toward graphic violence in horror cinema.

By contrast with scholars in film studies, researchers in psychology and communication have been quite interested to measure viewers' bodily responses in reaction to film content. Some of their findings may have significant import for explaining the upsurge of graphic violence in recent horror and suggest that it may have a sustaining psychophysiological basis in personality traits among the genre's core fans. I turn now to this issue.

IV

Considerable evidence exists showing that viewers respond to media violence with increases in their levels of heart rate, skin temperature, and blood pressure, and that these responses have some duration – that they linger after the stimulus is gone.[9] Cantor and Oliver have provided evidence of the long-term effects (years in some cases) of fright reactions to horror films (75–78). For viewers, the fright and excitement that horror films produce – experienced as an increased level of physiological response – is pleasurable and rewarding. Otherwise, audiences would not consent to viewing this type of material.[10] As one writer puts it, "when we are afraid, adrenaline surges through our bloodstreams, accelerating our heartbeats and giving us a rush of energy. We're left feeling more alert, our senses operating at their peak" (Rickey: 169).

Recognizing that violent, suspenseful, or frightening media produce physiological changes in their viewers, researchers have postulated a variety of motives and appeals that may underlie this process, that watching violence or terror may hold for movie and television audiences. In most cases, these involve the manner in which a cognitive or social label is attached to the base-level physiological response. Motives thus include a desire to experience aggression vicariously, to be rebellious by watching forbidden or stigmatized categories of programming, to calm apprehensions and anxiety, and to learn about a world that is perceived as threatening.[11] Zillmann has offered a gender-socialization theory to account for the prevalence of young audiences at horror movies, according to which the carnage and distressing imagery on screen enables young viewers to practice and master socially conditioned and gender-typed displays of emotion. "Boys . . . must prove to their peers, and ultimately to themselves, that they are unperturbed, calm and collected in the face of terror; and girls must similarly demonstrate their sensitivity by being appropriately disturbed, dismayed, and disgusted. Such demonstration seems important enough to adolescents to make them seek out cinematic horror and to subject themselves to emotional torment" (1998: 197).[12]

In addition to these hypotheses, Marvin Zuckerman's notion of "sensation-seeking" has stimulated considerable research. This notion describes a personality trait that is oriented to seeking out and maximizing emotional arousal. Sensation-seeking, in Zuckerman's formulation, has three dimensions, which are measured on a scale that plots an individual's overall SS level: (1) thrill and adventure seeking, (2) disinhibition (the seeking of sensory and sensual pleasures), and (3) a susceptibility/aversion to boredom. Sensation-seekers aim to achieve an optimum level of arousal, which can sometimes be more important than its positive or negative emotional content. As Zuckerman notes, "sensation-seekers are attracted to stimuli that are arousing regardless of whether they stimulate negative or positive affect systems. Sensation-seekers prefer being frightened or shocked to being bored" (1996: 155). He suggests that this personality trait varies with age, developing in children and peaking in adolescence – the latter group being the primary audience for horror films – and then diminishing in adulthood. The induction of intense, albeit negative, emotions by horror films might be an effective means for achieving an optimum level of arousal.

An important caveat is in order here. Zuckerman did not devise the notion of sensation-seeking, or its scalar dimensions, with reference to cinema, and thus there is a "goodness of fit" question that arises in work that seeks to apply the concept or the scales to film studies. A risk-taking individual, for instance, who seeks sensation by skydiving, would not necessarily be the same type of person to seek sensation vicariously through cinema. Nevertheless, a number of researchers have used the construct of "sensation-seeking" to explore individuals' preferences in visual media, and the outcome of the studies suggests that it would be fruitful to further refine the construct in ways amenable to the study of vicarious domains of conduct, such as moviegoing.

Zuckerman's work, and the concept of sensation-seeking, belongs to the field of *psychophysiology* – the study of the physiological responses accompanying psychological states. This field examines the biological basis of emotions and personality in an effort to understand the relation between mental and bodily processes.[13] Psychophysiologists view personality as consisting of a set of basic traits or groups of related habits, which combine to form "supertraits" at the highest level of organization. Competing models within the field describe personality in terms of a limited number of three, five, or seven supertraits; one example would be Hans Eysenck's three-supertrait model of extraversion (sociability), neuroticism (emotionality), and psychoticism (asocial tendencies). A psychophysiological approach to personality assumes that traits, such as sensation-seeking, are rooted in the operations and biochemistry of the central nervous system, have an evolutionary basis (arising via natural selection to facilitate survival and reproduction), and show up in other species besides the human. They are inherited characteristics and have biological markers (e.g., patterns of cortical activity, cardiovascular response, etc.).[14]

A number of studies have pointed to the associated biological markers of sensation-seeking, which are understood as a kind of orienting response directed at the environment. Individuals scoring high on the sensation-seeking scales show stronger physiological orienting responses than do low scorers. The response measures are patterns of cortical reaction following a visual or auditory stimulus. Sensation-seekers show a positive slope (an increase in the amplitude of response following the stimulus), whereas low sensation-seekers show a negative slope. These response measures have been demonstrated in numerous studies and have also been shown in cats and correlated with their individual tendencies to be active or withdrawn in reaction to the environment.[15] Other biological markers explored in relation to sensation-seeking include skin conductance response and heart rate. High sensation-seekers, for example, show more rapid heart rate deceleration, whereas low sensation-seekers show a stronger acceleratory response to auditory stimuli, consistent with a distinction between orienting and defensive responses. Zuckerman notes, furthermore, that high sensation-seekers have higher thresholds for pain and for intense auditory stimulation: "the high sensation-seeker would correspond to what has been called the 'Strong Nervous System' or 'Non-Reactive' type, characterized by an insensitivity to weak stimulation and a tolerance for high levels of stimulation" (1991: 340).

The duration and intensity of fright-inducing elements in contemporary horror films would seem to provide the kind of material appealing to viewers with "strong nervous systems" and, indeed, sensation-seeking has been found to correlate with preferences for horror movie watching. Before turning to that evidence, however, it should be noted that this personality trait has been correlated in a number of studies with preferences for style and content in visual media that are highly arousing. High sensation-seekers tend to prefer paintings with aggressive content[16] and paintings in an expressionistic style that features a lot of compositional tension.[17] Zaleski (607–08) found low sensation-seekers preferring positively arousing pictures (scenes of celebration and mild lovemaking) and high sensation-seekers preferring these pictures as well as negatively arousing ones (scenes of torture, hanging, and corpses). Male high sensation-seekers actually preferred the negatively arousing scenes to the positive ones.

Numerous studies have found sensation-seeking to be associated with preferences for horror films and with horror movie attendance; the personality trait seems to have predictive value in ascertaining a given viewer's preference for or against this type of material.[18] Tamborini and Stiff sampled viewers who had just left a screening of *Halloween II* (1981), asking them about their movie preferences and why they liked or disliked horror films. The categories, developed in previous research, were a liking for fright, for violence and destruction, for satisfying story resolution, and for humor. Through their influence on sensation-seeking, age and gender were found to predict the frequency of horror movie attendance. Sensation-seeking was related to gender (being strongest for males) and age (strongest for young viewers in the sample, which included viewers up to age forty-five), and it predicted a liking for fright and excitement as well as the enjoyment of violence and destruction (higher among male viewers). The preference for fright and excitement, in turn, was the variable that most predicted attendance at horror movies.

In another study, Tamborini, Stiff, and Zillmann gave their subjects descriptions of thirteen films containing graphic violence and asked them to rank the films according to which they would like to see most. The subjects' past viewing history predicted preferences for graphic horror: subjects preferring graphic horror had a history of viewing such films as well as films of violent drama, and these preferences were predicted by performance on the researchers' Sensation Seeking Scale.

If, as the empirical evidence suggests, sensation-seeking is one of the personality traits associated with preferences for horror films, these members of the genre's audience would have the "strong nervous system" that the enjoyment of graphic gore would otherwise imply, including a high sensory threshold for visual and auditory stimuli, a rapid habituation to such stimuli, and a susceptibility to boredom. Taken together, these personality characteristics in core audience members for graphic horror films provide an excellent incentive for filmmakers to keep expanding the level of graphic violence and fright-inducing elements. Expanding the level of cinematic jolts provides an excellent means for retaining this core group of viewers, and the net result of such expansion may help to account for one of the genre's fundamental transformations, namely a shift from the meta-physics of horror in films from earlier decades, where the uncanny and transgressive is implied, to the literalization of shock and fright and its location in imagery of graphic violence and extended scenarios of stalking and murder.[19]

V

As noted above, the amplification of grotesque imagery in post-1970s horror films is tied to a revolution in special effects make-up and the innovations of a new generation of effects artists. These artists are very conscious of "pushing the envelope," of trying to surpass the level of illusion and the types of imagery in previous films, and this underlying dynamic in their work addresses itself eloquently to the personality traits of the core audience. They also derive tremendous fun from fashioning grotesque effects and speak about their work in a manner that suggests (as one would expect) a very high tolerance for the gruesomeness of their products – a tolerance that matches the high sensory thresholds of the genre's viewers.

Tom Savini is one of the kings of splatter film make-up, designing effects for *Dawn of the Dead, Friday the 13th, Maniac, Creepshow* (1982), *Friday the 13th – The Final Chapter* (1984), *Day of the Dead* (1985), and *Texas Chainsaw Massacre 2* (1986), among many others. Savini was a combat photographer in Vietnam, and he believes that his make-up effects have an important root in some of the violence he witnessed during the war. His job was to photograph the violence done to people and buildings, and he thinks that it rarely affected him because of a kind of protection, a distancing, he felt from being behind the camera.

Once I was walking along and changing film, and I almost stepped on an arm. An arm, severed from the elbow down . . . and it was clenched in a tight fist. I remember looking at it and it was dusty, it had some road dirt on it, and there wasn't any blood around it. I could see the viscera coming out of the elbow, and it was like an effect. If I had to make it, it would look exactly like what I just saw! I paused, and I took a picture of it – and I actually kind of studied it a bit. (Timpone: 65)

As a make-up artist for horror movies, Savini excels at designing convincing imagery of mutilation – scalping, decapitation, gunshot wounds – and he loves concocting outré effects: "A third of *Dawn of the Dead* was improvised. We'd be sitting around thinking of ways to kill a zombie. We'd go to [director] George [Romero] and say, 'How 'bout if we drive a screwdriver through some zombie's ear?' 'Yeah, OK, Great!'" (66). One of Savini's most gruesome effects is a shotgun to the head at close range in *Maniac*,

for which he himself served as both victim and executioner. He made
a hollow plaster-of-Paris model of his own face and head, filled it with
blood, shrimp dip, vegetables, and apple cores, and stuck it on a dummy.
He then dressed as the killer in the scene and blasted the dummy: "Here
I was, firing a double-barreled shotgun with live magnum pellet ammu-
nition through the windshield of a car and a fake head of myself, with
four or five cameras rolling . . . It was very weird looking down the barrel
of the shotgun at *me* and then *blasting* me" (70–71).

The pleasure and emotional disassociation displayed by Savini in relation to his work is characteristic of other horror film effects artists. Chris
Walas designed a complex set of transformations for David Cronenberg's
The Fly (1986), which reach a climax when the insect's eyes burst forth,
rupturing the eyes of the human host. "Popping the eyeballs was just a
fun thing to do," Walas recalls. "It gave us the option of being gooey
and yucky without being bloody" (120). Describing his training at a low-
budget effects house, Howard Berger says, "I was paid a ridiculous rate a
week, but I was there to make monsters and have fun" (145).

Bob Keen, who partnered with Clive Barker on four films, traces his
work to a childhood delight in magic: "It started off with my wanting to be
a magician, and the main element of being a magician is to fool people
into believing they're seeing something that they aren't. That grew into
wanting to change people into werewolves, or making them look like
they'd been beaten up, or they'd been in a road accident." Keen and
Barker's motto for their trend-setting work on the *Hellraiser* series was
"There Are No Limits," and Keen took special pleasure in designing a
gluttonous demon with a ripped-open stomach: "the torn-open stomach
was a fun idea: that someone that fat would have direct access to his
stomach, he could probably reach in and pull out the nasty stuff" (164).

For *Return of the Living Dead* (1985), Tony Gardner designed a con-
vulsing, undead torso strapped to an undertaker's table, and the boldness of the conception taught him the importance of working in broad,
aggressive strokes: "It was really fun to build that thing. And then the
performance was very broad, too: 'Brains, brains, give me brains,' with
the spine flopping around and fluid leaking out of it. Maybe it burned
into *my* brain or something, but from that point on, I've tried to design
my creations with big broad visual strokes" (186).

Everett Burrell, who designed zombies for the Tom Savini–directed remake of *Night of the Living Dead* (1990), has pointed out the importance
of surpassing previous conceptions and designs – it was essential to attracting viewers. Failure to surpass previous work would entail a loss of

audience. About the zombies, "we tried real hard to make those things as different as possible. We knew that if we just did 'whatever,' we wouldn't get any attention" (207).

These remarks by the artists whose work is responsible for the upsurge of graphic violence in modern horror cinema suggest that they are aware, at varying levels of self-consciousness, of the personality traits of their core audience, and that they understand the need to fashion their work for the high threshold sensitivities of these viewers, sensitivities that the artists themselves seem to share. It is important that there be, in their work, "no limits."

To the extent, then, that the violence and fright in modern horror gratifies a sensation-seeking motive in viewers, the genre's escalation of violence and grotesquerie is comprehensible as part of an ongoing transaction between horror filmmakers and their core audience, a transaction that may have an important basis in the latter's biologically determined response characteristics. These shared and relatively unchanging personality traits are ones that the film industry has significant institutional investment in maintaining due to their revenue-generating potential. Because sensation-seeking may be understood as a dynamic trait, requiring a relatively high level of stimuli and which habituates to that level, it is the kind of motive that can exert a continuing upward pressure on the boundaries of style and content, a pressure toward their continuing transgression. This is precisely what we have seen in the evolution of the subset of contemporary horror cinema that has come to showcase graphic violence. The genre's effects artists understand the importance of maintaining this state of transgression for horror's ability to attract viewers.

To the extent that this ongoing transaction between filmmakers and audience shapes the nature of violence in contemporary horror, we are not likely to see abatement in the level of gruesomeness that the genre has today achieved. The hackings and dismembering will likely continue, provided that they can be visualized in continuously novel ways. The population of teenagers who are the genre's mainstay gets renewed each year, as does the imperative for horror films to provide these viewers with sensational entertainment.

One of the issues posed by the 1930s Payne Fund Studies was whether films that push the boundaries of acceptable content are inherently attractive to viewers. Are such films more enticing for audiences than those that stay within the boundaries of established norms? Or as Charles Peters put it, "Do people like better to attend motion pictures that are 'naughty'?" (142). Peters found no unequivocal evidence to support this idea and left it as a relatively open, if (for him) distasteful, possibility. By contrast, some of the evidence reviewed above suggests that in horror cinema, at least, a fundamental appeal lies in the transgression of established content boundaries – in showing, broadly and aggressively, new methods of maiming, dismembering, or mutilating. To the extent that the genre's viewers look to new horror movies for the provision of intense sensation, their expectations furnish the dynamic that drives this appeal.

The shape of contemporary horror cinema thus suggests a significant intersection of personality, institutional, and cultural variables. For the horror genre and its viewers, the attractions of sensational violence may have a significant source in psychobiology, which the film industry has learned to tap because the personalities that house this trait number in the millions, as do the dollars that can be earned by appealing to them.

NOTES

1. For such a critique, see Prince (1996).
2. *Variety*, June 8, 1988: 24.
3. Carroll (1990) discusses distortions of natural form from a philosophical standpoint, and I have examined the issue (Prince 1988).
4. Skal (1993) summarizes the alarm that 1930s horror films generated in social watchdogs.
5. Other types of monsters in the genre disturb because they are so deceptively ordinary in appearance, e.g., Norman Bates.
6. This study found a total of 1,573 violent acts in the sample, 52 acts per film on average.
7. See especially Grant (1996).
8. See Prince (1996) for such a critique.
9. Zillman (1971; 1991); Zillman, Hay, and Bryant; Wilson and Cantor.
10. Michael Levine makes a similar point in his essay in this volume.
11. Cantor (1998) summarizes research on these hypotheses.
12. Cf. Zillmann and Weaver.
13. Andreassi provides a succinct introduction to psychophysiology.
14. See Zuckerman (1991: 1–43).
15. Zuckerman (1991) provides a review of these studies.
16. See Tobacyk, Myers, and Bailey.
17. See Zuckerman, Ulrich, and McLaughlin.
18. See Edwards; Tamborini and Stiff; Zuckerman and Litle.
19. Again, this is not to imply that this shift typifies all films in the genre.

NOËL CARROLL

Afterword: Psychoanalysis and the Horror Film

Because I have expressed reservations about the application of psycho-analysis to film studies in general (Carroll 1988) and to the horror film in particular (Carroll 1990), I have been invited to contribute a comment to this volume on the relevance of psychoanalysis to the horror film. The editor's intention to include dissenting voices in this anthology is as laudable as it is generous and frankly unexpected. But I don't know for whom this opportunity is scarier: me or the psychoanalysts. For I must enter the lair of the Other, while they must suffer the presence of a wolf in philosopher's clothing. I guess it all depends on who you think the monster really is.

Is psychoanalysis relevant to the analysis of the horror film?[1] I think that the simple answer to this question is "Of course." It is certainly relevant, even apposite, to the analysis of many horror films, because many horror films presuppose, implicitly or explicitly, psychoanalytic concepts and imagery. *Forbidden Planet* (1956), for example, is frankly Freudian. Its monster is called the Id, a phenomenon explained in explicitly psychoanalytic terms within the world of the fiction. Anyone interpreting *Forbidden Planet* is thereby licensed to explicate the film psychoanalytically for the same reason that an exegete of Eisenstein's *The General Line* (1929) would be correct in adverting to Marxist ideology. In both cases, the hermeneutical warrant is historicist. If interpretation is, at least in part, the retrieval of a film's intended meaning and an explanation of its design, then, where a filmmaker intends psychoanalytic significance, it is incumbent on the interpreter to attempt to unravel it.

This does not mean that one must interview the filmmaker to establish that she intended her work to carry psychoanalytically inflected significance. The best evidence for such a message is the film itself. One can infer a psychoanalytic intention on the basis of the film, just as an interpreter of Thomas Mann's *Doctor Faustus* might appeal to Nietzsche's philosophy to explicate some of the more obscure aspects of the text. For some authors, like Norman Mailer, psychoanalytic concepts so infuse their writing that, were they to deny it, we would suspect irony, if not downright lying.

Similarly, an example is the horror filmmaker and author Clive Barker. His writing and imagery show familiarity with psychoanalysis at every turn. He wears it on his sleeve, so to speak, which is where Dante shows his Thomism and Brecht his Marxism. Using these frameworks interpretively, including psychoanalysis, with respect to the relevant texts need not involve going outside of the text, as they used to say, but is grounded by attention to the text.

So far my examples have been of filmmakers and authors who are rather self-consciously psychoanalytic. However, psychoanalytic interpretation may also be plausibly warranted with regard to less self-conscious filmmakers and authors. For in addition to being a medical practice, psychoanalysis has also become a common idiom of thought throughout Western culture; its concepts, scenarios, and metaphors have seeped into everyday language. Just as ordinary speakers may employ psychoanalytic frameworks without being aware of doing so, so may artists.

Psychoanalysis, understood as a cultural myth, like Christianity, pervades the thinking of literate Westerners (and many non-literate ones as well); we can overhear it in elevator conversations between people who can neither spell "psychoanalysis" nor differentiate it from any other form of psychology. Likewise, we can see its concepts, scenarios, and imagery in the work of filmmakers and authors with no express commitment to psychoanalysis.

In a Christian culture like ours, we can attribute Christ-imagery to a film – e.g., call a character a "Christ-figure" – even where that might not be the description the filmmakers would have offered. We can do this because we presume it is likely that the filmmaker arrived at this pattern because he is steeped in a culture where Christ-imagery is pervasive. Thus, we infer that the filmmaker tacitly or unself-consciously intends his character to have a Christ-like effect, though this is not how he might put it. Likewise, psychoanalytic imagery and concepts are so culturally widespread that we may infer psychoanalytic significance to films that are not fully self-conscious about its presence.

One last analogy: The idiom of Social Darwinism has suffused our culture since the late nineteenth century. People who may never have heard of Darwin mouth its platitudes. Thus, it makes sense to interpret a film like *King Kong* (1933) – which drips with pop-Darwinian imagery – in terms of evolutionary metaphors, despite the fact that the filmmakers, in all likelihood, would not have described them as such. Nevertheless, they did access from the ambient cultural atmosphere readily available material vibrating with Social Darwinian resonances, and they did intend it to move audiences who were prepared culturally to respond to it in certain predictable ways. And this is what licenses bringing to bear the framework of Social Darwinian concepts, scenarios, and imagery in an explication of *King Kong*.

Similarly, it is reasonable to hypothesize that, given the pervasive psychoanalytic coloration of our culture, often filmmakers and filmgoers share enough tacit, albeit generally vague and fragmented, knowledge of psychoanalytic concepts, scenarios, and imagery and, consequently, that they can be said to be trading in psychoanalytic meanings, even if that is not how they would put the matter. Hence, for the purpose of explaining the design and the uptake of such films, exegetes may resort to explicit psychoanalytic terminology, and this can be unexceptionable, even on historicist grounds. For example, calling Luke's relation to Darth Vader "Oedipal" should raise no hermeneutical eyebrows.

This defense of the relevance of psychoanalysis to the horror film, however, does not entail that psychoanalysis is relevant to the interpretation of *all* horror films. For, pervasive though psychoanalytic thought may be, it is not the case that in every horror film one will find evidence of psychoanalytic concepts, scenarios, and/or imagery. And where there is no evidence of the pertinent authorial intentions, either explicit or tacit, psychoanalytic interpretations cannot be warranted on historicist grounds.

Moreover, this sort of defense also places limitations on the specificity of the psychoanalytic framework one may mobilize with respect to a given horror film. As indicated, many of the psychoanalytic ideas available to filmmakers and their audiences are extremely general, rather vague, and even inchoate. These the interpreter must approach gingerly. In such cases, one's deployment of psychoanalytic concepts should be correspondingly general. For on historicist grounds, it will not do to apply a piece of recondite Lacanian conceptual machinery to a film whose only psychoanalytic commitment is something like the nostrum that sexual repression is unhealthy.

For example, a Lacanian analysis of the original *Cat People* (1942) could not be motivated on historicist grounds, though a specific psychoanalytic interpretation could be defended on the grounds of the film itself and the popularity of certain watered-down psychoanalytic ideas in the culture from which it emerged.[2]

This is not to say, I hasten to add, that there could not be a Lacanian horror film worthy of a Lacanian interpretation. But that would depend on whether Lacanian concepts, scenarios, and imagery were sufficiently evident in the film such that it is plausible to hypothesize that the film-maker intended them as such. Moreover, I have no doubt that we will be seeing many Lacanian horror films soon as more and more filmmakers and filmviewers are trained in university programs with film analysis classes where Lacanese is the vernacular.

The conclusion that psychoanalysis is relevant to the analysis of *some* horror films seems unavoidable, if only on historicist grounds. Lest my use of the qualifier "some" sound too grudging, let me explicitly state that I think that probably *many* horror films warrant psychoanalytic interpretations for the reasons I've given, just as many Italian Renaissance paintings warrant the use of interpretive frameworks informed by Catholic theology. The interpreter need not embrace these interpretive frameworks because they are true or because she believes them to be true, but only because psychoanalysis and Catholicism are sources of concepts, scenarios, and imagery that so suffuse their respective cultures that they can be postulated as influencing artists, audiences, and their mutually adaptive responses.

But just as not every Italian Renaissance painting mandates an interpretation informed by Catholicism, not every horror film warrants a psychoanalytic interpretation. Many space invasion films, like *Independence Day* (1996) – which agitate literally for the survival of the species – may be more fruitfully examined from a Darwinian perspective than from a psychoanalytic one (not because Darwinism is true and psychoanalysis is not, but because Darwinian concepts, narratives, and imagery also suffuse the culture *and* are more evident in *Independence Day* than psychoanalytic ones).[3]

This hermeneutical defense of the relevance of psychoanalysis to horror films grants the psychoanalytic critic a field of study. Indeed, I suspect that many psychoanalytic interpretations of horror films, though undertaken by exegetes convinced of the truth of psychoanalysis, could, without much strain, be recuperated instructively as the observations of participant-observers in a culture suffused with psychoanalytic thinking. However, I also suspect that many psychoanalytic critics are likely to spurn this concession, because, though I agree that *many* horror films deserve a psychoanalytic interpretation (at least in part), they believe that *all* horror films should be interpreted psychoanalytically.

One reason why many psychoanalytic critics are apt to reject what I've called the hermeneutical defense of their practice is that they believe that psychoanalysis is true, whereas the preceding hermeneutical defense does not require that psychoanalysis be any less wacky than scientology to be apposite in a given case. That is, the preceding hermeneutical defense only asks that psychoanalysis be culturally pervasive. Moreover, it is because the psychoanalytic critic believes that psychoanalysis is a comprehensive theory that she believes its laws apply to everything in its putative domain; whereas, according to the preceding hermeneutical defense, the warrant for psychoanalytic interpretations only extends as far as the historically concrete distribution of psychoanalytic ideas across filmmakers, films, and their intended audiences. That is why, under its aegis, one would look to scientology to initiate an interpretation of *Battlefield Earth* (2000) and not to psychoanalysis.

Insofar as psychoanalytic critics defend their practice with regard to the horror film on the grounds of the truth of psychoanalysis as a general theory of human nature, the debate is clearly too gigantic to be engaged here. There are too many different brands of psychoanalysis and too many different claims to be adjudicated *ad seriatim*. So, for the sake of argument, let us suppose that there is some truth to psychoanalysis. Is this enough to warrant a psychoanalytic approach to all horror films?

If we assume that whatever is true about psychoanalysis is universally true – in the sense that it applies to every aspect of human behavior – then we might suppose that psychoanalysis will always have something to say about every horror film, inasmuch as every horror film is a specimen of human behavior. However, I predict that this assumption will be too heady for even most, if not all, of the friends of psychoanalysis. Some human phenomena are not on the psychoanalytic radar screen. Surely, Freud thought this. Consequently, the case for explicating all horror films psychoanalytically will depend on showing that there is something in the very nature of the horror film that is peculiarly suited for psychoanalysis. That is, the psychoanalyst needs to establish that there is something in the essence of horror – something without which a film would not be a horror film – that is only explicable or that is best explained psychoanalytically.

This defense of the psychoanalytic interpretation of horror would not be based on interpretive protocols, like historicism. Rather, it would be a theoretical defense. It relies on identifying a comprehensive feature of all horror films, which feature, in turn, is theorized most compellingly by psychoanalysis.

In the past, I've denied that psychoanalysis has succeeded in adducing such a feature. For example, one of the most persuasive attempts to advance such a generalization can be derived from Ernest Jones's *On the Nightmare.* Jones argues that the horrific creatures of folklore are symbolic expressions of repressed wishes. This hypothesis, if convincing, would do a nice job of explaining the ambivalent reaction of horror fiction audiences – their tendency to be both attracted and repelled by horror films. The attraction comes from the fact that a wish is being manifested and thereby gratified, while the repulsion springs from the fact that it is a *prohibited* wish, a wish that occasions psychic punishment. So, for Jones, a vampire figure expresses the desire of the living for the return of a deceased loved one for the purpose of sexual congress, a wish that then elicits disgust from our psychic censor.

However, though this repressed-wish hypothesis promises certain explanatory advantages, it does require that we be able to locate in every horror film a symbolic expression of a repressed wish. And this, I have argued, cannot be done. Many horror films do not contain enough of the relevant kinds of details to motivate the postulation of any latent content, such as a repressed wish. A radioactively enlarged anything, tramping about the countryside killing everything, suffices to make a horror film, but neither the language or the imagery of the film has to suggest any repressed psychosexual portent, let alone a wish. The monster need only be abnormally large and lethal to be horrific; it may not be connected to anything psychically deeper than that. Therefore, the hypothesis that all horror shares the feature of expressing a repressed wish, insofar as it is insufficiently comprehensive, cannot support the conviction that all horror films are to be psychoanalyzed.

That is, horrific creatures can be manufactured formulaically through various strategies, including combinatory ones (for example, put an insect's head on a dog's body). With a specific film or text, this anomaly need not be associated with anything further to be horrifying. Hence, the horrific beings who serve to identify instances of the horror genre can be contrived disconnected from any wishes, repressed or otherwise. And yet the films in which they figure will still count as horror films – indeed, horror films immune from psychoanalysis – for anyone not in the thrall of Jones's theory.

Of course, this argument, if it is convincing, only shows that the universal applicability of psychoanalysis to the horror film cannot be derived from Jones's initially seductive proposal that all horror traffics in the fulfillment of repressed wishes. Yet might there be other psychoanalytic hypotheses that will succeed where the one derived from Jones failed?

Recently, such a proposal has been offered by Steven Jay Schneider. Schneider returns to Freud's 1919 essay "The 'Uncanny'" for inspiration. Schneider points out that in Freud's characterization of the uncanny, which he finds useful for modeling horror, Freud indicates that not only repressed wishes, but also surmounted beliefs, can function to trigger the sense of uncanniness (2000: 172). These surmounted beliefs include things like infantile beliefs in the omnipotence of the will and the belief that the dead can return to life. By portraying possessed children with telekinetic powers or revenants from the crypt, horror films reconfirm such surmounted beliefs, thereby presumably affording pleasure. Moreover, Schneider goes on to develop an interesting typology of horrific creatures in terms of the surmounted beliefs they reconfirm (183).

Schneider's conception of horror in terms of repressed wishes *and* surmounted beliefs is certainly more comprehensive than the account derived from Jones. However, it is plagued by a serious incongruity. If horror is a function of the reconfirmation of surmounted beliefs, then how can it be possible for people who have not surmounted the beliefs in question to be susceptible to horror fictions? A leading example of surmounted belief for Schneider is that the dead can return to life. This archaic belief underwrites all sorts of horrific beings, from zombies and vampires to ghosts and haunted houses. But, of course, many horror viewers believe that the dead can return to life.[4] They believe in channeling, and séances, not to mention ghosts, haunted houses, and zombies, and some perhaps even believe in vampires. Because these folks have never abandoned (or surmounted) these beliefs, then they should not be horrified by horror movies. But this prediction seems improbable.[5]

Under this category of horrific beings, Schneider includes "embodied souls," of which the demonically possessed are the prime example. Should we then suppose that a screening of *The Exorcist* (1973) in the church basement to an audience of Catholics who believe in possession will evoke no tremor of horror? Not very likely.

Another important family of reconfirmations of surmounted belief for Schneider comprises figures that embody the omnipotence of thought. But again there are horror fans who believe in the omnipotence of thought; for example, there are people who believe in voodoo. When such a person reads a horror novel, like Hugh Cave's *The Evil Returns*, in which the nefarious borcor Margal controls minds from afar, how will

Schneider explain the horror they feel, or the horror felt by reverential Fundamentalists who read Christian horror novels like *The Mark?* Surmounted belief just does not seem to be the elusive secret of horror that Schneider takes it to be.[6]

Nor does it appear to be the case that horror films that fail to be explained in terms of surmounted belief will nevertheless be explicable in terms of repressed wishes. To see this, we need only combine the counterexamples we used to challenge Jones and Schneider. Imagine a horror film, watched by believers in ghosts, about a spirit of whom not enough is said, shown, or implied to allow us to infer anything about its latent import. Nor is enough psychosexual detail indicated about the humans it besets to enable one to isolate a network of psychic associations. In such a case, the generalization that all horror films involve either the expression of repressed wishes or surmounted beliefs would seem to be falsified.

There does not appear to be a general feature, or disjunctive set of features, shared by all horror films such that they are always best explained by psychoanalysis. Needless to say, I've only canvassed two proposals about what that general feature might be – Jones's and Schneider's. But because these are among the strongest contenders, noting their limitations should indicate that the burden of proof here rests with the psychoanalysts. It is up to them to produce the relevant sort of general feature before they lay claim to being the privileged interpreters of all horror films.

Of course, that psychoanalysis might not be applicable to all horror films does not entail that it cannot clarify some. Psychoanalysis is a vast and complex body of ideas, including not only meta-psychological theories but also observations of hithertofore scarcely noticed patterns of human behavior. Some of these ideas, if they are well founded and if they track the phenomena on the screen, may illuminate otherwise perplexing aspects of particular horror films.

Consider, for example, James Whale's *Bride of Frankenstein* (1935), the sequel to *Frankenstein* (1931). On the eve of Henry Frankenstein's (Colin Clive) marriage, the wizened Dr. Septimus Pretorius approaches him in the hope of enlisting the younger scientist to experiment once again in the creation of life. Ernest Thesiger plays Pretorius in a style that we have since come to call camp. He tries to charm, cajole, and tempt Henry, though Henry resists, having had an unhappy experience with reanimation in the previous film. Pretorius flirtatiously importunes, promising knowledge and grandeur; Henry fidgets, nervously and darkly. If you turn off the soundtrack it is easy to imagine that we are witnesses to an attempt at homosexual seduction. But, of course, the object of the seduction is not directly sexual, but rather involves the prospect of two men creating life together.

Another notable feature of Pretorius's mien is his sneering attitude toward Henry's wife-to-be, Elizabeth (Valerie Hobson), and the upcoming nuptials. Indeed, Pretorius behaves almost as though he is jealous of Elizabeth, as if she were a rival. In any case, there is an undeniable sexual undercurrent here.

Part of what film interpretation is about concerns making sense of characters, explaining why they are as they are, notably where there is something mysterious and opaque in their behavior. With respect to *Bride of Frankenstein*, one question that arises about Pretorius is why he is so venomous about Henry's prospective mate and their marriage. Of course, part of the reason for Pretorius's opposition is that it may deter Henry's participation in the experiment. But Pretorius's dripping sarcasm is so marked and excessive that it suggests that something deeper is at stake. What could it be?

Here psychoanalysis may suggest an answer. In *Symbolic Wounds*, Bruno Bettelheim cites evidence for the existence of what might be called womb envy, a recurring male desire to possess the reproductive power of women. This longing, Bettelheim maintains, is re-enacted in the symbolism of many puberty rituals. Supposing the behavioral pattern to be well founded, the interpreter of *Bride of Frankenstein* might conjecture that Pretorius's animus is energized by the desire to realize this male "birth" fantasy. He wants to bring forth life, but with a man as his partner rather than a woman. The notion of subtracting the woman from the conventional birth equation is perhaps accentuated by the pointedly fey mannerisms that Thesiger brings to his role.

But, in any event, the logic of the admittedly weird plot of *Bride of Frankenstein* and Pretorius's pronounced aversion to marriage can be rendered intelligible interpretively by speculating that the film is underwritten by a male, in this instance possibly homosexual, desire to appropriate the female powers of reproduction. Indeed, this might even be an example of the kind of surmounted belief that Schneider emphasizes.

This use of a psychoanalytic concept to clarify an opaque pattern in a horror film would not be defended on the grounds of historicism. It is unlikely that the creators or the intended audience of *Bride of Frankenstein* had the concept of birth envy in their conscious cognitive stock. Nor is the preceding interpretation grounded in the supposition that all horror fictions can be interpreted psychoanalytically. Rather, this interpretation is motivated by the need to explain certain specific incongruities in the film. That those incongruities can be made intelligible by reference to a recurring behavioral pattern that has been recognized by psychoanalysis counts in its favor.

It need not be the case that the creators of *Bride of Frankenstein* be aware of the pattern as discovered by Bettelheim. They may be enacting it through the partnership of Pretorius and Frankenstein without realizing that that relationship struck them as comprehensible, intelligible, and fitting because it adhered to an unacknowledged psychic scenario. They had access to it, albeit unconsciously, because, *ex hypothesi*, it rehearses a naturally recurring form of envy. Here interpretation retrieves their unconscious intentions.

So if a psychoanalytic interpretation rests on empirically well-founded observations and theories of human behavior, if it accords with the details of the film, if it does not ignore or contradict countervailing evidence, and if it explains the incongruities of the film better than or equally well as competing interpretations, it will be well warranted. That may sound like a lot of "ifs," but it is by no means obvious that these conditions cannot be met in a particular case. Moreover, these conditions are pretty much default conditions that we expect to be met by any interpretation of fictional representations of fictional affairs. So if the preceding psychoanalytic interpretation of *Bride of Frankenstein* meets these conditions, all things being equal, it should be acceptable.

Thus far, we have found two ways in which psychoanalysis is relevant to the analysis of horror films: where it is motivated by historical or contextual considerations, and where it otherwise meets our general interpretive protocols. My own suspicion – and it is only a hunch – is that where most psychoanalytic interpretations of horror films succeed, it is on historicist grounds, but that may only reflect my skepticism about how many well-founded, uniquely psychoanalytic observations there are to be had about recurring patterns of human behavior. But since I concede that there may be some, then it follows that there may be some well-warranted interpretations of horror films that rest on them. This has to be the case, because in general, we allow as a default presupposition, that interpreters, including ordinary viewers, may legitimately make reference to well-founded, general patterns of human behavior when attempting to make sense of fictional representations of human action, including horror films.[7]

Before concluding, it may be useful to offer some brief remarks about two tendencies in psychoanalytic film criticism that have not yet been mentioned. We might call these illustrative criticism and demonstrative criticism. By illustrative criticism, I mean the use of fictional examples to serve as illustrations of psychoanalytic concepts. Perhaps Freud's use of Sophocles' play to explicate the "Oedipal complex" is an example of this. A more recent example, and one closer to the topic of this article, is Slavoj Zizek's employment of Robert Heinlein's novel *The Unpleasant Profession of Jonathan Hoag* to exemplify the notion of the Lacanian Real.

After quoting a passage from the novel, Zizek writes: "What is this 'grey and formless mist' if not the Lacanian Real – the pulsing of the pre-symbolic substance in all its abhorrent vitality? But what is crucial for us here is the form, or more precisely the place, in which the Real interferes; it irrupts on the very boundary separating the 'outside' from the 'inside', materialized in this case by the car window" (1999: 18–19). Henlein's imagery here is used to indicate something about the Lacanian Real, its liminality.

Zizek's purpose does not seem to be to explain Heinlein's text, but to give his audience a concrete handle on a difficult piece of Lacanian terminology. In this, Zizek strives to make the text fit the concept, rather than to find a concept that models the text. Given Zizek's aims, this is not an error – but, let me suggest, neither is it textual criticism. It has the wrong direction of fit: the concepts in question need not illuminate the text; the text is supposed to illuminate the concept. Likewise Freud's use of Sophocles' play tells us little about the specific texture of *Oedipus Rex*. Would we even say, on the basis of the play, that Oedipus had the famous complex that bears his name, since he did not know that Laius was his father and Jocasta his mother?

The use of films to illustrate psychoanalytic concepts can be found frequently in books devoted to introducing readers to poststructuralist ideas.[8] That this practice can have heuristic value should not be denied. Just as the preacher may use some current event to elucidate a theological doctrine, so a film instructor may turn a film or a part of a film into a parable about some psychoanalytic concept. But insofar as parables take the phenomenon at hand out of context and shape them for their own heuristic purposes, we do not count them as analytic, because the direction of fit between the concept and the phenomenon runs in the wrong direction.

Applying these observations about illustrative criticism to the question of the relation of psychoanalysis to the horror film, we can say that where the psychoanalytic criticism in question is essentially illustrative in nature, it is, strictly speaking, irrelevant to the analysis of the horror film. For in most cases, the illustrative criticism at issue will not be about the horror film; it will be about psychoanalytic concepts. That is, it will have the wrong object of inquiry. On the other hand, where examples of

illustrative criticism do tell us something about how a specific horror film
or subgenre works, that will be due to the fact that, in addition to pursuing illustrative purposes, they also abide by the protocols of interpretation
discussed above. But the bottom line is that illustrative criticism need not
abide by those protocols and, therefore, criticism that is as such merely
illustrative of psychoanalytic concepts guarantees little insight into the
horror film.

One last species of psychoanalytic criticism that deserves mention is
what I call demonstrative. Demonstrative criticism in general is criticism
aimed at getting people to notice features of artworks, including films.
The demonstrative critic may achieve her aim by pointing to an artwork –
getting us to feel the tension in the painting by pointing to one part of
it and then to another so that the imbalance between two figures jumps
out at us. Or the demonstrative critic may redescribe the work, perhaps
using metaphors, analogies, and comparisons to other artworks and the
like to bring certain qualities of the work to our notice. A dance critic, for
example, may call a movement "silky" to draw our attention to important
features of the choreography, such as its smoothness, seamless transitions,
and lightness.

Psychoanalytic concepts can also be used in this way. Steven Schneider
(1999: 72) calls attention to the repetition in the shower sequence in
Psycho (1960) by reminding readers of what Freud said about repetition.
Rhetorically, this gets one to see and to appreciate an important structural feature of the scene. And I suspect that many film instructors use
psychoanalytic concepts as a way to begin to encourage students to notice
cinematic articulations that would most likely go unheeded. In this way,
as an instrument of demonstrative criticism, psychoanalysis may be a very
serviceable medium for film pedagogy.

Demonstrative criticism is a very important, though frequently overlooked, form of criticism. One is truly fortunate when one has a good
demonstrative critic as a guide. However, the aim of demonstrative
criticism is not analysis or interpretation. It employs redescription,
metaphors, analogies, comparisons with other works, allusions, and so
forth to get us to notice what we might otherwise overlook. Its aim is pragmatic, not analytic. It succeeds if it enables audiences to grasp features of
works that might ordinarily be neglected. To that end, the demonstrative
critic can employ almost whatever it takes to get the job done, including
exaggeration. The output of demonstrative criticism is not ultimately a
meaning or an interpretation, but an experience – the viewers' coming
to take note of the pertinent features of the work.

And for that to occur, a false theory may be serviceable. For example, though arguably flawed, Freud's work alerts us to many important joke structures. That is one reason that I frequently teach it. It directs my students' attention to what they ought to be thinking about, even if I believe they should not be thinking about it Freud's way. Sometimes a weak theory can provide useful demonstrative criticism.

But, then, even if the psychoanalysis of horror films can function heuristically as salutary demonstrative criticism, that does not entail that it is directly relevant to the *analysis* of the horror film. Getting people to see what needs to be analyzed and analyzing it need not converge. And, for that reason, I would caution the friends of psychoanalysis against counting the pedagogical advantages psychoanalysis may afford them as evidence of its relevance to the analysis of the horror film. For in many cases, their successes may be better described as a function of their excellence as demonstrative critics.

I began with the question of the relevance of psychoanalysis to the analysis of the horror film. I have argued that one cannot presuppose that psychoanalysis has any proprietary authority when it comes to analyzing horror. Though many practitioners more or less presume that psychoanalysis is relevant to the analysis of all horror films, I think this presumption is mistaken. I have also denied that certain psychoanalytic practices with respect to the ostensible criticism of the horror film – notably illustrative criticism and demonstrative criticism – need not be regarded as contributions to the analysis of the horror film.

But these negative conclusions do not foreclose the possibility of the relevance of psychoanalysis to the horror film, especially on a case-by-case basis (film by film, and perhaps cycle by cycle, and maybe even subgenre by subgenre) – for psychoanalytic analyses of selected horror films can be supported on the basis of our standard interpretive protocols, including historicist ones.

How many of the thousands of psychoanalytic interpretations of horror films meet those standards? Who knows? The prospect of doing the work necessary to determine that is beyond my resources. Indeed, the very thought of it is horrifying.

NOTES

1. Because I have discussed the relevance of psychoanalysis to film theory at length elsewhere, here I will focus primarily on its relevance to interpretation. Consequently, the sentence above should be read as "Is psychoanalysis relevant to the *interpretation* of the horror film?"

2. The relevance of the surrounding culture and the cognitive stock of the audience to the retrieval of authorial intentions is that these factors are indicative of what the filmmaker intends to communicate for two reasons: (1) because the filmmaker is a similarly informed participant in that culture, and (2) because it is most plausible to assume that she means to exploit what she shares with viewers to secure audience uptake of her film. That is, the currency of certain ideas in a culture, or a significant segment thereof, is a fairly reliable indicator – where the film in question bears the stamp of said ideas – that the filmmaker intends to communicate them to her public (which is also her market).

3. Another constraint on psychoanalytic interpretations arises because psycho-analytic imagery often overlaps with imagery from other cultural sources. In a given film, imagery of a self divided between a bestial component and a saintly part may owe less to psychoanalysis and more to Christianity. Whether the appropriate hermeneutic framework in such a case is Christianity or psychoanalysis will depend on the specific spin the film gives this imagery. That is, if it is to be defended on historicist grounds, a psychoanalytic interpretation requires as a pretext that there be some feature or features of the film that call upon its special resources rather than upon some other, perhaps more general, equally available cultural myth, like Christianity.

4. Evidence for this includes the program *Crossing Over* with John Edward. This program is so popular that it is crossing over itself from the Sci-Fi Channel to network televison.

5. Also, many viewers believe in aliens from outer space. If aliens are thought by Schneider to embody surmounted beliefs, then such viewers should not be horrified by extra-terrestrial monsters. But aren't the believers in life out there as horrified as the non-believers?

6. This problem also challenges Schneider on another front. He maintains that there is "realistic horror" – horror films whose antagonists are neither supernatural nor sci-fi beings, but ordinary psychos, like serial killers (such as Henry in the film that bears his name). But what beliefs are surmounted here since probably nearly everyone believes that there are sociopaths?

7. I say that this is a "default presupposition." By that I mean to signal that it can be overridden. A text may be at odds with what we know of human behavior. It may advance a palpably false, obsolete, or completely ungrounded view of human life or some aspect of it. At that point, we do not use what we know about human life in general to fill in the text. That is, our interpretations are constrained by the text; we do not normally, knowingly contradict it by projecting our own beliefs onto it, except cautiously in very special circumstances (as when the text is internally incoherent). Where a text contradicts our knowledge of human life, we typically attempt to reconstruct it from an insider point of view, appealing to what was believed about human life in the original context of its production or appealing to the *données* of the genre to which it belongs. Nevertheless, where the text is consistent with what we believe about human life and feeling, our default assumption is that we are warranted in using that knowledge to fill in the text.

8. See, e.g., Silverman (1983).

About the Contributors

LINDA BADLEY is Professor of English at Middle Tennessee State University, where she teaches courses in Victorian and modern literature, film studies, and women's studies. She is the author of *Film, Horror, and the Body Fantastic* (Greenwood) and *Writing Horror and the Body: The Fiction of Stephen King, Clive Barker, and Anne Rice* (Greenwood), and has published essays in fantasy, science fiction, and horror literature, film, and television.

NOËL CARROLL is Monroe C. Beardsley Professor of the Philosophy of Art at the University of Wisconsin–Madison. He is the author of numerous books, including *The Philosophy of Horror* (Routledge), *Theorizing the Moving Image* (Cambridge University Press), and *Philosophical Problems of Classical Film Theory* (Princeton University Press). He has also written scores of articles and reviews for academic journals and such publications as *The Village Voice, Art Forum,* and *The Boston Review.*

JONATHAN L. CRANE is Assistant Professor in the Department of Communication at the University of North Carolina at Charlotte. He has published widely on such topics as Top 40 radio, horror film spectatorship, and music censorship and is the author of *Terror and Everyday Life: Singular Moments in the History of the Horror Film* (Sage).

BARBARA CREED is Associate Professor in the Department of Fine Arts, Melbourne University. She is the author of *Horror and the Monstrous Feminine: Film, Feminism, and Psychoanalysis* (Routledge) and has published widely in the areas of film and feminist theory.

CYNTHIA FREELAND is Associate Professor of Philosophy and Director of Women's Studies at the University of Houston. She has published widely on topics in ancient philosophy and aesthetics, is the author of *The Naked and the*

Undead: Evil and the Appeal of Horror (Westview Press) and *But Is It Art?* (Oxford University Press), and is coeditor of *Philosophy and Film* (Routledge).

MICHAEL GRANT is Senior Lecturer in Film Studies at the University of Kent–Canterbury. Publications include studies of contemporary poets, essays on philosophy and the horror film, a monograph on *Dead Ringers* (Flicks Books), and a collection entitled *The Modern Fantastic: The Cinema of David Cronenberg* (Praeger). He has also edited *The Raymond Tallis Reader* (Macmillan).

HARVEY ROY GREENBERG, MD practices psychiatry and psychoanalysis in Manhattan and is Clinical Professor of Psychiatry at the Albert Einstein College of Medicine at Yeshiva University in New York City, where he teaches medical humanities and adolescent psychiatry. Dr. Greenberg is author of *The Movies on Your Mind* (Saturday Review Press) and *Screen Memories: Hollywood Cinema on the Psychiatric Couch* (Columbia University Press), and his work has appeared in a wide variety of periodicals.

MATT HILLS is the author of *Fan Cultures* (Routledge) and is currently working on a research monograph entitled *The Pleasures of Horror* (Continuum). He has written for *Foundation – The International Review of Science Fiction, New Media and Society*, and *The Velvet Light Trap*. Matt is the coeditor of *Intensities: The Journal of Cult Media*, available at http://www.cult-media.com. He is a lecturer in the School of Journalism, Media, and Cultural Studies at Cardiff University, Wales.

MICHAEL LEVINE is Professor of Philosophy at the University of Western Australia. He has written widely in metaphysics, ethics, and philosophy of religion, and is the coauthor of *Integrity and Self-Knowledge* (Ashgate). He is editor of *The Analytic Freud: Philosophy and Psychoanalysis* (Routledge) and coeditor of *Racism, Philosophy and Mind* (Cornell University Press).

WILLIAM PAUL is Director of the Film and Media Studies Program at the University of Washington, St. Louis. He is the author of *Laughing Screaming: Modern Hollywood Horror and Comedy* and *Ernest Lubitsch's American Comedy*, both published by Columbia University Press. He is currently working on *Movies/Theaters: Architecture, Exhibition, and Film Technology* for The Smithsonian Press.

STEPHEN PRINCE is Professor of Communication Studies at Virginia Tech. He is the author and editor of numerous books of film history and criticism, including *Savage Cinema: Sam Peckinpah and the Rise of Ultraviolent Movies* (University of Texas Press), *Screening Violence* (Rutgers University Press), and *Movies and Meaning: An Introduction to Film*, 2nd edition (Allyn and Bacon).

STEVEN JAY SCHNEIDER is a PhD candidate in Philosophy at Harvard University and in Cinema Studies at New York University's Tisch School of the Arts. He has published widely on the horror film and related genres, and is author of the forthcoming *Designing Fear: An Aesthetics of Cinematic Horror* (Routledge). Steven is editor of *New Hollywood Violence* (Manchester University Press) and coeditor of *Understanding Film Genres* (McGraw–Hill), *Traditions in World Cinema* (Edinburgh University Press), and *Horror International* (Wayne State University Press).

ANDREW TUDOR is Senior Lecturer in Sociology at the University of York. Film critic for New Society from 1975 to 1982, Tudor was also chairman of the York Film Theatre for more than ten years. His books include *Monsters and Mad Scientists: A Cultural History of the Horror Movie* (Basil Blackwell), *Image and Influence: Studies in the Sociology of Film* (St. Martins), and *Beyond Empiricism: Philosophy of Science in Sociology* (Routledge and Kegan Paul).

MALCOLM TURVEY was formerly managing editor of *October* and currently teaches Film History at Sarah Lawrence College. He has published essays on film theory and avant-garde film and is coeditor (with Richard Allen) of *Wittgenstein and the Arts* (Routledge).

COSIMO URBANO received his PhD in Cinema Studies from New York University's Tisch School of the Arts in 2002. He is the author of "Projections, Suspense, and Anxiety: The Modern Horror Film and its Effects," in *The Psychoanalytic Review* (1998).

ROBIN WOOD is the author of several books, including *Ingmar Bergman* (Praeger), *Hollywood from Vietnam to Reagan* (Columbia University Press), and *Hitchcock's Films Revisited* (Columbia University Press). Before retiring, Wood taught at Atkinson College, York University, Toronto. He is a founding member of the *CineAction* editorial collective.

Bibliography

Abbott, Andrew (2001). *Chaos of Disciplines*. Chicago: University of Chicago Press.

Allen, Richard (1995). *Projecting Illusion: Film Spectatorship and the Impression of Reality*. Cambridge, UK: Cambridge University Press.

—— (1999). "Psychoanalytic Film Theory." *A Companion to Film Theory*, ed. Toby Miller and Robert Stam. Oxford: Blackwell: 123–45.

Allen, Richard and Murray Smith, eds. (1997). *Film Theory and Philosophy*. Oxford: Oxford University Press.

Anderson, Joseph (1996). *The Reality of Illusion: An Ecological Approach to Cognitive Film Theory*. Carbondale, IL: Southern Illinois University Press.

Andreassi, John L. (1989). *Pyschophysiology*. Hillside, NJ: Laurence Erlbaum.

Arnzen, Michael, ed. (1997). "Special Issue on the Uncanny." *Paradoxa: Studies in World Literary Genres* 3.3–4.

Arthur, Paul (1999). "Quickies: *American Movie*." *Film Comment* 35 (6): 78–79.

Audi, Robert (1998). "Intending, Intentional Action, and Desire." *The Ways of Desire: New Essays in Philosophical Psychology on the Concept of Wanting*, ed. Joel Marks. Chicago: Precedent Publishing: 17–38.

Austin, J. L. (1971). "Performative-Constative." *The Philosophy of Language*, ed. John Searle. Oxford: Oxford University Press.

Bansak, Edmund G. (1995). *Fearing the Dark: The Val Lewton Career*. Jefferson, NC: McFarland.

Battersby, Christine (1995). "Stages on Kant's Way: Aesthetics, Morality, and the Gendered Sublime." *Feminism and Tradition in Aesthetics*, ed. Peggy Brand and Carolyn Korsmeyer. University Park, PA: Penn State University Press: 88–114.

Benjamin, Walter (1972). "A Short History of Photography (1931)." *Screen* 13 (1): 5–26.

Benshoff, Harry (1997). *Monsters in the Closet: Homosexuality and the Horror Film*. Manchester: Manchester University Press.

Berks, John (1992). "What Alice Does: Looking Otherwise at *The Cat People*." *Cinema Journal* 32 (1), Fall: 26–42.

Bettelheim, Bruno (1962). *Symbolic Wounds*. New York: Collier Books.

Biskind, Peter (1983). *Seeing is Believing: How Hollywood Taught Us to Stop Worrying and Love the Fifties*. London: Pluto Press.

Black, Joel (1991). *The Aesthetics of Murder: A Study in Romantic Literature and Contemporary Culture*. Baltimore, MD: Johns Hopkins University Press.

Booth, Wayne C. (1974). *A Rhetoric of Irony*. Chicago: University of Chicago Press.

Bordwell, David (1989). *Making Meaning: Inference and Rhetoric in the Interpretation of Cinema*. Cambridge, MA: Harvard University Press.

(1996). "Contemporary Film Studies and the Vicissitudes of Grand Theory." *Post-Theory: Reconstructing Film Studies*, ed. David Bordwell and Noël Carroll. Madison: University of Wisconsin Press: 3–36.

Bordwell, David and Noël Carroll (1996). "Introduction." *Post-Theory*, ed. D. Bordwell and N. Carroll, op. cit.: xiii–xvii.

Bordwell, David, Janet Staiger, and Kristin Thompson (1985). *The Classical Hollywood Cinema: Film Style and Mode of Production to 1960*. New York: Columbia University Press.

Bourdieu, Pierre (1990). *Homo Academicus*. Cambridge, UK: Polity Press.

(1993). *The Field of Cultural Production*. Cambridge, UK: Polity Press.

Bouveresse, Jacques (1995). *Wittgenstein Reads Freud: The Myth of the Unconscious*. Princeton, NJ: Princeton University Press.

Braddock, Jeremy and Stephen Hock, eds. (2000a). *Directed by Allan Smithee*. Minneapolis: University of Minnesota Press.

(2000b). "The Spectre of Illegitimacy in an Age of Disillusionment and Crisis." *Directed by Allen Smithee*, ed. J. Braddock and S. Hock, op. cit.: 3–27.

Bram, Christopher (1996). *Father of Frankenstein*. London: Plume.

Britton, Andrew, Richard Lippe, Tony Williams, and Robin Wood, eds. (1979). *American Nightmares: Essays on the Horror Film*. Toronto: Festival of Festivals.

Brophy, Philip (1986). "Horrality – The Textuality of Contemporary Horror Films." *Screen* 27 (1): 2–13.

Brottman, Mikita (1996). "Once Upon a Time in Texas: *The Texas Chainsaw Massacre* as Inverted Fairytale." *Necronomicon: The Journal of Horror & Erotic Cinema 1*, ed. Andy Black. London: Creation: 7–21.

Brubaker, Rogers (1993). "Social Theory as Habitus." *Bourdieu: Critical Perspectives*, ed. Craig Calhoun, Edward LiPuma, and Moishe Postone. Cambridge, UK: Polity Press: 212–34.

Brugger, Peter, Reto Agosti, Marianne Regard, Heinz-Gregor Wieser, and Theodor Landis (1994). "Heautoscopy, Epilepsy, and Suicide." *Journal of Neurology, Neurosurgery & Psychiatry* 57 (7): 838–39.

Brugger, Peter, Marriane Regard, and Theodor Landis (1996). "Unilaterally Felt 'Presences': The Neuropsychiatry of One's Invisible Doppelganger." *Neuropsychiatry, Neuropsychology, and Behavioral Neurology* 9 (2): 114–22.

Cantor, Joanne (1998). "Children's Attractions to Violent Television Programming." *Why We Watch: The Attractions of Violent Entertainment*, ed. Jeffrey H. Goldstein. New York: Oxford University Press: 88–115.

Cantor, Joanne and Mary Beth Oliver (1996). "Developmental Differences in Responses to Horror." *Horror Films: Current Research on Audience Preferences and Reactions*, ed. James B. Weaver III and Ron Tamborini. Hillside, NJ: Lawrence Erlbaum: 65–69.

Carducci, Mark Patrick, dir. (2000). *Flying Saucers over Hollywood: The Plan 9 Companion*. Image Entertainment.

Carroll, Noël (1981). "Nightmare and the Horror Film: The Symbolic Biology of Fantastic Beings." *Film Quarterly* 34 (3): 16–25.

(1988). *Philosophical Problems of Classical Film Theory.* Princeton, NJ: Princeton University Press.

(1990). *The Philosophy of Horror; or, Paradoxes of the Heart.* New York: Routledge.

(1992). "Cognitivism, Contemporary Film Theory and Method." *Journal of Dramatic Theory and Criticism* VI (2): 199–219.

(1994). "The Paradox of Junk Fiction." *Philosophy and Literature* 18: 225–41.

(1995). "The Image of Women in Films: A Defense of a Paradigm." *Feminism and Tradition in Aesthetics*, ed. P. Brand and C. Korsmeyer, op cit.: 371–91.

(1996). "Prospects for Film Theory: A Personal Assessment." *Post-Theory*, ed. D. Bordwell and N. Carroll, op. cit.: 37–68.

(1997). "Art, Narrative, and Emotion." *Emotion and the Arts*, ed. Mette Hjort and Sue Laver. New York: Oxford University Press: 190–211.

(1998). *Mystifying Movies: Fads and Fallacies in Contemporary Film Theory.* New York: Columbia University Press.

Castle, Terry (1995). *The Female Thermometer: 18th Century Culture and the Invention of the Uncanny.* Oxford: Oxford University Press.

Cavell, Marcia (1993). *The Psychoanalytic Mind: From Freud to Philosophy.* Cambridge, MA: Harvard University Press.

Cavell, Stanley (1979). *The Claim of Reason: Wittgenstein, Skepticism, Morality, and Tragedy.* Oxford: Oxford University Press.

(1987). *Disowning Knowledge In Six Plays of Shakespeare.* Cambridge, UK: Cambridge University Press.

(1996). *Contesting Tears: The Hollywood Melodrama of the Unknown Woman.* Chicago: University of Chicago Press.

Charney, Leo (1995). "In a Moment: Film and the Philosophy of Modernity." *Cinema and the Invention of Modern Life*, ed. Leo Charney and Vanessa Schwartz. Berkeley: University of California Press: 279–94.

Chodorow, Nancy (1987). *Feminism and Psychoanalytic Theory.* New Haven, CT: Yale University Press.

Cioffi, Frank (1970). "Freud and the Idea of a Pseudo-Science." *Explanation in the Behavioural Sciences*, ed. Robert Borger and Frank Cioffi. Cambridge, UK: Cambridge University Press: 471–99.

(1985). "Psychoanalysis, Pseudo-Science and Testability." *Popper and the Human Sciences*, ed. Gregory Currie and Alan Musgrave. Dordrecht: Nijhoff: 13–44.

(1988). "'Exegetical Myth-Making' in Grünbaum's Indictment of Popper and Exoneration of Freud." *Mind, Psychoanalysis and Science*, ed. Peter Clark and Crispin Wright. Oxford: Blackwell: 61–87.

Clark, Peter and Crispin Wright, eds. (1988). *Mind, Psychoanalysis and Science.* Oxford: Blackwell.

Clover, Carol (1987). "Her Body, Himself: Gender in the Slasher Film." *Representations* 20: 187–228.

(1992). *Men, Women, and Chain Saws: Gender in the Modern Horror Film.* Princeton, NJ: Princeton University Press.

Cohen, Jeffrey Jerome (1996). "Monster Culture (Seven Theses)." *Monster Theory: Reading Culture*, ed. Jeffrey Jerome Cohen. Minneapolis: University of Minnesota Press: 3–25.

Cohen, Margaret (1995). "Panoramic Literature and the Invention of Everyday Genres." *Cinema and the Invention of Modern Life*, ed. L. Charney and V. Schwartz, op. cit.: 227–52.

Colby, Kenneth and Robert Stroller (1988). *Cognitive Science and Psychoanalysis*. Hillside, NJ: Lawrence Erlbaum.

Collins, Randall (1998). *The Sociology of Philosophies: A Global Theory of Intellectual Change* Cambridge, MA: Belknap Press of Harvard University Press.

Condon, Bill (1999). "Director's Commentary" (*Gods and Monsters* DVD, Collector's Edition), Universal Studios.

Cook, David (1998). "Auteur Cinema and the 'Film' Generation in 1970s Hollywood." *The New American Cinema*, ed. Jon Lewis. Durham, NC: Duke University Press: 11–37.

Cook, Pam (1999). "Part Six: Authorship and Cinema." *The Cinema Book*, ed. Pam Cook and Mieke Bernink. London: BFI: 233–310.

Copjec, Joan (1982). "The Anxiety of the Influencing Machine." *October* 23, Winter: 43–59.

(1995). *Read My Desire: Lacan Against the Historicists*. Cambridge, MA: MIT Press.

Corrigan, Tim (1998). "Auteurs and the New Hollywood." *The New American Cinema*, ed. J. Lewis, op. cit.: 38–63.

Cowan, Gloria and Margaret O'Brien (1990). "Gender and Survival vs. Death in Slasher Films: A Content Analysis." *Sex Roles* 23: 187–96.

Craib, Ian (1998). *Experiencing Identity*. London: Sage.

Crane, Jonathan Lake (1994). *Terror and Everyday Life: Singular Moments in the History of the Horror Film*. London: Sage.

Creed, Barbara (1986). "Horror and the Monstrous-Feminine: An Imaginary Abjection." *Screen* 27 (1): 44–70.

(1990a). "Phallic Panic: Male Hysteria and *Dead Ringers*." *Screen* 31 (2): 125–46.

(1990b). "Review Article: Andrew Tudor, *Monsters and Mad Scientists: A Cultural History of the Horror Movie*." *Screen* 31 (2): 236–42.

(1993). *The Monstrous-Feminine: Film, Feminism, Psychoanalysis*. New York: Routledge.

Crews, Frederick (1995). *The Memory Wars: Freud's Legacy in Dispute*. New York: New York Review of Books.

Culler, Jonathan (1980). "Literary Competence." *Reader Response Criticism from Formalism to Structuralism*, ed. Jane Tompkins. Baltimore, MD: Johns Hopkins University Press: 101–117.

Currie, Gregory (1995). *Image and Mind: Film, Philosophy, Cognitive Science*. Cambridge, UK: Cambridge University Press.

Dadoun, Roger (1989). "Fetishism in the Horror Film." *Fantasy & the Cinema*, ed. J. Donald. London: BFI: 39–62.

Day, William P. (1985). *In the Circles of Fear and Desire: A Study of Gothic Fantasy*. Chicago: University of Chicago Press.

Derrida, Jaques (1987). "The Parergon." *The Truth in Painting*. Chicago: University of Chicago Press.

Dika, Vera (1990). *Games of Terror: Halloween, Friday the 13th, and the Films of the Stalker Cycle.* London: Associated University Presses.

Doane, Mary Ann (1982). "Film and the Masquerade: Theorising the Female Spectator." *Screen* 23 (3–4): 74–88.

(1987). *The Desire to Desire: The Woman's Film of the Forties.* Bloomington: Indiana University Press.

(1993). "Subjectivity and Desire: An (other) Way of Looking." *Contemporary Film Theory,* ed. Anthony Easthope. London: Longman: 161–78.

Donald, James, ed. (1989). *Fantasy and the Cinema.* London: BFI.

(1991). "On the Threshold: Psychoanalysis and Cultural Studies." *Psychoanalysis and Cultural Theory: Thresholds,* ed. James Donald. Basingstoke, UK: Macmillan Press: 1–10.

Douglas, Mary (1966). *Purity and Danger: An Analysis of Concepts of Pollution and Taboo.* Harmondsworth: Penguin.

Dyer, Richard (1999). *Se7en.* London: BFI.

Edmondson, Mark (1997). *Nightmare on Main Street: Angels, Sadomasochism, and the Culture of Gothic.* Cambridge, MA: Harvard University Press.

Edwards, Emily (1984). "The relationship between sensation-seeking and horror movie interest and attendance." University of Tenessee, unpublished doctoral dissertation. Knoxville, TN.

Ekelund, Bo G. (2000). "Space, Time and John Gardner." *Pierre Bourdieu: Fieldwork in Culture,* ed. Nicholas Brown and Imre Szeman. Lanham, MD: Rowman & Littlefield.

Elsaesser, Thomas (2001). "Six Degrees of *Nosferatu.*" *Sight and Sound* 11 (2): 12–15.

Erwin, Edward (1993). "Philosophers on Freudianism: An Examination of Replies to Grünbaum's 'Foundations'." *Philosophical Problems of the Internal and External Worlds: Essays in the Philosophy of Alfred Grünbaum,* ed. John Earman, Allen I. Janis, Gerald J. Massey, and Nicholas Rescher. Pittsburgh, PA: University of Pittsburgh Press: 409–60.

(1996). *A Final Accounting: Philosophical and Empirical Issues in Freudian Psychology.* Cambridge, MA: MIT Press.

Evans, William (1984). "Monster Movies: A Sexual Theory." *Planks of Reason: Essays on the Horror Film,* ed. Barry Keith Grant. Metuchen, NJ: Scarecrow Press.

Fasolo, F. and G. Filidoro (1986). "A Case of Doppelganger Delusion Treated with a Fluphenazine Compound." *Psichiatria Generale e dell'Eta Evolutiva* 24 (2): 21–25.

Feagin, Susan (1992). "Monsters, Disgust and Fascination." *Philosophical Studies* 65: 75–84.

Ferris, Paul (1998). *Dr. Freud: A Life.* Washington, DC: Counterpoint Press.

Fish, Stanley (1980). *Is There a Text in This Class? The Authority of Interpretive Communities.* Cambridge, MA: Harvard University Press.

Flanagan, Kieran (1999). *The Enchantment of Sociology.* London: Macmillan.

Foley, Catherine, ed. (2000). *Facets Movie Lovers Video Guide.* Chicago: Facets Video.

Forgays, Donald, Tytus Sosnowski, and Kazimierz Wrzesniewski, eds. (1992). *Anxiety: Recent Developments in Cognitive, Psychophysiological, and Health Research.* Washington, DC: Hemisphere Publishing Corporation.

Freeland, Cynthia (1996). "Feminist Frameworks for Horror Films." *Post-Theory*, ed. D. Bordwell and N. Carroll, op. cit.: 195–219.
(1999a). *The Naked and the Undead: Evil and the Appeal of Horror.* Boulder, CO: Westview Press.
(1999b). "The Sublime in Cinema." *Passionate Views: Film, Cognition, and Emotion*, ed. Carl Plantinga and Greg M. Smith. Baltimore, MD: Johns Hopkins University Press: 65–83.
Freud, Sigmund (1900). *The Interpretation of Dreams.* New York: Avon Books, 1965.
(1901a). "Childhood Memories and Screen Memories." *The Psychopathology of Everyday Life. The Penguin Freud Library* 5. London: Penguin Books, 1975: 83–93.
(1901b). *The Psychopathology of Everyday Life. SE* 6.
(1905). *Jokes and Their Relation to the Unconcious. SE* 8.
(1907). "Delusions and Dreams in Jensen's *Gradiva*." *SE* 9: 7–93.
(1908). "Creative Writers and Day-Dreaming." *SE* 9: 141–54.
(1911). "On Narcissism: An Introduction." *A General Selection from the Works of Sigmund Freud*, ed. John Rickman. Garden City, NY: Doubleday Anchor, 1957: 104–23.
(1912). "On the Universal Tendency Towards Debasement in the Sphere of Love (Contributions to the Psychology of Love)." *SE* 11: 178–90.
(1913). "Animism, Magic and the Omnipotence of Thoughts." *Totem and Taboo: Some Points of Agreement between the Mental Lives of Savages and Neurotics*, ed. James Strachey. New York: W.W. Norton, 1989: 75–99.
(1915a). "A Case of Paranoia Running Counter to the Psychoanalytic Theory of the Disease." *The Psychopathology of Everyday Life. The Pelican Freud Library* 10. London: Penguin Books: 145–58.
(1915b). "The Unconscious." *Collected Papers* 4, ed. James Strachey. New York: Basic Books, 1959.
(1917a). "Introductory Lectures on Psychoanalysis." *SE* 16–17.
(1917b). "Mourning and Melancholia." *SE* 14.
(1917c). "The Paths to the Formation of Symptoms." *SE* 16: 358–77.
(1919a). "A Child is Being Beaten: A Contribution to the Study of the Origin of Sexual Perversion." *SE* 17: 175–204.
(1919b). "The 'Uncanny'." *The Penguin Freud Library Volume 14: Art and Literature*, ed. James Strachey. London: Penguin, 1990: 335–76.
(1920). "Beyond the Pleasure Principle." *The Standard Edition of the Complete Psychological Works of Sigmund Freud* 18. ed. J. Strachey. London: The Hogarth Press, 1953–74: 7–64.
(1921). "Psychoanalysis and Telepathy." *SE* 18: 178–81.
(1926). *Inhibitions, Symptoms, and Anxiety.* New York: W.W. Norton, 1959.
(1927a). "Fetishism." *SE* 21: 147–57.
(1927b). "The Future of an Illusion." *Civilization, Society and Religion. The Pelican Freud Library* 12. London: Penguin Books, 1995: 200–242.
(1930). "Civilization and Its Discontents." *Civilization, Society and Religion.* London: Penguin Books, 1995: 243–344.
(1954). *The Origins of Psychoanalysis: Letters to Wilhelm Fleiss, Drafts and Notes (1887–1902).* New York: Basic Books.

Fujiwara, Chris (2001). *Jacques Tourneur: The Cinema of Nightfall.* Baltimore, MD: Johns Hopkins University Press.

Gabard, Glen and Krin Gabbard (1987). *Psychiatry and the Cinema.* Chicago: University of Chicago Press.

Gabbard, Glen and Krin Gabbard (1999). *Psychiatry and the Cinema.* Washington, DC: American Psychiatric Press. 2nd edition.

Galindo, Steve (1996). "The Church of the Heavenly Wood." Http://welcome.to/woodism (accessed 10/30/02).

Gardner, Sebastian (1993). *Irrationality and the Philosophy of Psychoanalysis.* Cambridge, UK: Cambridge University Press.

Gaut, Berys (1993). "The Paradox of Horror." *British Journal of Aesthetics* 33 (4): 333–45.

   (1994). "On Cinema and Perversion." *Film and Philosophy* 1: 3–17.

   (1997). "Film Authorship and Collaboration." *Film Theory and Philosophy*, ed. R. Allen and M. Smith, op. cit.: 149–72.

   (1999). "Identification and Emotion in Narrative Film." *Passionate Views: Film, Cognition, and Emotion*, ed. C. Plantinga and G. Smith, op. cit.: 200–216.

Gay, Peter (1988). *Freud: A Life for Our Time.* London: Papermac.

Geertz, Clifford (1973). "Religion as a Cultural System." *The Interpretation of Cultures.* New York: Basic Books: 87–125.

Gerstner, David (2003). "The Practices of Authorship." *Authorship and Film*, ed. David Gerstner and Janet Staiger. New York: Routledge: 3–26.

Giddens, Anthony (1984). *The Constitution of Society: Outline of the Theory of Structuration.* Cambridge, UK: Polity Press.

Glymour, Clark (1991). "Freud's Androids." *The Cambridge Companion to Freud*, ed. Jerome Neu. Cambridge, UK: Cambridge University Press: 44–85.

Gombrich, E. H. (1969). *Art and Illusion: A Study in the Psychology of Pictorial Representation.* Princeton, NJ: Princeton University Press.

Goodman, Nelson (1976). *Languages of Art: An Approach to a Theory of Symbols.* Indianapolis, IN: Hackett.

Gould, Timothy (1995). "Intensity and Its Audiences: Toward a Feminist Perspective on the Kantian Sublime." *Feminism and Tradition in Aesthetics*, ed. P. Brand and C. Korsmeyer, op. cit.: 66–87.

Grant, Barry Keith, ed. (1995). *Film Genre Reader II.* Austin: University of Texas Press.

   (1996). *The Dread of Difference: Gender and the Horror Film.* Austin: University of Texas Press.

Grant, Michael. (1997). *Dead Ringers.* Trowbridge: Flicks Books.

   (2003). "On the Question of the Horror Film." *Dark Thoughts: Philosophic Reflections on Cinematic Horror*, ed. Steven Jay Schneider and Daniel Shaw. Lanham, MD: Scarecrow Press: 120–37.

Greenberg, Harvey Roy (1970a). "The Sleep of Reason II: The Beast in the Boudoir – Or, You Can't Marry That Girl, You're a Gorilla!" *The Movies on Your Mind*, op. cit.: 219–31.

   (1970b). "The Sleep of Reason I: Drowing the Ceremony of Innocence – Or, How Not to Raise a Monster." *The Movies on Your Mind: Film Classics on the Couch from Fellini to Frankenstein.* New York: E.P. Dutton, Inc./Saturday Review Press: 213–18.

(1993). "Re-Imagining the Gargoyle: Psychoanalytic Notes on *Alien* and the Contemporary Horror Film." *Screen Memories: Hollywood Cinema on the Psychoanalytic Couch.* New York: Columbia University Press.

Greenberg, Harvey Roy and Krin Gabbard (1993). "Reel Significations: An Anatomy of Psychoanalytic Film Criticism." *Screen Memories,* op. cit.: 15–37.

Grimm, Brothers (1987). *The Complete Fairy Tales of the Brothers Grimm.* New York: Bantam.

Grixti, Joseph (1989). *Terrors of Uncertainty: The Cultural Contexts of Horror Fiction.* New York: Routledge.

Grodal, Torben (1997). *Moving Pictures: A New Thory of Film Genres, Feelings, and Cognition.* Oxford: Clarendon.

Grünbaum, Adolf (1984). *The Foundations of Psychoanalysis: A Philosophical Critique.* Berkeley: University of California Press.

(1988). "Precis of *The Foundations of Psychoanalysis.*" *Mind, Psychoanalysis and Science,* ed. P. Clark and C. Wright. Oxford: Blackwell: 3–32.

(1993). *Validation in the Clinical Theory of Psychoanalysis: A Study in the Philosophy of Psychoanalysis.* Madison, CT: International Universities Press.

Gunning, Tom (1988). "'Like unto a Leopard': Figurative Discourse in *Cat People* (1942) and Todorov's *The Fantastic.*" *Wide Angle* 10 (3): 30–39.

Haimes, Ted, dir. (1999). *Dial H for Hitchcock: The Genius Behind the Showman.* Universal TV.

Halberstam, Judith (1995). *Skin Shows: Gothic Horror and the Technology of Monsters.* Durham, NC: Duke University Press.

Hale, Nathan (1995). *The Rise and Crisis of Psychoanalysis in America: Freud and the Americans, 1917–1985.* New York: Oxford University Press.

Hanson, Patricia (1993). *AFI Catalog of Feature Films, 1931–1940.* Washington, DC: American Film Institute.

Hardy, Phil, ed. (1986). *The Encyclopedia of Horror Movies.* New York: Harper & Row.

Haskell, Molly (2001). "Life with Andrew...and Film." *Citizen Sarris: American Film Critic – Essays in Honor of Andrew Sarris,* ed. Emanuel Levy. Lanham, MD: Scarecrow Press: 3–5.

Hassold, Chris (1994). "The Double and Doubling in Modern and Postmodern Art." *Journal of the Fantastic of the Arts* 6 (2/3): 253–74.

Hawkins, Joan (2000). *Cutting Edge: Art-Horror and the Horrific Avant-garde.* Minneapolis and London: University of Minnesota Press.

Hebb, Donald (1946). "On the Nature of Fear." *Psychological Review* 53: 259–76.

Hertz, Neil (1985). *The End of the Line: Essays on Psychoanalysis and the Sublime.* New York: Columbia University Press.

Herzogenrath, Bernd (2002). "Join the United Mutations: Tod Browning's *Freaks.*" *Post Script: Essays in Film and the Humanities* 21 (3): Summer: 8–19.

Hillier, Jim (1985). "Introduction: Part II: American Cinema." *Cahiers du Cinema: The 1950s: Neo-Realism, Hollywood, New Wave,* ed. Jim Hillier. Cambridge, MA: Harvard University Press: 73–115.

Hjort, Mette and Sue Laver (1997). *Emotion and the Arts.* New York: Oxford University Press.

Holland, Norman (1992). *The Critical I.* New York: Columbia University Press.
   (2000). *Poems in Persons* Cybereditions. Christchurch, NZ.
Holland, Norman and Leona Sherman (1976–77). "Gothic Possibilities." *New Literary History* 8: 279–94.
Hollows, Joanne, Peter Hutchings, and Mark Jancovich, eds. (2000). *The Film Studies Reader.* London: Arnold.
Hopkins, James (1982). "Introduction: Philosophy and Psychoanalysis." *Philosophical Essays on Freud*, ed. James Hopkins and Richard Wollheim. Cambridge, UK: Cambridge University Press: vii–xiv.
   (1988). "Epistemology and Depth Psychology: Critical Notes on *The Foundations of Psychoanalysis.*" *Mind, Psychoanalysis and Science*, ed. P. Clark and C. Wright, op. cit. Oxford: Blackwell: 33–60.
   (1992). "Psychoanalysis, Interpretation, and Science." *Psychoanalysis, Mind and Art: Perspectives on Richard Wollheim*, ed. James Hopkins and Anthony Savile. Oxford: Blackwell: 3–33.
   (1996). "Psychoanalytic and Scientific Reasoning." *British Journal of Psychotherapy* 13 (1): 86–105.
Hoxter, Julian (1998). "Anna with a Devil Inside: Klein, Argento, and *The Stendhal Syndrome.*" *Necronomicon: The Journal of Horror and Erotic Cinema* 2, ed. Andy Black. London: Creation Books: 99–109.
Hultkrans, Andrew (1994). "Look Back in Angora." *Arforum International* 33 (4): 11.
Iaccino, James (1994). *Psychological Reflections on Cinematic Terror: Jungian Archetypes in Horror Films.* Westport, CT: Praeger.
Jackson, Rosemary (1981). *Fantasy: The Literature of Subversion.* London: Methuen.
Jancovich, Mark (1992). *Horror.* London: B.T. Batsford.
   (1995). "Screen Theory." *Approaches to Popular Film*, ed. Joanne Hollows and Mark Jancovich. Manchester, UK: Manchester University Press: 124–50.
   (2000). "'A Real Shocker': Authenticity, Genre and the Struggle for Distinction." *Continuum: Journal of Media and Cultural Studies* 14 (1): 23–35.
Jenkins, Richard (1992). *Pierre Bourdieu.* London: Routledge.
Jones, Ernest (1953). *Sigmund Freud: Life and Work: The Young Freud 1856–1900.* London: The Hogarth Press.
   (1955). *Sigmund Freud: Life and Work: Years of Maturity 1901–1919.* London: The Hogarth Press.
   (1957). *Sigmund Freud: Life and Work: The Last Phase 1919–1939.* London: The Hogarth Press.
   (1971). *On the Nightmare.* London: Liveright.
Jung, Carl (1981). "On Synchronicity" (1957). *The Portable Jung*, ed. J. Campbell. New York: Penguin: 505–18.
   (1959). "The Shadow." *Aion: Researches into the Phenomenology of the Self.* Collected Works, Volume 9. New York: Pantheon.
Kant, Immanuel (1957). *The Critique of Judgment.* Oxford: Clarendon Press.
Kaplan, Morton (1973). "Fantasy of Paternity and the Doppelganger: Mary Shelley's *Frankenstein.*" *The Unspoken Motive: A Guide to Psychoanalytic Literary Criticism*, ed. Morton Kaplan and Robert Kloss. New York: Free Press: 119–46.

Kapsis, Robert (1992). *Hitchcock: The Making of a Reputation*. Chicago: University of Chicago Press.

Kavanaugh, James (1980). "'Son of a Bitch': Feminism, Humanism, and Science in *Alien*." *October* 13: 91–100.

Kawin, Bruce (1995). "Children of the Light." *Film Genre Reader II*, ed. Barry Keith Grant. Austin: University of Texas Press: 308–29.

Kendrick, Walter (1991). *The Thrill of Fear: 250 Years of Scary Entertainment*. New York: Grove Weidenfeld.

Kepler, C. F. (1972). *The Literature of the Second Self*. Tucson, AZ: University of Arizona Press.

Kieslowski, Krzysztof (1993). *Kieslowski on Kieslowski*. London: Faber & Faber.

King, Noel (1999). "New Hollywood." *The Cinema Book*, ed. P. Cook and M. Bernink, op. cit.: 98–106.

King, Noel and Toby Miller (1999). "Authorship in the 1990s." *The Cinema Book*, ed. P. Cook and M. Bernink, op. cit: 311–15.

Kivy, Peter (1997). "Music in the Movies, a Philosophical Enquiry." *Film Theory and Philosophy*, ed. R. Allen and M. Smith, op. cit.: 308–28.

Klevan, Andrew (2000). "The Mysterious Disappearance of Style: Some Critical Notes about the Writing on *Dead Ringers*." *The Modern Fantastic: The Films of David Cronenberg*, ed. Michael Grant. Trowbridge, UK: Flicks Books.

Knight, Deborah (1994). "Making Sense of Genre." *Film and Philosophy* 2: http:// www.hanover.edu/philos/film/vol_02/knight.html (accessed 12/5/02).

Krauss, Rosalind (1993). *The Optical Unconscious*. Cambridge, MA: MIT Press.

Kristeva, Julia (1979). "Ellipsis on Dread and the Specular Seduction." *Wide Angle* 3 (3): 42–47.

(1982). *Powers of Horror: An Essay on Abjection*. New York: Columbia University Press.

Lacan, Jacques (1979). *The Four Fundamental Concepts of Psychoanalysis*. New York: Norton.

(1987). *Ecrits: A Selection*. London: Tavistock.

(1988). *The Seminars of Jacques Lacan: Book II*. Cambridge, UK: Cambridge University Press.

LaCaze, Marguerite (2002). "The Mourning of Loss in *The Sixth Sense*." *Post Script: Essays in Film and the Humanities* 21 (3): Summer: 111–21.

Lakatos, Imre (1970). "Falsification and the Methodology of Scientific Research Programmes." *Criticism and the Growth of Knowledge*, ed. Imre Lakatos and Alan Musgrave. Cambridge, UK: Cambridge University Press.

Laplanche, Jean (1974). *The Language of Psychoanalysis*. New York: Norton.

Larouche, Michel (1985). *Alexandro Jodorowsky: Cineaste Panique*. Paris: Editions Albatros.

Lear, Jonathan (1990). *Love and Its Place in Nature: A Philosophical Interpretation of Freudian Psychoanalysis*. New York: Noonday Press.

Leibowitz, Flo (1996). "Apt Feelings, or Why 'Women's Films' Aren't Trivial." *Post-Theory*, ed. D. Bordwell and N. Carroll, op. cit.: 219–29.

Levine, Michael, ed. (2000a). "How Right Does Psychoanalysis Have to Be?" *The Analytic Freud*, ed. M. Levine, op. cit.: 1–8.

(2000b). *The Analytic Freud: Philosophy and Psychoanalysis*. New York: Routledge.

(2001). "Depraved Spectators and Impossible Audiences." *Film and Philosophy* 5: 63–71.

Levinson, Jerrold (1996). "Film Music and Narrative Agency." *Post-Theory*, ed. D. Bordwell and N. Carroll, op. cit.: 248–82.

Levy, Emanuel (2001). *Citizen Sarris, American Film Critic: Essays in Honor of Andrew Sarris*, ed. Emanuel Levy. Lanham, MD: Scarecrow Press.

Linderman, Deborah (1990). "Cinematic Abreaction: Tourneur's *Cat People*." *Psychoanalysis and Cinema*, ed. E. Ann Kaplan. New York: Routledge: 73–97.

Lopate, Phillip (2001). "The Gallant Andrew Sarris." *Citizen Sarris*, ed. E. Levy, op. cit.: 57–62.

Lyons, William (1980). *Gilbert Ryle: An Introduction to His Philosophy*. Atlantic Highlands, NJ: Humanities Press.

Lyotard, Jean-Francois (1994). *Lessons on the Analytic of the Sublime: Kant's Critique of Judgment, Sections 23–29*. Stanford, CA: Stanford University Press.

Macmillan, Malcolm (1997). *Freud Evaluated*: The Completed Arc. Cambridge, MA: MIT Press.

Mank, Gregory William (1994). *Hollywood Cauldron: Thirteen Horror Films from the Genre's Golden Age*. Jefferson, NC: McFarland & Co.

Marcus, Steven (1974). "Freud and Dora: Story, History, Case History." *Partisan Review* 41: 12–23, 89–108.

Masters, Brian (1985). *Killing for Company: The Case of Denis Nilsen*. London: J. Cape.

Mayer, Mercer (1968). *There's a Nightmare in My Closet*. New York: Dial.

Mendik, Xavier (1998). "From the Monstrous Mother to the 'Third Sex': Female Abjection in the Films of Dario Argento." *Necronomicon: The Journal of Horror and Erotic Cinema* 2, ed. Andy Black. London: Creation: 110–33.

Merhige, E. Elias (2000). "Interview with E. Elias Merhige." (*Shadow of the Vampire* DVD) Saturn/Lion's Gate.

Metz, Christian (1982). *Psychoanalysis and Cinema: The Imaginary Signifier*. London: Macmillan Press.

Mishra, Vijay (1994). *The Gothic Sublime*. Albany, NY: SUNY Press.

Molitor, Fred and Barry Sapolsky (1993). "Sex, Violence and Victimization in Slasher Films." *Journal of Broadcasting and Electronic Media* 37: 233–42.

Moretti, Franco (1983). "Dialectic of Fear." *Signs Taken for Wonders: Essays in the Sociology of Literary Form*. London: Verso.

Morgan, Jack (2002). *The Biology of Horror: Gothic Literature and Film*. Carbondale, IL: Southern Illinois University Press.

Morris, Gary (2000). "Graverobbers and Drag Queens from Outer Space! Four Ed Wood Greats on DVD." *Bright Lights Film Journal* 28: http://www.brightlightsfilm.com/28/edwood1.html (accessed 12/5/02).

Mulhall, Stephen (2002). *On Film*. London: Routledge.

Mulvey, Laura (1975). "Visual Pleasure and Narrative Cinema." *Screen* 16 (3): 6–18.

Neale, Stephen (1980). *Genre*. London: BFI.

(1989). "Issues of Difference: *Alien* and *Blade Runner*." *Fantasy and the Cinema*, ed. James Donald. London: BFI: 213–23.

Neill, Alex (1992). "On a Paradox of the Heart." *Philosophical Studies* 65: 53–65.

Nichols, Bill, ed. (1976). *Movies and Methods.* Berkeley: University of California Press.

Oakley, Justin (1993). *Morality and the Emotions.* London: Routledge.

O'Hehir, Andrew (2001). "Blood, Breasts and Beasts." *Salon* (26 January): http://www.salon.com/ent/movies/2001/01/26/kaufman/print.html (accessed 12/5/02).

Osborne, Peter (2000). *Philosophy in Cultural Theory.* New York and London: Routledge.

Paini, Dominique (2001). "The Wandering Gaze: Hitchcock's Use of Transparencies." *Hitchcock and Art: Fatal Coincidences,* ed. Dominique Paini and Guy Cogeval. Montreal: Montreal Museum of Fine Arts.

Parker, Ian (1997). *Psychoanalytic Culture: Psychoanalytic Discourse in Western Society.* London: Sage.

Paul, William (1994). *Laughing Screaming: Modern Hollywood Horrory and Comedy.* New York: Columbia University Press.

Penley, Constance (1989). "Feminism, Film Theory, and the Bachelor Machines." *The Future of an Illusion: Film, Feminism, and Psychoanalysis.* Minneapolis: University of Minnesota Press.

Perez, Gilberto (2000). "Toward a Rhetoric of Film: Identification and the Spectator." *Senses of Cinema* 5: http://www.sensesofcinema.com/contents/00/5/rhetoric2.html (accessed 12/5/02).

Perry, David (1967). *The Concept of Pleasure.* The Hague: Mouton & Co.

Peters, Charles C. (1970). *Motion Pictures and Standards of Morality.* New York: Arno Press.

Peterson, James (1996). "Is a Cognitive Approach to the Avante-garde Cinema Perverse?" *Post-Theory,* ed. D. Bordwell and N. Carroll, op. cit.: 108–29.

Pinedo, Isabel (1997). *Recreational Terror: Women & the Pleasures of Horror Film Viewing.* Albany, NY: SUNY Press.

Plantinga, Carl and Greg Smith, eds. (1999). *Passionate Views: Film, Cognition, and Emotion.* Baltimore, MD: Johns Hopkins University Press.

Polan, Dana (2001). "Auteur Desire." *Screening the Past: An International, Refereed, Electronic Journal of Visual Media and History* 12: http://www.latrobe.edu.au/screeningthepast/firstrelease/fr0301/dpfr12a.htm (accessed 12/5/02)

Prawer, S. S. (1980). *Caligari's Children: The Film as Tale of Terror.* Oxford: Oxford University Press.

Prince, Stephen (1988). "Dread, Taboo, and *The Thing*: Toward a Social Theory of the Horror Film." *Wide Angle* 10 (3): 19–29.

    (1996). "Psychoanalytic Film Theory and the Problem of the Missing Spectator." *Post-Theory,* ed. D. Bordwell and N. Carroll, op. cit.: 71–86.

    (1998). *Savage Cinema: Sam Peckinpah and the Rise of Ultraviolent Movies.* Austin: University of Texas Press.

    ed. (2000). *Screening Violence.* New Brunswick, NJ: Rutgers University Press.

Punter, David (1996). *The Literature of Terror: A History of Gothic Fictions from 1765 to the Present Day.* London: Longman.

Rank, Otto (1989). *The Double: A Psychoanalytic Study* (1925). London: Maresfield Library.

Ray, Robert B. (2001). "The Automatic Auteur; or, A Certain Tendency in Film Criticism." *Directed by Allan Smithee*, ed. J. Braddock and S. Hock, op. cit.: 51–75.

Reik, Theodor (1941). *Masochism in Modern Man*. New York: Grove.

Rickels, Laurence (1999). *The Vampire Lectures*. Minneapolis, MN: University of Minnesota Press.

Rickey, C. (1982). "Hooked on Horror: Why We Like Scary Movies." *Mademoiselle*: 169.

Rieff, Philip (1959). *Freud: The Mind of the Moralist*. Chicago: University of Chicago Press.

Ringel, Harry (1974). "*The Exorcist.*" *Cinefantastique* 3 (2) (Spring): 24–40.

Robinson, Paul (1993). *Freud and His Critics*. Berkeley: University of California Press.

Rogers, Robert (1970). *The Double in Literature: A Psychoanalytic Study*. Detroit, MI: Wayne University Press.

Roose, Steven and Robert Glick, eds. (1995). *Anxiety as Symptom and Signal*. Hillsdale, NJ: Analytic Press.

Routt, William D. (2001). "Bad For Good." *Intensities: The Journal of Cult Media* 2: http://www.cult-media.com/issue2/Aroutt.htm (accessed 12/5/02)

Russell, David (1998). "Monster Roundup: Reintegrating the Horror Genre." *Refiguring American Film Genres: History and Theory*, ed. Nick Browne. Berkeley: University of California Press.

Russell, Vito (1981). *The Celluloid Closet: Homosexuality in the Movies*. New York: Harper & Row.

Russo, Mary (2000). "Freaks" (1994). *The Horror Reader*, ed. Ken Gelder. London: Routledge: 90–96.

Rycroft, Charles (1970). *A Critical Dictionary of Psychoanalysis*. London: Penguin.

Ryle, Gilbert (1954). "Pleasure." *Dilemmas*. Cambridge, UK: Cambridge University Press.

Saper, Craig (2001). "Artificial Auteurism and the Political Economy of the Allen Smithee Case." *Directed by Allen Smithee*, ed. J. Braddock and S. Hock, op. cit.: 29–49.

Sarris, Andrew (1968). *The American Cinema: Directors and Directions, 1929–1968*. New York: Da Capo.

(1992). "Notes on the Auteur Theory in 1962" (1962). *Film Theory and Criticism: Introductory Readings*, ed. Gerald Mast, Marshall Cohen, and Leo Braudy. New York: Oxford University Press: 585–88.

(2000). "Allen Smithee Redux." *Directed by Allen Smithee*, ed. J. Braddock and S. Hock, op. cit.: vii–xvi.

Schneider, Steven Jay (1997). "Uncanny Realism and the Decline of the Modern Horror Film." *Paradoxa: Studies in World Literary Genres* 3 (3/4): 417–28.

(2000). "Monsters as (Uncanny) Metaphors: Freud, Lakoff, and the Representation of Monstrosity in Cinematic Horror." *Horror Film Reader*, ed. Alain Silver and James Ursini. New York: Limelight Editions: 167–91.

(2001). "Killing in Style: The Aestheticisation of Violence in Donald Cammell's *White of the Eye*." *Scope: An Online Journal of Film Studies*: http://

www.nottingham.ac.uk/film/journal/articles/ killing-in-style.htm (accessed 12/5/02).

(2001–02). "Van Sant the Provoca(u)teur." *Hitchcock Annual:* 140–48.

(2002). "Barbara, Julia, Myra, Carol, and Nell: Diagnosing Female Madness in British Horror Cinema." *British Horror Cinema,* ed. Steve Chibnall and Julian Petley. London: Routledge: 117–30.

(2003a). "'Suck . . . Don't Suck.' Framing Ideology in Kathryn Bigelow's *Near Dark.*" *The Cinema of Kathryn Bigelow: Hollywood Transgressor,* ed. Deborah Jermyn and Sean Redmond. London: Wallflower Press: 72–90.

(2003b). "Murder as Art/The Art of Murder: Aestheticizing Violence in Modern Cinematic Horror." *Dark Thoughts,* ed. S.J. Schneider and D. Shaw, op. cit.: 174–97.

(1999). "Manufacturing Horror in Hitchcoch's *Psycho.*" *Cineaction* 50: 70–75.

Seltzer, Mark (1998). *Serial Killers: Death and Life in America's Wound Culture.* New York: Routledge.

Sendak, Maurice (1963). *Where the Wild Things Are.* New York: Harper & Row.

Showalter, Elaine (1997). *Hystories: Hysterical Epidemics and Modern Culture.* New York: Columbia University Press.

Siegel, Joel (1973). "Tourneur Remembers." *Cinefantastique* 2 (4).

Silverman, Kaja (1983). *The Subject of Semiotics.* Oxford: Oxford University Press.

(1988). "Masochism and Male Subjectivity." *Camera Obscura* 17: 30–67.

(1992). *Male Subjectivity at the Margins.* New York: Routledge.

Simpson, Philip (1999). "The Politics of Apocalypse in the Cinema of Serial Murder." *Mythologies of Violence in Postmodern Media,* ed. Christopher Sharrett. Detroit, MI: Wayne State University Press.

(2000). *Psycho Paths: Tracking the Serial Killer in Contemporary American Film and Fiction.* Carbondale, IL: Southern Illinois University Press.

Skal, David J. (1993). *The Monster Show: A Cultural History of Horror.* New York: Norton.

(1999). "The World of Gods and Monsters: A Journey with James Whale Narrated by Clive Barker." (*Gods and Monsters* DVD, Collector's Edition). Universal Studios.

Smith, Jeff (1996). "Unheard Melodies? A Critique of Psychoanalytic Theories of Film Music." *Post-Theory,* ed. D. Bordwell and N. Carroll, op. cit. 230–47.

(1999). "Movie Music as Moving Music: Emotion, Cognition, and the Film Score." *Passionate Views,* ed. C. Plantinga and G. Smith, op. cit.: 146–67.

Smith, Murray (1995). *Engaging Characters: Fiction, Emotion, and the Cinema.* Oxford: Clarendon Press.

(1997). "Imagining from the Inside." *Film Theory and Philosophy,* ed. R. Allen and M. Smith, op. cit.: 412–30.

(2000). "A(moral) Monstrosity." *The Modern Fantastic: The Films of David Cronenberg,* ed. M. Grant, op. cit. 69–83.

Sokolov, E. N. (1963). *Perception and the Conditioned Reflex.* New York: Macmillan.

Sontag, Susan (1966). *Against Interpretation and Other Essays.* New York: Dell.

Spitz, Ellen Handler (1998). *Inside Picture Books.* New Haven, CT: Yale University Press.

Spolsky, Ellen (1993). *Gaps in Nature: Literary Interpretation and the Modular Mind.* Albany, NY: SUNY Press.

Spoto, Donald (1983/1999). *The Dark Side of Genius: The Life of Alfred Hitchcock.* Boston: Little Brown.

Stabile, Carol A. (2000). "Resistance, Recuperation, and Reflexivity: The Limits of a Paradigm." *Pierre Bourdieu: Fieldwork in Culture,* ed. Nicholas Brown and Imre Szeman. Lanham, MD: Rowman & Littlefield.

Staiger, Janet (2000). *Perverse Spectators: The Practices of Film Reception.* New York: New York University Press.

(2003). "Authorship Approaches." *Authorship and Film,* ed. D. Gestner and J. Staiger, op. cit.: 27–57.

Stringfellow, Frank, Jr. (1994). *The Meaning of Irony: A Psychoanalytic Investigation.* Albany, NY: SUNY Press.

Stuart, Jan (2001). "The Vampire Strikes Out (Rev. of *Shadow of the Vampire*)." *The Advocate*: (January 30): http://www.advocate.com/html/video/849-Vampire_830.asp (accessed 12/5/02).

Sulloway, Frank (1992). *Freud, Biologist of the Mind: Beyond the Psychoanalytic Legend.* Cambridge, MA: Harvard University Press.

Tamborini, Ron and J. Stiff (1987). "Predictors of Horror Film Attendance and Appeal: An Analysis of the Audience for Frightening Films." *Communication Research* 14: 415–36.

Tamborini, Ron, J. Stiff, and D. Zillmann (1987). "Preference for Graphic Horror Featuring Male versus Female Victimization." *Communication Research* 14: 415–36.

Tan, Ed (1996). *Emotion and the Structure of Narrative Film: Film as an Emotion Machine.* Mahwah, NJ: Lawrence Erlbaum.

Tarratt, Margaret (1971). "Monsters from the Id." *Films and Filming* (January): 40–42.

Tatar, Maria (1992). *Off with Their Heads: Fairy Tales and the Culture of Childhood.* Princeton, NJ: Princeton University Press.

Telotte, J.P. (1985). *Dreams of Darkness: Fantasy and the Films of Val Lewton.* Urbana, IL: University of Illinois Press.

(1994). "In the Realm of Revealing: The Technological Double in the Contemporary Science Fiction Film." *Journal of the Fantastic of the Arts* 6 (2–3): 234–52.

Thompson, David (1991) *"The Silence of the Lambs." Sight and Sound* (includes p. 20). (May): 19–20.

(2000). "The Riddler Has His Day." *Sight and Sound* 11 (4): 118–21.

Thornton, Tim (1998). *Wittgenstein on Language and Thought: The Philosophy of Content.* Edinburgh: Edinburgh University Press.

Timpone, A. (1996). *Men, Makeup and Monsters: Hollywood's Masters of Illusion & FX.* New York: St. Martin's.

Tobacyk, J. J., H. Myers, and L. Bailey (1981). "Field-Dependence, Sensation Seeking and Preference for Paintings." *Journal of Personality Assessment* 45: 270–77.

Todorov, Tzvetan (1975). *The Fantastic: A Structural Approach to a Literary Genre.* Ithaca, NY: Cornell University Press.

Torrey, E. Fuller (1992). *Freudian Fraud: The Malignant Effect of Freud's Theory on American Thought and Culture*. New York: HarperCollins.
Travers, Peter (1995). "Auteur in Angora (Review of *Ed Wood*)." *Rolling Stone* 511: http://www.rollingstone.com/reviews/movie/review.asp? mid=72991 (accessed 12/5/02).
Trosman, Harry (1985). *Freud and the Imaginative World*. Hillsdale, NJ: Analytic Press.
Tuan, Yi-fu (1979). *Landscapes of Fear*. Oxford: Basil Blackwell.
Tudor, Andrew (1974). *Theories of Film*. London: Secker & Warburg.
    (1980). *Beyond Empiricism: Philosophy of Science in Sociology*. London: Routledge.
    (1989). *Monsters and Mad Scientists: A Cultural History of the Horror Movie*. Oxford: Basil Blackwell.
    (1995). "Unruly Bodies, Unquiet Minds." *Body and Society* 1 (1): 25–41.
    (1997). "Why Horror? The Peculiar Pleasures of a Popular Genre." *Cultural Studies* 11 (3): 443–63.
Twitchell, James B. (1985). *Dreadful Pleasures: An Anatomy of Modern Horror*. Oxford: Oxford University Press.
Tyson, Jeremy (1997). *Bright Darkness: The Lost Art of the Supernatural Horror Film*. London: Cassell.
Urbano, Cosimo (1998). "Projections, Symptoms, and Anxiety: The Modern Horror Film and Its Effects." *The Psychoanalytic Review* 85 (6): 889–908.
Vale, V. and Andrea Juno, eds. (1983). *Incredibly Strange Films*. San Francisco: RE/SEARCH.
Von Wright, G.H. (1963). *The Varieties of Goodness*. London: Routledge & Kegan Paul.
Waller, G., ed. (1987). *American Horrors: Essays on the Modern American Horror Film*. Urbana, IL: University of Illinois Press.
Walton, Kendall (1997). "On Pictures and Photographs: Objections Answered." *Film Theory and Philosophy*, ed. R. Allen and M. Smith, op. cit.: 60–75.
Watkins, Roger (1980). "'Demented Revenge' Hits World Screens." *Variety* (October 29): 3.
Weaver, James B., III (1991). "Are 'Slasher' Horror Films Sexually Violent? A Content Analysis." *Journal of Broadcasting and Electronic Media* 35: 385–93.
Webber, Andrew (1996). *The Doppelganger: Double Visions in German Literature*. Oxford: Clarendon Press.
Weiskel, Thomas (1976). *The Romantic Sublime: Studies in the Structure and Psychology of Transcendence*. Baltimore, MD: Johns Hopkins University Press.
Weldon, Michael (1983). *The Psychotronic Encyclopedia of Film*. New York: Ballantine.
Wells, Paul (2000). *The Horror Genre: From Beelzebub to Blair Witch*. London: Wallflower Press.
Williams, Linda (1996). "When the Woman Looks" (1984). *The Dread of Difference*, ed. B. K. Grant, op. cit.: 15–34.
    (1999). "Film Bodies: Gender, Genre and Excess" (1984). *Film Theory and Criticism*, ed. Leo Braudy and Marshall Cohen. New York: Oxford University Press: 701–15.

Wilson, B. J. and J. R. Cantor (1987). "Reducing Children's Fear Reactions to Mass Media: Effects of Visual Exposure and Verbal Explanation." *Communication Yearbook* 10. 553–73.

Winter, Sarah (1999). *Freud and the Institution of Psychoanalytic Knowledge.* Stanford, CA: Stanford University Press.

Wollen, Peter (1969). *Signs and Meaning in the Cinema.* Bloomington, IN: Indiana University Press.

Wollheim, Richard (1991). *Freud.* London: Fontana Press.

Wood, Robin (1978). "Return of the Repressed." *Film Comment* 14 (4): 25–32.

   (1979). "An Introduction to the American Horror Film." *American Nightmare Essays on the Horror Film,* ed. Andrew Britton, Richard Lippe, Tony Williams and Robin Wood, op. cit.: 7–28.

   (1986). "The American Nightmare: Horror in the 70s." *Hollywood from Vietnam to Reagan.* New York: Columbia University Press: 70–94.

Woolery, George (1983). *Children's Television.* Metuchen, NJ: Scarecrow Press.

Wright, Elizabeth (1984). *Psychoanalytic Criticism: Theory in Practice.* London: Methuen.

   (1998). *Psychoanalytic Criticism: A Reappraisal.* Cambridge, UK: Polity Press.

Yaeger, Patricia (1989). "Toward a Female Sublime." *Gender and Theory: Dialogues on Feminist Criticism,* ed. Linda Kauffman. Oxford: Blackwell: 191–212.

Young, Robert (1999). "Freud's Secret: *The Interpretation of Dreams* was a Gothic Novel." *Sigmund Freud's The Interpretation of Dreams: New Interdisciplinary Essays,* ed. Laura Marcus. Manchester, UK: Manchester University Press.

Young-Breuhl, Elisabeth (1996). *The Anatomy of Prejudices.* Cambridge, MA: Harvard University Press.

Zaleski, Zbigniew (1984). "Sensation Seeking and Preference for Emotional Visual Stimuli." *Personality and Individual Differences* 5: 609–11.

Zillman, Dolf (1971). "Excitation Transfer in Communication Mediated Aggressive Behavior." *Journal of Experimental Social Psychology* 7: 419–34.

   (1991). "Television Viewing and Physiological Arousal." *Responding to the Screen,* ed. Jennings Bryant and Dolf Zillmann. Hillside, NJ: Lawrence Erlbaum.

   (1998). "The Psychology of the Appeal of Portrayals of Violence." *Why We Watch: The Attractions of Violent Entertainment,* ed. Jeffrey H. Goldstein. New York: Oxford University Press.

Zillman, Dolf and James B. Weaver III (1996). "Gender-Socialization Theory of Reactions to Horror." *Horror Films: Current Research on Audience Preferences and Reactions,* ed. James B. Weaver III and Ron Tamborini. Hillside, NJ: Lawrence Erlbaum: 81–101.

Zillman, Dolf, T. A. Hay, and J. Bryant (1975). "The Effect of Suspense and Its Resolution on the Appreciation of Dramatic Presentations." *Journal of Research in Personality* 9: 307–23.

Zizek, Slavoj (1993). *Tarrying with the Negative: Kant, Hegel, and the Critique of Ideology.* Durham, NC: Duke University Press.

   (1994). "The Spectre of Ideology." *Mapping Ideology,* ed. Slavoj Zizek. London: Verso.

(1999). "The Undergrowth of Enjoyment: How Popular Culture Can Serve as an Introduction to Lacan." *The Zizek Reader*, ed. Elizabeth Wright and Edmond Wright. Oxford: Blackwell.

(2001). *The Fright of Real Tears: Krzysztof Kieslowski Between Theory & Post-Theory*. London: BFI.

Zuckerman, Marvin (1990). "The Psychophysiology of Sensation Seeking." *Journal of Personality* 58: 313–45.

(1991). *Psychobiology of Personality*. New York: Cambridge University Press.

(1996). "Sensation Seeking and the Taste for Vicarious Horror." *Horror Films*, ed. J. B. Weaver III and R. Tamborini, op. cit. 147–60.

Zuckerman, Marvin and A. P. Litle (1986). "Personality and Curiosity about Morbid and Sexual Events." *Personality and Individual Differences* 7: 49–56.

Zuckerman, Marvin, R. S. Ulrich, and J. McLaughlin (1993). "Sensation Seeking and Reactions to Nature Paintings." *Personality and Individual Differences* 15: 563–76.

Index